Listening for
Africa

Listening for
Africa

Freedom, Modernity, and

the Logic of Black Music's

African Origins

David F. Garcia

Duke University Press Durham and London 2017

Cover design by Matthew Tauch. Interior design by Courtney Leigh Baker
Typeset in Garamond Premier Pro and Futura by Westchester Publishing Services

Library of Congress Cataloging-in-Publication Data
Names: Garcia, David F., author.
Title: Listening for Africa : freedom, modernity, and the logic of Black music's African
    origins / David F. Garcia.
Description: Durham : Duke University Press, 2017. | Includes bibliographical references
    and index.
Identifiers: LCCN 2017006461 (print) | LCCN 2017009241 (ebook)
ISBN 9780822363545 (hardcover : alk. paper)
ISBN 9780822363705 (pbk. : alk. paper)
ISBN 9780822373117 (e-book)
Subjects: LCSH: African Americans—Music—History and criticism. | Blacks—Music—
    History and criticism. | Dance music—History and criticism. | Music—Africa—
    History and criticism.
Classification: LCC ML3479 G37 2017 (print) | LCC ML3479 (ebook) |
    DDC 780.89/96073—dc23
LC record available at https://lccn.loc.gov/2017006461

COVER ART: A group of Katherine Dunham Dancers shown in mid rehearsal in
New York, 1946. Courtesy Library of Congress, Prints & Photographs Division.

Duke University Press gratefully acknowledges the support of the University Research
Council at the University of North Carolina at Chapel Hill, which provided funds
toward the publication of this book.

FOR NELSON MY BROTHER

I began the research for this book soon after moving to North Carolina in 2003. Originally, I planned to write a book on the history of the mambo and its social and cultural significance in various parts of the Americas. Starting my research with materials published and produced in the United States, I was struck by the prevalence of the notions "primitive," "savage," and "Africa" in describing mambo and related styles of music, including Afro-Cuban music. I had encountered similar terms in some of the Cuban materials I used for my research on Arsenio Rodríguez. I soon shifted my focus to researching the epistemological nature of these terms, primarily in anthropological thought of the 1940s in the United States, which led me to the work of Melville J. Herskovits and his archival collections at Northwestern University and the Schomburg Center for Research in Black Culture. From that point forward, I followed many of the direct connections Herskovits had made during his acculturation and New World Negro research, and the project shifted focus accordingly from the mambo to an epistemological study on these and related notions as understood and used not only by academics but also by musicians, dancers, and others as well.

The need I felt to understand the prevalence of the notions "primitive," "savage," and "Africa" in public discourse of the 1930s through the 1950s was indeed great. I wanted to write a book that explained why these notions were so prevalent in public discourse including but not limited to academia. My interests in this problem, however, extended beyond my research to include specific experiences I had throughout much of my own academic life. During a personal trip to visit my extended family in Quito, Ecuador, in 1996, I decided to wander into the Centro Cultural Afroecuatoriano. I had completed my first year of graduate school in the ethnomusicology program at the University of California at Santa Barbara, and I was planning to conduct doctoral research on an Andean topic. Upon recounting my visit to my cousins, one asked, "Why did you go there? Are you visiting your ancestors?" The racist implication of the joke was clear to me, and it was a stark reminder that Darwinist evolution had so deeply engrained itself across societies throughout different parts of the world, or at least the Americas.

One other experience occurred much more recently, the effects of which convinced me of the importance that the work of Henri Lefebvre, Michel de Certeau, and Gilles Deleuze had on attempting to theorize the implications of place and history in understanding and explaining the workings of political and ideological power. While on a short family trip in the mountains of western North Carolina, my wife and I began a friendly conversation with a gentleman and local resident, who eventually came around to asking us where we were from, to which we replied, Los Angeles. Not satisfied, he asked, "No, where are you really from?" My wife, whose father and mother are from Peru and Guatemala, respectively, and I had been asked this type of question many times before, and I suspect that my two children will be asked the same question—if they haven't already. Our obvious Latin@ ethnic features, it was clear, marked us as *not possibly being from here* (western North Carolina) or even our place of birth, Los Angeles! My daughter, who was in fact born in Durham, will particularly have a lot of explaining to do going back three generations.

I can't help but think about and feel the ideological violence that such questions whip up, especially during the course of a friendly chat among strangers. I also understand that such experiences do not compare with those of others who are in a much more vulnerable position, as, for instance, undocumented immigrants, transgendered people, and so on. In many ways, then, this book is about how the notion of someone's origins, regardless of racial, ethnic, sexual, or political status, is indeed a double-edged sword; my wife and I are very proud of our familial origins in South and Central America, and the histories of our parents' immigration to Los Angles, and we want our children to also be proud and claim these origins and histories at every opportunity, without, however, ever ceding their rightful place where they call home, wherever they happen to be.

There are many individuals and organizations to thank and recognize for their assistance in the completion of this book. I was awarded research fellowships from several entities, beginning with a visiting scholar fellowship in 2006 from the Cristobal Díaz-Ayala Cuban and Latin American Popular Music Collection at the Cuban Research Institute, Florida International University. Veronica González, director of the Cristobal Díaz-Ayala Collection, and Jaime Jaramillo were especially helpful in providing me with research copies of many recordings. Research awards from the Associate Professor Support Program of the College of Arts and Sciences (2011–2015), Moore Undergraduate Research Apprentice Program (2011, 2012), IBM Junior Faculty Development Award of the Office of the Executive Vice Chancellor and Provost (2009), and Small Grant Program of the University Research Council (2009), all at the University of North Carolina at Chapel Hill, greatly enabled the bulk of my archival research.

A fellowship from the National Endowment for the Humanities (2014–2015) was absolutely key in the completion of my manuscript. Any views, findings, conclusions, or recommendations expressed in this publication do not necessarily reflect those of the National Endowment for the Humanities. A subvention award from the University Research Council at the University of North Carolina at Chapel Hill also assisted greatly in the publication of the book. I want to thank my recommenders Kenneth Bilby, Peter Manuel, and Robin Moore for supporting my many fellowship applications.

I thank my colleagues at the University of North Carolina at Chapel Hill, whose support of my work carried me through various stages of my research. These include Annegret Fauser, Mark Evan Bonds, and Severine Neff. I thank as well our graduate students in the Graduate Program in Musicology at Carolina, especially Christopher Wells for our discussions about the broader goals of the book, and Megan Eagen for her assistance in translating Mieczysław Kolinski's letters from German into English.

I thank the many archival and library staff throughout the country, including Kevin Leonard and the entire staff of the Northwestern University Archives; Marilyn Graff, Archives of Traditional Music, Indiana University; Kristin Heath and Andrew Perlman, Hunt Library, Carnegie Mellon University; Cecilia Peterson, digitization archivist, Center for Folklife and Cultural Heritage, Ralph Rinzler Folklife Archives and Collections, Smithsonian Institution; Donella D. Maupin, archives manager, Hampton University Museum; Valerie Harris, associate special collections librarian, Special Collections and University Archives Department, University of Illinois at Chicago; and Kathleen Sabogal, Carnegie Hall Archives.

I thank my editor, Courtney Berger, for working diligently with me throughout all of the stages of the book's preparation. Her support of the project from the beginning was vital indeed. I thank Bonnie Perkel for her assistance during preproduction, and especially my four anonymous readers for their thoughtful and thorough commentary on drafts of the manuscript.

I thank friends and other colleagues who took an interest and assisted in my work, including Jacky Ávila, Andy Kleindienst, Robin Moore, Marysol Quevedo, and Bradley Simmons.

Finally, I thank my wife, Rose Delatorre, my son Benicio, and my daughter Adriana for their support and understanding, especially during the year in which I completed writing the manuscript. I love you.

Between the thirties and the end of World War II, there was perhaps as radical a change in the psychological perspective of the Negro American toward America as there was between the Emancipation and 1930. —AMIRI BARAKA (LeRoi Jones), *Blues People*, 1963

Like race, time is a social construct. And as a social construct it seems natural, never making itself appear indispensable while structuring much of what we do and think, when we do and think, and most importantly how we do and think. When time is coupled with space, also a social construct, together they determine how we understand where we come from, where we are now, and where we might be going next and thereafter. Such operations fulfill a limitless number of purposes, not least of which is in the ways we think of our own place in history and in the world. What relationship does music have in the service of these temporal and spatial operations? In the epigraph above, Amiri Baraka, still writing as LeRoi Jones, reflected back in time to the interwar period and claimed an ontological shift had occurred among African Americans in regard to their relationship to the nation. He made his claim inspired no doubt by the political transformations in American society of the early 1960s during which he wrote *Blues People*. Such transformations from slave to citizenship, he argued, are most graphic in black music.[1]

We also encounter music having a formative place in James Weldon Johnson's statement from 1925, "As the years go by and I understand more about this music and its origin, the miracle of its production strikes me with increasing wonder."[2] We know Johnson was writing about the Negro spiritual during the height of the Harlem Renaissance. We may also take his statement as evidence supporting Baraka's claim that black music has had the capacity like no other form of expressive culture to record how African Americans have forged their place in history and the nation.

But is there more to be said about black music in this regard, especially given the immensity of the literature on black music history? In historical terms, what Baraka claimed to have occurred among African Americans in the 1930s was plausible, but thinking of Johnson's and Baraka's claims in historicist terms raises a different set of questions altogether concerning the deeply precarious implications of situating oneself within music bounded by modernity's social and historical frameworks of race and history.[3] Although the spiritual's origin was an empowering topic of debate for African Americans and others at the time (and would continue to be in the 1930s), what often goes unexplained is how and why Johnson, Baraka, and others took black music as a medium to understand the historical past and place of origin in the first place. What was it about the historical period that Johnson anticipated and Baraka reflected back upon that ushered in much reflection and work on the social and political status of black Americans, Africans, and Caribbeans via their shared origins in music?

By way of an answer, consider the headline on the front page of New York City's *Sun* on April 19, 1940, which reads, "Jungle Drums Sound as Africans Wed atop Skyscraper."[4] The musical items captured in this image are the three "jungle drums" that are being made to sound by three individuals who, along with the rest of the group, are identified as Africans. According to the caption, this wedding party, which includes newlyweds who are "natives of Nigeria" in addition to a "witch doctor" and a "witch woman," is atop the Chanin Building, located on East Forty-Second Street and Lexington Avenue in Manhattan, and in the distance is the Empire State Building, located on Thirty-Fourth Street and Fifth Avenue, southwest of the Chanin Building. The primitivist symbolism of the image and caption surely appear to us today as obvious enough and might have even appeared as such to some readers of the *Sun* in 1940, for the caption also clarifies that the newlyweds are "appearing with other native Africans" in *Zunguru*, an African dance drama produced by the choreographer Asadata Dafora from Sierra Leone.

Putting aside questions of representation and the group's promotional intentions, the image itself reproduces conceptual dichotomies integral to modernity's formations of history and geography in music and dance. It is a logic that enabled the "jungle drums" to not simply sound as such but to bring sound from the historical past to the modern present. The group of musicians and dancers also occupied the modern present, but like their drums they simultaneously embodied the ancestral origins whose music and, dance James Weldon Johnson, Melville J. Herskovits, Katherine Dunham, Fernando Ortiz, Asadata Dafora, and so many others sought to understand, explain, and perform at the time. Moreover, those pictured on the *Sun*'s front page, their drums, and the sounds of the drums all materialized in temporal and spatial opposition to the Chanin Building upon which they sat and stood, the Empire State Building whose top floors and antenna peer from behind, and the metropolis of Manhattan in which they lived. The caption reads, "In the distance is the Empire State Building." It is *distance* temporally and spatially conceived that distinguishes the group of African musicians and dancers from modernity's monuments of its own progress. The image, in other words, constitutes an assemblage of practices of mapping people and their music within Cartesian space (the jungle and the modern metropolis) and time (the primitive and the modern). It is in fact a visual materialization of the logic of black music's and dance's African origins, prompting as it has vast temporal and spatial distances for many generations of writers, listeners, and observers, including James Weldon Johnson as well as Amiri Baraka when he stated, "There are definite *stages* in the Negro's transmutation from African to American. . . . I insist that these changes are most graphic in his music."[5]

Listening for Africa: Freedom, Modernity, and the Logic of Black Music's African Origins critically analyzes how and why the African origins of black music and dance mattered during the historical period that Johnson, Baraka, and many others marked as significant in the history of African Americans. The 1930s through the early 1950s was a politically turbulent time indeed, bridging the Harlem Renaissance, the Great Depression, World War II, the Cold War, the civil rights movement, and African decolonization, when modernity's promises of freedom and progress were at their most vulnerable or near collapse. During this time ethnomusicology, dance studies, and African diasporic studies in the United States emerged in conjunction with interrelated developments not readily recognized as such, including Nazism in Europe, anticolonialism in Africa, and black nationalism in the Caribbean and United States. Not only Americans but Africans, Caribbeans, and others as well promulgated a revaluation of the African origins of black music and dance in order to sway entrenched attitudes toward race and Africa or the so-called Dark Continent in the face of a troubled modern world.

This book focuses on some of these key figures—Melville J. Herskovits, Katherine Dunham, Richard Waterman, Zoila Gálvez, Fernando Ortiz, Harold Courlander, Modupe Paris, Luciano "Chano" Pozo, Asadata Dafora, Edward Kennedy "Duke" Ellington, Harry Smith, and Dámaso Pérez Prado. Whether they were anthropologists, comparative musicologists, dancers, musicians, artists, or political activists, they all looked toward black music's and dance's trajectories from their origins in Africa to the New World to address or, in some cases, help solve modernity's shortcomings. For some the goal was to resolve racism in Europe and the United States by scientifically discovering black American music's origins in ancient African civilization and its survivals in the Caribbean; for others it was to raise political support among Americans for Africa's decolonization and modernization by performing in music and dance their shared histories of oppression and liberation; while for others it was to assuage anxieties about modernity's threat of nuclear annihilation by rediscovering humanity's redeeming qualities in black music itself.

Their research, performances, and activism did indeed mark significant shifts in attitudes toward Africa and racial Others. But when considered in historicist terms, these shifts in the end did not entail a definitive break from modernity's trappings, which would have truly been transformative if not for their continued dependence on modernity's notions of the modern city and Africa as epistemological axes (Cartesian coordinates) of human history and progress. Instead, their work prolonged and remade modernity's paradoxes, differences, and disagreements with the cultures of black internationalism established during the interwar period as put forth by Brent Hayes Edwards.[6] More than documenting and performing the fact of black music and dance, their work entailed modernity's practices of listening to and embodying a historical past that made racialized living compelling and empowering, yet precarious all the same.

In taking a historicist approach in analyzing the logic of black music's and dance's African origins, this book challenges the persistence of national and ethnic boundaries that circumscribe the scope of most studies on black American music and dance history. It does this by uncovering a rich historical archive of Africans, Americans, Cubans, and others who, in the two decades leading up to the civil rights movement, African independence from colonial rule, and the Cuban Revolution, addressed questions of racism and colonialism in conversation with each other and with a strategic eye toward music's and dance's potential to inspire social and political change. It follows the ideological and political forces that shaped their activities and receptions in varying locales throughout North and South America as well as the Caribbean and West Africa. The decision to pursue a transnational and interdisciplinary perspective is guided by the most recent scholarship on the black power movement by Peniel E. Joseph, Jeffrey O. G. Ogbar, and Robin D. G. Kelley, among others, and scholarship on the African diaspora by Frank Andre Guridy, Kevin Yelvington, J. Lorand Matory, Lisa Brock and Digna Castañeda Fuertes, and Brent Hayes Edwards, all of whom bypass nationalist and ethnocentric perspectives on black culture and history in order to get at its transnational flows of racial difference that Paul Gilroy theorized in *The Black Atlantic*. Indeed, *Listening for Africa* sheds light on one of Gilroy's more recent challenges in the critical examination of race by taking that step from analyzing the "ways that particular 'races' have been historically invented and socially imagined" to explaining how "modernity catalyzed the distinctive regimes of truth" (or that which Gilroy calls "raciology") such that a logic of origins and of race itself was made epistemologically viable in music and dance.[7]

Thus this book addresses the following main questions: When black music and dance sounded and embodied its African origins—whether from recordings and films made in Suriname, Martinique, New York, and Mexico City, or public performances in Havana, Chicago, and Lima—exactly how, why, and for whom were those soundings and embodiments materializing? What did it mean when listeners and audiences perceived those performing black music and dance as modern man's ancestors or primitives? And how did such practices of racial and historical listening and embodying serve as empirical and aesthetic sustenance for modernity itself? Addressing this final question in particular necessitates interrogating whiteness as well, not as the supposed beneficiary of modernity's racial regimes, as Gilroy questions, but as modernity's way of preempting un-raced and un-sexist living for men and women.[8] For, as this book will explore, whether Negro spirituals, jazz, cubop and bebop, Yorubá *toques* (rhythms) and *cantos* (chants), black modern and African folkloric dance, or mambo, these fields of music and dance compelled from people a wide range of human emotions, actions, and interactions, from the most intense feelings of degradation and disavowal to the most uplifting, empowering, and liberating sense of self and community.

When such music and dance compelled academics, activists, and performers, as well as their audiences, to move discursively back and forth from savagery to civilization, from the bush to the city, and from Africa to the New World and back, these distances were not matters of human history and geography but rather forged by the weight of modernity's axes of time, space, and race.[9] The radical change Amiri Baraka pointed to in the psychological perspective of African Americans toward the United States was even more profound in that, through the early 1950s, Africans and Caribbeans, as well as Americans, put forth music and dance to reconfigure Africa as origin with the expressed intention of staking their claim on modernity's promises of freedom and equality, usually in very subtle yet unmistakably real ways as only can be achieved in music and dance. Real ways, that is, that inhabited the interstices between real and fantasy, past and present, observation and participation, primitive and modern, and black and white. Interstices that they oriented toward freedom and that were often racially inclusive, which provoked modernity's machines—among them psychoanalysis, the Catholic Church, nationalism, and especially capitalism—to react rather hysterically but swiftly nonetheless.[10]

Although the book's chapters move from the late 1920s through the early 1950s, the presentation of these temporal and spatial reconfigurations in black music and dance is not intended to imply a teleology leading ultimately to the emergences of the use of "diaspora" in the 1950s or the black power movements of the 1960s.[11] For in this book's broader proposal to reconfigure how and why we think of history in music and dance, each of the case studies analyzed in the following chapters is revealed to constitute the ferment of agitation and activity that has been a constant part of the human condition under modernity regardless of race, gender, ethnicity, or nationality.[12] What this book will argue is that for these academics, performers, and activists, listening to, analyzing, sounding, embodying, and even resisting black music's and dance's African origins enabled their holding modernity's promises of freedom and equality to the fire usually as their acts of faith in modernity but also as acts of stepping inside and outside of its regimes of truth.

The following introductory remarks will explain the theoretical imperatives in unpacking the notions of black music, dance, and African origins as well as modernity's need for this logic, which will necessitate moving above, around, and through boundaries of many sorts. It is with such movements between music, dance, and film; black and white; urban and rural; and science, art, and magic that this book proposes a critique of the state of modernity at the mid-twentieth century, when its own excesses—through colonialism, capitalism, and science at a global scale—seemed to threaten its own collapse if not for the ideological hold its discourses of race and history had on those living in the modern world at the time. What is important to keep in mind throughout the many turns taken in this book is the premise that this logic of black music's and dance's African origins was fundamentally contingent on modernity's most deeply confounding paradoxes, freedom from which regardless of one's race was most improbable.

Modernity and Africa as Origin

This book's basic methodological premise is that music and dance embody a historically complex and contingent field of people's actions and interactions. I approach the music and dance studied here thus as constituting people's ways of having existed in the world during this particular historical period. By framing black music and dance in this way, I do not purport this book to be a study of Bush-Negro music of Suriname, African dance dramas, cubop, mambo, or any other black music or dance genre of the 1930s and 1940s. Attempting to do so would not only be an entirely different kind of project, it would trap us in modernity's orderings of historical time, space, and race. These are the very discourses that had disavowed Melville J. Herskovits's "Bush Negroes," Asadata Dafora, John Birks "Dizzy" Gillespie, and Chano Pozo from occupying the same historical place in the modern world.[13] Rather, I conceive of the music and dance studied here as having been significant occasions of musicking whose effects had assembled among its musicians, dancers, and observers, on the one hand, a consistent pattern of discourses about race and history, and, on the other, the socially sanctioned roles to operate within these discourses accordingly. Christopher Small defines musicking as "a way of knowing our world—not that pre-given physical world, divorced from human experience, that modern science claims to know but the experiential world of relationships in all its complexity—and in knowing it, we learn how to live well in it."[14] In spite of its suggestive utopianism, what musicking ensures is an analysis of music and dance not as genre but as human actions and interactions that encapsulated no doubt people's planning and desires, and that were entangled in modernity's ways of knowing, yet were also immanently about people's experiences in the world.

Said another way, there could be little or nothing shared in the sound or aesthetics of, for instance, Dámaso Pérez Prado's "Mambo del ruletero" and Asadata Dafora's *Kykunkor*, or among such musicians and dancers *without* modernity's discourses of race, Africa, and history. Like what Karl Hagstrom Miller does with southern music in *Segregating Sound*, this book is similarly about how a variety of people compartmentalized music and dance of many kinds not only according to race but most urgently along modernity's map-pings of history and geography, wherein the logic of black music's and dance's shared African origins was for most a matter of common sense.[15] What compelled people to compartmentalize black music and dance in these prescribed ways is a much more complex question altogether. To address these problems, this book insists on eschewing any transhistorical constructs of black music and dance, as Jonathan Sterne does with sound in his study of the history of sound reproduction, in order to get at the dispositions, practices, and techniques by which people formulated their responses to black music and dance in terms of African origins.[16] To conceive of music as a field of people's actions and interactions, or moving, sounding, and observing, which I will occasionally flag throughout the book as "dance-music," puts us in a position to situate their articulations of musicking to black music's and dance's African origins alongside the social and political imperatives shaping their historical and social contexts.[17]

Such articulations of black music and dance to their African origins had much to do with how people experienced and understood their own place in a world troubled by racism, fascism, war, and inequality. Becoming, as described by Gilles Deleuze and Félix Guattari, is a useful theoretical insight in this regard.[18] According to Deleuze and Guattari, becoming attempts to capture that "prepersonal intensity corresponding to the passage from one experiential state of the body to another and implying an augmentation or diminution in that body's capacity to act."[19] What I am after in using this notion of becoming is to historicize people's affective experiences in performing and observing black music and dance in their responses to Jim Crowism, Nazism, colonialism, and the dawn of the atomic age and the Cold War without taking for granted their capacity to articulate their experiences as anthropologist, comparative musicologist, African, American Negro, Afro-Cuban, artist, scientist, musician, dancer, activist, and so on. I approach these identifications as conditioned by the dispositions, practices, and techniques sanctioned to them by modernity. Recent scholarship in sound studies and aurality have shown that seemingly mundane actions such as listening are steeped in modernity's regimes of history, ideology, and physical practice or comportment. Jonathan Sterne draws from Pierre Bourdieu's notion of habitus to theorize styles of listening and beliefs in the efficacy of their techniques as learned, matters of education, or shared repeated practices, all of which are made actionable in a prescribed set of contexts.[20] Similarly, Ana María Ochoa Gautier suggests that particular styles of listening generate or constitute ideas about the world. Sound, in other words, is a medium for constructing knowledge about the world.[21]

Hence, by beginning the book's chapter titles with the terms "analyzing," "listening," "embodying," "disalienating," and "desiring," I intend to focus analytical attention on these actions as socially sanctioned, historically determined, and sometimes ideologically destabilizing. They involved prescribed techniques, compelling them (as a matter of habitus) to invoke the notions "bush," "origins," "native," "African," "Negro," "modern," "soul," and so on in their capacities to be anthropologist, comparative musicologist, African, modern listener, or simply in the modern world. Certain kinds of musicking constituted unique occasions in which people put into practice these notions and their associated techniques of action (analyzing, listening, embodying, and so on). What will become clear, then, is that their resolve to embark on engaging black music's and dance's African origins had little to do with the empirical question of their origins and more to do with their investments in the modern world and their precarious conditions in it.

In drawing from de Certeau's well-known axiom "space is a practiced place," we might best understand the modern world as materializing in people's practicing becoming scientists when listening in the anthropological field and laboratory, historians when lecturing in the hall, Africans when performing on stage, natives when acting on film, and modern when observing the primitive.[22] Such practices, with their associated techniques and fields of action, ensured the continuity and a degree of cohesion of people's place in the modern world and thus modern living itself. Perhaps most important to this book's theoretical imperatives is the proposition that the historical time line and geographic mapping invoked by the notion of African origins were revealed through such decipherings of the modern world.[23] Put simply, according to this logic, the geographic places where black music and dance were believed to have originated (Africa) and still survived (Caribbean and South America) were separate in every possible way—socially, economically, and temporally included—from the modern city or metropolis. Because of their privileged status in the workings of this logic, then, anthropologists, departments of tourism, historians, record company producers, and Africans as well were enabled to navigate the temporalized distantiation separating urban or modern from rural or premodern space. They held the capacity to listen and even travel back in time to the "jungle" or "bush," a fantastical feat that was in fact not fantastical at all but a matter of the spatial practices and becomings endowed to them by Hegelian, Comtean, Darwinian, and capitalist spatialized decipherings of the world and its history.

What is also essential to this proposition of the modern world is the notion of haptic perception in which all of the senses (optical, aural, tactile, etc.) were in operation independently as well as cross-referentially all the time.[24] When a sense organ was isolated for specialized perception or consumption, as with the comparative musicologist's listening to and analysis of the field recording's capturing of the African past, modernity's temporal and spatial mappings were operating especially formatively. It was the act of and belief in listening to and analyzing the African past that reinscribed one's belonging in the modern world. But my analysis also considers dancing within the framework of musicking because the tactile senses, including touch and interbodily movement, along with the aural and optical, served to reinscribe those participants and their observers that much more rigorously in the modern world. The costs of such investments in the modern world, however, were great in that modernity's temporal and spatial mappings, as made actionable through these fields of interaction and their associated practices and dispositions, entailed its discourses of race and history. Such mappings were indeed violent in that they were intended to striate people's places in the world in terms of difference and distance with the realization of freedom always at stake.

As modernity's striating technique par excellence, "Africa" conjured in people an authoritative list of interrelated techniques that included the "bush," "jungle," and "savage"; the "primitive" and "premodern"; and "origin" and "ancestral" with which people routinely reinscribed modernity's orderings of the world. Their discursive valences were far-reaching in that they helped unleash forces that, in W. E. B. Du Bois's words, tore asunder the racialized body into two irreconcilable existences.[25] There is no doubt that the work of Du Bois and many others, dating from the first half of the twentieth century, took to task modernity's violence on ontological as well as political grounds. Three works in particular, Du Bois's *The Souls of Black Folk* (1903), Oswald Spengler's *The Decline of the West* (1918), and Frantz Fanon's *Black Skin, White Masks* (1952), will emerge, especially Fanon's temporal critique of modernity's racial logic, throughout various chapters of the book as important signposts of just how precarious and at the same time forceful modernity's formations appeared to people, especially those racialized as black, at this time.

For now, it is worth noting briefly some of the ways in which Spengler, Du Bois, and Fanon critiqued modernity's formations of time and race. Spengler, for instance, characterized time and race as modernity's petty and absurd systems of truth and signs. "Time," he stated, "is a word to indicate something inconceivable, a sound symbol, and to use it as a concept, scientifically, is utterly to misconceive its nature."[26] After asserting that a "phantom time" satisfies the need of modernity's philosophers to measure and explain all things, he ends with the following: the "invention of a time that is knowable and spatially representable within causality is really wizard's gear." Spengler's suggestion that time, or that which is "bound up with the living and irreversible," is more clearly felt in music—and, I will add, dance—together with his critique of time's purported scientific uses as "wizard's gear," is significant. Not only does it lend historical grounding to this book's methodological use of musicking, it also puts forth the theoretical imperatives of time and space when conducting a historicist analysis of the ways analyzing, listening, and embodying (as social practices), and not music and dance itself, determine what history and place mean. In terms of race, Spengler states that "Race, like Time and Destiny, is a decisive element in every question of life, something which everyone knows clearly and definitely so long as he does not try to set himself to comprehend it by way of rational—i.e. soulless—dissection and ordering."

Spengler's remarks affirm the skepticism that writers before and after him expressed concerning time and race as arbitrary notions manipulated by social Darwinists among other purveyors of like-minded philosophical and scientific traditions of the nineteenth and early twentieth centuries. In fact, W. E. B. Du Bois had already proclaimed "the problem of the Twentieth Century is the problem of the color-line." As for the oppressive deployment of Western civilization's discourses of time and space, Du Bois's famous explication of double consciousness as that sense of having to *measure* "one's soul by the tape of a world that looks on in amused contempt and pity" poignantly describes the yoke of modernity's formations of time and space on the everyday life of racialized Others.[27] Yet, with all their critically and rhetorically compelling exegeses of the shortcomings of modern society, science, and history, both Du Bois and Spengler make ample use of modernity's temporalizing figure, the primitive. To the extent that evolutionism and Darwinism scientifically consummated history and primitive man, Spengler's theorization of "high Cultures" and "primitive Culture" becomes that much more confounding given his repeated rejections of Darwinism.[28] In fact, he made it the "task of the twentieth century . . . to get rid of this system of superficial causality [i.e., placing primitives or savages as the point of departure of modern humans] . . . and to put in its place a pure physiognomic," a deceptively promising proposal indeed since Spengler's formulation still spatialized groups of people and culture in terms of modernity's time.[29]

In reality, condemnation of Darwinism—not to mention Hegelianism and Comteanism and the unabated currency of their notions of the primitive in popular as well as scientific discourse in the United States, Mexico, and throughout Latin America as well as Africa—continued into the 1950s, which raises the question of that which Du Bois and Spengler named as the problem of the twentieth century.[30] Was it the color line as Du Bois posited, Darwinism as Spengler posited, or might we bracket these two problems within a deeper ontological problem of Western civilization's time line? Frantz Fanon was among the few twentieth-century theorists up until the 1950s who tackled precisely this problem of the time line, drawing primarily from the psychoanalytical and existential phenomenological works of Sigmund Freud, Jean-Paul Sartre, and Günther Stern Anders. Fanon acknowledges the "savage" and "African jungle" in the world as occupying modernity's primitive past, though he makes it clear that the need felt by the "modern Negro" to traverse the distance separating the African from himself (i.e., the Antilles Negro) and ultimately the European (becoming whiter, he claimed, in the process, or achieving embodiment of the Hegelian Spirit) is symptomatic of an inferiority complex or a psychopathological symptom "rooted in the temporal," that is, in colonialism's temporalizing logic of evolutionism.[31] He declares, "There is of course the moment of 'being for others,' of which Hegel speaks, but all ontology is returned unrealizable in a colonized and civilized society." It is Fanon's use of the Other, that is, as pertaining exclusively to the racialized and colonialized being-for-the-other distinct from "the other" of the Hegelian dialectical tradition, that is implemented most often in this book to signal not only this peculiar race-producing otherness but especially its effects among varying racialized groups. In fact, Fanon speaks of a "third-person consciousness" derived from ontological conflicts existing among black Americans and those of the Antilles (or black Others) to which he adds the ontologies of the individual and that forced upon him by the "white man's eyes."[32]

Du Bois, on the other hand, reflected on this unreconciled striving, a double consciousness, or "two warring ideals in one dark body," without hesitating to posit this struggle's eventual reconciliation within the grand dialectical tradition contrived by Hegel: "The history of the American Negro is the history of the strife . . . to merge his double self into a better and truer self. In this merging *he wishes neither of the older selves to be lost.* He would not Africanize America [nor will he] bleach his Negro soul in a flood of white Americanism."[33] Fernando Ortiz's transculturation is constructed, though in inverse form, on this same dialectical formulation of race and time. But for Fanon, this dialectical resolution would never be forthcoming in the modern world, whether in situations of colonialism or not. The answer to this problem, in Fanon's opinion, was refusing to be temporalized in the first place by modernity's spatial decipherings of the world, a resolution that was attainable but not sustainable by Katherine Dunham, Duke Ellington, Harry Smith, or the other case studies analyzed in this book given their preoccupations with redeeming their sense of Self within modernity's racialist, sexist, nationalist, capitalist, and historicist formations.[34]

Indeed, ontological freedom from modernity's formations was for most a disorienting or else an absurd proposition even as a broad range of contemporaneous thinkers from Mikhail M. Bakhtin, Kurt Koffka, and Martin Heidegger to C. L. R. James, Lydia Cabrera, and Gabriel García Márquez—in addition to Du Bois, Spengler, and Fanon—interrogated the ideologically and politically contingent nature of subjectivity in the modern world. As this book argues, it was this preoccupation with, or fear of losing (as Du Bois in fact noted), one's subjective anchorings in modernity's sanctioned and contingent identity formations that accounted for the profundity in analyzing, listening, embodying, disalienating, and desiring one's way in modernity. The fact that music and dance entailed prediscursive sounding, moving, and feeling bodies, capable at any time to confuse or, worse, unhinge modernity's hold—racialized, sexist, capitalist—on people, made rehearsing the logic of black music's and dance's African origins all the more urgent.

Du Bois's, Spengler's, and Fanon's insights, if anything else, provide the historically contemporaneous theoretical thrust to critically analyze the logic of black music's and dance's African origins as one of modernity's most natural and all-encompassing technologies in the orderings of people, place, and time. For this reason alone their theorizing of time and space is woven into this book's story and put into conversation with the work of a broad range of thinkers in their own right. This book is not simply a historical study of black music and dance, and though much of the material presented here locates the musicking in the United States, it is also not a historical study of African American music and dance in and of itself. In resolving to analyze this logic in the interstices of subject and object, modern and primitive, what can we learn about and from its racialized subjects? Specifically, what did they have to gain and lose artistically, ontologically, economically, ideologically, and politically with respect to their spatialized and temporalized places in the world at this time? And how did these exchanges impart a sense of their place in the world, in terms of their arbitrarily defined status, racially or otherwise? These are some of the questions this book seeks to answer.

The Pathways through the Work

In his *Representing African Music* (2003) Kofi Agawu perhaps best critiqued the problem of twentieth-century Africanist ethnomusicology beginning with comparative musicology as the problem of difference. In formulating this problem, he traverses the many ways in which non-African musicologists, from Erich von Hornbostel, Mieczslaw Kolinski, and Richard Waterman to Rose Brandel, John Chernoff, and David Locke, posited the differences separating African music and Western music (both of which are always conceived as homogeneous). These include differences in perception, as in Hornbostel's statement "We proceed from hearing, they from motion."[35] Agawu attempts to provide a resolution to this "somewhat paradoxical situation" in the following way:

> To say with the structuralists that meaning is difference is, in a sense, to do no more than identify a condition of language use. To say with [Johannes] Fabian that the production of ethnomusicological knowledge depends crucially on a denial of coevalness—a posture designed to keep the Other in a different time frame—is also to identify a condition of knowledge construction. The challenge, therefore, is not whether but *how* to construct difference. It is here that we need to attend to factors of an ethical, political, and ideological nature.[36]

Throughout the chapters of this book, I purposefully use the terms "sound," "movement," "musicking," "dance-music," "racialized as black," and temporalized and spatialized as "of African origins" as methodological gestures toward, but not solutions for, this problem of difference construction. I follow many occasions in which people were compelled to broach black music's and dance's African origins in order to analyze the systems of power—racism, sexism, colonialism, and classism—that were at the crux of these occasions' makings. Chapters 1 and 2 provide hitherto unknown insight into how Melville J. Herskovits, Mieczslaw Kolinski, and Richard Waterman (in addition to other analysts Agawu does not consider, namely, Katherine Dunham, Fernando Ortiz, and Harold Courlander) made some of their decisions to attend to ethical, political, and ideological factors not only affecting their subjects in the anthropological field and racialized modern Others in the city but themselves and each other as well.

Chapter 1 concerns the comparative analysis of music and dance of the New World Negro as this field of research emerged in the late 1920s from the work of Melville J. Herskovits, his colleagues Fernando Ortiz and Erich von Hornbostel, and eventually his collaborator Mieczslaw Kolinski and student Katherine Dunham. It is perhaps appropriate that this first chapter focuses on Herskovits's research activities and beliefs since his anthropological project was vexingly steeped in modernity's discursive paradoxes of race, sexism, and historical time. His belief in science's potential to objectively reason away the scourge of racist thinking did in fact steer many people's work, Kolinski's and Dunham's included, toward the same goals of racial understanding. Yet they predicated much of their work on traveling to, or listening in on, the historical past as it was retained, they believed, among premoderns living in the "bush." As other chapters will show, this technique of being transported back to Africa or the bush upon observing African dance-music and its survivals was shared among many kinds of moderns, anthropologists and comparative musicologists included. But science's precariousness also emerged in more material ways. As Kolinski's life was put increasingly at risk by the spread of Nazi control in Western Europe, Herskovits transgressed his own delineation between politics and scientific objectivity in his attempts to save him and thus their collaborative work on analyzing the African origins of New World Negro music. Whereas for Dunham, in dancing and musicking in the anthropological field, she actively blurred modernity's temporal and spatial formations of the modern and the premodern as well as its delineations of science and art, theory and practice. Dunham would continue to pursue her career in the interstices of science, art, theory, and practice, and in so doing anticipate the kind of feminist praxis that bell hooks and others would advocate for later generations of feminists of color.[37]

The historiographical thrust of chapter 2 provides further explanation of the circumstances surrounding listening practices in modern spaces as well.

Whether in lecture and concert halls and street celebrations in Havana, the Laboratory of Comparative Musicology at Northwestern University, or homes in cities throughout the United States, the practices of listening for the distance and direction from which musical sound traveled, and then measuring such perceived phenomena according to discourses of national history, psychology, and authenticity, factored deeply in how people oriented themselves in the modern world. We can readily detect these practices underlying the experiments in sound perception by German Gestalt psychologists, and though Herskovits chose to collaborate with Hornbostel and Kolinski on the basis of their training in Gestalt psychology, what chapter 2 argues is that these practices conditioned listening across varying social, cultural, and political arenas. Public debate surrounding Havana's carnival celebrations of 1937 was a fulcrum for the Cuban public, including Fernando Ortiz and other Cuban intellectuals as well as modernist composer Gilberto Valdés, to listen for both the African past of, and its presence in, Cuban music. Similar debates in the United States over the African origins of American Negro music continued into the 1940s. In transcribing and analyzing Herskovits's Trinidadian field recordings at Northwestern's laboratory, Waterman developed his theories of "hot" rhythm and metronome sense by listening his way into the mind of the black body to locate the site of black music's African aesthetic retentions.

Whereas Henry Edward Krehbiel had looked to the Negro mind as the location where memories of the African musical past persisted, Herskovits complained that Krehbiel "as with all later writers ... made no detailed study of African musical style, but relied mainly on what he could glean from travelers' accounts and other nonmusical works."[38] In fact, Waterman devised his theories in the laboratory in consultation with Abdul Disu and Julius Okala, two Northwestern students and research assistants from Nigeria who also worked to raise awareness among Americans of the oppressive conditions under colonialism in Africa. Disu and Okala, along with other African immigrants, worked to convince Americans of the myths of the savage and the jungle, whose circulation only intensified with the proliferation of new record disc formats and print media outlets. In helping to usher in the commercial consumption of field recordings, Harold Courlander serves as a particularly important figure in establishing the practices of listening for Negro authenticity via its African origins across not only the scientific and popular divide but also the black and white racial divide as well.

What ontological possibilities did Africans Modupe Paris and Asadata Dafora forge for themselves and African Americans by performing and lecturing about black music's and dance's African origins? How did Zoila Gálvez and

Chano Pozo in their performances of the American Negro mother and the African native foster political solidarity, professional opportunities, and artistic collaborations among Afro-Cubans and African Americans? And how did the engagements of Paul Robeson, Katherine Dunham, Duke Ellington, and Harry Smith with Africa, the Caribbean, and the nature of the modern world itself both shore up and destabilize modernity's promises of freedom? These are the questions that chapters 3 and 4 address, all of which have to do with raced and un-raced bodies as fundamental technologies of modernity's regimes of freedom and time.

Chapter 3's first case study is musician, dancer, and activist Modupe Paris. In his memoir *I Was a Savage* (1957), Paris chronicles his early life in French Guinea, including his first encounters with Western civilization's notions of the savage, historical time, and Christianity.[39] Upon arriving in Freetown, Sierra Leone, to attend missionary school, he was not only looked upon by urban Africans as a savage, stating, "I must have looked the savage that I was," he also quipped about the "hardships which seemed to go with being a Christian," saying, "being a savage was certainly more comfortable."[40] His discussions of space and time are equally insightful, describing his experience moving from his village in Dubréka to Freetown and then to New York City as feeling that he had traversed centuries of time; that time stretched spatially from the thatched-roof village of Dubréka to the skyscraper-studded seaboard of New York City.[41] Paris's observations provide an important framework with which to analyze how he, Dafora, and other African immigrants in the United States strategically maneuvered in, around, and back through differing temporal and spatial formations, including linear, cyclic, ancestral, colonial, and materialist time, in order to expose modernity's shortcomings and contradictions with respect to their own freedom as well as the freedom of other black Others. As racial and temporal Others under colonialism, Paris and Dafora became competent in, and thus acted on, the conceptual equipment of modernity's "native" and "savage" African, modifying them according to the occasion at hand, which often involved performing, researching, and lecturing on the modern American Negro's African ancestors and the African origins of black music and dance of not only the United States but also of the Caribbean and South America as well.[42]

Too often uses of time outside of capitalist and even Hegelian historical dialectical time are attributed exclusively to so-called primitive or non-Western cultures, but E. P. Thompson reminds us in his classic work "Time, Work-Discipline, and Industrial Capitalism" of people's movements from one temporal regime into another, such as "employer's time" to the "worker's own time."[43] Here, I follow the movements of Zoila Gálvez, Paul Robeson, and Chano Pozo to and from their performances of varying temporalized figures of the black body in the United States, Europe, and Cuba, all of which effected a manifold of ethical, political, and ideological consequences. In Gálvez's case, these included her forging among black Cuban and American women what bell hooks identified as the true meaning and value of Sisterhood.[44] With Robeson and Pozo, however, similar solidarities along anticolonial and anticapitalist values were complicated at best, if not deferred by their occasional realizations of the desires and imaginations of the British film industry and Russian modernist dancers.

According to Manthia Diawara, modernity for Africans was a matter of occupying its space, access to which was determined by its regimes of time, not only historical time but capitalist, socialist, and Christian time as well.[45] But the logics of these temporal formations were given to dialecticism's ruthless paths toward progress, which V. Y. Mudimbe critiqued as not actually speaking of Africa nor Africans but rather as justifying the "process of inventing and conquering a continent and naming its 'primitiveness' or 'disorder,' as well as the subsequent means of its exploitation and methods for its 'regeneration.'"[46] Thus, for Africans and others racialized as black, gaining ontological freedom under modernity's temporal formations came at an impossible cost, as Frantz Fanon had determined in *Black Skin, White Masks*. But while Fanon formulated his project of disalienation without much regard to music, its realization actually had been premised on the notion of "being in music" as theorized by Günther Stern Anders, from whose work Fanon drew to formulate his theory of disalienation in the first place.

Chapter 4 argues that, while the kinds of disalienation Fanon theorized did materialize in acts of "being in music" or musicking, such realizations were in fact contingent on modernity's indeterminacies and not merely a matter of rejecting its temporal formations. Through the 1940s, Katherine Dunham, Duke Ellington, and Harry Smith, in their own inimitable ways, affected fleeting moments of disalienation in their day-to-day work from one artistic creation to the next, from one performance to the next. Such moments of disalienation, in other words, were not necessarily limited to acts of musicking. Rather, we might also expect moments of disalienation to have materialized in the interstices of capitalism's, sexism's, and racism's striations through the thicket of everyday living, through their daily actions and the actions of those around them.[47] Dunham continued to operate in and around modernity's dissections of art from science, anthropology from entertainment, black from white, and woman from man, creating for herself along the way—in her work leading up to and out from her choreography *Heat Wave: From Haiti to Harlem*—fleeting moments of disalienation in the world. Ellington, similarly, operated in and around the limits imposed upon him and his musicians by segregation and civil rights activism, the jazz music industry, and directing a band, from one composition to the next. Along the way, in composing and premiering *Liberian Suite*, he alluded to Franklin D. Roosevelt's Four Freedoms by claiming his hope for a fifth freedom from, as I argue, modernity's contingencies. Harry Smith pursued his aim to disrupt visual, sonic, and temporal linearity in creating abstract films and screening them accompanied by recorded music by Dizzy Gillespie and Chano Pozo and by live jazz musicians. Smith's desire to cut off all of the modern world's representational devices might have materialized in his representation of black jazz musicians as being innately soulful if not for his prior anthropological training and, most imperatively, his privileged whiteness or un-raced self.

If during the 1930s and throughout World War II the psychological perspective of African Americans toward the nation changed radically, as Amiri Baraka proposed, then many people's psychological perspective of the modern world, and their sense of security in it, suffered an existential crisis from 1945 through the early 1950s. Chapter 5 homes in on modernity's precarious holds on those entering and moving through fields of black dance music by analyzing the mambo in its varying manifestations in Cuba, the United States, South America, and Mexico. The existential crisis here was affected not merely by the threat of nuclear annihilation but, more to the point of this book, also by the racial intensities whose practices of analyzing national histories in music, listening one's way in the modern present, and embodying the un-raced were disrupted to the point of collapse under the mambo's excesses. It is telling the number of points of convergence one encounters in mambo, from fields of thought and (threat of) action—*lo real maravilloso*, or magical realism; Sartrean existentialism; and atomic war—to a variety of twentieth-century figures: Alejo Carpentier, Dámaso Pérez Prado, Arthur Murray, Chano Urueta, Gabriel García Márquez, the cardinal Juan Gualberto Guevara, Amalia Aguilar, and Rita Montaner. It is important to understand its disparate reaches in terms not of style or influence but, I argue, of its capacity to metastasize to modernity's own regimes of truth formation. If mambo's unorderly, unpatriotic, and sinful movements and soundings threatened the integrity of capitalism's essential social unit, the modern (i.e., un-raced gendered normative) family, then why was capitalism itself the cause of its generative profitability?

In spite of the arbitrary nature of modernity's systems of logic, it is important to stress that black music's and dance's African origins were not a fiction. The connections between music and dance practices in Africa and the Americas were and continue to be real, whether historically, ideationally, stylistically, or experientially conceived. This book's aim, rather, is to situate the logic supporting black music's and dance's African origins within modernity's social and political imperatives of the 1930s through the early 1950s, revealing it to have been not so much a construct as to have involved individuated affects and desires taken up into the assemblage of modern living.[48] The rhizome, as proposed by Gilles Deleuze and Félix Guattari, is a particularly apt metaphor for explaining the paths taken in this book. Consider their definition of the rhizome as establishing "connections between semiotic chains, organizations of power, and circumstances relative to the arts, sciences, and social struggles."[49] The spatial distances across which the logic of black music's and dance's African origins had impressed itself in analyzing, listening, performing, resisting, and desiring is compelling enough to follow and to explore some of its otherwise limitless burrows of significance. Each realization of this logic, whether rendered by an anthropologist, dancer, musician, audience, listener, political activist, filmmaker, or critic, was as a result of deeply compelling human encounters with freedom (individual or political) ultimately at stake, a freedom that modernity promised yet deferred on the basis of people's relationships with its discourses of race, sex, and history.

Just as modernity afforded intellectuals to think, speak, and act in privileged ways, sanctioned by modernity's decipherings of legitimate knowledge production, Africa as Western civilization's Other afforded musicians, dancers, activists, and others to retrace, usually subversively, modernity's decipherings (temporal, spatial, and epistemological) of Africa and thus reconstitute its mattering maps across society along the way. In these ways, the logic of black music's and dance's African origins enabled a field of interaction for Africans, Americans, Cubans, and others to contest, arrest, or re-create flows of the Negro spiritual, jazz, calypso, mambo, and other New World Negro black dance and music. They did so not only to stake their claims in historicism's renderings of black music's and dance's African origins but also to step into each other's histories of oppression, both as the oppressed, as with the Scottsboro case of 1931, and as the oppressors, as in the Americo-Liberian history of minority rule over indigenous Liberians. What we are left with, thus, is a critical understanding of modernity's systems of power—time, space, and race—not merely as social constructs but, more importantly, how and why they operated as such during one of Western civilization's most precarious historical periods, the 1930s through the early 1950s. This was a period of savage oppression and barbaric warfare throughout much of the modern world, culminating in its invention of its own means of destruction (atomic weapons), yet, modernity's condition of unfreedom from identity's subjective assurances proved to be its most perniciously elusive.

Analyzing the African Origins of Negro Music and
Dance in a Time of Racism, Fascism, and War

The ritual drums were never touched by a woman, even the highest of the *mambos*. Many liberties were permitted me because of my unofficial position as emissary of the lost black peoples from *Nan Guinin*. —KATHERINE DUNHAM, *Dance of Haiti*, 1983

Following the end of World War II the urgency to resolve the ideology of racial superiority once and for all was palpable across various spaces of discourse, including international political bodies. Academics in particular continued to predicate their urgency to resolve this problem on their confidence in the natural and social sciences, even though their disciplines had long held opposing definitions of race, which seemed intractable. The statements on the nature of race and racial difference by the United Nations Educational Scientific and Cultural Organization (UNESCO) represent examples of the legitimating role natural and social scientists played in shaping the international community's responses following the end of the war to the Nazi death camps and to racism in general. Charged with redressing the causes of World War II through education, science, and culture, UNESCO convened a panel of mostly social scientists in 1949 in Paris to "adopt a programme of disseminating scientific facts designed to remove what is generally known as racial prejudice."[1] Its first statement published in 1950 resulted from the work of anthropologists, sociologists, and psychologists of different nationalities led by Brazilian anthropologist Arthur Ramos. Criticisms of this document came from human geneticists and physical anthropologists who complained that it "tended to confuse race as a biological fact and the concept of race as a social phenomenon."[2] They were particularly critical of the statement's assertion of the lack of biological or mental differences among racial groups, proof of which they declared had not been scientifically established. (Proof of biological differences had also not been scientifically established.) To address these complaints, UNESCO convened a second group of geneticists and physical anthropologists in 1951 to revise the original document. Before publishing it, however, the new statement was circulated among other biological and social scientists, one of whom was the American anthropologist Melville J. Herskovits; they were asked to submit their comments about the new statement.

In October 1952 Herskovits wrote his response in a letter to Swiss anthropologist Alfred Métraux, who was serving as the director of UNESCO's Social Science Department's race program.[3] His two reservations regarding the statement were based on the premises of cultural determinism. The first concerned the following passage from section one: "The concept of race is unanimously regarded by anthropologists as a classificatory device providing a zoological frame within which the various groups of mankind may be arranged and by means of which studies of evolutionary processes can be facilitated."[4] Herskovits objected to the phrase "by means of which studies of evolutionary processes can be facilitated" because it "suggests a possible implication that there are significant differentials in degree of evolution of different races, something I am sure there is no desire to imply."[5] His second reservation concerned the following passage from section five: "It has been recorded that different groups of the same race occupying similarly high levels of civilization may yield considerable differences in intelligence tests."[6] Herskovits lamented the wording in this paragraph, stating, "I miss the fine hand of a cultural anthropologist."[7] He recommended that the phrase "groups of the same race occupying similarly high levels of civilization" be substituted with "groups of the same race having similar cultures." Métraux did not make these changes to the statement but rather recorded Herskovits's objections, in addition to those of the other reviewers, in a separate section of the document titled "Comments and Criticisms on Different Items of the Statement."

The statements made by UNESCO on the nature of race and racial differences reveal the entrenched vexation that discussions of race still evoked among scientists of varying nationalities, research fields, and methodological approaches. Notions such as "evolutionary processes" and "high levels of civilization," when addressing questions of race, clearly persisted among international bodies of academics into the 1950s in spite of the genocidal practices that the Nazi regime rationalized based on these and other related scientific and historical ideas. For their part, black American writers W. E. B. Du Bois, George Schuyler, and Alain Locke had long discounted definitions of race based on biological determinants.[8] The second UNESCO statement of 1952, however, reveals that biological and evolutionary understandings of race and the authority by which these understandings were issued were as relevant as ever.[9] What is even more revealing is the advice the editor of the 1952 UNESCO statement gave to the reader, based on a dialectical viewpoint: "If confusion seems to be rife, we must not forget that it is precisely such differences of opinion and, indeed, such bitter attacks which give birth to what we call truth."[10]

Although it seems that the authors of UNESCO's statements on race held opposing views over the scientific suitability of evolution, civilization, and cultural relativism, the truth was that they were operating within the same logic of false oppositions (e.g., biological versus cultural determinism), the same race-producing or raciological regime.[11] We can consider the temporal implications in the deployment of these concepts in the name of science as the dominance of one system of historical time, in this case, Western evolutionary Time, "leveled off" as the world's time.[12] Thus, so long as Africa was posited within this temporal scheme, Africans racialized as black body by social and biological scientists alike had at least one foot in the modern's savage or primitive past. The spatialization of Africans and New World Negroes according to the significations of nonurban places was especially compelling when explaining the origins of black music, as even Du Bois demonstrated in *The Souls of Black Folk* (1903) when he turned back onto the "African forests, where its counterpart can *still be heard*" to mark the distance from which American Negro religious music had evolved to its civilized modern state.[13] Thus, regardless of the branch of science, we can attribute UNESCO's vexed statements on race to their temporalizing and spatializing practices, which were particularly productive in analyzing black music's African origins.[14]

Beginning in the late 1920s Herskovits and his Cuban colleague Fernando Ortiz, among others, aimed to deal with their respective society's long-held beliefs in African racial and cultural inferiority. By the early 1940s they each would publish their defining work on race—Herskovits's *The Myth of the Negro Past* (1941) and Ortiz's *El engaño de las razas* (The deception of the races, 1946)—in which they reaffirmed that objective scientific knowledge of both the African origins of the New World Negro and the nature of cultural retention and change would debunk those false theories of race (based on biological determinism and the ideology of racial superiority) to which they attributed the existence of racial prejudice, including toward black music and dance.

Herskovits and Ortiz drew from their capital as scientists to resolve racism in society, believing that their work would impart, on the one hand, a sense of indisputable fact among people holding racist views and, on the other, a sense of pride among society's black populations in their African pasts. They also believed, however, that objective scientific analysis of the African origins of New World Negro cultures must come a priori to any political activism if racist ideologies were to be debunked once and for all. In other words, the unearthing and collection of African retentions in the anthropological field was strictly a matter of scientific discovery for the benefit of all groups, wherein racism's pathologies would thereafter disappear.

This chapter begins with analyzing Herskovits's correspondence with Fernando Ortiz and Erich von Hornbostel regarding his research on the African origins of the spiritual as part of his program to debunk the mythologies surrounding American Negroes. It focuses on deconstructing the significance placed on contemporaries—that is, Herskovits toward Caribbean and West African people of the "bush"—as spatial and temporal substitutes for Africans of the past. Such projections of the historical and spatial past onto so-called primitives and their cultural practices have been critically analyzed, especially in critiques of Africanist anthropology of the nineteenth and early twentieth centuries.[15] What has escaped accountability, however, is how histories of whiteness as racially consolidating phenomena in North America and Europe further enabled the consolidation of black Others as either primitive or modern Negroes in Africa and in the so-called New World. For the purposes of this chapter the question of racially consolidating discourses invites analysis of not so much racial discourse *per se* as the ability of anthropologists and comparative musicologists to apprehend music both a priori and a posteriori on behalf of race, an ability that was indeed constitutive of Herskovits's project in toto in spite of his desire of scientific or a priori objectivity.

What this chapter also addresses are the day-to-day actions taken in a transnational social science industry that attempted to meet the need for the valuation of racial Others and their cultures in the face of fascism's growing threats. To this end, Herskovits's collaborations with German comparative musicologists Erich von Hornbostel and Mieczyslaw Kolinski are situated within the Nazis' rise to power in Western Europe.[16] The urgency Herskovits felt in saving Kolinski from the Nazis motivated him to maximize his social capital as a scientist in order to convince philanthropic and government agencies in the United States of the potential social breakthrough of Kolinski's comparative musicological work on the music that Herskovits himself recorded in Suriname, West Africa, and Haiti. It was this music, according to Herskovits, that would help not only provide American Negroes the history and aesthetic value as was wont of music and cultures deemed as modernity's standard-bearers of Western civilization but also wrestle the domains of civilization and evolution away from fascist claims of Aryan racial superiority for the benefit also of white Others, namely, Jews.

Of similar significance to the analysis of black dance music's African origins during the 1930s is Herskovits's relationship with dancer and anthropologist Katherine Dunham, which reveals science's power dynamics based on race, gender, and the privileging of science over performance as the appropriate mode of knowledge production. As was the case with other women anthropologists and comparative musicologists, Dunham's field methods and scholarship were simply downplayed by her white male colleagues.[17] In fact, Dunham's fieldwork and publications reveal instances in which her participation in dance and rituals generated haptically different spatial and temporal configurations, rendering inconsequential those "landmarks" orienting the Maroons of Accompong, Jamaica, or the "Bush Negroes" of Suriname as substitutes for historical Africans. Moreover, her correspondence with Herskovits from the anthropological field uncovers among her informants a suspicion of anthropologists along with other temporal and spatial configurations of the New World Negro from which Dunham benefited, as this chapter's epigraph demonstrates, in terms of gaining access to cultural practices, including those otherwise reserved for men. In other instances, however, she did not resist anthropology's temporalizing and spatializing practices in dealing with primitive dance's African influences, actions that she would also take in pursuing financial backing for her dance productions later in her career.

The postwar statements made by UNESCO on race state that racism is "the outcome of a fundamentally anti-rational system of thought and is in glaring conflict with the whole humanist tradition of our civilization."[18] Racism, it seems, was neither of science nor humanism, of which among the most revered endeavors were music and dance. Yet, as this chapter argues, some attempts made in the 1930s to prove racism's irrational foundations looked toward the scientific analysis of black music and dance's African origins, fraught as this endeavor was with contradictory practices stemming from Western civilization's inscriptions of historical time and space, along with its racial and gendered norms. Whether they conceived of race as biologically or culturally determined, and accessible a priori or a posteriori, anthropologists and comparative musicologists did not take account of the paradox in inscribing the temporal past onto singing voices and dancing bodies when searching for evidence of their music and dance's aesthetic value and historical integrity.[19] Nor were their objective scientific analyses unaffected by the turbulent political situation instigated by the rise of fascism in Europe. In the end, the pursuit of science regarding the African origins of black music and dance occupied a rung interlaced with, or adjacent to, notions of African inferiority, Eurocentrism, and UNESCO's statements on race and racial difference, all of which constituted the same sign chain and practices of listening to, seeing, and rationalizing race.[20]

"This Problem of Race That Has Plagued Us So"

In a letter addressed to Fernando Ortiz on June 12, 1946, Melville Herskovits thanked the Cuban scholar for sending him his book *El engaño de las razas*, stating, "It is a magnificent analysis of this problem of race that has plagued us so, and will undoubtedly take a very high place among the books that have attempted to set people right in this difficult field."[21] Five years earlier, in 1941, before the United States entered World War II, Herskovits published *The Myth of the Negro Past*, which served as the culmination of his work begun in the 1920s in which he similarly posited the practical social effects of the scientific study of the New World Negro's African heritages. Herskovits summarized the rationale for *The Myth of the Negro Past*: "It must again be emphasized that when such a body of [scientific] fact, solidly grounded, is established, a ferment must follow which, when this information is diffused over the population as a whole, will influence opinion in general concerning Negro abilities and potentialities, and thus contribute to a lessening of interracial tensions."[22]

Based on his fieldwork in the Caribbean and West Africa, Herskovits intended *The Myth of the Negro Past* to debunk racist myths commonly held in American society that he believed were the source of interracial tensions; these myths included that Negroes were descended from inferior African slaves; that slaves of different ethnic groups lacked common languages and customs; that slaves and their descendants gave up their inferior cultures for superior European customs; and that the modern Negro had no past. In fact, Herskovits's dissertation advisor, Franz Boas, had similarly intended his work to debunk such myths as early as 1904 by pointing to African accomplishments in iron technology, law, trade, and culture.[23] For Ortiz's part, he synthesized the latest scientific literature on race in *El engaño de las razas* to dispel similarly held racist beliefs for the benefit of the public not only in Cuba but in all of the Americas. In spite of their varying scopes, Herskovits and Ortiz believed that the scientific study of the African origins of their society's black populations would help discredit theories of these populations and, thereafter, resolve race prejudice among whites and inspire race pride among blacks.

Both Herskovits and Ortiz were adamant that their scholarship was not to be guided by any social or political agenda. As Walter Jackson shows, by the late 1920s, after having conducted physical anthropological studies of racial miscegenation among American Negroes and championing racial and cultural assimilation to combat the tenets of scientific racism and racial prejudice in the United States, Herskovits believed that pursuing only objective studies of the history of American Negroes detached from any political activism would provide the scientific basis upon which claims of racial equality could then be put forth.[24] Current racial politics nationally and internationally, in fact, shaped Herskovits's and Ortiz's desire to proclaim their work to be a priori scientific. Jerry Gershenhorn suggests that Herskovits "emphasized his professional legitimacy by wrapping himself in the mantle of science" because of American academia's anti-Semitic environment and the suspicion of Jewish scholars having a subjective, minority agenda.[25] Indeed Herskovits hesitated to associate himself with the National Association for the Advancement of Colored People, which had invited him to write an appreciation of the organization on the occasion of its twentieth-anniversary conference in 1928. Two years later, in his landmark article "The Negro in the New World: The Statement of a Problem," he laid out in detail for the first time his acculturation methodology for studying the New World Negro and only vaguely implied the "far-reaching practical significance" of his research.[26] Beginning in 1935, however, Herskovits increasingly transgressed this principle as a result of actively advocating for Mieczyslaw Kolinski's escape from Nazi-controlled Western Europe. With this in mind, Herskovits's work on the New World Negro, among other avenues of historiography, lends insight into the peculiar alchemy by which American Jews became Caucasian in the decade leading up to World War II.[27]

Similarly, by 1930, Ortiz had rejected his earlier notions about the relationship between black Cubans, cultural decadence, and social deviance and began to address questions of Cuban race relations, as Boas and Herskovits had been doing in the United States.[28] As early as 1928, while in Madrid, Ortiz attacked formulations of race purity and superiority, believing that racism was a "barbaric anachronism, incompatible with the present demands of culture and an enemy of the Cuban nation."[29] In 1942, in a speech he delivered to Havana's Club Atenas, he outlined the stages of interracial relations Cuba had undergone, proclaiming that "we are at last on the road to mutual understanding in spite of prejudices which have not been eradicated and are even aggravated today by foreign political ideologies whose principal exponent is Hitler with all his brutal race theories. This is today's phase." Indeed, for both Herskovits and Ortiz, Nazism would become the most immediate threat to the problems of race plaguing the United States and Cuba. Yet while they attempted to disprove the biological basis of the binary racial logic of black and white, in addition to ideologies of racial superiority and purity, they never questioned this logic's temporal underpinnings.

Ortiz initiated correspondence with Herskovits, writing to his American colleague in October 1930, shortly before he went into exile as a result of the oppressive policies of the Cuban dictator Gerardo Machado.[30] At first they exchanged publications with little discussion of the specifics of their work apart from their common interest in studying the cultures of New World Negroes. Then Herskovits received a letter written by Ortiz from New York City in December, notifying Herskovits that he had "emigrated, fleeing Machado's tyranny." He ends the letter by indicating that he is finishing a book on Afro-Cuban musical instruments.[31] In the following year Ortiz was still in exile, now living in Washington, DC, and making plans to either stay in the United States or move to Spain.[32] Meanwhile, Herskovits was attempting to secure funds in order to invite Ortiz to deliver a lecture at Northwestern University but to no avail, given the university's budgetary limitations due to the ongoing effects of the Great Depression.[33] Eventually, after the Machado regime fell in September 1933, Ortiz returned to Cuba and his teaching post at the University of Havana. Initially, Ortiz was unable to continue his work on Afro-Cubans, a theme that he described to Herskovits as that about which he was most passionate.[34] This situation changed, however, in 1936, when Ortiz helped organize and was named president of the Sociedad de Estudios Afrocubanos (Society of Afro-Cuban Studies).

By 1935 Nazi Germany's implementation of the Nuremberg Laws, which deprived Jews of German citizenship and outlawed marriages between Aryans and non-Aryans, along with continuing racial tensions in American and Cuban society, compelled Herskovits as well as Ortiz to make pronounced announcements about the urgency in scientifically studying the African origins of black cultures, including in the field of comparative musicology. For instance, the second statute of the Sociedad de Estudios Afrocubanos reads: our "goal . . . will be to study with objective criteria the phenomena (demographic, economic, juridical, religious, literary, artistic, linguistic and social in general) produced in Cuba by the tolerance of distinct races, particularly the so-called black race *of African origin*, and the so-called white race or Caucasian, with the goal to accomplish with knowledge of the facts, of their causes and consequences, and the most egalitarian mutual understanding of the diverse integral elements of the Cuban nation toward the happy realization of its common historical destinies."[35] Ortiz would continue to argue for the nonexistence of racial purity through the end of the war in his scholarship as well as in editorials published in Havana's dailies.[36] But the speculation over so-called races did not extend, it seems, to the temporal and spatial construct of "African origin," whose analogue "European origin," significantly, does not appear in that statement's formulation.

Racism's plague indeed vexed these social scientists and their fellow citizens not merely because their scholarship failed to ferment a new knowledge of Negro abilities, potentialities, and history. In fact, African, African American, and Afro-Cuban musicians and dancers, too, were working in the United States and Cuba to affect a shift in popular knowledge of their respective population's historical and cultural legitimacy (see chapters 3 and 4). Rather, because these performers and social scientists projected Africa as point of origin, the goal toward affecting a true ontological shift would remain elusive. The next chapter will explore this problem in further detail as it unfolded in Havana in the late 1930s. What follows here is a closer look at the temporal implications of searching for origins as these pertained to Herskovits's work on the Negro spiritual and the rise of Nazism in Germany.

Early on in his research Herskovits believed in the significance music, in addition to folklore and religion, had in not only studying the processes of acculturation but also furthering a culturalist definition of race against, for instance, its psychophysical definition as proposed by Gestalt-trained comparative musicologists.[37] His correspondence with the comparative musicologist Erich M. von Hornbostel between 1927 and 1933 proves particularly insightful in regard to the ideological impact scientific practice had on shaping the discourse on race and the African origins of the Negro spiritual as well as determining whose work in these areas was scientific in the first place. Herskovits wrote to Hornbostel in April 1927 after reading his article "American Negro Songs" (1926) in which the author argued that American Negro music, particularly the spiritual, was of European origin, yet the style in which Negroes performed it was of African origin.[38] In his initial reply to Herskovits's letter, Hornbostel claimed that he had developed the idea of motor behavior as being a characteristic of race after hearing Franz Boas "many years ago" remark that it was fundamentally characteristic of style.[39] Indeed, throughout his career when addressing issues of race Boas wrestled with reconciling the methodologies of physical anthropology (which assumed differences of mental aptitude between races), cultural anthropology, and his liberal values, which informed his initiation of a cultural and social determinist outlook. Boas also realized that racial prejudice and discrimination toward American Negroes were ultimately the results of notions of white social and economic privilege and racial supremacy and purity.[40] Although Hornbostel conceived of motor behavior and musical style as racially determined, he theorized it not exactly in physical anthropological terms but rather in psychophysical terms; as such, he presented black music making, regardless of the racial or national origins of the melodic and rhythmic content, as a Gestalten, divorced from any cultural influence.[41] Accordingly, in his article Hornbostel argued: "Not what [an African Negro] sings is so characteristic of his race, but the way he sings. This way of the Negro is identical in Africa and in America and is totally different from the way of any other race, but it is difficult, if not impossible, to describe or analyse it. . . . Motor behaviour, then, proves to be the psycho-physical basis on which, independent of culture and surroundings, racial physiognomy rests."[42]

Herskovits, however, pointed to his prior anthropometric research on race mixing among American Negroes to challenge Hornbostel's Gestalt-based understanding of race and motor behavior, arguing instead that motor behavior, and thus musical style, is in fact conditioned by culture. As for race, he wrote: "I must confess that I conceive human beings as being very fundamentally conditioned (this in the sense of the word as used by the behavioristic psychologists) by the manner of behavior of the people among whom they happen to be born."[43] In his response to Herskovits's point about race mixing, Hornbostel suggested that motor behavior might belong "to those hereditary traits which keep more constant in one race than in the other."[44] Once again, Herskovits refuted this explanation and held to his original argument, writing, "The motor behavior of the American Negro in singing his Spirituals could well, it seems to me, be carried over as a behavior pattern handed down thru imitation and example from the original African slaves who were brought here."[45] Hornbostel's Gestalt-based theorizing of musical style and racial homogeneity pointed to the kind of racial mythologizing that Herskovits and Ortiz perceived to be complicit in society's rationalization of racist attitudes. Herskovits, however, revealed his own complicity in perpetuating the truth of time by constructing a lineage of musical style (regardless of whether it was culturally conditioned or psychophysically determined) as a subject of history rather than an object of his own acculturation method's spatialization of the historical past. In either case, what differentiated Herskovits's and Hornbostel's claims from scholars such as James Weldon Johnson, who as late as 1925 had already asserted that the spiritual was "purely and solely the creation of the American Negro" and the "Negro brought with him from Africa his native musical instinct and talent," was Herskovits's belief in particular that Johnson's claims had not been subjected to scientific study beginning with doing fieldwork.[46]

Herskovits's practice of temporalizing the New World Negro and spatializing the historical past onto the bush was evidenced in his selection of Suriname as the location to start his fieldwork in order to contribute his own scientific study of the African origins of American Negro culture, including the spiritual. The methodological importance of (supposedly) isolated New World Negro groups weighed heavily on Herskovits's thinking as early as 1927, when he consulted with Elsie Clews Parsons, an anthropologist and folklorist who suggested to him he research the "Bush-Negro" population of Suriname. The historical record confirmed that the Bush Negroes were "descended from escaped slaves who had established their own communities during the late seventeenth century."[47] Herskovits's desire to adapt the notions of the laboratory and controlled, repeated experimentation from the natural sciences—as had also been done by Gestalt psychologists in Europe—to his study of the African origins of the New World Negro factored fundamentally in the methodological importance he placed on knowledge of African cultural traits coupled with the study of New World Negro populations spatially isolated from European and American Indian cultures. As he noted in 1930, "The only way in which problems of this sort are ever to be answered is through searching out situations in which we find the necessary controls presented to us, and studying these."[48] But isolated places such as the bush alone did not constitute Herskovits's laboratory of black cultural controls against which he would then study the process of acculturation. As he posited in his article "Social History of the Negro" (1935): "History sets up experiments for the social scientists that can be regarded as more comparable to the laboratory experiments set up by the natural and exact scientists than is ordinarily thought to be the case."[49] Historical time, therefore, in conjunction with isolated locations served as the conceptual planes upon which Herskovits, anthropology, and modern society in general mapped the New World Negro as historically and spatially distant.

Herskovits and his wife Frances S. Herskovits made two research trips to Suriname, first in July 1928, and then again in the summer of 1929. Morton C. Kahn of the American Museum of Natural History accompanied the Herskovitses on their first trip. It was the material collected during the second research trip, however, that resulted in *Suriname Folk-lore*, the first two parts of which he coauthored with Frances Herskovits. In regard to their first trip, H. Gordon Garbedian reported in the *New York Times* that Kahn and the Herskovitses led a scientific expedition to a "little-known country" in South America where a "unique people which still adheres to the primitive culture of the African jungle [live] on the edge of Western civilization."[50] Garbedian describes the various items of Bush-Negro culture that Kahn and Herskovits collected, including their drums. "Strongly suggestive of the culture of the Dark Continent is the highly developed system of drum telegraphy found among the Suriname River Djukas." Garbedian identifies two other uses of the drum: communicating with spirits and inducing the "frenzy of religious fervor." In another issue of the *New York Times*, a reporter quoted the researchers: " 'An experience which we will never forget was the witnessing of an Obeah dance which was accompanied by chanting, beating of tom-toms and frenzied excitement,' the scientists said. 'The scantily clad natives, seized by the spirit of the drums and the gods of the place . . . dashed about in the frenzy of their religious fervor.' "[51] Even local newspapers published reports of the scientific expedition. Kansas's *Sun* titled one article "Two Scientists Back from Trip to Dark Africa" in which it is stated that they had returned from the Dutch Guiana jungle only later claiming that they had spent two months with the Bush Negroes "of the Submarine river valley in South Africa."[52]

These news reports in their entirety demonstrate that the Herskovitses' first research trip fell squarely within the spatial practice of traveling to, and reporting on, exotic places and relaying these adventures from the historical and geographical edge of Western civilization to newspaper readers in the modern world. The exact geographic location did not matter, for any location "on the edge of Western civilization"—whether Dark Africa, South Africa, Suriname, or Accompong, Jamaica (as we will see later)—occupied humanity's primitive and savage past. Nor did Herskovits's aim to produce scientific research that would have "practical significance" factor into the logic of reporting on such adventures. Newspaper reports published during and after their 1929 research trip did not differ from the previous year's, though some reported on Herskovits's hypothesis that the Bush Negroes were "descendants of former slaves and essentially of the same stock as the American negro."[53] The black newspaper *Philadelphia Tribune* titled one article "Throws New Light on Origin of American Negro" and quoted Herskovits saying "that the American Negro and that of the West Indies came from the same place in Africa as the former slaves of Dutch Guiana. As these Bush-Negroes know approximately the places in Africa whence their ancestors came, we have a new insight into the origin of the American Negro."[54] Baltimore's *Afro-American*, however, made no specific mention of his hypothesis, saying only, "Chicago savant thrilled by magic of natives."[55] As Richard Price and Sally Price note, Herskovits was all too eager to identify traits in the cultural practices of the Bush Negroes of Suriname as African retentions: he "wasn't just 'seeing' Africa. He was inducing it and insisting on it repeatedly."[56] Moreover, the fact that his hypothesis about the African origins of the spiritual went unreported in these black newspapers points to the general prejudice or apathy that many black Americans felt, as Alain Locke had noted in 1924, toward Africa.[57] This was, to Herskovits, one of the by-products of American society's ignorance of African culture and history, an ignorance that African anticolonial activists, musicians, and dancers would also attempt to reverse throughout the following decade (see chapter 3).

Herskovits first reported his findings "as music is concerned" to Hornbostel in November 1929, following his second trip to Suriname. He believed that the one hundred cylinder recordings he made "when [they] are worked up will go far to solve the problem you have stated so interestingly—that of the origins of the American Negro spiritual."[58] He considered asking comparative musicologist George Herzog to transcribe and analyze the recordings had he been available, thus, he continued, "I would count it an honor for you to transcribe them and I realize they would receive their full scientific consideration." As the director of the Phonogramm-Archiv of Berlin, Hornbostel had at his disposal the equipment necessary to produce electrotyped copies of Herskovits's field recordings. Furthermore, in spite of his disagreements with Hornbostel's Gestalt-based viewpoints on race and motor behavior in music, Herskovits regarded him as an able scientist and leader in the field of comparative musicology, which he believed to be as scientifically rigorous in its methodologies as acculturation and thus crucial to his study of the New World Negro. It is important to note, however, that Herzog was not the only American comparative musicologist able to transcribe and analyze his recordings.

Before Herskovits's field trip to Suriname, Helen H. Roberts had not only published scholarship on African survivals in Jamaican music, she had also conducted her own fieldwork and made field recordings in the United States and in Jamaica in 1920 and 1921. In her article "Possible Survivals of African Song in Jamaica" (1926), for example, she concluded that based on her transcription and analysis of her field recordings, which she collected in and around Accompong, the occurrences of part singing, the mixed minor scale (i.e., scales with a minor third and raised sixth), and repetition of phrases are of African origin.[59] That Roberts had already made some of the conclusions Herskovits and Hornbostel's student Mieczyslaw Kolinski would make nearly ten years later raises the issue of sexism in the history of comparative musicology and New World Negro studies, an issue that will receive further attention in the following sections. In this instance, Herskovits's intrigue with Hornbostel's application of his Gestalt-based methodology toward the question of motor behavior, a problem Roberts did not address in her scholarship, probably accounted more for his decision to approach Hornbostel than any considerations of gender. Moreover, Hornbostel's and

Herskovits's methodologies were confluent in the same temporal and spatial epistemology, wherein the theoretical imperatives of comparative musicology and acculturation induced them in hearing Africa, in addition to Herskovits hearing the spiritual, in the singing and drumming of the Bush Negroes.

Hornbostel encouraged Herskovits to send his cylinders to the archive in Berlin but declined the offer to transcribe and analyze them because of his busy work schedule.[60] Eventually, in July 1930, he recommended Kolinski to Herskovits for the job of transcribing and analyzing the Suriname field recordings.[61] Kolinski had completed his doctoral dissertation in comparative musicology under Hornbostel's supervision earlier that year and was now serving as his assistant at the Phonogramm-Archiv. Before receiving Hornbostel's recommendation, Herskovits wrote him in May, identifying the recordings whose contents struck him as "resembling our American Negro spirituals very closely."[62] The fact that these recordings were of the Bush Negroes of the Saramacca tribe, and not the Town Negroes of Paramaribo, further demonstrates the spatial and temporal logic of Herskovits's selection of research sites and in how he listened to his field recordings.

Thus, by 1935, Herskovits felt able to proclaim the following: "Because in Dutch Guiana the Bush Negroes were able to muster sufficient forces to revolt and thus to attain complete freedom, their culture is the most African that exists in the Western Hemisphere." "In accordance with the cultural conservatism that is a concomitant of isolation, *these Negroes, therefore, have the same cultural patterns that marked the life of their ancestors in Africa*, so that the civilization of the Guiana Negroes reflects more faithfully than any other modes of life *as lived in Africa three centuries ago*."[63] Indeed, the spatial and temporal significance that Herskovits attributed to the Bush Negroes also helps explain how their music as recorded by Herskovits functioned as sonic indexes of the distant African past. That is, both Hornbostel and Herskovits deduced that the more an African or New World Negro group was isolated from modernity, the more their music was *contiguous* with, and thus an index (rather than merely a survival or icon) of, seventeenth-century Africa.[64] Writing in September 1930, Hornbostel advised Herskovits: "The comparison with the music actually to be heard in West Africa will somewhat be complicated by the fact that in the meantime—since their forefathers went to America—African singing itself has been influenced by the White, especially on the Guinea cost [*sic*]. But it may be that some tribes in the bush have escaped both European and Islamic influence and will show what genuine West-African Negro Music really sonds [*sic*] like."[65] That both Herskovits and Hornbostel determined the auditory significance of the field recordings based largely on spatial and temporal factors points to a habitus of listening scientifically in the social science's equivalent to the laboratory that induced them to hear genuine African singing and drumming patterns dating as far back as the seventeenth century.

By 1931 Herskovits's laboratory for studying the African origins of New World Negro music extended well beyond Suriname and the United States to include Nigeria, Dahomey, and the Gold Coast. He continued to collect field recordings and send them to the Phonogramm-Archiv to be copied, transcribed, and analyzed. As with the Suriname recordings, he listened for stylistic resemblances, writing to Hornbostel that "the correspondence between these [African] songs and the Suriname music of the bush comes out very strikingly."[66] Time and space factored fundamentally in Herskovits's scientific methodology, which he began to refer to as the historical-ethnographic method by 1933. He even credited Ortiz's work as "one of the few examples available of the utilization of the historical-ethnographic method employed here."[67] In fact, the historical-ethnographic method was essentially a version of the Boasian diffusionist paradigm that, based on the comparative method, conceived cultural history as fundamentally spatial and thus used the present spatial distribution of folklore elements or traits to reconstitute the historical past.[68]

As a result, and as Herskovits's own correspondence and reports of his research trips show, he conceived of black Surinamese, West Africans, and other black populations throughout the New World, who otherwise were his contemporaries as well as contemporaries of American Negroes, as "controls" in his study of African retentions, such that by 1945 he felt that he stood on enough objective scientific ground based on fieldwork to publish in the short-lived journal *Afroamérica* a comprehensive table listing various areas of social life and organization of these so-called controls and grading the "intensity" of their Africanness (figure 1.1). Thereby, Herskovits joined his evolutionist and pre-evolutionist anthropological ancestors of the eighteenth and nineteenth centuries in employing "contemporary primitive peoples to stand in for historical primitives in the absence of adequate historical evidence."[69] He did try intentionally not to set these "contemporary primitive peoples" against moderns as less "evolved" by adopting a cultural relativist viewpoint. It was this rhetorical tactic, Herskovits believed, that would have a practical effect on the problem of racism and notions of racial inferiority. What he seemed to be disavowing, however, was that the temporal myths that sustained, for example, the notion of evolutionary progress, were the same upon which he based his scale of New World Africanisms. Acculturation, he believed, was measurable

	Technology	Economic Life	Social Organization	Non-kinship Institutions	Religion	Magic	Art	Folklore	Music	Language
Guiana (bush)	b	b	a	a	a	a	b	a	a	b
Guiana (Paramaribo)	c	c	b	c	a	a	e	a	a	c
Haiti (peasant)	c	b	b	c	a	b	d	a	a	c
Haiti (urban)	e	d	c	c	b	b	e	a	a	c
Brazil (Bahía)	d	d	b	d	a	a	b	a	a	a
Brazil (Porto Alegre)	e	e	c	d	a	a	e	?	a	c
Brazil (north-urban)	e	d	c	e	a	b	e	d	a	b
Brazil (north-rural)	c	c	b	e	c	b	e	b	b	d
Jamaica (Maroons)	c	c	b	b	b	a	e	a	a	c
Jamaica (general)	e	d	d	d	c	b	e	a	b	c
Trinidad (Toco)	e	d	c	c	c	b	e	b	b	d
Trinidad (Port-of-Spain)	e	d	c	b	a	a	e	b	a	c
Cuba	?	?	?	c	a	a	?	?	b	?
Virgin Islands	e	d	c	d	e	c	?	b	?	d
Gulla Islands	c	c	c	d	c	b	e	a	b	d
United States (rural south)	d	e	c	d	c	c	e	c	b	e
United States (north)	e	e	c	d	c	c	e	d	b	e

a : very African
b : quite African
c : somewhat African
d : a little African
e : trace of African custom, or absent
? : no report

FIG. 1.1 "Scale of Intensity of New World Africanisms," prepared by Melville J. Herskovits. From "Problem, Method and Theory in Afroamerican Studies," *Afroamérica* I, no. 1 (1945): 14.

temporally, as implied in the scalar spectrum "a" to "e" (or "very African" to "trace of African custom, or absent") and spatially as that marking the distance between the bush or rural and urban.

Through 1932 Herskovits's correspondence with his Berlin-based colleagues regarding his field recordings concerned mostly the methodological challenges in transcribing and analyzing their contents. By spring 1933 political events in Germany put Hornbostel, Kolinski, and millions of other Jews living in Germany in danger of their livelihood, freedom, and lives. For instance, the passing of the Law for the Reestablishment of the Professional Civil Service called for the removal or forced retirement of non-Aryan state officials, including professors.[70] Like many of his colleagues, Hornbostel decided to leave Berlin immediately after the passing of this law; he went first to Zurich, where he eventually received safe entry into the United States. Herskovits read of Hornbostel's move to Zurich in a letter written to him by Herzog in which he expressed his sadness over the fact that "a man of his caliber, the authority in a number of fields, should find it difficult to devote his time and peace of mind to teaching and work."[71] He asked Herskovits if Northwestern University could invite him to the United States to deliver a lecture, saying "As you probably know, he is the best man there is also in the fields of the Psychology of Music, Physiological

Acoustics and Comparative Physiology of the Sense-Organs. The fact that he is one of the Gestalt men, in close touch with [Wolfgang] Köhler, ought to add interest to his lectures on the Psychology of Music."[72] Hornbostel eventually wrote to Herskovits in September, happily announcing that the "New School for Social Research has given me an appointment for two years and we shall leave old Europe tomorrow."[73] He, too, asked Herskovits if he saw any possibility for him to receive an invitation from Northwestern to deliver a lecture.

Kolinski, like his mentor, left Berlin in April 1933 and went to Prague, where he felt safe enough to continue working with field recordings, including those from Herkovits's Dahomean and Ashanti collection, as well as composing and performing. But in the immediate aftermath of Adolf Hitler's rise to power as chancellor of Germany, confusion over Kolinski's whereabouts and speculation about his ethnicity settled over Herskovits and Herzog. In a letter to Herskovits, Herzog appended the following postscript: "Hornbostel also wrote me that he has left his assistant in charge of the Archive so that I am quite confident Kolinsky's [sic] work for you is not suffering any through the conditions. I rather doubt it that he is even a Jew."[74] In May, Herskovits replied with more troubling news: "Kolinski has written me from Zurich that as a 'non-Aryan' he finds it advisable to live outside the borders of the third Reich."[75] In fact, Kolinski would remain in Prague until August 1938, when Nazi aggression, after the invasion of Austria in May of that year, threatened his safety in Czechoslovakia. Kolinski was indeed Jewish, having been born in Warsaw, but he renounced his Polish citizenship when he became a citizen of Germany before 1933.[76] In 1935, after officially losing his German citizenship due to the passage of the Nuremberg Laws, Kolinski became in effect a citizen without a nation. Thus began an intensely distressful period of frantic letter writing on the part of Herskovits, extolling the scientific and thus the social significance of Kolinski's work and of comparative musicology in general in order to secure his safe exit from Europe. Indeed, Herskovits's New World Negro acculturation research (not to mention the discipline of comparative musicology itself) was now irrevocably bound up with political events in Europe. Meanwhile, regular communication between Kolinski and Herskovits was frequently interrupted by eerie periods of no response from the exiled comparative musicologist.

Comparative Musicology in Exile

The 1930s were a decisive decade in the history of comparative musicology in Germany and the United States. In February 1933 Henry Cowell, George Herzog, Dorothy Lawton, Helen H. Roberts, and Charles Seeger founded the

American Society for Comparative Musicology in New York City.[77] That same year the Gesellschaft zur Erforschung der Musik des Orients (Society for the Exploration of the Music of the Orient), which was formed by Hornbostel, Kolinski, Herzog, Curt Sachs, Robert Lachmann, Georg Schünemann, Marius Schneider, and Johannes Wolf in Berlin in 1930, changed its name to Gesellschaft für vergleichende Musikwissenschaft (Society for Comparative Musicology). According to Charles Seeger, in response to the growing threat of Nazism in Germany, members of the American society, which included Herskovits, chose to affiliate with, and enroll in, the German society "with the aim to strengthen the parent group to withstand the onslaughts of National Socialist fanaticism."[78] Members of the American society also received a free subscription to *Zeitschrift für Vergleichende Musikwissenschaft* (Journal of comparative musicology), the German society's quarterly. By 1935 all of the Jewish members of the society had fled Germany.[79]

As a member of the American society, Herskovits received a letter in April 1934 from the society's secretary, Helen Roberts, announcing among other items the arrival in the United States of Hornbostel, who had "joined the Graduate Faculty of Political Science ('University in Exile') at the New School for Social Research . . . where he is conducting in English a Seminar in 'Problems of Musicology' and a Lecture Course in Comparative Musicology—both for advanced students only."[80] Comparative musicology in the United States seemed to be strengthening its presence in academia and other institutions. In January 1935 Roberts mailed to members the society's constitution, which included fourteen sections detailing the society's bylaws. The first section listed the four objectives of the society, the first of which was to advance musicology by research into and comparative study of the music of all peoples, primitive and barbaric, Oriental and European, for the purpose of preserving it and making it accessible to all. Meanwhile, the impending demise of comparative musicology in Germany continued with the dissolution in 1935 of the Gesellschaft für vergleichende Musikwissenschaft. Then, in November 1935, Hornbostel died in Cambridge, England, where he had moved after only one year in New York City.[81] By 1937 the American society, now known as the American Section of the International Society for Comparative Musicology, began to dissolve because of the lack of financial support and organizational cohesion as well as the political climate internationally.[82] Amazingly, in spite of the discipline's institutional demise and the ever-growing dangerous political situation in Europe, Kolinski continued to work transcribing and analyzing Herskovits's field recordings and publishing his own work while in exile in Prague from 1933 to 1938. We can attribute his persistence to both his need for income and

Herskovits's need to answer the question of the African derivation of New World Negro music, which factored fundamentally in his acculturation studies of New World Negro cultures and his goal for his research to have a practical impact on social issues concerning race.

Kolinski's analysis of Herskovits's Suriname field recordings, as it appears in the manuscript *Suriname Folk-lore* (1936), took approximately two and a half years to complete. With the initial support of a grant from Northwestern University, Herskovits contracted Kolinski in September 1930, while he was still working at the Berlin Phonogramm-Archiv, to begin transcribing and analyzing his recordings. At the time Kolinski was the only German scholar to have earned his doctorate in comparative musicology under Hornbostel's supervision at the University of Berlin's Psychological Institute.[83] Initially, Herskovits and Kolinski's collaboration took place through regular correspondence, usually via Hornbostel. Herskovits even asked Hornbostel to supervise Kolinski's work and to offer his own thoughts about the "relationships which the music may have with African or European songs."[84] Hornbostel did this, and, in fact, in March 1931 he asked Herskovits on behalf of Kolinski for additional grant money, because both of them had miscalculated the amount of time and work it would take to properly transcribe the recordings. As he explained, "The number of different songs amounts to more than 200, and, during Kolinskis [sic] work the bulk of the material proved to be in a rather African stile [sic] and rhythmically very intricate."[85] By September 1931 Kolinski had transcribed more than 150 of the 270 total recordings, in spite of the fact that Herskovits had not yet secured additional grant money to pay him.[86] Both Herskovits and Kolinski planned to have their sections of the manuscript completed by the spring of 1932.[87]

Herskovits and Hornbostel also discussed plans for Kolinski to transcribe his field recordings from West Africa, which he made in the summer of 1931, and compare these with his Suriname transcriptions. As with his Suriname recordings, Herskovits commented on his African records upon receiving copies of the original cylinders in March 1932, saying, "It is, of course, interesting to hear them once more and at this distance from the music the correspondence between these songs and the Suriname music of the bush comes out very strikingly."[88] The very next month Herskovits wrote Kolinski directly, saying, "I am sending you . . . copies of a few papers of mine which may perhaps make clear to you the point I am taking in my research. I would appreciate it if, in your discussion, you would have it always in mind that this music like all other aspects of the culture of the Negroes of Suriname is derived from African and European sources, and that it is of the utmost importance for us to know to what extent such of these two elements is found in the songs."[89] At this point, Kolinski was nearly finished with the transcriptions of the Suriname recordings, the notations of which would constitute sections F ("Bush-Negro Songs") and G ("Town-Negro Songs") of *Suriname Folk-lore*, but he had not yet begun to write his analysis and findings.

Six months later Kolinski mailed to Herskovits the section that would become section B ("Musicological Analysis"), which he described as "the part that has cost me much [effort] most of the time."[90] Herskovits replied that he was enormously pleased with his work, adding, "I find myself fascinated by the technique of analysis you have employed and deeply interested in your conclusions. I only hope that some day it may be possible for you to record and analyze some West Indian and American Negro music in the light of this Suriname and our African data."[91] Kolinksi's analysis followed the conventional techniques of comparative musicology, which included the measurement and classification of the songs' tonal range, melodic movement, scalar and melodic intervals, melodic combinations of thirds and fourths, scalar types, meter and melodic rhythm, drum rhythms, song structure and form, part singing, and tempo. These musical elements constituted the traits with which Kolinski, as per Herskovits's instructions, compared the musical characteristics of the Bush Negroes and Town Negroes. Here, again, Herskovits and Kolinski colluded in spatializing geographic places in ways that manifested race and historical time in the music of their inhabitants (figure 1.2). In fact, Herskovits eventually reworked portions of Kolinski's text, sometimes considerably, so that his findings better accorded with Herskovits's research goals.

By January 1933 Herskovits had received from Kolinski a draft of the section that would constitute section C ("Ethnological Evaluation") of the manuscript.[92] In this section Kolinski first of all determined that the African derivation of the Suriname songs could not be fully assessed until he analyzed Herskovits's West African field recordings. As a substitute for Herskovits's African recordings, Kolinski reviewed other African recordings held at the Berlin archive in order to make preliminary conclusions. Next, he stressed that the music of the Bush Negroes and Town Negroes was not homogeneous but rather varied according to the musical traits listed above, even among songs of the same genre. Then Kolinski summarized his methodology in interpreting the ethnological derivations of the recordings based first and foremost on the principle of observation, which formed the crux of his training in experimental psychology at the Berlin Institute under Hornbostel and his teacher Carl Stumpf.[93] It is also significant that he was able rather seamlessly to apply the principle of observation to the study of acculturation:

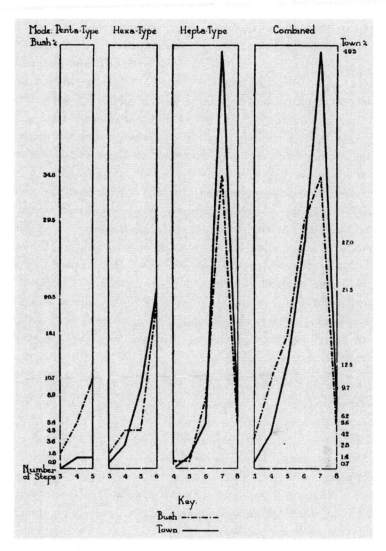

FIG. 1.2 "Number of Steps (Excluding Octaves)," prepared by Mieczslaw Kolinski. From Herskovits and Herskovits, *Suriname Folk-lore*, figure 7.

For the problems of acculturation, it is of great importance to see to what extent and in what manner European influence may be detected in this music. Before this is attempted, the criteria which determine whether or not a song is African, European, or a combination of both African and European elements, must be considered. Theoretically, two methods are possible. The first is synthetic; one listens to the record of the song in question, and the resulting judgment is prompted by the total impression [i.e., Gestalten]. *Naturally, this method can be employed only by one who for years has studied primitive music,—including also the music of African Negroes,—and who has acquired the ability when hearing primitive music, to recognize instantly the European elements.* The second method is analytical. After the recording of a song has been transcribed, its melody, rhythm, form, and other characteristics are analysed, and those features which are typical of African or European music are segregated. The exclusive use of either of these methods is, however, inadvisable; for only through employing both the synthetic and the analytic approach will the student be led to reasonably valid results. In this investigation, therefore, both general impressions and detailed analyses have been taken into account.[94]

That the synthetic method's reasoning was deductive and a posteriori enabled Kolinski to easily apply his comparative musicological approach to Herskovits's acculturation program in that both operated on the premise that African and European elements or traits consisted of opposites. Therefore, he asserted unsurprisingly that the musical traits of the Bush Negro are also typical of "African Negro music," and that those of the Coastal Negroes "show a strong European influence."[95] He supplemented his impressions by analyzing the frequency in which African and European traits appeared in the recordings of these two groups, thus supplementing the scientific rigor of his methodology with inductive and a priori reasoning. In other words, Kolinski's analytical method depended on modern aurality's habitus of listening, which determined the field recording's scientific essence and imbued the comparative musicologist and his laboratory with their scientific credentials (see chapter 2). He, for instance, claimed that his findings gave "insight into the direction of the change from African to European elements." The frequent appearance of melodic passages of a major and a minor third in the Bush-Negro recordings did not necessarily indicate the European influence of broken chords or triads but rather the African influence of melody structured on "filled-out fifths" or "enlarged" minor thirds, leaving it to the listener to determine whether this kind of passage constitutes a broken chord (European perspective) or filled-out fifth (African perspective).[96] The ambiguity of this synthetic method notwithstanding, he prepared proportional tables showing the results of his analyses of the music's modal structures. Marking off the Bush Negro from the Town Negro with dotted and solid lines, many of the proportions seem to coincide, hence revealing the arbitrary nature of these two categories.

Kolinski's most striking conclusion, however, contradicted Herskovits's own impressions regarding the resemblances between the Bush-Negro recordings and the spiritual: "The Negro spirituals have very little resemblance to the songs of the Suriname Negroes. However, the Suriname music helps to throw light on the question as to whether or not some features of the spirituals can be traced to Africa."[97] Naturally, Herskovits was disappointed that he did not say more about the relation of these results to the spiritual, to which Herzog, in a letter written to Herskovits, attributed "chiefly to modesty" on Kolinski's part.[98] As a result, Herskovits felt compelled to revise and add text to this part of the manuscript. It is likely, for example, that Herskovits wrote the sentence concerning the Suriname music, helping to shed light on the possible African derivation of the spiritual. He also more than likely wrote the sentence addressing the ethnological significance of the melodic occurrence of thirds or broken chords as "forming a bridge between European and Negro music," an insight that seemed to be informed by syncretism, the theory of which he would not fully formulate until 1937.[99]

Kolinski's conclusion, however, did not seem to dampen Herskovits's desire to scientifically prove the African sources of the spiritual. On the contrary, soon after reading the first draft of his analysis, Herskovits received a grant from the American Council of Learned Societies to fund the comparative musicological analysis of his West African field recordings. By now he was concerned as much, if not more, with the African sources of Negro music in the United States and New World Negro music in general as with the spiritual only. In a letter written to Hornbostel, Herskovits expressed his hope that the "analyses of these two sets of songs [i.e., his Suriname and West African recordings] will give a new impetus to the investigation of the sources of New World Negro music in general. For despite everything that has been done with Negro music in the United States, I am not satisfied that we are anywhere near an understanding of its sources, since the spirituals, I have found, are only one of several quite different types of music sung by the Negroes of this country."[100] Kolinski began work on Herskovits's West African recordings after leaving Berlin in April 1933 and settling in Prague. As their correspondence shows, Kolinski's work continued with little interruption until May 1938.

Kolinski had started to transcribe Herskovits's West African recordings by March 1934, when he wrote to Herskovits sharing his initial impressions about the extent to which these recordings sounded African. In his reply, Herskovits admitted that he was "a bit puzzled at your statement that the songs are more African than the African songs in other collections. My only explanation for this would be that those who recorded the music had made merely casual contacts with coastal Negroes who [sang] songs for them which were not strictly aboriginal."[101] Once again, the spatial and temporal properties of the bush determined for Herskovits the African essence of its music. A year later, Herskovits expressed much more than bewilderment in his reaction to Kolinski's challenge to his mentor's hypothesis regarding the derivation of syncopation in Negro music. In a letter from February 1935, Kolinski wrote: "Something else that would likely interest you: In contrast to the Surinamese bush songs, in the jazz music here, characteristic syncopations such as ♩♩♩♩♩ occur very often; thus we can scarcely maintain that jazz syncopations are derived from European rhythms and above all from Scottish songs."[102] The rhythm that Kolinski notated in his letter contains the so-called Scotch snap that Hornbostel had argued was "so prominent in all American Negro music, in the old spirituals as well as in rag-time and other dance tunes," and that was "so typical of Scotch folk tunes."[103] Hornbostel suggested that syncopation is only one of the hundred different forms of African polyrhythmy such that "nobody would call the 'Scotch snap' an outstanding feature" of African music. Therefore, he argued, "This very simple figure was the only one in European tunes that could remind the Negro of those rhythmical devices in which his own music abounds. It was a white achievement, though a black commonplace."

In his response, Herskovits seemed to feel vindicated by, and even contemptuous of, what he described as "the tendency in recent years in this country . . . increasingly to ascribe European origin to our Negro music."[104] He admitted to have had accepted Hornbostel's hypothesis when he "first went into the field of Negro research," and only after having "more and more experience with African music, I have come to have increasing doubts in the matter." He further explained his reasons for doubting Hornbostel's interpretation by drawing from key aspects of his acculturation theory: "That, for example, the Negroes who, in the matter of rhythm, had such a complex tradition, should not have retained anything of it, but should have given way before casual contacts with whites, whose songs were occasionally syncopated, has impressed me more and more as an untenable proposition." Besides pointing to retention, Herskovits alludes to the notion of cultural focus that he introduced in collaboration with anthropologists Robert Redfield and Ralph Linton as a key aspect of the process of acculturation in "Memorandum for the Study of Acculturation."[105] The authors first published this memorandum in the October 1935 issue of *Man*, seven months after Herskovits wrote his letter of vindication to Kolinski. Whereas the mention of cultural focus in this article lacked any detail whatsoever, Herskovits articulated the fundamental premise of this notion in his letter to Kolinski, which involved the cultural import rhythm and syncopation had for Negroes such that they would retain these musical traits in spite of contact with whites and others, whether the contact was casual or otherwise.[106]

In spite of his differences with Kolinski, Herskovits moved forward with the *Suriname Folk-lore* manuscript, asking Herzog and Roberts to review Kolinski's transcriptions and analysis. Herzog considered Kolinski's analysis to be excellent. He also advised Herskovits not to remove Kolinski's footnote citing the work of Guy Johnson on the Negro spiritual to his sentence regarding the lack of resemblance between the spiritual and the songs of the Suriname Negroes.[107] Herskovits followed his advice but he then revealed the following: "[I] toned down what he had to say because I am of the opinion that he is beginning to see something that I have felt to be the case for some time, namely, that both these gentlemen [i.e., Guy Johnson and George Pullen Jackson] [know] so little of anything having to do with African music that their judgments are not overly significant." He continued: "Kolinski is beginning to discover that perhaps some of Hornbostel's ideas about the spirituals are not so valid, now that he is working on the Dahomean and other West African music that we collected. Thus he has just written me in great excitement that he has found the typical jazz rhythm in Dahomean music; incidentally, I am going to tone down considerably his preliminary statement on the same lines—tone it down, that is, by simply omitting one or two sentences of general statement concerning the relationship between American Negro, African, and non-European musical styles."[108]

Indeed, the tone of the paragraph constituting section A, General Statement of the manuscript's Part III Suriname Music, is noticeably tinged with Herskovits's acculturation outlook.[109] The section stresses the need to analyze American Negro music for its ethnological and musical significance, attributing the contributions of this methodological approach to clarifying "some of the important problems of acculturation." The paragraph also emphasizes the "value of the data presented here" due to the lack of research of "New World Negro musical forms," apart from spirituals and jazz. Finally, the concluding sentence alludes to the notion of cultural focus and thus clearly reveals Herskovits's hand: "In spite of the sudden uprooting of the Dutch Guiana Negroes from their native soil, the decisive change that took place in their conditions of life, and their contact with foreign races, this element [i.e., music] of their culture has been preserved partially unchanged for centuries."

After receiving the manuscript of Kolinski's part back from Herzog, Herskovits mailed it to Roberts for her review.[110] Roberts quickly wrote her review for Herskovits.[111] She, too, supported the publication of this part of the manuscript but pointed out that its technical content lacked clarity. She also pointed to the lack of "explicit references" to relevant publications, including her three articles on folk music of Jamaica as well as her article "Melodic Composition and Scale Foundation in Primitive Music," which she had published in 1932. She suspected that Kolinski's criticism of the simplistic uses of the terms "pentatonic" and "anhemitonic" in his introductory remarks to section B ("Musicological Analysis") might have been inspired by her own criticism of the Eurocentric as well as simplistic uses of the concept pentatonic scale.[112] Herskovits's stated theoretical interests in the concept of motor behavior as applied to music accounts for his initial interest in collaborating with Hornbostel, but neither Kolinski nor Roberts dealt with this concept. What is more, Roberts's comparative musicological scholarship was not only as rigorous as Kolinski's, but many of its contributions predated it, which adds to the speculation that sexism was indeed a factor in Herskovits choosing to work with Kolinski. To his credit, however, he did ask Roberts to assess his work, recognizing her credibility and good standing in the field.

After the manuscript was approved for publication later that month, Herskovits asked both Herzog and Roberts to add their comments for revision to the margins of the manuscript, which they completed by June.[113] In the following month Herskovits wrote Kolinski about his ongoing work on the West African recordings as well as the revisions to his sections of the *Suriname Folklore* manuscript. Concerning the latter, he expressed his gratitude to Kolinski for not objecting "to my having tempered your remarks concerning the African influences to be seen in the spirituals; you may be sure that my revision has not committed you anything that is not most tentative."[114] As for his West African field recordings, he instructed Kolinski to emphasize the range of variation in the musical styles represented within each cultural group. Once again Herskovits attributed the "confusion of thought about the relationship between American Negro music and African music" in part to the lack of knowledge among American scholars (e.g., Henry Edward Krehbiel, as well as Guy B. Johnson and George Pullen Jackson) regarding the "enormous variety of song types in West Africa." He concluded by stating that "the complexity of the problem of determining origins of American Negro music would be much more readily understood than it is at present." Of course, he had in mind Hornbostel and

Kolinski as well as American scholars among those whose scholarship he felt had not benefited sufficiently from studying the vast amount of West African music available to them by conducting fieldwork. Herzog made the same point in his review of the book published in the *Journal of Negro History*, concluding, "For this very reason the Suriname material is important. It could be used for a study of musical hybridization; both African and European melodies were affected by changes, but the results of this process did not produce types comparable to the Spirituals."[115]

In August, one month before Germany's passing of the Nuremberg Laws, Kolinski traveled to Salzburg, Austria, to attend a performance of a ballet he had composed.[116] It had been six months since he wrote to Herskovits, questioning Hornbostel's hypothesis about the European origins of Negro syncopation. Now he was in full agreement with Herskovits and, in particular, with his revisions to section A, "General Statement" of *Suriname Folk-lore*, stating "I am also, of course, of the opinion that the paragraph on the issue of non-European influences in the spirituals should be revised, and am very grateful that you have already made this correction." Although Kolinski did not abandon the comparative musicological method and its Gestalt underpinnings, breaking ranks with his teacher over such a significant piece of scholarship in his oeuvre was noteworthy. We may, however, attribute Kolinski's shift in thinking to not only his ongoing analysis of an increased number and variety of African field recordings but also the growing political and social pressures of Nazi Germany's Aryan supremacy propaganda felt particularly among German-Jewish scholars in exile, such as Franz Boas. As Vernon Williams Jr. argues, Boas's "positions on race were dynamic: they evolved . . . Boas's political awakening," particularly after 1933, "and empirical research were mutually reinforcing. That is, 'political beliefs' were as salient as 'scientific commitments' in countering the claims of overt racists."[117]

Like Boas and Herskovits, Kolinski, perhaps, began to consider the need to scientifically prove the African origins of New World Negro music in order to help combat discourses of racial superiority, whether these were directed toward New World Negroes or Jews in the Old World. It is also worth considering his precarious situation in terms of his livelihood as a German Jew in exile whose future in Europe was, to say the least, uncertain. Gaining the support of Herskovits, whether on pure humanitarian grounds or also based on their agreement over key issues concerning the African origins of New World Negro music, was certainly not unreasonable.

For his part, Herskovits made one of his earliest published declarations of the social import of Kolinski's work in his article "The Significance of West

Africa for Negro Research," which he published in the *Journal of Negro History* in 1936. Herskovits originally presented this article as an address delivered to the Association for the Study of Negro Life and History in Chicago in September 1935, several months after *Suriname Folk-lore* was approved for publication. In his paper he discussed the advances made in the field of Negro research through the ethnohistorical method, but he also stressed the need for more "concentrated study of West Africa" in order to better address questions concerning Negro-White racial mixing and the origins of Negro speech and music.[118] In regard to music, Herskovits claimed that "the analysis and transcription by Dr. M. Kolinski, an expert in the study of primitive music, of songs recorded by myself in various field trips to Dutch Guiana, West Africa, and Haiti, already shows results which assure us that their publication will alter profoundly our theories of the derivation of the spirituals." Clearly, he had not given up on Kolinski, his methodological techniques, or his own impressions about the African derivations of the spiritual.

Indeed, Herskovits felt more and more compelled to extol the practical social benefits of comparative musicology regardless of the occasional finding contradicting his impressions and hypotheses. As he concluded in his presentation to the association, "Facts will be at hand not only of inestimable value in giving basic information to those concerned with the practical problems of race relations, but also for the study of one of the most important scientific problems known at the present time—the study of the processes and results of cultural and physical contacts between peoples of different races and differing traditions."[119] Five days after Herskovits delivered his presentation in Chicago, Nazi Germany's Reichstag passed the Nuremberg Laws, stripping Kolinski of his German citizenship. In the months leading up to this devastating legislation, and as Herskovits and Kolinski worked on revising *Suriname Folk-lore* and transcribing the West African field recordings, tension and concern among these scholars, in particular Kolinski, were rising on account of the Nazis' increasing control over everyday life in Germany.

As early as June 1935 Herskovits expressed concern over Kolinski's well-being. He encouraged Herzog to "look up Kolinski" in Prague while he was in Europe, saying that a "visit with you would do a great deal for his morale and would be a merciful act for you to go and see him."[120] Without any hope of returning to Berlin, Kolinski remained in Prague for another two years, completing his transcriptions and analysis of Herskovits's West African field recordings in November 1937.[121] He was now preparing to begin work on the Haitian field recordings that Herskovits collected in 1934 until an alarming chain of political events, starting with the German annexation of Austria in March 1938 and followed by the Sudeten crisis in April, compelled Kolinski to flee Prague and find safety outside of the sphere of Nazi aggression. In May he wrote multiple letters to Herskovits, who was in Paris, asking for his assistance in securing an invitation for him to go to France. Kolinski's prospect of securing a work visa in a European country that at the time was safe from Nazi persecution of Jews was indeed bleak.

By August, as British representative Lord Walter Runciman was leading negotiations between the Czechoslovak government and Nazi sympathizers in the Sudetenland, Herskovits began to write letters to colleagues in Europe and the United States petitioning them for assistance in securing Kolinski a work visa. In August Herskovits wrote Boas, giving him an update on Kolinski, who had secured a transit visa and was currently in Paris with Herskovits.[122] He had also secured a three-week visa for Belgium and permission to go to England for three months. "After that," Herskovits reported, "unless he can be taken care of somewhere, he will have to go back to Prague—and no job, for by then the research funds I have for him will have run out. I shall do what I can for him; anything you can do from your end will also be appreciated." On the same day he wrote a letter to Georges Smets of l'Institut de Sociologique Solvay in Brussels, asking the Belgian sociologist if "anything could be done, with him [Kolinski] on the spot, to keep him in Belgium, and perhaps even find something for him to do there?"[123] In the letters to both Boas and Smets, he credited Kolinski with being "one of the best men in his field in the world, and has had more experience with primitive Negro music than anyone else." He described his musicological analysis of his field recordings as "brilliant" and "beautiful," and stressed the importance it will have on the "question of the origins of American Negro spirituals."

Kolinski was in Brussels by December 1938 with no prospects of ever returning to Prague, as the Czechoslovak government had begun to expel Jewish refugees from the city. Meanwhile, Herskovits continued to write to colleagues, including Boas and Herzog; directors of societies and institutes, such as Waldo G. Leland of the American Council of Learned Societies and Abraham Flexner of the Institute for Advanced Study in Princeton; and administrators at Northwestern University, hoping to gather support to bring Kolinski to the United States.[124] At first, in addition to humanitarian reasons, Herskovits cited Kolinski's specialization in a "method for the study of primitive music that is generally held to be the most valid and scientific one that has yet been devised" as justification for financially supporting his invitation to the United States.[125] He recognized, however, the two challenges he and Kolinski faced: the American economy's strain on university budgets and the difficulty of securing a tenured position after initial financial support was expunged. Flexner, who was known for helping to bring German-Jewish scientists to the Institute for Advanced Study at Princeton University during the 1930s, recommended to Herskovits that he contact Howard University, Hampton Institute, Fisk University, and Tuskegee Institute in order to offer Kolinski a post financed with a subvention from the ACLS. On March 2, 1939, with the threat of a Nazi invasion of Czechoslovakia growing stronger, Kolinski applied for a visa under the Polish quota at the American Consulate General in Antwerp.[126] Thirteen days later, on March 15, the German Army invaded Czechoslovakia.

Meanwhile, the Board of Trustees at Northwestern University approved a lecturer position for Kolinski in the Department of Anthropology for the academic year of 1939–1940 provided the financial support come from outside sources.[127] Moving quickly to secure funding for Kolinski's teaching appointment, Herskovits wrote to Samuel A. Goldsmith, the director of the Jewish Welfare Fund of Chicago, citing his qualifications in the field of primitive music and the "music on which Dr. Kolinski has worked [holding] particular interest for this country" as justifications for procuring financial support for Kolinski's academic position.[128] He further explained: "In his analysis of the West African songs I collected he has been able to amass an impressive series of correspondences between this African music and the published collections of Negro spirituals which I sent him while he was engaged in this work." He also wrote to Edwin R. Embree of the Julius Rosenwald Fund, asking for matching funds, which Goldsmith stipulated that Herskovits procure in order to receive funds from his organization.[129] Goldsmith also advised Herskovits to apply to the Emergency Committee in Aid of Displaced Foreign Scholars of New York City for possible financial sponsorship, which Herskovits did.[130] The secretary of this committee, Betty Drury, responded positively to Herskovits, indicating, however, that the committee required a letter from the president of the university or dean of the College of Liberal Arts detailing the amount of money needed from the committee and information about Kolinski's chances in securing a permanent appointment.[131] The dean of the College of Liberal Arts immediately wrote a letter.[132] Momentum was clearly building to successfully bring Kolinski to the United States to continue his research, but not without some glitches, one of which would eventually derail the entire process.

Goldsmith wrote to Herskovits in April, announcing that his committee approved a one-time subsidy for $1,800 for one year. He then explained to Herskovits that "an important member of our committee raised serious objections to the granting of this gift in the light of the terrific strain under which we have been to raise funds for helping the large number of Jewish and other refugees who are now virtually without help, except that which comes from the American Jews. We have a very decided feeling that we should help those scholars, the continuance of whose work will be of direct material benefit to the United States."[133] With the funds already secured from the Jewish Welfare Fund, Herskovits nevertheless felt compelled to address the reservations this committee member expressed about the relevance of Kolinski's field to the United States and Jewish Americans. He explained:

> I can understand how the study of Negro music must seem remote from our concerns, but on the basis of the considerable number of years' study in this field, I am convinced that investigations of this kind are of great practical importance when we take a long-term view of the questions involved in the solution of our American race problem as it affects the Negro. One of the matters in which people are most prone to admit Negro ability is in music, particularly religious music. A flank attack on the race problem, so to speak, which shows the African derivations of this music will, I think, in time tend to affect general attitudes and in this way cut under some of the fallacious assumptions concerning the nature of Negro cultural origins that perhaps more than we have hitherto suspected give sanction to fundamental points of view on this and wider phases of race relations.[134]

That Herskovits heard resemblances of the American Negro spiritual in his Bush-Negro and West African field recordings was as much a manifestation of the spatializing practices of doing science at the edge of civilization as it was a result of the habitus of listening scientifically to the African past. But science as a social practice, its materials (i.e., field recordings), and methods (i.e., comparative musicology, Gestalt psychological theory, and ethnohistorical method), did much more for Herskovits, as made clear in his statement above, and in the context in which it was produced. For the practice of science enabled Herskovits to redress the committee's doubts about the "direct material benefit to the United States" that, in their mind, the study of Negro music lacked. Given that the Jewish Welfare Fund had been under "terrific strain" to raise funds for Jewish and other European refugees, and that the resources the committee did manage came largely from American Jews, such doubts were reasonable. Indeed, what could the social benefits for Jews in the United States possibly be in studying the African origins of the American Negro spiritual? For Herskovits, the answer was a "flank attack" on the notions of racial inferiority and purity, the plague of which was destroying modern society and its promise of freedom and equality, throughout the Western hemisphere. With the comparative musicological method, Kolinski was showing the African derivations of the Negro spiritual, and because Negro religious music was one of the areas in which white Americans were "most prone to admit Negro ability," such musical qualities would have to be attributed to their African sources, thus lending Africa a degree of legitimacy in matters belonging to civilized culture. By virtue of their scientific methods, their scholarly results would give "sanction" to other musicological studies addressing race and racial discrimination elsewhere, including those societies under the political and ideological thumb of Nazism and fascism.

While Herskovits was successful in securing employment and funding for Kolinski, obtaining a visa that would allow him to enter the United States proved elusive. Commencing in earnest in May 1939, efforts to secure a nonquota visa for Kolinski were undertaken by president Walter Dill Scott and Dean Hibbard of the College of Liberal Arts of Northwestern University.[135] Meanwhile, Herskovits assigned Kolinski to teach two courses for the following academic year of 1939–1940, one in comparative musicology, and the other in the "methods of studying primitive music."[136] Events continued to move quickly, as the American Consulate General in Antwerp, acting on President Scott's request, called Kolinski in for an interview in May to consider him for a nonquota visa under section 4(d) of the Immigration Act of 1924, which provided nonquota status for an "immigrant who continuously for at least two years immediately preceding the time of his application for admission to the United States has been, and who seeks to enter the United States solely for the purpose of, carrying on the vocation of minister of any religious denomination, or professor, or a college, academy, seminary, or university."[137] Unfortunately, Kolinski was unable to prove ever having had a teaching position at a university, and, in fact, he provided the officials with a letter written by Hornbostel dated August 19, 1933, which stated that he had worked voluntarily at the Staatliche Akademische Hochschule für Musik in Berlin.[138] In addition, his passport listed his occupation as composer, not professor or teacher. His never having had a teaching position in Berlin, let alone in Prague, where he had lived for the previous five years, forced Kolinski to have to wait for a quota visa, a process he knew could take years.

As Kolinski and Herskovits continued to work on securing his safe exit from Brussels, the German Army invaded Luxemburg, the Netherlands, and Belgium on May 10, 1940. Herskovits wrote Kolinski on May 14, saying, "I do not know if this letter will ever get to you, but I am writing to you at your Brussels address in the hope that it will eventually reach you, and to advise you to keep me informed by letter or, if urgent, by cable of your whereabouts, if this is at all possible. If you are in serious need of funds you can cable me collect, and I will see that the money here for you is cabled back to you immediately. There remains nothing at the moment but to hope that you are able to make some kind of an adjustment."[139] Through August 1941, Herskovits continued to work to raise funds and obtain Kolinski's transit visa out of Europe. In one letter he reasoned that "Kolinski's peculiar value to American musicology and in the field of new world Negro studies is such as perhaps to justify the making of an exception in appropriating the funds necessary to save him."[140] But the political situation continued to get bleaker, as consulates of allied nations in Europe closed in the summer of 1941.

Undoubtedly frustrated, Herskovits gave interviews and lectures on his research and the practical problems of race relations. His university newspaper, the *Daily Northwestern*, published an interview with him in March 1940 in which he espoused a cultural relativist perspective on the study of primitive people, saying, "Don't get the idea that we're superior to primitive people. Oh, we have more gadgets, more tools, more implements of destruction. . . . But every people think their ways are best."[141] The reporter concluded the article with the following statement, no doubt inspired by Herskovits's insight: "Today with a new 'anthropology' as the spearhead of Nazism, with the concept of race superiority as the basic ideology of half of Europe, an understanding of anthropology becomes even more significant." But the plane in which racial superiority operated also encompassed those mechanisms such as cultural relativity and temporal spatialization that anthropologists and others used and consumed in their everyday practices, including in listening to as well as writing and reading about black music. The *Indianapolis Star* reported on Herskovits's keynote lecture of April 1940 to the Central States Branch of the American Anthropological Association, in which he played some of his field recordings from Suriname and Trinidad or "straight out of the bushes," which is how Herskovits "put it," according to the reporter Lloyd Wilkins.[142] Titling the article "Jungle Jive Pans of Roving Savant Monopolized for Anthropologists," Wilkins quoted Herskovits as saying, "People frequently laugh at the music and the songs . . . when actually the music is highly serious and reverent to the natives." Herskovits's relativist perspective, in this instance, operated along with the spatializing and temporalizing of the native and the bush, in effect sequestering these natives away from modernity's present.

On the other hand, in their presentation of their acculturation program, Redfield, Linton, and Herskovits introduced the notion of contra-acculturative movements as one of three possible results of acculturation, the other two being acceptance and adaptation. According to the authors, contra-acculturative movements arise as a reaction against acculturation "because of oppression, or because of the unforeseen results of the acceptance of foreign traits."[143] Such movements "[maintain] their psychological force (a) as compensations for an imposed or assumed inferiority, or (b) through the prestige which a return to older pre-acculturative conditions may bring to those participating in such a movement." Their decision to include acts of psychological and political resistance in their formulation of acculturation is not to be underestimated even though Herskovits and his coauthors did not pursue much research or publish scholarship addressing this particular aspect of the acculturative process.

Other anthropologists and sociologists, however, did research so-called contra-acculturative movements of the 1930s and early 1940s, identifying Father Divine and his Peace Mission of Harlem, the Malê of Bahia, and Igbo groups of Nigeria as examples of contemporary groups reacting against American, Western, modern, and colonial cultures for their oppressive ideologies and political practices.[144] Even one of Herskovits's students, Katherine Dunham, pursued research on the Nation of Islam in Chicago, whose political and social program also fell within this definition of contra-acculturation. To their credit, therefore, Redfield, Linton, and Herskovits's acculturation program did allot conceptual space for the practices of these groups as not only deeply political and ideological but also ongoing and situated in the present, in addition to groups in the spatially and temporally distant bush. Indeed, Dunham documented strains of such contra-acculturative movements not only in the city but also in the bush, which were as suggestive of black nationalism and race pride as was Dunham's anthropological research on, and choreographical work inspired by, the dances of Haiti, Martinique, Jamaica, and Trinidad. Such strains, however, also revealed its purveyors' chauvinistic faith in their own panracial temporal and spatial formations, however subversive they were.

Gender, Race, and "The PhD Urge"

Katherine Dunham's road to becoming a pioneer in applied and self-reflexive anthropology was not an easy one to travel, due not least of which to the gendered and racialized discourses and practices of anthropology at the time of her training.[145] Dunham's arrival in Chicago in 1928, the year before the department of anthropology formed at the University of Chicago, and her subsequent enrollment at the university were timely due to the presence of some of the seminal theorists in anthropology at the time, including Alfred Radcliffe-Brown, Robert Redfield, and Edward Sapir, as well as Herskovits at Northwestern University.[146] During this time the University of Chicago upheld a liberal humanist philosophy, encouraged independent and interdisciplinary study, and supported a racially progressive environment, qualities that resonated with the young African American student.[147] Moreover, the university's humanist and liberal arts mission also resonated with Dunham's interests in modern dance, ballet, and non-Western dance forms, which she pursued professionally while as an undergraduate student.

Dunham began merging her professional and academic interests in dance after consulting with Sapir and Redfield, when she first realized the potential and need for studying the connections between dance, culture, and society. She also received assurances from Herskovits about the academic viability of studying dance in spite of its novelty. As she wrote in 1942, from the start Dunham felt the stress in "trying to bring about this extraordinary marriage of two seemingly unrelated interests."[148] The fact that she considered these two endeavors unrelated, at least initially during her student career, was a result of not only practical reasons—she led a busy teaching and performance schedule, the logistics of which kept her away from campus and in a precarious financial situation—but also epistemological ones, with which she would struggle into the 1940s. For in spite of the university's liberal and progressive mission academically, and her professors' support of both her academic and professional activities, Herskovits and the others continuously impressed upon her an irreconcilable separation between dance as art and entertainment and dance as a subject of scientific study, wherein she often sensed doubts in them as to her intellectual capacity to become a true scientist. This, in addition to power imbalances in terms of gender and race, not only shaped the trajectory of her academic career but also inspired her to make choices in the anthropological field that at the time were considered unconventional, or else inconsistent with the scientific goals of Herskovits's acculturation program.

Dunham first wrote to Herskovits in March 1932, asking him for his thoughts on the potential contribution of the study of primitive dance to anthropology. In his response Herskovits confirmed in his opinion the viability of primitive dance as a specialized topic of study, but he stressed that such a "study must be predicated on work in the field and, as I said, based upon a very broad general anthropological background."[149] Not until 1935, however, did Dunham start formal training in fieldwork methodology with Herskovits at Northwestern and theory with the anthropology faculty at the University of Chicago. But Dunham and Herskovits remained in contact in the interim, during which they attended each other's performances and lectures. For example, in April 1933, Dunham attended a lecture that Herskovits gave at the University of Chicago in which he spoke about his research in Nigeria and Dahomey, and on the Gold Coast in 1931.[150] The program included what the *Chicago Daily Tribune* called an "exhibition of the ancestral dance of the Swasidei ceremony by Kwesi Kuntu and his tribe of Ashantis."[151] Two months later, upon hearing that Herskovits had attended the premiere of Ruth Page's *La Guiablesse*, a ballet in which Dunham performed in June, she wrote to him, saying his attendance reminded her to share with him her appreciation for his lecture in April, particularly the pictures he showed of West African rituals and art.[152] She then asked him for suggestions regarding "two African numbers" that her dance company, the Negro Dance Art Studio, was developing. She continued, "I'd like very much to have my instructor [Luda Paetz] see something really authentic. We are working just now on 'Bamboula' but I am not exactly satisfied ... seeing Kuntu's group and your pictures offered a lot of practical inspiration, but I'm afraid that the Bamboula may have a particular significance that we are overlooking."[153]

Although he did not give any explicit suggestions in his response, Herskovits did imply that such choreographies should remain separate from authentic dances. Thus, after complementing Dunham on her dancing in *La Guiablesse*, he stated, "The performance achieved one of the things that I feel artistic performances should do, namely, giving the 'feel' of an exotic situation without attempting a realistic presentation."[154] Herskovits's differentiation between the "feel of an exotic situation" and a "realistic presentation" exemplifies anthropology's epistemology that undergirded its distinction as science. An artistic performance could certainly be informed by the exotic effects of primitive dance, but it ought not be presented as, or be mistaken for, authentic primitive dance. In the political economies of race in American and Cuban society, however, the racializing practices of dancing bodies, as we will see with Dunham, Asadata Dafora, and Chano Pozo in the 1940s, usually did not attend to such distinctions.

Herskovits's remarks also remind us of the full range of anthropology's spatializing practices, whereby his lecture and the lecture hall itself, and not merely the intentions of the dancer, iconically helped determine the dance as "realistic presentation." He is also shortsighted in terms of the potential social benefits of dance as science, art, or both, which Dunham would begin to realize by 1939. Clearly, she did not consider research on primitive dance as exclusively belonging to the domain of science. Indeed, many of her contemporaries associated with the New Negro and Harlem Renaissance movements, including Zora Neale Hurston, had already begun to realize the import of dance and the arts in general toward affecting the resolution of their social, cultural, political, and economic status. Thus, in beginning formal training in anthropology to buttress her work in dance in 1935, Dunham continued the principles of the New

Negro and the Harlem Renaissance beyond its supposed historical decline by pursuing the study and production of black dance as a mode of expressing resistance, hope, race pride, and ultimately freedom.[155]

After all, this was one of Herskovits's goals. As Walter Jackson shows, Herskovits had consistently intended his scientific work, unhampered by political and social ends, to nevertheless "impart to blacks in the United States pride in the African past."[156] But his response to Dunham's request for guidance also points to the doubt he harbored concerning the ability of black academics to do scientific work a priori of racial pride. According to Kevin A. Yelvington, Herskovits "saw himself as upholding objective scientific standards" and thus, for example, behind the scenes actively undermined W. E. B. Du Bois's proposal to edit an *Encyclopedia of the Negro* in 1931 because he "worried that activists would be involved and would be less than scientific."[157] Yet by 1938, Herskovits himself espoused publically and in his scholarship the social and political benefits of comparative musicology in particular, and New World Negro studies in general, as a result of his efforts to secure Kolinski an exit visa from Europe. In regard to Dunham, however, he was careful to advise her against being distracted by activities such as her interest in undergoing initiation rites in Vodun in Haiti that deviated, in his mind, from her scientific work as strictly observer in the anthropological field. Dunham herself wrote, "It is necessary for me to remember often that my business here [in Haiti] is to know dances. But being a Negro forces many aspects of the various strata of society to come to my attention."[158]

In fact, Dunham's and Herskovits's field notes and letters reveal informants' own articulations of their cultural, political, and religious realities to African history that drew equally from contemporary movements and events such as Garveyism and Haile Selassie's war of resistance against Italian fascism as from what Herskovits regarded as retentions of African religious belief.[159] Only Dunham's affinity racially with her informants, as she noted, in addition to some informants' rejection of anthropology's "shadows" cast by the first generation of New World Negro studies scholars made it impossible for her to stay put in her role as the objective scientist. Additionally, in her materials we observe both her articulations of a feminist subjectivity to her activities in the field and, if not a protothick description style of ethnographic writing later advocated by Clifford Geertz, then fieldwork and ethnographic strategies that escaped the spatializing and temporalizing imperatives of Herskovits's acculturation methods.

To support her studies with Herskovits and subsequent ten-month field trip to Haiti, Jamaica, Martinique, and Trinidad, Dunham successfully applied

for a "Negro Fellowship" with the Julius Rosenwald Fund.[160] Her first stop
was Haiti, where she arrived in June 1935. In three letters to Herskovits from
Haiti, two of which she wrote during her second visit beginning in November,
Dunham commented on one of his more important contacts, Jean Price-Mars,
and his social standing among some of her informants. At the time Price-Mars
was Haiti's foremost ethnologist, a sitting senator, and one of the leaders of the
Haitian black middle class–inspired *indigènisme* movement.[161] In the third letter,
which she wrote in December, she described her plans to attend a "Mystere" in
Cul de Sac upon the invitation of a "very strong Papaloi" or Vodun god, and then
stated: "Perhaps I overstep tact and ethics in repeating this, but he [Reiser] told
me much about P. M. [Price-Mars] and D. [Justin-Chrysostome Dorsainvil]
and their errors because they really don't attend such things [alluding to the
Mystere], never being informed because they are known to write books. This
particular service, for example, has never been seen by either one of them he
tells me."[162]

A medical doctor by training, Jean Price-Mars published *La vocation de
l'élite* (The purpose of the elite) around 1920, in which he blamed Haiti's Eurocentric elite for not resisting the American occupation of the country, which
lasted from 1915 to 1934. In his next book, *Ainsi parla l'oncle* (So spoke the
uncle), published in 1928, he drew from his ethnohistorical and ethnographic
interests in Haitian peasant folklore to extol the nation's African heritage and
pointed to the Harlem Renaissance, instead of French culture, as an example
for Haitians to reverse feelings of racial inferiority.[163] Also a member of the
indigènisme movement, Justin-Chrysostome Dorsainvil had published *Vodou
et névrose* (Vodou and neurosis) in 1931 in which he made the claim that "possession [in Vodun] was the result of widespread psychopathology in the countryside, which, far from being the result of individual and social experience, was in
fact related to the genetic characteristics of the Haitian people."[164] Unsurprisingly, Herskovits rejected Dorsainvil's "hypothesis of an inherited racial psychosis," basing this on his cultural determinist perspective.[165] Moreover, as was the
case among the black Cuban peasantry, members of the Haitian peasantry—
particularly religious leaders, as Dunham's reports indicate—objected to the
divulging of their cultural practices in print and, furthermore, questioned the
accuracy of these publications and the political and financial motives of their
authors and American collaborators.[166]

Her next stop in Jamaica lasted about a month, during which time she
drafted what she called a "Journal of thirty days in Accompong," eventually
to be published as *Journey to Accompong* in 1946. In a letter to Herskovits, she
explained that the journal "cover[s] everything from typography to land ten-

ure, and [I] am reserving my discussion of the dance to be written after I have settled down for a while, perhaps here [in Martinique]."[167] The dances she observed on her twenty-seventh day in Accompong were a Myal dance, a male cockfight dance, and Koromantee dance. She also described making "nightly excursions at twelve o'clock to the graveyard to be washed in rum and obi-weed" by Ba' Weeyums, one of her Maroon informants who was also "an obea man." In fact, she described in vivid detail in *Journey to Accompong* one of these excursions as having taken place on the twenty-ninth day of her stay. This was to be one of Dunham's first of many acts of participation in religious practices while conducting fieldwork, to which Herskovits objected not only because he believed participation to be of no benefit to his acculturation methodology but also out of his genuine concern for her physical safety.[168] As part of Herskovits's approved methodological program, Dunham took at least four reels of film of the dancing, which she sent to Herskovits to be developed and reviewed.[169]

In his reply, Herskovits described the contents of the reels containing the Myal dance as a "perfect amalgam of the European where men and women touch one another and the Ashanti pattern where they dance opposite each other."[170] Throughout their correspondence, Herskovits regularly made attempts to identify the African ethnic provenance of dance traits. Dunham, on the other hand, did occasionally comment on the traits' possible African ethnic origins, but her ethnographic writing displayed much more descriptive detail of the dancing, drawn not only from her observations but also her participation, and often included explications of the meanings of the dances and accompanying music. As a result, her writing in these instances conveyed a haptic closeness to her informants or dance partners empty of the temporal distance inlaid by the observer's and the evolutionist perspectives, which is all the more significant considering that her ethnographic descriptions of dances appeared in magazines rather than academic periodicals.

For instance, in her 1945 article "Goombay," readers of *Mademoiselle* magazine learned about the practice of baptizing drums, common among many Caribbean cultural traditions, as conducted by individuals whose representation by Dunham is characterized by her acknowledgment of their cultural knowledge and traditions.[171] "There he [Ba' Weeyums] poured rum on the goatskin head, rubbed it in, took a long drink himself, then spat a mouthful at the drum again. Between times he mumbled in a tongue which I recognized as Koromantyn. Then he poured a few drops of rum on the ground, and the baptism was over. This was for the spirit of the drum, he explained. Then he squatted over the drum again, and indeed it seemed to me that it was suddenly alive."[172] Also characteristic of Dunham's writing are her vivid descriptions of the physicality involved and required in the dances, insights that she linked to her own knowledge and experience as a dancer, in addition to being based on her own participation. "Then Henry Rowe and I are facing each other doing a step which could easily be compared to an Irish reel. Hands on hips, we hop from one foot to the other, feet turned out at right angles to the body, or well 'turned out' in ballet vernacular. This hopping brings us nearer to each other, and I must closely watch the rest to keep up with Henry. [. . .] a moment later we are 'bush fightin,' crouching down and advancing in line to attack an imaginary enemy with many feints, swerves, and much pantomime."[173]

Dunham continued to produce films of dancing, in addition to keeping field notes, in Martinique, where she worked from August through October. Initially, she had trouble finding opportunities to study and film dances, but eventually she filmed examples of *belaire* and *l'ag'ya*, the latter of which she described to Herskovits as an "acrobatic dance that much resembles the Dahomean thunder dance (could be taken for it)" (figure 1.3).[174] After watching her film of the l'ag'ya dance, Herskovits replied, "I rather imagine it is a survival of something like the Nigerian wrestling match, which in Africa is held in honor of the earth mother."[175] He continued, "I think the Ag'ya is one of the most finished and exciting dances I have ever seen and you have enough of it so that you should have no difficulty in training people to do it." In fact, in October, by which time Dunham had begun fieldwork in Trinidad, Dunham had started to choreograph *Ballet of the Antilles*, which included "principle dances and discussions of Jamaica, Haiti, Martinique [and] Trinidad."[176] Each of her engagements with dance in the anthropological field—as observer, participant, and choreographer—amounted to distinct temporalizations materialized within the otherwise perceived temporally static bush, that is, temporalizations that exceeded the limitations of anthropology's scientific purview at the time.

For example, in 1939, Dunham published an ethnographic description of the l'ag'ya dance in *Esquire* magazine, titling it "L'ag'ya of Martinique." Here, she distinguishes the dance as performed for tourists and perceived in primitivist terms: "I continue to think of the sons of Nigeria. This is the *l'ag'ya* as I know it. As I love it. No lurid spectacle under flickering kerosene torches, while callow-faced men place a piece for the breaking of a companion's skull. No exhibition for the tourist to come and see and feel a little ill and go away and write about the savage beat of the tom-tom, the bloody attacks of the two naked combatants, and the mad, primitive frenzy of the onlookers."[177] She compares this with the "real *l'ag'ya*," the fascination of which "lies not in the lust of the combat, but in the finesse of approach and retreat, the tension which becomes almost a hypnosis, then the flash of the two bodies as they leap into the air, fall in a

FIG. 1.3 "Ag'ya," Jamaica & Martinique Fieldwork, 1936, film still from video clip #19. Music Division, Library of Congress.

crouch, and whirl at each other in simulated attacks, only to walk nonchalantly away, backs to each other, showing utter indifference before falling again into the rocking motion which rests them physically but excites them emotionally." This is indeed an important example of personal observations of dances that predate the "new" ethnography of the 1980s but whose writing style at the time restricted its publication to magazines.[178] Dunham's thick description, coupled with a critical analysis, of the l'ag'ya dance simply inhabits an epistemology distinct from contemporaneous (and soulless) anthropological and comparative musicological orderings of Africanisms and musical scales (cf. figures 1.1 and 1.2).

Yet in other instances in which Dunham acted as choreographer and anthropological observer, her work activated or reinforced the temporal strictures of racial difference in exoticism and anthropology. As we will see in chapter 4, Dunham's choreography L'ag'ya as performed in the 1940s often evoked in writers the kinds of primitivist images she critiqued in her Esquire article (figure 1.4). As an anthropologist, Dunham was sometimes unable to escape the questions concerning culture as enculturation or racial inheritance as proposed

FIG. 1.4 *Lag'ya*, scene 3, film still of the Katherine Dunham Company, Studebaker Theater, Chicago, 1947, filmed by Ann Barzel. Ann Barzel Dance Research Collection, Newberry Library.

to her, for instance, by Margaret Mead and Franz Boas. In early June, during Dunham's stopover in New York City on her way to Haiti, Margaret Mead, Ruth Benedict, and Erich Fromm hosted a soiree in her honor, at which Boas and "any number of artists and psychiatrists and sociologists," Dunham wrote, were also in attendance.[179] Upon describing to Herskovits the film she took of belair dancing in Martinique, she recalled the conversations that she had with Mead and Boas in which "Miss Mead was particularly anxious that I notice the training of children and Dr. Boas raised the question of whether or not the rhythm of the Negro is inherent or acquired . . . that is, just how much is due to outside influence."[180] Her description of the dancing in question follows: "[Reel] 15 I think was a master stroke of luck. Did you notice the child dancing? The drums were going and out of a clear sky he began and couldn't be stopped until we paid too much attention to him, then he began to cry. [. . .] When you notice that the woman who dances the Belair with such feeling is seven months pregnant (she danced from eight in the morning until one thirty in the afternoon, scarcely stopping) I would of course say that there is a tremendous balance on the latter side [i.e., rhythm as acquired]."

In response to Mead's concern, Dunham implicitly acknowledges the significance of enculturation in the retention of not only dance patterns but also the values that give it meaning, whereas concerning Boas's question, Dunham explicitly favors the cultural determinist perspective in regard to the "rhythm of the Negro," but she seems not to completely reject the physical anthropological perspective. Boas's question to Dunham regarding the possibility of music's racial inheritance is indeed striking given that since 1933 he had continued to publically speak out against popular and pseudoscientific notions of race and racial superiority in his attempt as a scientist to undermine both racial prejudice in the United States and the Nazi regime's claims to political legitimacy. In this context, Boas was unequivocally clear: "There is no 'German race'; there are only local types which are very different one from another, each of which comprises individuals of different characteristics"; and, in regard to intelligence tests administered in the United States, "the learned scholar has no confidence in [them] because such tests cannot be divorced from environment and experience."[181]

Was there a difference between music and dance, on the one hand, and intelligence tests, on the other, in terms of the impact of environment and experience on black Americans? The answer seemed to be yes, particularly when the discourse turned to primitive people. In a draft version of her *Journey to Accompong*, Dunham slips into the discourse of primitivism in describing musical encounters between Jamaican Christian revivalists and the descendants of Accompong's runaway slaves: "When the travelling band of 'revivalists' visits, they join in the rhythmic clapping to the drum, bouncing and swaying along with the old folk [i.e., the Maroons], receiving here the foundation for that remarkable sense of rhythm which seems to characterize the more primitive peoples."[182] It is worth noting that this excerpt from the draft text of *Journey to Accompong* does not appear in the published version. Regardless, Dunham's writing in this instance assumes the perspective of the distant observer who spatializes and temporalizes the inhabitants of Accompong, creating primitives or black Others as opposed to individual dance partners and, as we will see next, cohabitants of multiple temporalities who offer their own gnostic insight as remedies for the social ills affecting American Negroes in the United States.[183]

In October and November, Dunham continued her fieldwork in Trinidad, where, in addition to filming local versions of the belair, *bonga* (or bongo), and *cariso* dancing, she asked for a sacrifice to be done "to pacify the spirit of one of my ancestors who persisted in troubling me. This is the Shango crowd."[184] She also confessed to Herskovits the following: "If all goes well in Haiti, I shall have a little controversy with you, I think. I shall try to be initiated, which means that I will probably have to do away with typewriter and picture machine for a while." She returned to Haiti in November, once again informing Herskovits, "I shall start initiation when I feel better and hope that before leaving Haiti I can reach the second stage, or Hounci Conzo. The fact that my great grandparents were Haitian (well, mayn't they have been) wins me many friends in the cults. They are amazed at my dancing. All of which will facilitate initiation."[185] Until receiving this letter, Herskovits had not addressed Dunham's previous intimations about undergoing initiation rites. Finally, writing in January 1936, Herskovits warned Dunham that the amount of her traveling and work was contributing to the decline of her health, and advised her against undergoing the *hounci kanzo* initiation ritual.[186]

In her response, Dunham related to him details of the consultation she received from a *houngan* (or male priest of Vodun), 'ti Couzin, who advised her to first undergo the *lave-tête* ritual, which marks the first level of initiation in Vodun, before undergoing the hounci kanzo.[187] At the time, Dunham seemed to be inspired to receive these initiation rites to be enabled to address the malevolence affecting her family members as well as other American Negroes: "I talked with him at length about the difficulty in my land where the tradition is broken and when people are possessed they don't know what to do nor do they understand it. He pitied them a great deal, and is much concerned over me [. . .] The loi is running loose because we have not done the right things. He told me about my brother . . . that the loi is making him do all sorts of things and that if it is not appeased there will be no help, he will be definitely insane." Her houngan settled on seeing "what the loi says through me, then lave tete at the prescribed time. The Conzo not till I go back home and take care of the things with my family and loi, because I'll die undergoing it if no. [. . .] When I am ready to go he will show me how to lave tete my family and brother, and just what ceremonies to do, then conzo when I return. He actually convinced me." In her memoir *Island Possessed*, published in 1969, Dunham provides more detail in regard to this fascinating consultation session: "He ['ti Couzin] nodded in agreement when I explained my theory that people deracinated, denied full participation in a society in which they are obliged to live, inevitably turn backward to ancestral beliefs or follow any leader who can propose a solution to their immediate distress, who can offer a future if not a present. I mentioned the disorientation of the German people after World War I and their subsequent need for a leader such as Hitler, non beneficent as he was. Then I returned to the Black Muslims, American Negroes seeking social and economic stability."[188]

The Nation of Islam, founded in 1930 in Detroit, and later reestablished in Chicago in 1934, indeed attempted to appeal to all nonwhite peoples to resist the indignities of white racism and imperialism in the United States and beyond.[189] Dunham herself indicated to 'ti Couzin that she had researched the "Black Muslims," including attending "several meetings in the temple with Mohammed Elijah presiding," and acknowledged that she had "always respected their unity, faith, economic and spiritual ambitions and recently their journalistic skills."[190] She added that " 'ti Couzin was interested in the military training, schooling, black nationalism, and secret-society aspects of the Muslims." Could Herskovits have encountered the Nation of Islam in Chicago and thus been inspired to account for the resonance of its political and ideological program among black Americans with the notion of contra-acculturation? It is curious indeed that Dunham left out her conversation with 'ti Couzin about the "Black Muslims" in her letters to Herskovits. She also left out the conflicted feelings she was harboring toward pursuing Vodun as a student of anthropology as well as a source of spiritual guidance. "I was, in short, not at all sure of my sincerity in these pursuits and there seemed to be no way to put myself to the test, to find out."[191]

Kate Ramsey characterizes this moment as Dunham's ethnographic crisis, attributing it to her experiences in participating in Vodun rituals out of which she ultimately came to reject the "claims of both an objectifying ethnographic authority on the one hand, and a mystifying experiential authenticity on the other."[192] What is significant to this historiographical analysis of Dunham's fieldwork, but thus far overlooked, are the discursive unfoldings of her and her Haitian and Jamaican informants' diagnosis and prognosis of the social and supposed spiritual predicaments of New World Negroes, including black Americans. It is curious, for instance, that Dunham attributed her brother's pathologies, and those of American Negroes in general, to their lack of knowledge of the Vodun loi. Is this not the kind of practical social problem Herskovits hoped to solve with his acculturation research? The seemingly obvious answer in the affirmative, however, turns out to be highly problematic at best when taking into account the analogy Dunham then draws between the deracinating conditions leading to the rise of black nationalism and the disorienting conditions that had similarly been leading to the rise of Aryan fascism in Germany. This is indeed a "gnawingly uncomfortable" instance of the "commanding power of raciology" that, according to Paul Gilroy, undergirds all forms of fascisms, not least of which is its materialization as racial-nationalist movements, whether black or Aryan.[193] But Dunham's ethnographic crisis was actually symptomatic of a deeper ontological problem of freedom not merely from feelings of racialized distress and indignation but also from freedom itself, that is, from what German philosopher Günther Stern Anders theorized as the "pathology of freedom" (see chapter 4).

For the moment Dunham's maneuvering in multiple spatial and temporal formations remains the focus of this chapter's deconstruction of Herskovits's acculturative project. For although she did not divulge in her letter to Herskovits all of the details of her conversation with 'ti Couzin, Dunham did relay to him other instances in which her informants, sometimes in passing, expressed an outlook based not only on the notion of a shared African origin but also on a concern for the social well-being of their "brothers" in the United States. While in Haiti in June 1935, Dunham attended a Vodun ceremony in which the host allowed her to "shake the rattle over [bottles of water prepared for the ancestors] after a long discourse in Creole to the effect that we were all of the same origin, and since I too was from African descent, he was glad to let me be present so that I would be able to tell the brothers in America."[194] In July, while in Jamaica, she documented Ba' Weeyums's similar worldview: "One's ancestors are very important in controlling the destiny of the world. As for Christianity . . . well, it was alright, but the people who turned from obi, who refused to recognize the importance of the spirit world, the ancestors, and the powers concealed in nature for man to use, were in error. Things are getting worse and worse in the world. More unhappiness, more strife, more discontentment. Particularly difficult is the way of the black man. This because he has forsaken the teachings of his fathers . . . was ashamed of them."[195] Ba' Weeyums is critical of Jamaicans who have turned away from Obeah practices as well as others of the black diaspora who have similarly turned away from their ancestral practices out of shame of their African origins. While Vodun, Obeah, and acculturation all recognized the existence of African ancestors, the way in which they spatialized them differed greatly. Moreover, it was evolution's temporal dominance that determined in large part why black moderns turned away from these socalled primitive spatializations.

Indeed, Dunham encountered and commented on Martinicans, who "as usual resent my bringing up what they'd like to forget."[196] She initially felt that Martinique was a "very difficult country. It is small, and the people are much amalgamated. Perhaps I repeat myself, but there is much more to be done here psychologically than artistically or anthropologically. The country is slowly decaying, and the people with it."[197] Dunham's sentiments about Martinique could be attributed in part to the extreme physical fatigue she was experiencing at the time, for, as she and Herskovits would eventually conclude, the films she took of dancing in Martinique were invaluable to her research and choreographies. Nevertheless, her comment about the imperative to study the "amalgamated" people of Martinique from a psychological perspective anticipated Frantz Fanon's psychoanalytical study of Martinican race identity in *Peau noire, masques blancs* by more than fifteen years. Whereas Herskovits, Ortiz, and others believed that scientifically proving the African origins of New World Negro cultural practices would inspire race pride and debunk popular beliefs undergirding racial prejudice, Dunham's informants in the anthropological field broached these same challenges from no less contemporaneous metaphysical methodologies that they believed were also equipped, perhaps exclusively so, to assuage the social and psychological conditions of black people. What held all of this together, as Gilroy has argued, is race thinking.

Not only did race reveal itself to Dunham in the field in scientific and metaphysical ways, but gender did as well, often in tandem with race. Dunham's confrontation with anthropology's gendered discourse in the field commenced even before she left the United States for Haiti, her first destination. Preparations for Dunham's fieldwork began in April 1935, when, for instance, Herskovits wrote to Helen Roberts, asking if she would lend his student her "field machine." After explaining how the machine was "in great demand," Roberts admitted the following: "I am a little reluctant to let it go out of the country and in the hands of a negro student, but on the other hand, dislike to refuse it to anyone who can make good use of it. . . . Its original cost was $250.00."[198] In a postscript, Roberts clarified her reasons for feeling reluctant: "Only because most of the negroes are a little careless, perhaps, and not good mechanics, at best, in my observation." She also reminded Herskovits of the "500 songs [she collected] in Jamaica in 1920, which for the most part have never been published." Surprisingly, Herskovits avoided addressing Roberts's racism. Instead, he clarified that Dunham's purpose is to study "Negro dancing so that her findings can be used in developing choreographic presentations and is not making an anthropological study except incidentally, either of the music or the dances."[199] This sequence of correspondences demonstrates, on the one hand, the kinds of racist stereotypes that shaped everyday practices for students of color and, on the other, the gender discrimination that similarly structured everyday practices for women scholars in general. Of course, Negro women students such as Katherine Dunham were subjected to both forms of oppression by their white male and female counterparts.[200]

That Roberts would question Dunham's reliability and abilities, pertaining to the costs and technological demands of the recorder, was an outcome of, to be sure, the very racist ideology in American society that Herskovits, Boas, Du Bois, Locke, and many others intended to change. Moreover, Herskovits's response to her reference to her Jamaican research points to Robert's own marginalized and exploited status in the field of comparative musicology.[201] In attempting to reassure Roberts of her work's protection from encroachment by his student, Herskovits noted: "I know of your Jamaica collection of songs, and I hope it will be possible to bring them out soon. Whatever [Dunham] would get would be used to an entirely different end." In her response, Roberts clarified that she had "no 'dog in the manger' attitude in regard to it, merely thinking it might save some duplication of effort if Miss Dunham were going there for collecting similar to mine."[202] Nevertheless, in suggesting that Dunham would use her results for her choreographies and not for anthropological study, Herskovits exposes himself, in turn, to doubting the scientific import of Dunham's research. This would not be the only time that Herskovits downplayed the scientific import of a woman anthropologist's work.

As Sally Cole points out, Herskovits's stinging review of Ruth Landes's *City of Women* (1947) "had a permanent effect on [Landes's] career and effectively excluded her from participation in African American culture studies in anthropology."[203] Herskovits's student Richard Waterman also criticized Dunham's *Journey to Accompong*, published the year before Landes's groundbreaking work, on the same grounds that Herskovits critiqued Landes's work—that is, what they both perceived to be nonconventional methods of conducting fieldwork and ethnographic writing. Waterman thus concluded that *Journey to Accompong* was "not a scholarly work, and does not pretend to be. Instead, it offers warm pictures of the friends Miss Dunham made, the gossip she heard, the traditional practices she unearthed, and the festivities in which she shared, so that the reader is likely to end up with at least the feeling that he understands Maroon life because he knows a good many Maroons personally."[204] There is no doubt that Dunham was aware of the conventions of anthropological fieldwork, based on her training under Herskovits, and thus presented the early drafts of the journal as something that would "amuse" Herskovits and "merely a personal account of observations."[205] He wrote, "[If you] continue with your diary in the same form you will have something that will be worth publishing."[206] To Dunham, however, a "journal" carried more intellectual weight than a "diary," to which she objected as a (gendered?) descriptor of her work, regardless of its ethnographically nonconventional style.[207]

After eleven months of fieldwork, Dunham returned to New York City in April 1936 and to Chicago in May. By the next month, she was performing in addition to teaching ballet as well as Caribbean dances, the experience of which would eventually lead her to develop the Dunham technique.[208] She also took two summer courses with Radcliffe-Brown at the University of Chicago. In anticipation of completing her master's degree, she prepared a paper titled "Dances of Haiti," which she submitted to Radcliffe-Brown in early August and, later that month, to Herskovits, for their assessment. Herskovits held her writing to his highest scholarly standards, as demonstrated in his critical remarks in regard to her use of source material, her treatment of Vodun terminology, and her theoretical explanations, all of which he said needed "a lot of work."[209] He did, however, complement her writing in the sections where, he wrote, "you actually describe the details of the dance-patterns and the modes of dancing . . . without any very fancy vocabulary of the dance, since you seem to have done quite well with ordinary words." This aspect of her scholarship indeed contributed to Dunham's long-term significance to the field, as well as to her short-term success publishing articles in nonacademic periodicals beginning in 1939.

Although Dunham had planned to take a seminar with Herskovits at Northwestern and a linguistics course at the University of Chicago in the fall of 1936, the stress of her summer schedule, along with her tight budget, convinced her that doing so was impossible.[210] She decided to focus her winter's work on dancing, including completing her choreography of *Martinique ballet*, which she would later title *L'ag'ya* and premiere in January 1938. Herskovits supported Dunham's decision to take time off to concentrate on dancing. She planned to continue her studies during the following spring semester.[211] Indeed, her financial needs in terms of completing her anthropological studies for the master's degree were resolved as a result of being awarded a fellowship from the Rockefeller Foundation. Both Redfield and Herskovits were pleased with her receiving the fellowship and eager for her to complete her degree, which she planned to do by fall 1937. In his response to Redfield's request that he serve on her committee, Herskovits stated, "She is an excellent person and deserves the help of us all in getting the training she needs to carry on her program."[212]

Everything seemed to be in order, and Dunham recommenced her coursework in January 1937, but by April her ongoing busy performance schedule, which included performances in New York City in February and March, in combination with taking classes and the prospects of preparing for her master's examinations, began to weigh heavily on her.[213] Specifically, her complaints about pursuing anthropology touched on issues of gender and the regiment of seminars required in order to return to the field. In May Dunham wrote Herskovits a rather frankly worded letter, which addressed these and other issues. "I suppose like all women anthropologists (would be) I have had my dreams of museum or institute connections, inspired, no doubt, by our energetic fellow sister of the Pacific [i.e., Margaret Mead]. Anyway, after the masters' (if—the exams are increasingly trickier) I shall concentrate a while on the dance, hoping for field work in this connection in some way. Frankly, I could be made into a good field worker and shouldn't be forever lost to science!"[214] Then, after indicating that Redfield had urged her to continue her "artistic emphasis" in studying anthropology, rather than pursue her new interests in physical anthropology, Dunham asked Herskovits, "By stressing the artistic do you people mean to discard a scientific approach? I have an uncomfortable feeling that it is merely a polite way of telling me that I'm too stupid to be an anthropologist!"

Back in February of that year, Dunham had asked Herskovits for his advice regarding her interest in pursuing a study of foot measurements (i.e., from ankle bone to heel projection), as a component of her research on dancers' abilities to leap and spring.[215] After citing the names of some physical anthropologists who had conducted such research and reading a paper she had written on the topic for a seminar with Fay-Cooper Cole, he confessed to her that he "should very frankly regard it as unfortunate if you went off on this tack for too great a time—unless, of course, you are intrigued by the problem and really want to get into a serious study of physical anthropology."[216] In addressing Dunham's charge toward him and Redfield regarding her intellectual capacity, or lack thereof, as a woman, to be an anthropologist, Herskovits reassured her that "neither Redfield nor I have any feeling that you should give up the scientific approach on which you have started . . . but that your most important contribution because of the nature of your abilities, must be through your choreographic work."[217] But by August, she had decided that she was "cured of the Ph.D. urge," namely because pursuing "both artistic and scholastic urges [was] fast reaching a climax."[218]

In reality, Dunham merely stopped matriculating at the University of Chicago, but she continued to advance in her pursuit to merge her academic and artistic endeavors in dance with her ultimate goal being to have a practical social impact on American Negroes, which she would also accomplish in the 1940s. She even continued to pursue independent field research, as demonstrated in her fellowship application to the Rosenwald Fund in March 1939. Her proposed project was to continue the "creative-academic" work she had started in 1935, under the auspices of the Rosenwald Fund, the significance of which "carries with it not only the benefits of a new and dynamic theory into the artistic world, but implies a social benefit to the Negro in general because of the nature of the source material and the medium of expression."[219] Her actual research proposal was to join sociologist Robert Park and anthropologists Donald Pierson and Ruth Landes in Bahia, Brazil, where they were conducting research on the African influences of Brazilian culture. As mentioned above, Landes published her book *City of Women* based on this research. Dunham indicates that Park had invited her to join their general acculturation study and contribute her research on dance. In addition to publishing this material as scholarship, she proposed to publish her work in "semi-popular form" and use it "for the theatre and concert stage, and the continuation of the development of a primitive technique for use in the teaching of the dance." This statement is significant because it is one of, if not the earliest indication of her development of the Dunham technique. It is also significant because she explicitly situates the development of her technique within the context of her fieldwork and presents it as a product of her academic and artistic work, tying it to the goals of the Rosenwald Fund in regard to improving race relations.

George M. Reynolds of the Rosenwald Fund wrote Herskovits, asking him to assess Dunham's project proposal.[220] After prefacing his remarks by saying that he had not "seen a great deal of her [since she returned from her field trip in May 1936], and it is therefore somewhat difficult" to assess her proposal, he stated that the films she took were "of interest" but that he had not seen her dance group perform and thus could not comment on the results of her research in terms of her choreographic work.[221] He also indicated that she had no publications, and that the draft of her Jamaican journal "needed considerable working over," presumably to make it scientifically rigorous. He continued, "There is no question that Brazilian Negro dances offer an interesting and significant field for study. I must confess, however, that I am a little hesitant to recommend a study of acculturation in the field of the dance, when this is to be carried on by a person who does not know the African base. The project would be a stronger one if phrased not in terms of acculturation, but of a comparison between Haitian, Jamaican and Trinidad dancing on the one hand, and this other type of New World Negro dancing on the other."

Dunham's proposal to conduct research on dance in Bahia and Herskovits's criticisms of her proposal point to the broader issues explored in this chapter in regard to the significance of anthropology, gender, and race in the analysis of black music and dance's African origins during the 1930s. Although Dunham actively used participation as an alternative mode to study dancers, dance patterns, and their significances in the field, she on occasion resorted to the discourse of primitivism in writing her field notes and submitting proposals for fellowship support to conduct acculturation research. The epistemological shortcomings of the term "primitive" was clearly evident to Dunham, as can be observed in her attempt to clarify her use of the term in her application to the Rosenwald Fund: "By 'primitive' is meant here cultures of folk or less developed status."[222] Yet there seemed to be no other option to characterize such groups of people when conducting acculturation research on the African origins of New World Negro culture. To pursue the scientific goals of his acculturation program, Herskovits, too, resorted to conceiving black populations of the bush in Suriname and elsewhere as, if not "less developed" culturally, then frozen in time and space. But primitivism's pernicious temporalizing and spatializing effects drove not only the work of these anthropologists but also the imaginations of popular musicians, folkloric dancers, and their audiences, as the following chapters will show.

Gender, as well, factored at least implicitly in Herskovits's indifference toward Robert's comparative musicological scholarship in the early stages of his acculturation work, in addition to his criticisms of Landes's work, as well as Dunham's, particularly in regard to his dismissal of the former's research on sexuality and, in general, the methodology of participation. At best, he could credit Dunham only for attempting to "*begin* comparative study of dancing among Negro folk of the New World."[223] It is, however, noteworthy that he criticized Landes and Dunham for lacking knowledge of the African background of those traditions they aimed to research, whereas he did not criticize the comparative musicological work of his student Richard Waterman or of his colleagues Hornbostel and Kolinski, neither of whom conducted fieldwork in Africa.[224] Although Herskovits's sexism bias in this regard cannot be overlooked, his belief in the scientific legitimacy of the comparative musicological method explains in large part why he was not critical of his male counterparts. For instance, in *The Myth of the Negro Past* he writes, "Approaches to the study of the dance comparable to those worked out for music by such musicologists as von Hornbostel or by such psychologists as [Carl E.] Seashore and [Milton] Metfessel are entirely lacking; other than a general recognition that motion pictures should be useful, almost no scientific approach has been devised."[225] Once again, he unjustifiably downplays Roberts's groundbreaking comparative musicological research from the 1920s by relegating her scholarship to an endnote. Moreover, it appears that having access to field recordings made in the bush in Africa could substitute for conducting fieldwork in order to gain the requisite background of music of the New World Negro. As chapter 2 will show, however, the African past that anthropologists and comparative musicologists articulated to the sonic content of field recordings was similarly articulated to performances and commercial recordings of dancers and musicians racialized as black.

As for race, Herskovits's belief in the practical social benefits of scientifically studying the African origins of black music and dance only got stronger as the

Nazi regime's control of Western Europe spread beyond the borders of Germany and threatened the work and safety of his collaborator Kolinski. In contrast, he merely implied the social benefits of Dunham's research when noting that other dancers and even laymen were able to detect in her choreographies familiar dance patterns, the reactions of which, in spite of their "impressionistic nature," pointed "to the rich returns to be gained from systematic scientific analysis, on the basis of comparative studies, of the tenacity of African dance styles and the effect of acculturation on New World Negro dancing."[226] Besides Dunham's early work, he supported the work of other anthropologists, such as Lorenzo Dow Turner, while remaining suspicious of those such as W. E. B. Du Bois whose research and scholarship he considered to be corrupted by subjective and political goals. To Herskovits, there was a clear distinction between conducting scientific research a priori to race pride and having the results of that research engender racial pride and equality. Dunham's fieldwork experiences, on the other hand, and even Kolinski's synthetic and analytical techniques, challenged his distinction.

Even though Herskovits aggressively posited his acculturation program as a scientific endeavor free of political agendas, ironically, it helped uncover a transnational race consciousness shared among many inhabitants of the bush who were willing to enter the anthropological field. Indeed, the voices of these informants from the New World Negro's past, steeped in mystical, metaphysical, and modern epistemologies, were rarely if ever given access to media outlets controlled by the black literati predating and even during the various negritude movements of the 1920s. In the chapters that follow, more of these will emerge, as well as African voices, whose perspectives will lend further critical insight into the logic of black music's and dance's African origins.

Listening to Africa in the City, in the Laboratory, and on Record

These experiments also indicate descriptively the existence of an auditory space-level; for when the noise of a metronome stroke occurs, it enters into a thus far empty, yet phenomenally existing, auditory space. [...] The conclusion is that normally we possess a general spatial level within which we are anchored. When we lose this anchorage, we are practically lost. —KURT KOFFKA, "Perception: An Introduction to the *Gestalt-Theorie*," 1922

Kurt Koffka was one of three German experimental psychologists—the other two were Max Wertheimer and Wolfgang Köhler—whose innovative work on Gestalt theory revolutionized psychology and greatly influenced other disciplines in the humanities and social sciences, including comparative musicology.[1] This chapter's epigraph is from Koffka's first publication in English ("Perception: An Introduction to the *Gestalt-Theorie*"), dating from 1922, in which he gave American readers a detailed introduction to the Gestalt movement in psychological thought that had been developing in Germany during the previous ten years.[2] Koffka, along with his colleagues Wertheimer and Köhler, focused on developing a theory of perception that took into account the phenomenological whole of an auditory or visual experience. In "Perception," for instance, he proposed that the apprehension of "stillness," as in the silence in between beats, or "white spaces," as in the space between shapes, are integral to the entirety of an experience. No pattern of sounds (or figure) could thus occur without its contingent silences or background noises (or ground).[3] Moreover, as the spatial conditions surrounding the perception of a figure become unstable (as in seeing a flashing light in total darkness) or manipulated (as in effecting the direction in which a sound reaches the ear) the more unstable that figure and the perceiver's orientation become in that space.[4]

Koffka's observations concerning the perception of sound in particular serve as a productive introduction to this chapter for several reasons. First, German and American comparative musicologists drew from the work of Gestalt psychologists not only for their hypotheses concerning perception of sound but also because Gestalt psychologists set forth to establish Gestalt psychology as a rigorously empirical science on a par with the natural sciences.[5] As Melville Herskovits's correspondence and work with Erich von Hornbostel and Mieczyslaw Kolinski demonstrate, measurement was the methodological activity by which Gestalt psychologists as well as comparative musicologists and anthropologists working on black music's and dance's African origins could claim scientific reliability. Second, Koffka's invocation of the notion of Gestalt qualities in the analysis of sound perception resonates with the notions of habitus of listening and affect, both of which enable a nuanced critical analysis of those phenomenological principles of listening to music as black and of African origins that were specific to this historical moment. Third, and most importantly, he asserts what was at stake if a perceiver of sound were to lose any relationship with a fixed level of coordinates (physical or ideational) within an auditory space. Citing Hornbostel and Wertheimer's experiments in directional listening, Koffka relates that the "left-right localization of sound depends upon the time difference with which the sound wave strikes the two ears, localization occurring towards the side whose ear is struck first."[6] He goes on to explain how locating a sound to fixed coordinates in front or "straight ahead" of the listener (or observer) depends on her or his orientation within a physical space, such as within the four walls of a room.[7] When not squarely facing one of the walls, a listener, according to Koffka, is unable to successfully determine the sound's location of origination and, as a result, she or he loses "subjective assurance."[8]

This final observation is significant for analyzing the phenomenological, not to mention historical, factors that conditioned how, where, and why listeners observed music and dance as black and of African origins. For, as this chapter's case studies will show, listeners of music as performed by bodies racialized as black, whether on the streets or on stage in Havana, as recorded in the anthropological field in Trinidad, Brazil, and Cuba or in studios in New York City and Havana, and listened to in the laboratory or domestic spaces, were disposed to localizing that music in temporally and spatially distant locations, the effect of which was that the listener remained anchored in, or at least aware of, their physical modern present. Sometimes listeners, particularly comparative musicologists, used headsets to get closer to the music (produced as field recordings) in order to better determine the distance that it had traveled in time and space by virtue of measuring the intervals separating its scalar, rhythmic, and harmonic elements. In other contexts, listeners such as concert goers, music critics, and record reviewers were momentarily transported in time and space by the music to primitive or savage Africa, or they heard the threat of disorder of a bygone stage of humanity's or the nation's social evolution, the experiences of which signaled varying possibilities of the listener's subjective assurance within the modern present. Regardless of the physical locale in which the listening took place, most listeners perceived musical sound of certain qualities and especially as produced by black bodies, in accordance with modernity's striating temporal and spatial horizons, orientations, and distances.[9] Because without being anchored in the present or modern metropolis with a clear perception of temporal and spatial coordinates, one's subjectivity as a *modern* white or black citizen was indeed threatened or altogether lost. For other listeners, however, their dislodgment from modernity into an antimodern or "smooth" space, no matter how momentary, was in fact desirable (see chapter 5).

In further exploring the contours of this historical moment's logic of black music's and dance's African origins, the listening practices of modern aurality emerge as crucial activities of analytical and theoretical inquiry. Who was listening? What was being listened to? How and where was the listening taking place? With whom was the listener listening? When was it occurring? And why were listeners listening in these ways in the first place? Because access to this insight for the purposes of historical studies in particular is primarily obtained from text-based materials, such sources as articles, correspondence, and field notes require that we account for the listener's translation of sound, hearing, and listening into written texts via the dominant discourses in circulation at that time, the process of which nevertheless resulted in the listener imbuing sound and the act of listening with profound meaning.[10] In addition to text-based sources, the materiality of sound, too, helped determine this historical moment's listening practices, sensory experiences, and reliance on certain discourses. Indeed, the 1930s and 1940s was a time when the pace of the materiality of sound increased exponentially such that new formats, including ten-inch and twelve-inch 78-RPM disc albums and 33 1/3 long-play records (LPs) necessitated sound's mediation by the auditory together with the visual and tactile senses, lending therefore increased haptic depth to a listener's listening experience.

As Veit Erlmann has recently noted, "The modern era without question witnessed the massive dissemination of new patterns of sensory consumption marked by distraction and the atrophy of concentrated listening, but this new way of hearing was also the result of efforts to sharpen the ears of modern subjects and to turn them into more finely calibrated and ever-ready receivers of signals and codes."[11] This crisis of twentieth-century listening that Erlmann analyzes was in fact central to how and why modern listeners listened to or for Africa in the ways they did. It helps contextualize not only the importance Koffka places on the subjective assurance of the listener—given the anxiety-producing distractions from the mass dissemination of radio, films, and record players, not to mention the inhumane sounds of World War I and the rise of fascist governments—but also the growing emphasis of listening scientifically in comparative musicology, as we have already seen with Kolinski's synthetic and analytical methodology of listening to field recordings. Chapter 1 analyzed the temporal and spatial significance of traveling to the bush to locate and document African music and dance of the past as hearkening to Auguste Comte's positivist philosophy and sociology, wherein, Comte argued, human and social development passes through three stages, the third of which—the Positivist stage—enables the scientist "to take a comprehensive and simultaneous view of the past, present, and future of Humanity."[12]

This chapter will explore how this "view" of the past in particular also enabled listeners, whether scientists or otherwise, to hear the past in not only the recorded products of such research trips in the laboratory but also music as performed by black Cubans and other black Others in the streets, on stage, and on records produced in the studio or field, played on the radio, and listened to in domestic spaces. Such listening practices undergirded a habitus of listening to music as black and of African origins regardless of who the listener was or where and how the listening took place. The notion of habitus, as proposed by Pierre Bourdieu, is crucial here because it asserts that individuals internalize practices (thoughts, perceptions, expressions, and actions) as a result of historically, socially, and politically conditioned principles, the process and results of which, accumulating over time, appear as reasonable, commonsensical, or natural.[13] In methodological terms Bourdieu advises that to explain such practices, one must relate the "social conditions in which the *habitus* that generated them was constituted, to the social conditions in which it is implemented."[14]

For the purposes of this chapter we can readily point to Johannes Fabian's discussion of the naturalization of Judeo-Christian and Western time in his historiographical critique of anthropology's emergence in the nineteenth century in order to historically situate listening to music as black and of the distant African past in the mid-twentieth century, especially as practiced by comparative musicologists.[15] As Fabian explains, the modern Western notion of time developed as a system of temporal and spatial coordinates, with the Western metropolis operating as the spatial center and temporal present, onto which "given societies of all times and places [have been] plotted in terms of relative distance from the present."[16] The disposition to locating one's subjectivity within modernity's geographic center and temporal present—as is indicative of the scientist in Comte's theory of human and social development—was fundamentally operational when listening to music during this historical moment.

Whereas the habitus of listening in general terms, as Judith Becker has proposed, is quite "tacit, unexamined, seemingly completely 'natural,'" the habitus of listening to music as black and of African origins often involved a disposition to listen for particular sonic characteristics—for example, hand drums, syncopation, offbeat phrasing, and nonharmonic singing—and interpret the meanings of these sounds and one's affective responses to the musical event itself in varying yet rather predictable ways.[17] Underlying this disposition were the metropolis and the bush, operating as one set of opposing coordinates in time and space, as the previous chapter demonstrated. It is thus not a coincidence that Gestalt psychologists, anthropologists, comparative musicologists, and historians tended to articulate sound to coordinates of time and space, for in doing so they perpetuated the practice of reifying their presence as listeners in modernity. Insofar as listening to music as black and of African origins anchored the nationalist listener in the modern present, it involved a rendering of African music as having contributed to the formation of what Hegel called the "Spirit of a people."[18] Indeed, listening to music as black and of African origins was for listeners a powerful way to appropriate to themselves the ideals of science, modernity, and the nation, making modern life, with all its technologically induced sonic distractions, navigable and livable and thus "enabling [modern listeners] to have a definite place in the world."[19]

So, what was it about music's soundings that engendered these dispositions of listening? And how did the materiality of the music in performance and on recorded formats contribute to and expand the viability of these dispositions? An analysis of the public debate in Havana surrounding the question of African influence in Cuban music will begin to address these questions. This analysis will focus on the organization, content, and reception of three lecture-concerts, two featuring the music of Gilberto Valdés and the third the drumming, singing, and dancing of Santería, which took place in the months leading up to and following the celebration of carnival in Havana in February 1937.[20]

During this time a contentious public debate emerged surrounding the city government's reauthorization of *comparsas*, the celebratory music, dance, and parading of which for many, including some black intellectuals, embodied the worst ramifications—chaos, violence, and immorality—of Africa's presence in an earlier stage of Cuban society's development. The lecturers, Salvador García Agüero and Fernando Ortiz, aimed to lend the audience's listening experience a sense of rationalism based on Hegelian, Comtean, and anthropological notions of the spirit, art, history, and cultural survivals of African civilization. García Agüero also accused those who denied Africa's presence in Cuban music as, on the one hand, harboring repressed anxieties toward modern society's black presence and, on the other, symptomatic of Cuban society's classism, whereas for Alberto Arredondo the lingering African presence in Cuban music was a sonic marker of the nation's ongoing colonial status under American imperialism. In either case, articulations of the sounds and movements of contemporaries to Cuba's racial pasts, whether African or European, Congo or Spanish, Masinga or Gallego, were bounded by modernity's political, economic, and cultural imperatives brewing in Cuba, the United States, and especially Europe in the late 1930s.

Rationalized listening to music as black and of African origins, as put on display at these lecture-concerts, was at its most scientifically compelling among comparative musicologists in the laboratory, where music originally recorded in the field was made, in Jonathan Sterne's words, "cellular, cut into little pieces, and reassembled" for intense listening.[21] When transcribed and analyzed in the laboratory, this kind of listening made the recording a crucial gauge in determining its content's sonic historical and spatial coordinates. Herskovits set up the Laboratory of Comparative Musicology at Northwestern for his student Richard Waterman so that his work on the acculturation of African music in the New World could continue in Kolinski's absence. Waterman listened to transcribe and analyze Herskovits's field recordings from Trinidad and Brazil, doing so at times with Nigerian university students who were working as research assistants at Northwestern. He also drew from Gestalt, behavioral, and psychoanalytical psychology, from which he would develop his theories of "hot" rhythm and metronome sense, thus contributing significantly to the ongoing debate among American academics regarding the African presence in American Negro music. Waterman, like Kolinski before him, certainly fit the profile of the modern audile wherein listening was the privileged sense for knowing or experiencing. Only, for Waterman, his notions of "hot" rhythm and metronome sense reveal an eclectic application of psychological theories marked particularly by Sigmund Freud's topography of the mind, wherein his interlocution with Nigerian students, as they listened to field recordings together, opened to Waterman access to the African musician's unconscious. Thus the unconscious region of the musician's mind served for Waterman as that which the bush served for Herskovits, that is, a topographically determined spatial level, previously unexplored scientifically, in which Waterman oriented his listening *in* the past as stored in the black mind.[22]

In analyzing black music and its African origins as the product of certain listening dispositions, instead of as materializations of African musical retentions, the distinctions made between, on the one hand, modern and superficial black music and, on the other, orthodox and authoritative black music erode altogether. Thus, by deconstructing these otherwise historically and ideologically formative dichotomies, we are able to further study the habitus of listening to music as black and of African origins in other contexts. Whether purchasing from Decca, Victor, DISC, or Ethnic Folkways Library, a record buyer was already disposed to listening to the recorded music of Cuba or the Caribbean as emanating from a distant and often dangerous past, in large part as a result of the disc's promotion and packaging, not to mention record reviews published in widely read American magazines and newspapers. Even before placing the disc on the record player and hearing the music's sonic characteristics, the listener was preparing to go, as one reviewer put it, on an adventure. This, along with the music's effect, tended to evoke in the listener predictable kinds of emotions, meanings, and discourses, oftentimes regardless of the musician—folk, traditional, cult, jazz, white, or black—who happened to be captured playing music on disc. What was certain was the listener's desire to remain in, or momentarily escape from but always return to, her or his subjective assurance in the modern present.

Locating Africa's Presence

Havana's carnival season of 1937 was a unique moment in twentieth-century Cuban social history during which the city's residents partook in a celebration that provoked an impassioned debate over the nation's musical identity and, in particular, black music's effects on the public's well-being. The editors of *Adelante*, a black social club's periodical, described it as the "most notorious [event] . . . since the matter has provoked a troubling and animated debate."[23] This debate centered on the decision by Havana's mayor, Antonio Beruff Mendieta, and the Advisory Committee on Municipal Tourism to reauthorize the participation of comparsas, or performance groups, that its supporters considered beautiful and respectable examples of folkloric culture to parade as

part of the city's carnival celebrations.[24] Robin Moore explains that munici
pal authorities lifted the twenty-five-year-old ban of these groups for at least
three reasons: to bolster tourism during carnival in February; to feature it in
response to the international vogue of black primitivist music and dance; and
to recover the collective past during a heightened degree of Cuban nationalist
sentiment following the overthrow of the Gerardo Machado dictatorship in
1933.[25] Because comparsas, along with rival neighborhood performance groups
known as *congas*, were originally banned in 1912 for the occurrence of violence,
particularly among the latter groups, the fear among those who objected to the
comparsa's reinstatement, as well as those who supported it, was that congas,
with their "vulgar music, devoid of any beauty in their dancing and singing,"
would spontaneously form and mix with the comparsas, thus inciting violence
once again.[26]

The mayor's detractors articulated the specter of the "repulsive" conga's reemergence among the orderly comparsas to its origins among African slaves in
the colonial period, and thus reason enough not to lift the ban, while his
supporters proposed to revive the comparsas, "elevating them to the category
of folkloric art representative and evocative of customs and popular traditions of
the past born from our nation's core ... [that is] from the mixture and fusion
of the diverse races integrating this core."[27] Moore has considered this debate's
racial implications in regard to the ideological underpinnings of the formation
of Cuban cultural nationalism. Historians of Cuban labor in the early twentieth century similarly point to business practices, state immigration policy, and
labor organizing to explain the contradictory definitions of racial difference
at this time, all the while noting the dominant ideology equating whiteness
with progress and modernity and denigrating blackness as inferior, atavistic,
and savage.[28]

For the purposes of this chapter, Cuban race history, along with the debate
surrounding the inclusion of comparsas and the threat of the conga's unsanc-
tioned reemergence in the city's carnival celebration, provide the discursive and
spatial backdrops for the analysis of a set of lecture-concerts programmed in
1936 and 1937 to address the question of Africa's presence in the nation's music
and in the character of the Cuban people. These lecture-concerts provide invaluable openings into understanding the reasons why listening to music as
black, of African origins, degrading, or respectable empowered social, cultural,
and municipal organizations to form alliances, and these lecturers, musicians,
and critics to act, discursively or otherwise.[29] Whether the comparsa's and
conga's sonic and performed characteristics were African retentions biologically or culturally determined was beside the point. What mattered more was

the reconciliation of the African primitive past with, or its condemnation as a detriment to, Cuban society's modernizing present, which for either perspective hinged on the desire for a culturally assimilated or racially homogeneous nation.

Havana's preparations for the 1937 carnival season began almost a year before its official start when the city's Department of Tourism approved the formation of the Advisory Committee on Municipal Tourism in March 1936.[30] This committee was charged with the responsibility of approving the expenditure of forty thousand dollars of municipal funds by the department and mayor to support the organization and promotion of carnival events. The promotion of the events took place via newspapers, cinemas, radio, and posters. The committee also approved expenditures for the construction of public stages and dance floors, musical groups, prizes, concerts, costumes, and the formation of two comparsas, Los Guajiros (Country Folk) and El Barracón (The Hut), to participate with other comparsas in the carnival parade. Three of the concerts, featuring the music of thirty-two-year-old Cuban composer Gilberto Valdés, took place in the Anfiteatro Nacional (National Amphitheater); the first two, on February 18 and 25, occurred at the height of carnival celebrations, and the third followed on March 11.[31]

Before scheduling Valdés's concerts, the advisory committee had attended a lecture-concert featuring his music in November 1936 at the Institución Hispano Cubana de Cultura (Hispanic Cuban Institute of Culture), an association that the Department of Tourism recognized as "highly prestigious" and having "authority" in matters concerning the nation's Hispanic folkloric roots.[32] Club Atenas (Club Athens), a black middle-class social club also regarded by the department as being of "well-known prestige," had invited the committee to attend this event with the hope that its members would invite Valdés to participate in programs scheduled for the upcoming carnival season. Preceding the performance was a lecture delivered by Salvador García Agüero, an educator, member of the Cuban Popular Socialist Party, and treasurer of the Sociedad de Estudios Afrocubanos (Society of Afro-Cuban Studies), an association concerned with the African folkloric roots of Cuban culture. In his lecture, titled "Presencia africana en la música nacional" (The African presence in the nation's music), García Agüero stressed Valdés's "veracious ability" to give voice to the "black emotion" in Cuban music for all Cubans to appreciate, thereby constituting in his music the promise of a racially unified Cuban society:

> White *criollo*, Gilberto S. Valdés has, in addition to his musical genius and vigorous sincerity, a singular sensibility to receive, understand, and

interpret the black emotion in rhythm and harmony. And, in doing so, he remains faithful to the spontaneity of the themes that he pulls out from the very life of the black man: pain, jubilation, rebellion, faith. . . . It is not by stabbing the drum and strangling the black song that he elevates the height of art and Cuban society, but by lifting the yoke of hostilities and reserved worries that attempt to keep the black man in the shadows of an unjust omission.[33]

Throughout his lecture García Agüero referred to the "emotional tone of the Negro," which represented, he argued, the essence of the soul of the black composer and musician dating to the colonial period and thus serves as the undeniable evidence, no matter how "latent" in modern Cuban music, of Africa's presence in contemporary Cuban music and society.[34] He pointed to the historical record to assert that music making throughout colonial society was "in the hands of the black man" or "in the hands of the descendants of Africa." Now, with Cuban society having progressed from slavery and colonialism to freedom and a republic, García Agüero believed that "music is, certainly, the collective manifestation in which we can *best* observe the mental evolution of a human group (and even much of its material transformation) from the shadows of its primitive stage to the supreme stage of its civilization."[35] Thus García Agüero, like so many other Latin American intellectuals before him, took the positivist view that music, as the most social, resonant, and reasoned of the arts, rendered in the most vivid way the consolidation of the nation's consciousness.[36] But the realization of Cuban society's evolution, he believed, was being hampered by the persistence of racism and classism, as was evidenced by some critics who "denied the African influence in our nation's traditional music."[37]

This alliance between these diverse public entities to install Valdés and his music in the city's sanctioned carnival events (where not only Havana's residents but also the nation's rural visitors, or guajiros, as well as foreign tourists would watch and hear the sounds of modern Cuba) formed in large part from his music's resonance with their own conviction in seeing the completion of the nation's progress toward modernity without, however, denying the presence of its African past in its musical and cultural soul. Identified as white, Valdés was born in Jovellanos, a rural town in the province of Matanzas that Cuban folklorist Herminio Portell Vilá characterized as "one of the strongest nuclei of Cuba's African populations."[38] By 1924, Valdés had moved to Havana, where he eventually studied composition with Spanish-born composer Pedro Sanjuán.[39] Indeed, Valdés's advocates, both black and white, mapped the evolution of Cuba's progress from its colonial origins to its modernized status onto the composer's biographical trajectory from rural Jovellanos to modern Havana, as well as onto the sonic resonances of his music. As the discourse surrounding his concerts and music demonstrates, they also pointed out, or else alluded to, his whiteness as material evidence of the nation's synthesis of the primitive African's spirit into the modern Cuban's emotion.

In a statement dedicated at Valdés's concerts at the National Amphitheater in February 1937, the Department of Tourism declared, "Because Gilberto Valdés's orchestra, who will tonight offer the performance of the director's original black poems, is, certainly, the admirable vehicle that brings to us all that which for some time now was due to foreigners, that is, the profound vibration of that spiritual chord that can give them with maximum veracity the intimate sentiment of the Cuban emotion; and to us [Cubans] . . . he hands over in the rhythm inherited from Africa the deepest impulse of our ardent and sensual exaltation."[40] The rhetoric of this introduction certainly drives home the municipal government's goal to present the city as racially inclusive and modern. But it also prepares the audience, both Cuban and foreign tourist alike, to locate the presence of Cuba's African past as sounded in Valdés's "black poems" in the spirit, sentiment, emotion, exaltation, and soul of the modern Cuban citizen. In addition, mayor Beruff Mendieta, in a report to the advisory committee, plainly stated that "one [of Valdés's three concerts at the National Amphitheater] will be offered free to the people, in accordance with our plan of cultural dissemination and to put the masses in contact with *correct interpretations* of their very own music."[41] The mayor was explicit in identifying the altruistic nature of the city's plans and those whom they targeted as the recipients of the aesthetic veracity in Valdés's music, but he was less explicit in critiquing the deniers of African influence in Cuban culture and music, for it was they presumably who were to be the recipients, he and the advisory committee hoped, of its goal to disseminate the music of the masses as interpreted "correctly" by Valdés and his orchestra.

It is not known to what extent the masses populated Valdés's audience at the amphitheater. We do know, however, that among the audience's tourists were Beatrice Wilson from New York and Helen Cooper of Washington, DC, two black American women who were visiting Havana and were in attendance at the concert accompanied by Zoila Gálvez, Cuba's most popular soprano at the time. According to Gálvez, Wilson and Cooper were "surprised that the musical spectacle, which [they] had described as something traditional of ours, was for them familiar from the melodic and rhythmic point of view."[42] Gálvez's recollection of Wilson's and Cooper's hearing Valdés's music as melodically and rhythmically familiar must be interpreted in the context of the formation of her own identifications with African and American Negro music based on her performance career in Europe and the United States (see chapter 3). What is important here is the Department of Tourism's intention in contracting Valdés to prepare a series of concerts exhibiting the nation's modern status in music. The advisory committee, following Valdés's concert in November 1936, approved an advance for the composer to "organize an orchestra with all of the elements necessary for the exact interpretation of his creations."[43] With this advance he orchestrated his music for a symphonic orchestra with the addition of, according to the Department of Tourism, "a chorus of twenty vocalists and a battery of [batá] drums, both authentically black, recruited from genuine cultivators of this musical modality," that is, musicians of the Santería religion. The batá drummers were Jesús Pérez (okónkolo), Aguedo Morales (itótele), and the leader Pablo Roche (iyá).[44] In addition, the performance featured two Cuban vocal soloists, Rita Montaner (soprano) and Alfredo Valdés (tenor).[45] Montaner had by 1937 attained national and international popularity as a vocalist and actress of the theater and film, having appeared on stage in the United States with Al Jolson and in Paris with Josephine Baker.[46] While not as well known internationally as Montaner, Alfredo Valdés had gained national popularity in his own right performing with Cuban popular dance bands, including the Septeto Nacional.[47]

Thus, with the participation of "authentically black" and "genuine" batá drummers and singers of Lucumí, the Yoruba-based language of Santería, along with popular singers of the stage and film, Valdés's music better enabled his audience the vantage point of listening to Cuba's African past without having to leave the city's aesthetically or geographically modern present. Indeed, in choosing the recently constructed national amphitheater, located adjacent to the waterway entrance to the Port of Havana, through which the tourist members of the audience probably arrived and left the city, the Department of Tourism further prepared the audience to listen to a "fusion of what some might call 'cultured music' and 'savage music,'" reassuring them, however, that they would try to explain the "exact technical criteria" of Valdés's music.[48] The program notes follow with a somewhat detailed explanation, most likely prepared by Valdés himself, of the tuning system of each of the three double-headed batá drums (okónkolo, itótele, and iyá), identifying their pitch placements on the musical staff.[49] The purpose of this musically technical explanation was twofold: first, to show that the rhythms of these African drums, as heard in the introduction to Valdés's "Tambó" (Drum), the opening piece of the program, were "at once, melodic and harmonic"; and, second, to show that the orchestra "executes variations without changing the notes inside the same rhythmic and harmonic complex" set by the batá.[50] This presentation of African rhythm's commensurability with Western music notation, harmony, and melody seemed appropriate, since Valdés's music satisfied the concert organizers' desires to harness Cuban music's African origins within a modern musical and social setting. What is more, the first section of "Tambó," following the introduction, is set in a 6/8 meter wherein the batá, piano, bass clarinet, and double bass alternate ostinato phrases in duple and triple, thus creating a hemiola, which the program notes are careful to explain lacks syncopation: "The batá, in reality, do not execute syncopation. The listener *thinks* he is hearing syncopations as a consequence of the rhythmic combination of the drums that proceed, one in triple time and the other in duple."[51]

Of all the qualities of rhythm, syncopation had carried in it an overwhelming power to affect the perception of it as quintessentially black, African, or savage and threatening to the body politic, psychologically and biologically. As Ronaldo Radano points out in regard to the emergence of ragtime in the United States, its xenophobic detractors equated its syncopated rhythms with other epidemics or contagions endangering the health of whites and thus threatening the integrity of the (white) modern social order.[52] This discourse of black rhythm as pathological to the morality of whites and blacks and the civilized status of American society continued through the Jazz Age in the 1920s but it was certainly not unique to the United States. For, in addition to some of the American tourists in the audience, Cuban listeners might have also harbored qualms about listening to black syncopated music. In fact, García Agüero made sure to stress to the advisory committee, which attended Valdés's concert in November, that the composer "evades syncopation. What fundamentally preoccupies him [instead] is the development of the rhythmic phrase."[53] With this, the department in its program notes was able to reassure their audiences that what they might hear as syncopation was in fact not that at all. As was the case with nineteenth-century spirituals and musical notation in the United States, the discourse of notation in the department's program notes became "a way of encouraging a particular way of hearing," in this case, hearing Valdés's music as simultaneously modern and of African pedigree.[54] However, since notation was perceived as unable to fully harness African rhythm, as Kolinski complained in transcribing Herskovits's field recordings, so were municipal officials, Valdés's music, and its advocates unable to convince all listeners of the African presence in, or its value to, modern Cuban music and society.

One of the most vocal critics of the reinstatement of comparsas, Valdés's music, and its advocates was journalist and economist Alberto Arredondo, who identified himself as an anti-imperialist.[55] Drawing rather poignantly from Hegel, Marx, and Comte, Arredondo asserted the following:

> In terms of "afrocubanismo" we repeat that it is as absurd as "hispano-cubanismo." The Cuban nation cannot afford the likes of Fernando Ortiz who, on the one hand, flatters Hispanicists with the distinguished "Hispana Cubana de Cultura," and, on the other, flatters blacks and *mestizos* with the "Sociedad de Estudios Afrocubanos." [. . .] Our nation is such because it has stopped being the nation of Africans or the nation of Spanish. Both, Africans and Spanish, brought to a geographic zone (space) and evolving into a distinct society (time) *dialectically* shaped a distinct nationality.[56]

Modernity's spatial and temporal coordinates, in this instance, functioned in plain sight and sound, for, as Arredondo states, they measure how and when the modern Cuban materialized. It is important to clarify that García Agüero and Arredondo, both of whom were black Cuban intellectuals, theorized Cuban society based on the "internal laws of history" or Comtean positivism and Marxian material dialecticism in economic as well as historical terms.[57] In his Marxist-inspired characterization of the comparsa as a "drug" of the "lumpen-proletariat," however, Arredondo relates what he claims to have overheard spectators—"not only politicians, journalists, and capitalists but also those of the working classes"—say of the comparsa participants from various vantage points along the parade route: "And then they say that the black man has evolved! . . . They are degenerates! They're in the jungle! In plain barbarity, the blacks need to be civilized!"[58] Where Arredondo and Valdés's advocates parted ways was thus in regard to the viability of the nation's African past in modern Cuban society and culture. For Arredondo, the nation's African past was dead and, at best, Valdés's music could be considered African but not Cuban or, worse, Afro-Cuban: "Those rhythms that Valdés resuscitates constituted a stage of our musical development. [. . .] One may maintain that Gilberto S. Valdés's artistic dedication should be known as 'African' since its rhythms are refined of all other influences."[59] In his book *El negro en Cuba* (The black man in Cuba), published in 1939, Arredondo reiterated his condemnation of *afro-cubanismo*, whose racist imperatives, he proclaimed, "seek to divide the black man from the Cuban."[60] In terms of music, could he have really meant unhinging the black man from modernity?

Following his concerts at the National Amphitheater, which the Havana weekly magazine *Carteles* proclaimed were "triumphant," Valdés's orchestra performed again on March 24, a concert organized by the Sociedad de Estudios Afrocubanos and hosted by Club Atenas in honor of a visiting cohort of French dignitaries, among whom was the author André Demaison.[61] Demaison's descriptions of the effect that listening to Valdés's music had on him provides yet another occurrence of modernity's habitus of listening to music as black and of African origins, in this instance from the perspective of a French author who, according to *Carteles*, had "written and published six very important books about African life and dramas and novels about African themes."[62] Demaison published his impressions of Valdés's music in the edition of the French periodical *Les Nouvelles littéraires, artistiques et scientifiques* (Literary, artistic, and scientific news) that appeared on January 29, 1938.[63] Titling his article "Musique Afro-Cubaine: Souvenirs de La Havane" (Afro-Cuban music: Souvenirs from Havana), the author reveals that after listening to "Tambó" and "Sangre africana" (African blood), he felt

> once again, *a shake*, the one that invades me when I listen to the great ancient and modern works. . . . As the chorus, orchestral themes, and solos develop, they launch, they mutually penetrate, I do not know in which continent I find myself, *at this hour.* And as to intensify *my strange disturbance,* the faces of those women who balance themselves singing leitmotifs, evoke the diversity of the African populations. . . . One comes from Egypt; that other one is a Somalian, that one, a little stocky, a Makua; this one is from Dahomey, without a doubt; a Yoruba is together with a Mandinga; and not even their suits of diverse colors . . . managed to separate *those distant presences* that have materialized before my eyes.[64]

Demaison's rhetoric seems reminiscent of accounts of travel to Africa written by European explorers, dating back to as early as the seventeenth century.[65] But there is much more to analyze in his rhetoric's temporal and spatial implications, such as in the becomings before his eyes of "those distant presences" or African ethnicities embodied by the singers. Not only the music's sound but also the singers' faces and bodily comportment contributed to this performance's affect, producing in Demaison, among other physical sensations (e.g., "shakes"), a "strange disturbance," only to result in his seemingly ecstatic relocation to Africa and, simultaneously, the "materialization" of Africa and its populations in Havana. In an interview published in *Carteles* Demaison explained, "We feel the nostalgic and sensual tropic in the broken yell of Jorgelina singing 'Sangre africana,' or in the melancholic drum of Pablo [Roche] when his artistic hands play 'Tambó.'"[66] In describing his listening to "Ilé-nko Ilé-nbe," Demaison asserts, "In a hurry, Africa *reveals itself.* [. . .] These three drummers [Pérez, Morales, and Roche] are

terribly curious! I observed them, before they started to play, indifferent, simi
lar to all of the other Negroes in Havana."[67] Such musical performances listened
to and observed by Demaison and those spectators whom Arredondo reportedly overheard commenting on the comparsas exemplify the kinds of temporalizing that were undertaken by individuals in general on a moment-to-moment,
everyday basis. In other words, at the micropolitical level, the temporalizing in
these spectators' utterances reveals the functionality they sought from particular
conceptual equipment (i.e., black man, evolve, degenerate, barbarity, the jungle,
Africa, Egypt, Yoruba, and so on) that they deemed singularly handy at that moment in order to best allow what they were seeing and hearing to be given to
them and others (in Demaison's case, his readers) in homogeneous, appropriate, and familiar ways.[68]

Moreover, what seems to escape commentary by Demaison—that is, Valdés's use of modernist compositional techniques to include inflections of the
whole-tone scale, modal harmonic patterns, and the "mystic chord" heard at
the beginning and at the end of "Sangre africana"—might in fact have been
functioning, in Gestalt terms, as the sonic ground from which the perception
of its temporalizing features ("nostalgic and sensual tropic in the broken yell")
took maximum effect.[69] Although this conceptual equipment as projected in
these instances suggests that these performers share a common distance and
pastness (i.e., one Africa accessible along the same evolutionary trajectory), we
must take into account those subjective assurances from which the temporalizing is occurring in the first place. For Demaison's colonialist perception of
the African presence in Cuba as that derived from his experiences traveling in
Africa beforehand differed from García Agüero's Hegelian perception of another Africa's metaphysical presence in the constitution of the modern Cuban's
spirit, which equally differed from Arredondo's Comtean perception of yet another Africa relegated to an earlier stage of the modern Cuban's evolution but
whose reappearances are the results of racially divisive and politically exploitive
imperatives.

In still another temporalized Africa, Fernando Ortiz projects Africa's presence in Cuba based on the current anthropological notions of retention and
survival, undergirded nonetheless by his own positivist perspective on Cuban
history.[70] As a founding and active member of both the Sociedad de Estudios
Afrocubanos and the Institución Hispano Cubana de Cultura, Ortiz had assisted in organizing Valdés's concerts in November and March. Following these
concerts, Ortiz organized his own lecture-concert program, which took place
on May 30, 1937, at the Institución Hispano Cubana de Cultura. Titling the
program "La música sagrada de los negros yorubá en Cuba" (The sacred music

of the Yoruba Negroes in Cuba), Ortiz aimed for his lecture presentation to be a "simple exhibit of the instruments, rhythms, songs and dances constituting one of the most primitive religious liturgies of the black Yoruba and of their Cuban descendants, *as is conserved here in its ancestral purity*, without contamination of European music, nor with vernacular decorations that would corrupt its sacred feeling."[71] There was no being transported to Africa here. Rather, the cultural practices of Africa's Yoruba, Bantu, Calabari, Ganga, and Dahomey had remained fixed, unchanged, and isolated from modern Cuba since slavery—proof positive scientifically of Africa's presence in Cuba. Indeed, Ortiz promised his audience that "they would hear and see" Yoruba religious music and dance, which is "conserved pure and orthodox in Cuba. [. . .] Until today they have not left the temples of the Negroes."[72]

In his introduction Ortiz declared that his lecture-presentation on the musical and ethnographic qualities of Cuba's Yoruba was to be "the extreme opposite" of Valdés's November program, which presented the "extreme advancement of modernity" by featuring his compositions "of the modern musical technique."[73] But to demonstrate Africa's presence in the music featured in both presentations (modernist and sacred orthodox), Ortiz invited Pablo Roche's batá ensemble, the same one that had performed with Valdés's orchestra in the National Amphitheater, to participate in his program (figure 2.1). The lecture itself, as published in the *Estudios Afrocubanos* volume of 1938, is quite remarkable for Ortiz's emic descriptions of the music and dance of Santería. For instance, he discussed the *añá*, or sacred force, residing in consecrated batá drums; he gave careful attention to the Yoruba terms for the drums, players, Orishas (gods), and other aspects associated with the music; and he described in fluid detail aspects of playing the drums, including methods of producing the tones necessary to make the batá speak "in the Lucumí language," as well as tuning the drums; the mimetic aspects of the dances dedicated to the Orishas Babalú Ayé, Ochosi, Changó, and Yemayá; and the Orisha's characteristics. In regard to explaining the music itself, however, he confessed that he was insufficiently prepared to do so; instead he cited Gilberto Valdés's conclusions about the music, one of which concerned the lack of syncopation in batá drumming that had already appeared in the Department of Tourism's program notes prepared for Valdés's concerts at the National Amphitheater. Ortiz, however, gave a more thorough and accurate explanation of Valdés's conclusion, which is equally remarkable since it anticipates Richard Waterman's theory of metronome sense by at least six years.

According to Valdés, songs and rhythms in the music of "black Africans" do not accent strong beats; particularly in rhythms, strong beats are "represented

FIG. 2.1 Fernando Ortiz, lecturing on Afro-Cuban music, is helped by three drummers playing itótele (Aguedo Morales), iyá (Pablo Roche), and okónkolo (Jesús Pérez), the three drums of a batá, Havana, May 30, 1937. Photographs and Prints Division, Schomburg Center for Research in Black Culture, New York Public Library.

as silences." These silences, Valdés continued, are "registered mentally by the instrumentalist for the complete integration of the rhythm," and "reflected by the musician, we might say instinctively or unconsciously, in the movements of their body, their gestures and postures, or by certain soundless contacts of their hands with the drum."[74] As we will see, Waterman's theory of metronome sense was based on similar musical and psychological explanations, with the addition of his suggestion that dancers, too, accented strong beats with their steps. For his part, Ortiz also anticipated Waterman's work in discussing the percussiveness, antiphony, and timbral density of Santería music.

Following the lecture, an *ankoori* (choir) of sixteen women and men, including soloists Benito "Roncona" González and Alberto Angarica, sung chants of the Santería liturgy. Other members of the choir included Alberto Zayas, who would appear on field recordings made by Harold Courlander in 1941 and on the booklet cover of the album *Music of the Cults of Cuba* produced in 1947 (see figure 2.4). The final part of the presentation, a *luluyonkori,* involved a complete performance of drumming, song, and dance, featuring four dancers who demonstrated the sacred mimetic significances dedicated to the Orishas (figure 2.2). But Ortiz made sure to clarify for the audience that the batá were not consecrated, which, he noted, is required for actual ceremonies. In addition, the dancing was "without abandoning itself to the emotional frenzy that provokes the experience of possession, which is beyond the purpose of this lecture."[75] For our purposes, this is a crucial moment in the lecture because, in spite of his earlier claim of the "orthodoxy" and "purity" of the African music and dance the audience members were about to hear and see, he confesses to its necessarily artificial nature in recognition of the secular or modern space of the lecture-concert hall. But he also refers to Cuban society's anxieties about Santería by virtue of his attributing its process of possession to the "emotional frenzy" of the dancers rather than to the presence of the Orishas invoked in the drumming, singing, and dancing in their entirety. In other words, Africa's presence in such emotional frenzy was decidedly unmodern, as opposed to its presence in the emotion of the modern Cuban citizen. We can further pry loose this contradictory moment in Ortiz's text by examining other texts (both recorded and written) pertaining to this event's intended orthodoxy and purity in contrast with Valdés's concerts.

For example, among the *toques* (rhythms) performed for Ortiz's audience were "Ilé" and "Yemayá," which Valdés used in "Sangre africana" and "Tambó," respectively. Set in the colonial period, according to the Department of Tourism's program notes, "Sangre africana" is a dramatic rendition of slaves at work who throw down their tools at the sound of distant singing and drumming. At specific moments of the performance, the program notes continue, the batá and tympani initiate the "rhythmic phrase" (i.e., toque for "Ilé") along with the cellos and bassoons. Later, "in the middle of a cadence of the violins, a violent percussion and a silence denote the rebellion of those who have hurled their irons to the ground."[76] In the recorded version of "Tambó," the toque for "Yemayá" is played at a fast tempo, as it is in the sacred context, according to Ortiz, who describes it as a "singularly vigorous rhythm."[77] It is unknown how many of the audience members, if any, might have recalled Valdés's "Sangre africana" and "Tambó" upon listening to the toques for "Ilé" and "Yemayá," but for Ángel Lázaro, whose review of Ortiz's lecture-concert, titled "The Academy and the Drums," appeared in *Carteles,* the performance portion transformed the stage of the Institución Hispano Cubana de Cultura into a "jungle": "the jungle suddenly arose imaginatively under the spell of the ancestral voices. And the noble audience . . . felt that unknown gods had entered the temple of the

FIG. 2.2 Fernando Ortiz, the Cuban ethnologist, in Havana presenting a *luluyonkori* with singers, dancers, and drummers to illustrate before an audience the survival of African cultural traits in Cuba. Photographs and Prints Division, Schomburg Center for Research in Black Culture, New York Public Library.

theater. [...] A voice started the song, and the others followed it pushed by the jungle's black wind. [...] There were two worlds facing each other."[78]

As the noble audience sat in their seats located in the academic world, squarely facing the stage, the jungle materialized once again from the distant sounds and frenzied movements of the black bodies on stage. Indeed, such materializations of Africa and the jungle on stage or in the streets of Havana reveal modern aurality's practices, which together with modernity's conceptual equipment for dealing with dance music's affects, racialized as they were in the black body, made these practices tacit, unexamined, and completely natural to Cubans and foreigners alike. The fact that modernity's power brokers (such as municipal officials, intellectuals, and musicians) enacted what Jacques Attali said about music's power of "making people believe by shaping what they hear" is beside the point of modern aurality's privileging of the ear as a form of embodied knowledge.[79] But the significance of listeners' subjective assurances in the act of projecting such listening practices onto others is, in the end, what matters most if we are going to take seriously Martin Heidegger's claim that time is "intrinsically self-projection pure and simple."[80] The debate among Cubans over Africa's presence in the spirit, culture, and music of the nation continued into the 1940s, as did the debate about Africa's presence in American Negro music and culture in the United States. Although distinct in regard to each nation's history with colonialism, slavery, and race relations, these debates were undergirded fundamentally by the same dispositions of listening to music as black and of African origins, wherein Freudian psychology provided a particularly apt, if new, set of conceptual equipment to map the topography of anxiety toward and repression of black music's and dance's African origins.

Habitus of Listening Scientifically

At the American Folklore Society annual meeting in 1960, Richard Waterman presented a paper titled "On Flogging a Dead Horse: Lessons Learned from the Africanisms Controversy" in which he presented five factors that he argued contributed to the resolution of what he called the Africanisms controversy as it pertained to black American music in particular.[81] As he makes clear in the title, Waterman considered the controversy a settled issue and thus felt a "distaste" when he was asked, once again, to broach the "importance of the African cultural background for certain present-day characteristics of the music and the folklore of the American Negro."[82] Indeed, as we have seen in this chapter thus far and in the previous chapter, this debate had raged among Waterman's colleagues in comparative musicology since at least the 1920s. Among the five factors of the acculturation method that he credited with contributing to the resolution of this controversy, the second—knowledge of the characteristics of West African music, namely via phonograph record and magnetic tape—is especially relevant not merely to the historiographical study of comparative musicology of New World Negro music but more importantly to this chapter's analysis of the practices of listening to music as black and of African origins. Whereas the analysis of the debate in Havana focused on explaining the spatially and temporally demarcating principles of listening to Africa's sonically embodied presence in music as performed in Havana in 1936 and 1937, this section takes into account these demarcating principles as evoked primarily by sound recording technology as utilized by Richard Waterman in the 1940s, the comparative musicological work of which, as he argued, definitively settled the question of the African origins of black music.

By the time Waterman began his graduate studies in anthropology at Northwestern University in 1941, researchers in the fields of anthropology, folklore, and comparative musicology had used sound recordings for the scientific study of primitive music for about fifty years. During this time, sound recording technology changed, but the scientific motivation in using this technology to study primitive music changed little from its study in the prephonographic era.[83] Writing in 1903, for example, Otto Abraham and Erich von Hornbostel reiterated the Comtean notion that the music of primitive peoples can "provide us with criteria for a way of looking at the music practice of [European music] antiquity" so long as comparative musicologists can "securely establish" their common factors and analogous contexts of musical development.[84] The fact, according to Abraham and Hornbostel, that music transcription and phonographic recording are the two best methods available to comparative musicologists to establish these criteria not only bolsters the comparative musicologist's viewpoint of music's past and present but in the case of the phonograph makes her or his scientific task easier to accomplish: "With the phonograph one can record a piece of music and study it at leisure in the studio, where attention is not so much distracted visually as it is at performances by exotic peoples. Moreover, the phonograph has special advantages."[85]

These special advantages afforded by the phonograph, realizable only in the studio or laboratory, included adjusting the speed of the playback to "bring within the ear's comprehension" music that is too quick; splitting the music into fragments for better measurement in terms of pitch distribution and tuning; and securing a lasting document for repeatable and comparative listenings. The sound recording for Abraham, Hornbostel, and the next generation of comparative musicologists carried in it, as Jonathan Sterne points out, a triple temporality of linear-historical time, geological time, and fragmented time.[86] That is, in belonging to the equipmental contexture of measuring time and space (along with the conceptual equipment discussed above), recording technology enabled the anthropologist and comparative musicologist to not merely record the voices of dying cultures, archive the sound recording, and listen to it repeatedly in the laboratory in temporal fragments for analysis; it also allowed for the preservation, and thus control, of time writ large. It was these dispositions toward the field recording that compelled Herskovits to not only go to the bush to preserve the origins of American Negro music but also to establish the Laboratory of Comparative Musicology at Northwestern and eagerly recruit Richard Waterman to matriculate in the graduate program in anthropology so that his entire collection of field recordings could be analyzed.

In his attempts to recruit Waterman (who had also been accepted to Yale University), Herskovits wrote to him in June 1941 expressing his support of Waterman's dual interests in anthropological theory and musicology by suggesting he could work on his discs from Trinidad, which Herskovits had recorded during the summer of 1939.[87] Herskovits even hoped that Kolinski would be at Northwestern that academic year, and he suggested to Waterman that Kolinski could help train him in the methods of comparative musicology. At the time, Herskovits was still writing letters to raise financial support to help save Kolinski from Nazi-occupied Belgium. The most recent letter Herskovits had received from Kolinski was written on March 24, 1941, in Brussels, informing Herskovits of the possibility of receiving a regular visa from the US consulate in Antwerp.[88] That summer Herskovits worked persistently to secure another lecturer appointment for Kolinski at Northwestern, which was granted, and to raise money to pay for his transportation and salary, but to no avail. By June all US consulates and embassies had closed in Germany and in all German-occupied territories, thus closing off the official channels to secure Kolinski's transport out of Europe and to the United States. In addition, Herskovits had received a grant from the Rockefeller Foundation to conduct research in Brazil for twelve months, starting in September 1941, and with the United States' entrance in the war that December, Kolinski's only chance for survival was to hide, which is what he did, in Ghent, Belgium. Unbeknownst to Herskovits, his letter of March 24 was the last he would receive from Kolinski until Ghent's liberation in 1944.

As for Waterman, Herskovits informed him that in his absence during the academic year of 1941–1942, William R. Bascom and Herbert Passin were "going to be in charge" in the Department of Anthropology and "will be able to give you stimulating work."[89] Waterman completed his master's in anthropology with Morris E. Opler at Claremont College in June 1941.[90] With Opler's input, Herskovits designed Waterman's program for his first year at Northwestern. He advised Waterman to take Social Organization, Folklore, and Political Institutions with Bascom, and Primitive Economics with Passin.[91] He also encouraged him to take courses in the Department of Psychology, specifically Social Motivation and Conflict and Psychological Foundations of Social Sciences with Donald T. Campbell, and to pursue independent study with Robert H. Seashore, who was "carrying further," Herskovits noted, "his father's [Carl E. Seashore's] studies of the psychology of music."[92] Based on Waterman's use of concepts such as "subliminal perception," "subconscious, " "unconscious," and "Gestalt," beginning in his dissertation, in addition to Seashore's publications dating from this time, Waterman clearly and eagerly drew from Seashore's instruction in various fields of psychology, which included psychoanalysis, Gestalt psychology, and behaviorism.[93] Herskovits, as well, had applied the Freudian concepts of repression, compensation, and the unconscious in his attempt to put forth an analysis of "primitive psychology" among the Dahomey and the Bush Negro of Suriname. Thus, Freudian, Gestalt, and behavioral psychology played a formative role in Waterman's training as a graduate student.

Waterman began to inquire about a dissertation topic by the end of his first year of study. With Herskovits still in Brazil conducting fieldwork, Waterman asked Bascom for advice on possible topics; he expressed interest in studying the Negro in Mexico, of which Bascom disapproved for the lack of existing scholarship on, and thus the low probability of receiving research support for, this topic. Bascom suggested that Waterman wait until Herskovits returned, and in the meanwhile encouraged him to contact historian Fernando Romero of Peru to inquire about the possibilities of doing research on black populations of Colombia, Peru, Argentina, Uruguay, or Chile. He also discouraged Waterman from considering Cuba since he himself was planning to conduct research on the "Yoruba influence" there, adding, "I think I could do better work there than someone who hasn't been with the Yoruba."[94] In the end, Waterman completed his dissertation, "African Patterns in Trinidad Negro Music," working with Herskovits's Trinidadian field recordings and notes, and defended it in February 1943, less than a year after initially consulting with Bascom. His dissertation committee included Robert H. Seashore and John Eberhart from the Department of Psychology, linguist Werner F. Leopold, and sociologist Ernest R. Mowrer, in addition to Herskovits.[95] After Waterman successfully defended his dissertation, Herskovits secured a position for him as interim instructor and, starting in the fall of 1944, as regular instructor in the Department of Anthropology.[96] Herskovits also established the Laboratory of Comparative Musicology in January 1944, of which Waterman served as director until 1956.[97]

Thus Waterman's program of comparative musicological research and teaching at Northwestern was established by January 1944. With the war ongoing, no word from Kolinski had reached Herskovits until November, when he received a letter from a British lieutenant, N. T. Rider, informing him that Kolinski was "in very good health and that he was married a few weeks ago."[98] Kolinski had been in hiding in Ghent at the home of painter Fritz van den Berghe.[99] While in hiding, he continued to work on "new and detailed methods to analyze the structure of primitive music." The British Army had liberated Ghent in September, and now Kolinski was very eager to immigrate with his wife, Edith van den Berghe, to Evanston and proposed to start an Institute of

Comparative Musicology with a record and film archive, a staff to complete transcriptions and analysis, a journal, and sponsored research trips, all based on the work and activities done at the Berlin Phonogramm-Archiv before 1933.[100] Herskovits expressed to Kolinski his elation about and congratulations on his safety and marriage, but he also quelled his proposal by updating him on the comparative musicological work Waterman had already started and planned to continue at Northwestern.[101] It would be another seven years before Kolinski would arrive in the United States. In the interim, he remained in Belgium, where he continued his scholarship, including publishing articles, and his career as a composer and pianist.[102]

As for Waterman, it is important to note that his first experience of field-work did not occur until 1946, despite his having expressed an interest in doing fieldwork as a graduate student.[103] There is no indication, however, that he complained about the lack of opportunities to do fieldwork. On the contrary, his comparative musicological work in the laboratory not only led to conference presentations and published articles but also facilitated a wartime research opportunity for the State Department. In planning his research activities for the summer of 1944, Waterman received a grant from the American Council of Learned Societies (ACLS) to compile a bibliography of archival collections in the United States containing records of non-European music.[104] This project was originally conceived by the Advisory Committee on Music of the State Department's Division of Cultural Relations, the members of which included Herskovits, Gilbert Chase, Charles Seeger, and committee chair Harold Spivack, who was also serving as chief of the Music Division of the Library of Congress.[105] With Herskovits's encouragement, both Spivack and Seeger read Waterman's dissertation and based on its merits decided to assign Waterman to complete this bibliography of records for the purposes of their possible "use in propaganda programs" in addition to providing documentary information on extant recordings of non-European music for researchers in the country.[106] As part of his research, Waterman was charged with submitting a report indicating "the reception of native music and its meaning to the inhabitants" as well as "their response to occidental music." After completing this project, he returned to Northwestern for the fall semester to continue his teaching and research at the laboratory.

Among the classes he taught was Primitive Music, which in the course description was described as a "survey of the musical styles of native peoples of Africa, Asia, Oceania, and the New World, and analysis of foreign musical idioms, based on records in the departmental collection."[107] In addition to covering musical instruments, their uses, and the role of music in "primitive societies,"

Waterman taught "techniques in the recording and study of non-European music." Thus his work in the Laboratory of Comparative Musicology informed his teaching as well as his research, which in large part followed the conventional techniques of transcribing and analyzing recorded music as established by Hornbostel and further developed by Kolinski. One of the clearest examples of this is a worksheet that Waterman presumably designed for his use in the laboratory (figure 2.3). Like his predecessors, Waterman believed that "modern techniques of musical analysis [had] reached the point in development where they can be used to characterize musical styles in strictly objective fashion."[108] He distinguished the musicologist, who among other subjects studies music in its cultural context, from the comparative musicologist, whose work "calls for such a high degree of technical specialization that the [comparative] musicologist cannot always be expected to be an ethnologist as well." What Waterman said distinguished his approach from his German colleagues' approach, however, was his belief that music's patterns were culturally rather than biologically or psychophysically determined. In fact, his approach was very much shaped by Freudian psychology as well, but his use of Freud's topographical system of the mind to locate the retention of African rhythm in the unconscious went far beyond what Herskovits had attempted with Freudian theory. Regardless, they all rendered recordings and transcription as the best equipment to subject music, a cultural "intangible," according to Waterman, to "objective analysis," even as the music resided in the African musician's unconscious mind.

The worksheet demonstrates how recorded music enabled the manipulation of time on multiple levels. The recorded "song," as identified by its number, informant, song name, collector, location, and date of recording, guaranteed the preservation of the music as it existed at that particular date and place, which for Herskovits, however, meant not so much the present as it did his informant's "present," that is, the African past shared among Negroes living in the bush throughout the New World. For example, while making his field recordings in the rural village of Toco, Trinidad, in 1939, Herskovits complained to Harold Courlander that the "much touted calypsos are learned from the phonograph records that the commercial bands make! There are plenty other kinds [of music], however, that are well worth while [sic]."[109] To George Herzog, he wrote, "The Calypsos are pretty synthetic; I have quite a number of the commercial ones, but they are not as good as some of the older ones in Creole. The whole Calypso tradition is a carry-over of the African custom of improvising songs for purposes of social comment, usually adverse."[110] Of course, the desire for authentic songs was not unique to Herskovits. But his selection of Toco as a research site because of its predominantly Negro population, "far

Laboratory of Comparative Musicology

Northwestern University   Department of Anthropology

Song No.............................Record No............................Informant ....
Name of Song..Collector ....
Location ....Transcriber ....
Date of Recording..Date of Transcription..

Instrumentation:

Time Signature: Original Key: Tempo:

Phrase-length: Pattern of Phrases:

Scale: Mode: Tonal Range:

Melodic Direction (Differences in semitones): B-E............, B-H............, B-L............, E-H............, E-L............,

Intervals:

ascending (semitones)	descending (semitones)	Repetitive Monotone (4 or more notes)...........................	
1...............	1...............	Tri- ⎧ dim r........	Two 4ths rf........
2...............	2...............	adic ⎨ dim f........	Two 4ths fr........
3...............	3...............	"Split ⎪ M r........	Linear 4ths rr........
4...............	4...............	5ths" ⎨ M f........	Linear 4ths ff........
5...............	5...............	⎪ m r........	Interlocked 4ths r........
6...............	6...............	⎩ m f........	Interlocked 4ths f........
7...............	7...............	Linear 3rds rrr........	Two 5ths rf........
8...............	8...............	Linear 3rds fff........	Two 5ths fr........
9...............	9...............	Interlocked 3rds r........	Add. larger-interval
10...............	10...............	Interlocked 3rds f........	patterns:
11...............	11...............	Pendular 3rds M rfr........	
12...............	12...............	Pendular 3rds M frf........	
....	....	Pendular 3rds m rfr........	
....	....	Pendular 3rds m frf........	
		Add. patterns of 3rds:	

Attack r:............ Attack f:............ Release r:............ Release f:............ Dumbell r:............ Dumbell f:............

Full Harmony:............ Sporadic Harmony:............Overlapping:............ Ldr.-Chor:............ Unis:............

Melodic Rhythm: Dotted Notes............ Syncopation............ Triplets............

Percussion Rhythm: Percussion Pitch:

Add. Characteristiccs and Remarks:

Function of Song:

Prescribed Time, Place, Personnel:

Context of Song:

Specific Use of Song:

Note: B—beginning tone, E—ending tone, H—highest tone, L—lowest tone, M—major, m—minor, r—rising,
    f—falling.
LA1130-6M

FIG. 2.3 Laboratory of Comparative Musicology worksheet (verso). From Afrobahaian Cult Music, Folder 12, Box 138, Series 35/6, Melville J. Herskovits Papers.

removed . . . from the capital in the northwest" and untouched by industrialization, pointed to, according to Herskovits, historical and economic factors that bound "the life of the Toco Negroes" with "Negroes in many other West Indian islands, and in the rural sections of [the] southern United States."[111] He wrote Courlander again with the following update: "The only ones I recorded were the pre-phonograph ones in Creole French. Many of them are interesting from a musical point of view and I hope eventually they will be worked up and analyzed."[112]

The worksheet also indicates how the recording rendered the music of the informant's distant past repeatable such that the music's traits (semitones, intervals, rhythm, syncopation, etc.) could be accurately represented in musical notation and objectively analyzed in the modern laboratory's perpetual present. Finally, the recording enabled the measurement of the spatial and temporal distance separating, in Waterman's terms, European from non-European or-primitive music, as inflected by the sheet's categories of distantiation, such as phrase length; tonal range; scale; mode; repetitive monotone; triadic split fifths; linear, interlocked, and pendular thirds; and full and sporadic harmony. In other words, the comparative musicologist's auditory detection of sporadic harmony, pendular thirds, or repetitive monotones, for example, was a good indication of not only the song's ethnic affiliation but also its distance from European music's modern status. In short, this worksheet graphically represents that which the comparative musicologist's technical specialization as a scientific listener was equipped to translate from recorded sound to text.

In his pursuit of determining the African background of Negro music, Waterman consistently stated the importance of not only the comparative musicologist's adequate application of this technical specialization but also the use of modern recording equipment.[113] Writing in 1949, he discussed how early researchers of African music might have mistaken recordings of individual singers for the absence of harmony in that music, explaining the limitations of early acoustic recording technology, which required that the musician be "carefully placed in front of the horn." He added, "Since the usual field musicological task is looked upon simply as the collection of melodies, it is not difficult to comprehend how choral backgrounds, possibly harmonized, could *elude the ear of the laboratory musicologist* who heard only the recorded result, although he might be making use of the best equipment available at the time."[114] In his dissertation, Waterman stressed the significance of Herskovits's use of an electric recording machine in Trinidad as assuring "material having the highest possible degree of fidelity."[115] Of the collection of 325 field recordings, Waterman transcribed a random selection of forty-five, encompassing styles identified by

Herskovits's informants as Baptist, *bele*, bongo, *calenda*, calypso, quadrilles, Shango, and Yariba. Expectedly, his presentation of his analysis is organized according to the categories listed on the worksheet, and, with the exception of his discussion of "percussion polyrhythms," his findings deal with these items in strictly technical musical terms.

Waterman's section titled "Percussion Polyrhythms" in chapter five stands out for several reasons. It is the first section in which he declared, "The music of Trinidad is strongly African," in particular the music of the Shango cult, which he identifies as Trinidadian culture's "most African" manifestation.[116] He also credits the electric phonograph recorder for its unique contributions to his analysis, namely, those recordings that Herskovits made of drummers alone, the discs of which Waterman characterized as invaluable "aids to the understanding of these rhythm patterns, since it was possible to separate individual drum-parts from the total rhythmic configuration." Finally, it is here that he enacts the kind of psychological theoretical eclecticism that Robert H. Seashore embraced to produce his most lasting, yet controversial, contributions to the study of black music's African origins.[117] In drawing from Gestalt psychology, behaviorism, and psychoanalysis, and from acculturation theory and his experience playing jazz, Waterman put forward a theory of African rhythm that necessitated a different kind of auditory space-level in which the analyst anchors his listening within that which "the African" holds "below the level of consciousness," the implications of which, nevertheless, perpetuated the temporal and spatial principles demarcating the modern auditor and laboratory from the primitive musician and the bush.[118]

Waterman's orientation of the analyst's auditory space-level within the mind of the African musician began with his attempt to explain what he termed the "off-beat phrasing" of melodies, which he detected in the majority of the forty-five Trinidadian field recordings that he transcribed. These were melodies lasting one or more measures whose beats were rendered syncopated given their displacement usually by an eighth note in relationship to the accompanying "steady and dependable" beat patterns of the three drum parts.[119] In recordings in which a solo vocalist accompanies himself with hand clapping, Waterman asserts that such melodies "could hardly have been performed without a 16/8 ostinato *in mind*, accented triply for the first twelve beats and duply for the remaining four."[120] What is significant here is his articulation of these field recordings' musical contents to Gestalt theory, specifically in terms of the dynamics between figure and ground. For example, in describing each drum part's relationship with the other two as well as with the sung melody, he identifies either its amplitude or its metric relationship with the other parts to explain why a part "fades in and out with regularity, psychologically if not acoustically." A part "fades in," or takes on the solid and coherent character of a figure, when it is set against the other parts.[121] It "fades out" when it takes on the loose and empty character of the acoustical space or ground, remaining, in Waterman's words, "in the background of the rhythmic gestalt." For Waterman, the ground of the music's rhythmic gestalt typically consisted of the highest two drum parts set in a 4/4 and 6/8 meter, respectively. It was the function of the third or lowest-tuned drum, "upon entering [this] rhythmic gestalt," to momentarily effect a "radical dislocation" in the listener without his mistaking this dislocation for a change in meter.[122]

Waterman presented his findings from his dissertation in a paper titled "'Hot' Rhythm in Negro Music," which he delivered on December 28, 1943, at the annual meeting of the American Musicological Society held at Schirmer Hall in New York City.[123] Among the musicologists whom Waterman consulted about his research at the conference was George Herzog, who apparently questioned his formulation of black music as constituting rhythmic Gestalts, proposing instead the existence of varying degrees of independence among the percussion and sung parts.[124] In a letter written after the conference, Waterman admitted to having pondered over Herzog's objection, but after listening again to field recordings in the laboratory with this in mind, he found himself "as firmly convinced as ever that, at least in the African music . . . there is a definite integration of melodic and percussion rhythms." Most convincing for Waterman were those "instances in which a singer himself plays [*sic*] the percussion rhythms, either on a drum or by clapping his hands," which indicate that the "rhythmic complex is perceived as a gestalt."[125] As mentioned above, six years earlier Gilberto Valdés had given a similar explanation of the psychological and physical processes involved in a musician mentally registering, and not actually accenting, strong beats for, in Valdés's words, "the complete integration of the rhythm." But Waterman did not stop with Gestalt theory in his analysis of these field recordings, for in his attempt to fulfill Herskovits's New World Negro acculturation program he drew from behaviorism as well as acculturation theory in order to define what he agreed to be the "essential homogeneity" of black music of Africa and the New World, offbeat phrasing being one of its defining characteristics.[126]

In the opening paragraphs of his "'Hot' Rhythm in Negro Music" paper, Waterman outlines his eclectically conceived theoretical framework for explaining this homogeneous rhythmic style heard by "those who have had opportunity to listen to Negro music in Africa or the New World." He labels this rhythmic style "hot," identifying its provenance as a "linguistic concept of West African tribesmen" used to describe a compelling or exciting rhythm. Because, as he notes, "hot" has "come to our own slang" to describe this rhythmic style's "overt manifestations" in Negro music everywhere, including jazz, Waterman argued that "hot" rhythm was an Africanism, or "one of those subliminal constellations of feelings, values, attitudes, and motor behavior patterns" that is not racially inherited but rather has survived as a "culture-pattern *carried below the level of consciousness*, often unrecognized by those who adhere to it."[127] This, in essence, is the eclectic framework that he had begun to construct as a student and attempted to collect more evidence for after completing his dissertation. But the sources for his use of the term "hot" rhythm were anyone but "tribesmen" from West Africa.

In addition to Herskovits's Trinidadian field recordings, Waterman in all likelihood had access to his field notes as well. It is in Herskovits's entry for August 20, 1939, that we read of his making reference to the "'jazzing' of a Sankey hymn" that he observed while attending a Shouters service in Toco. Herskovits writes of "the hymn . . . being sung over and over until it gradually went into a jazz rhythm which brought about the second possession of the evening"; he adds, "The song leader shook a bit and did a kind of foot-patting dance that gave a further basic rhythm to the massed song." Finally, he uses the term "hot": "The singing became hotter and hotter, the lad who had been dancing starting again. This time they went into full cry, and gave as 'hot' a performance as I have ever seen."[128] Then, in October 1944, Waterman wrote his colleague William Bascom, who had been drafted by the US Army and was currently working for the Foreign Economic Administration in West Africa, asking him to "collect five or six words, from different [West African] languages" that mean "'hot' as in 'hot music.'"[129] He continued, "The idea, of course, is to suggest that the concept of 'hot music' in this country is sort of an Africanism. If there aren't any African words with this meaning, my heart will be broken." He indicated to Bascom that he had received confirmation of this term's provenance as an African linguistic concept from Abdul Disu, a student of Yoruba background from Lagos, Nigeria, who had studied journalism at Lincoln University and the University of Wisconsin at Madison.[130] But, as Waterman stated, "like a dope I didn't ask him for the words."

Disu took up residence in Evanston in the spring of 1943 to work as a research assistant for Herskovits, Bascom, and Waterman at Northwestern.[131] His work included demonstrating Yoruba dances, which Waterman would later recall while observing Cuban dancers (presumably at a Santería ceremony) while making field recordings in Havana in 1946.[132] Disu returned to Evanston for two weeks in June 1943 to help Herskovits translate the Yoruba-based songs he had recorded in Bahia, Brazil, and to review his field notes for comparisons with similar customs among the Yoruba in Nigeria; Disu accepted this work to help pay for his matriculation at the Graduate School of Journalism at Columbia University that fall semester.[133] In addition to Disu, Waterman also credited Julius Okala for his work as an informant in the preparation of his dissertation and " 'Hot' Rhythm in Negro Music" paper. Born in Onitsha, Nigeria, of Igbo background, Okala applied to Northwestern also to work as a research assistant in the anthropology department. Like Disu, Okala studied at Lincoln, majoring in linguistics, but he arrived at Northwestern before Disu and worked during the fall semester of 1941, the same year Waterman started the graduate program.[134] Okala's work with Waterman included addressing the "problem of oblique expression or indirection in West Africa [i.e., Igbo derisive songs]" in addition to translating the Yariba songs in Herskovits's Trinidad field recordings, confirming their Yoruba texts for Waterman's dissertation.[135] Disu and Okala were two of a relatively small group of students from Nigeria and the Gold Coast studying in the United States who were also active in promoting African decolonization, activities that Herskovits and Waterman never acknowledged in their published work.[136]

In any event, Bascom, Disu, and Okala did not provide Waterman with specific West African words equivalent to "hot" rhythm. Without such evidence, he could not definitively establish this Africanism's linguistic origins, though he never completely abandoned the notion of "hot" rhythm, especially when discussing its significance in jazz performance and terminology. In reality, the notion of "hot" rhythm in jazz as delineating that which was believed to be authentically black and of African origins had continued to be disseminated widely via concert programs organized by John Hammond, Jr., in the 1930s and in published books and articles by Rudi Blesh in the 1940s (see chapter 4).[137] Instead, Waterman further pursued "hot" rhythm's psychological and behavioral qualities (and not its African origins per se), and by 1949, in a paper titled "African Influence on the Music of the Americas," which he delivered at the International Congress of Americanists, he substituted "hot" rhythm with "metronome sense" to hone in on the psychological and behavioral processes that he continued to argue constituted not only the musical foundation of African music's difference from European music but also that which any listener, even "the most careful investigator," must develop in order to comprehend those aspects of African music that are "most important to the African."[138] Central to his behaviorist argument of metronome sense was the importance of rhythm in many contexts of "native life," including the economic and religious as well as musical: the playing of percussion instruments, in particular, was formative in establishing the pace of work and affecting spirit possession, for example. Metronome sense was not limited to the drummer in musical contexts, however. As Waterman argued, "Signs ... of the African feeling for music are to be read ... likewise ... in the motor behavior of participants in African dance." The fact is he had asserted the importance of dance to his theory of "hot" rhythm as early as 1943, inspired no doubt by Herskovits's field notes from Toco: "The thread of each rhythmic element contributing to the thunderous whole of the percussion *gestalt* is followed in [the dancer's] movement without separation from its polyrhythmic context."[139]

Waterman's Gestalt-based explanations of the auditor's "subjective meter" in listening to African music when it is affected by an "objective stimulus" is strikingly reminiscent of Kurt Koffka's work on auditory space-level, as is the case in this statement: "The off-beat phrasing of accents [i.e., objective stimuli], then, must threaten, but never quite destroy, the orientation of the listener's subjective metronome."[140] But Waterman also stressed the conscious, subconscious, and unconscious in explaining African rhythm's diffusion and retention among black populations of the New World. In one instance, he declared that musical patterns "are formed, and are carried to a large degree, below the level of consciousness" (to wit, "the musical patterns stemming from Africa, and *passed down through several generations of Negroes to the present time*"), thus making the description of such "'unconscious' patterns in objective terms" a "major problem in studies of cultural dynamics."[141] This statement, too, is reminiscent of Freud's declaration of the importance of the person analyzed in order to make conscious that which is unconscious.[142]

In another instance, Waterman declared that whereas "conscious and unconscious aspects of the Negro rhythmic style are fully integrated" in Africa and, "for the most part," in Latin America, North American "slaves were forced to relinquish many of these conscious and material aspects [i.e., African drums] of their rhythmic tradition." Thus the "concept of 'hot' *went underground ... until it reappeared in jazz music*."[143] In the interim, the "process of inducing the Negroes to adopt behavior patterns befitting an inferior caste in white society was looked upon as a humanizing process, and the North American Negroes soon learned to be ashamed of their African heritage."[144] Waterman's equating of African musical patterns with repression in the unconscious (or "below the level of consciousness") of American Negroes is, in part, patterned after Herskovits's analysis of socially "sanctioned release[s] of inhibited feelings" such as "suppressed emotions" and "repressed grievances" among singers in Dahomey and Suriname.[145] His applications of the unconscious thus evoke its uses in Freudian and behavioral psychology, for he reads the contents, both admissible and inadmissible (or repressed), of the unconscious in social and historical terms, as had also García Agüero in reference to Cuban composers and music historians who denied Africa's presence in Cuban music. Ultimately, however, these archaeologies of the mind in their racializing and temporalizing capacities were continuations of the work of Henry Edward Krehbiel and his generation of musicologists, who helped carry forward from the nineteenth century into the twentieth the mining of the subconscious memory of the Negro's savage past.[146] In fact, these aurally induced excavations of the mind and soul belong to a much longer history of modern aurality that include the work of René Descartes.[147]

The debate over the African presence in black music of the New World persisted among intellectuals, economists, politicians, folklorists, anthropologists, comparative musicologists, and others in Cuba, Germany, Martinique, the United States, and elsewhere. For Waterman, his analysis of field recordings and field notes, as well as his consultations with Disu and Okala, in the Laboratory of Comparative Musicology at Northwestern University produced the musical and psychological evidence locating African music's retention in the mind of the African and his descendants, that is, regions that he seemed to believe could now be accessed through scientific listening given the methodological gains achieved in psychology and comparative musicology. The dynamics of the mind, he claimed, psychologically, socially, and historically explain how the retention and reinterpretation of "African musical formulae" occurred in varying acculturative contexts, a commonplace of culture contact that he felt by the late 1940s (and certainly by the 1960s) needed no explanation if "not for the fact that a sort of *academic* tradition has been in force which . . . has systematically denied both the fact and the possibility of such persistence of African tradition."[148] It bears pointing out that Katherine Dunham, Salvador García Agüero, and Richard Waterman all evoked psychoanalytical discourse (at varying levels of theoretical rigor) to address such denials as emanating from repressed anxieties harbored by black Martinicans; as symptomatic of a "black phobia in music" harbored by certain Cuban music historians and composers; and as either conscious feelings of inferiority or an unconscious inferiority complex as harbored by past generations of American Negro musicians, respectively.[149] Attention to such turns to psychoanalytical discourse as a mode of black musical and cultural listening, analysis, and commentary allows for an even fuller grasp of the temporal and spatial discrepancies between black music and its African origins rendered by other epistemologies, such as comparative musicology and acculturation theory.[150]

As these interlocutors' chosen methodologies varied—whether Hegelian phenomenology, Comtean positivism, Marxist historical and material dialecticism, acculturation theory, or Gestalt, behavioral, and psychoanalytical psychology— their practices of listening to music as performed and recorded by black bodies, whether in the streets, the amphitheater, the lecture hall, the bush, or the university laboratory, proved that much more decisive. Apart from their motivations, including those who denied Africa's influence in Cuban and American Negro music, what seemed always at stake was their urgency in not merely listening to music in racial terms but also in delineating its racial materializations and valuations for listeners. Thus, when García Agüero and other public speakers addressed music that sounded (or not) Africa's racial and historical presence in the Cuban nation's body politic, their articulations and textualizations of what they wanted their audience to hear operated so as to privilege their own presence in modernity's spatial and temporal center. Whereas for Waterman, his work in the modern laboratory—removed from the distractions of the bush or of bringing African "tribesmen" out of the bush and into the laboratory— was intended to enable listeners to access the unconscious mind of African musicians now temporalized in order to hear how their descendants, including jazz and boogie-woogie musicians, have perceived music for generations, all the while remaining physically in their own present.[151] The market for records, both field- and studio-produced, in the 1940s further enabled and perpetuated modernity's modes of listening among domestic record buyers.

Topographical Listening for the Home and Study

"Fighting a losing battle against time, and using the same weapon as the phonograph salesmen, anthropologists and folklorists the world over are doing what they can to salvage the remnants of primitive music."[152] This statement is taken from a *Time* article titled "Melody Hunters" published in 1937. Although the article's author is unnamed, in all likelihood it was written by *Time*'s music critic, Winthrop Sargeant, who conveyed to his readers the urgency felt by folklorists and anthropologists in making and preserving recordings of "fast disappearing" "native music" of "out-of-the-way parts of the world." This music, played by "woolly-headed blacks," "aging tribesmen," and "long headed Congo Negroes," is fast going "extinct," Sargeant warned, due in part to the phonograph, the very modern device that was at once helping to preserve "primitive music" and disseminate commercial phonograph records to record buyers in, for example, Toco, Trinidad to Herskovits's vexation. Sargeant mentions that the music on some of these records from Africa "shows rhythmic resemblances to jazz," noting also that the records, besides being collected by anthropologists for museums and universities including Northwestern and Columbia, are "now & then" put on sale. Ten years later, in 1947, the *Washington Afro-American* published a record review of two albums that Decca released that year, Katherine Dunham's *Afro-Caribbean Songs and Rhythms* and Miguelito Valdés's *Bim Bam Boom: An Album of Cuban Rhythms* (figures 2.5 and 2.6).[153] Both sets of records, according to the reviewer, "show examples" of the music "created in the Caribbeans [*sic*] when Africans and Europeans came in direct contact" by virtue of the musicians' uses of "authentic rhythm accompaniment" "stemming directly from Africa." Like the *Time* magazine article, this one too suggests that these records give some indication of the "kinship" between jazz, African music, and the music of the Caribbean, but both reviewers agreed that the rhythms on these records are "more complicated than Gene Krupa's randiest rataplan" and "far more complicated and animated than those of jazz," in general.

Decca producers recorded and designed the Dunham and Valdés albums in New York City. But readers of the *Washington Afro-American*'s review and Decca's record buyers may not have assumed so if we take into account the reviewer's impressions of the music contained on the albums and her or his prediction for the prospective record buyer: "Some of the Dunham numbers are chillingly weird, while Valdes is at times positively savage. If you haven't heard this music, you're due for an amazing experience." As this and the *Time* commentary demonstrate, the discourse of evolutionary time, as used by writers to convey their listening impressions and experiences to prospective record buyers, blurred the boundary between records made in the field, such as Harold Courlander's DISC album *Music of the Cults of Cuba* (figure 2.4), and those made in the studio by reinforcing the distance separating the record buyer and listener from the recorded music's place and time of origin. Also blurred, or altogether overlooked, were the performance contexts in which the music of these two albums originated: Dunham's album consisted of the songs included in *Tropical Revue*, which she and her troupe performed throughout the country between 1943 and 1945 (see chapter 4); and Valdés's album consisted of the music he performed at the time in nightclubs, mostly in New York City. Modernity's listening practices did indeed transcend such differences, including even album cover designs. The cover of the DISC album's booklet conveys a documentary aesthetic highlighted by the greyish tone and the image of an anonymous musician (cropped above the torso) playing a *marímbula*. In contrast, the Decca covers gesture toward entertainment and spectacle by featuring Dunham in an exotic headdress and neck covering, and Valdés, engulfed in a hellish fire, playing the savage conga drum.

FIG. 2.4 Alberto Zayas playing marímbula on the cover of *Music of the Cults of Cuba*, DISC Ethnic Album 131 (1947), booklet. From the Moses and Frances Asch Collection.

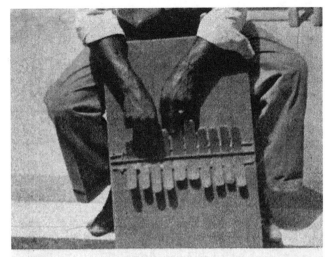

FIG. 2.5 Katherine Dunham, *Afro-Caribbean Songs and Rhythms*, album cover, 1947, Decca A-511.

FIG. 2.6 Miguelito Valdés, *Bim Bam Boom: An Album of Cuban Rhythms*, album cover, 1947, Decca 344.

Other reviews of Dunham's album, in addition to the music and production itself, are particularly insightful in indicating that listeners considered it a product of the scientific enterprise, if not to save primitive music from extinction, then to confirm jazz's origins. Will Davidson of the *Chicago Daily Tribune* credited Dunham's authority as an artist to her earlier "explorations of native Caribbean dance and musical forms, begun as part of her work for a degree at the University of Chicago."[154] Writing for the jazz monthly the *Record Changer*, John Lucas characterized Dunham's album as a "documentary and highly interesting set" of records whose "relation to jazz, though indirect and at times indistinct, is obvious enough."[155] The back cover of the LP version of the album released in 1950 summarized Dunham's activities as a student in Chicago and researcher in the Caribbean, including her initiation into "a Haitian voudun cult." It also gives detailed information about the various percussion instruments heard on the recordings, all of which shaped the listener's expectations and experience in ways and for reasons not unlike those pursued via the Cuban concert lectures and program notes discussed earlier.

Comparative musicologists and ethnomusicologists have acknowledged the interrelated histories, especially from the 1880s to the 1930s, of the commercial record industry and folklore, anthropology, and comparative musicology.

The American Society for Comparative Musicology's stated objectives, for instance, stressed not only the collection but also the issuing of phonograph records. Kay Kaufman Shelemay, however, suggests that by the end of the 1930s an "irreversible divide separated the record industry from the world of ethnomusicological field recording" due in part to the industry's marketing of the playback-only gramophone, which she argues "necessitated more sophisticated recording facilities to achieve 'professional' sound recordings" on the part of record companies.[156] In fact, this divide, in addition to differences in album design, seemed to have little bearing on listeners when listening to recorded music as black and of African origins—regardless of whether the record was produced in the field or in the studio—even though the temporal and spatial gulf separating the out-of-the-way field and the modern city, as Shelemay notes, continued through the 1940s to weigh heavily on ethnomusicologists wishing to preserve the former's dying music traditions. Indeed, certain performances as captured on discs made by Harold Courlander and Richard Waterman in Cuba document modernity's encroachment on Havana's outlying and rural towns, but for the critical listener they function to further destabilize the distinction between field and studio recordings and, in turn, the temporalizing and spatializing logic of Cuba's musical topography.

Funded by a grant from the American Council of Learned Societies, Harold Courlander traveled to Havana in April 1941 to make field recordings on behalf of Columbia University's Archive of Primitive Music using a windup recording machine loaned to him by George Herzog. Courlander, who had always considered himself primarily a novelist, had also pursued his research interests in American Negro culture.[157] Encouraged by Herskovits and Herzog, he set out to study African survivals by conducting fieldwork and, eventually, making field recordings in Haiti in 1939.[158] Courlander applied to the ACLS in January 1941, proposing to gather the folksongs of Afro-Cubans, "paying particular attention to the various cults," the recordings of which, he believed, "should prove of value to students of exotic music, particularly those studying the survival of Africanisms in America." After identifying Fernando Ortiz as his sponsor in Havana, he concluded his application by stating that the "bulk of the recording will be done *in remote and out of the way places* where the old cults are strong."[159] Once in Havana, Courlander met with Ortiz, who put him in contact with Alberto Zayas, who had participated as a singer in Ortiz's lecture-concert "The Sacred Music of the Yoruba Negroes in Cuba" four years earlier.[160] In addition to singing songs and playing marímbula for Courlander's recorder, Zayas assisted him in getting musicians in Guanabacoa to perform Abakuá and Santería music as well. Ortiz also encouraged Courlander to travel to Jovellanos to record musicians there as well. Since he had proposed to record the music of cults in "out of the way places," it is not surprising that Zayas and Ortiz recommended he go to Guanabacoa and Jovellanos, since both locations and their inhabitants lay beyond the modern city of Havana.

In total, Courlander collected about two hundred discs, most of which contained music of the Abakuá, Arará, Congo, Guajiro, and Lucumí repertories recorded in Havana, Guanabacoa, and Jovellanos.[161] Several, however, cannot be contained within these categories, representing instead recorded performances in excess of comparative musicology's field recording enterprise. While in Jovellanos, for instance, Courlander made copies of 78-RPM discs of commercially produced Cuban music using his recording machine, presumably in his hotel room. One of these field recordings consists of a one-minute excerpt of Orquesta Casino de la Playa's disc "Los venecianos" (The Venetians), which was recorded for the Victor record company in Havana in September 1938.[162] Courlander started the recorder about one minute and seven seconds into the disc, when the lead singer and future Decca recording artist Miguelito Valdés sings the final line of the first verse: "Ya a llegar a Caraguao, el mundo ahí se acabo porque gritaron así" (And in arriving in Caraguao, the world came to an end because they yelled out). The style of the music is a conga, and the song describes a nostalgic remembrance of the comparsas of the past as invoked in the protagonist upon hearing Los venecianos perform at carnival, parading through various neighborhoods of Havana, including Caraguao. Victor in fact recorded dozens of such congas as performed by Cuban-style big bands like Casino de la Playa following the reauthorization of comparsas in Havana in 1937.

Casino de la Playa and lead vocalist Valdés recorded many types of Cuban music, including songs from the Santería repertory. One of these is "Elube Changó," which the band recorded in June 1939. The sung melody and antiphonal responses heard on this record match with two performances of this song that Courlander recorded in Havana and Jovellanos, but apart from the phrase "elube Changó" the text of Valdés's performance does not match with those sung in Courlander's recordings. The instrumentation, of course, is distinct as well. The performance in Havana was given by a group of singers and batá drummers, while the one in Jovellanos was given by two singers accompanying themselves on *achere* (small rattle) and *bembé* drum. Casino de la Playa consisted of a big band format (trumpets, trombone, saxophones, piano, and double bass) with the addition of a bongo player. Another 78-RPM disc that Courlander copied was Chano Pozo's "Blen, blen, blen," which was recorded by Casino de la Playa and Orquesta Hotel Nacional in Havana and Xavier Cugat's Waldorf Astoria Orchestra in New York City, all in 1940. Eight years later, while conducting his own field recordings in Jovellanos, Richard Waterman recorded Alberto Brito singing "Blen, blen, blen" as a *columbia* (from the rumba repertory) accompanied by two drummers and two other percussionists playing claves and *palitos* (sticks).

This particular session recorded by Waterman generated twenty-six recordings of songs from the rumba (including the columbia and the *guaguancó*), conga, Congo, Santería, and Abakuá repertories. He collected a total of 118 performances on twelve-inch acetate discs from June through August 1948. Initially, Waterman settled in Manantiales Villiers, located on the border between Regla and Guanabacoa (just east of the Port of Havana), where he planned to make recordings of music from the Abakuá and Santería repertories.[163] By mid-July, however, he had made less than ten discs, none of which was of music from these repertories. Instead, two were of a male speaker reciting words in Abakuá with their Spanish translations; another of children singing children's songs; one of a woman named Hilda Miguel singing "La barca de oro" (The boat of gold) from the 1947 Mexican film *La barca de oro* starring Mexican singer and actor Pedro Infante; and one of a woman named Gume Sastre singing "Angelitos Negros" (Little black angels) from the 1948 Mexican film of the same title. Eventually, Waterman decided to relocate to Cárdenas, Matanzas, on the recommendation of William Bascom, who was also conducting fieldwork with Berta Montero-Sánchez, a Cuban graduate student in the anthropology program at Northwestern University, in nearby Jovellanos.[164] Once he was settled in Cárdenas, Waterman recorded dozens of discs there, in addition to those made in Jovellanos.

As these recordings of "Blen, blen, blen," "Elube Changó," and "Angelitos Negros" suggest, such categories as "popular" and "Santería" music, as well as "field," "studio" or "film" recordings, are unable to fully capture what was clearly a free-flow circulation of music whose radius not only undermined the notion of "remote and out-of-the-way places" but also stretched far beyond Cuba itself. It is important to stress that this circulation of music was induced not only by the market for 78-RPM discs or the Mexican film industry and radio broadcasts, but also by the everyday practices of individuals who made music, whether among friends in their home, for folklorists and comparative musicologists, or for American record companies. Just as "folk" or "cult" music from the field formed a significant part of music recorded in studios, such as with Casino de la Playa's "Elube Changó," records from the commercial music and film industries formed an equally important part of music making and listening in Guanabacoa, Jovellanos, and Cárdenas. In short, Cubans in remote and out-of-the-way places watched Mexican films, listened to the latest popular 78-RPM discs, and even incorporated some of these tunes into their performances for anthropologists, folklorists, and comparative musicologists. Still, such musical utterances, once captured on disc as a studio or field recording, were destined to be listened to in any number of modern spaces beyond Cuba itself, the effects of which involved familiar dispositions in listening to music as black and of African origins.

We have already read that one reviewer of Katherine Dunham's and Miguelito Valdés's Decca albums felt that some songs "at times" were "chillingly weird" and "positively savage." Although the reviewer does not specify in which songs these moments occur, utterances that had excited other listeners to similar effects also occur in some of these recordings. For example, Dunham's "Toitica la Negra" (Toitica the black woman) and Valdés's "Enlloro" exhibit sonic utterances that signaled for many American and Cuban listeners the "underworld" of "voodoo," *brujería*, and *ñañiguismo*, the latter two of which were stereotypical terms that Cubans used to criminalize the religious practices of Santería and Abakuá. Labeled a "ritmo santo-Cubano" (rhythm for a Cuban saint) on the disc's seal, "Toitica la Negra" begins with the beating of a low-pitched hand drum, followed by a male baritone voice (La Rosa Estrada) reciting a prayer in Lucumí for Changó.[165] Then the vocalist sings a salutation for Changó over a drum roll as other male vocalists add mocking laughter, woops, and other assorted vocables. Dunham begins singing halfway through the record, now over a steady beat on the hand drum, while the vocalized noises continue. Valdés's "Enlloro," similarly, begins with male voices singing a short, dirge-like chant punctuated by short and loud attacks—or sonic stabbings, as Salvador García Agüero would have it—by the big band.[166] Soon after, the band settles into a throbbing ostinato as Valdés sings the verse. For non-Spanish-speaking listeners, the verse's text would have been rather meaningless if not for Valdés's use of eerie laughter in addition to the dirge-like chorus sung in the lowest part of the bass range. For Spanish speakers, words such as *selva* (jungle), *sacrificio* (sacrifice), and *África* emerge from Valdés's exaggerated "black Spanish" speak. Listeners of jazz, regardless of language, might have instantly recognized the trumpet wah-wah growl at the end of the second verse as belonging to Duke Ellington's jungle music style.

For Cuban listeners, the song's title, "Enlloro," might not have been significant unless the listener was aware of the *enlloro* funeral ceremony of the Abakuá, to which the song makes vague reference.[167] Regardless, its sonic signifiers in all probability invoked the notions of *brujo* (witch) and *ñáñigo* (member of an Abakuá lodge), terms that, according to Cuban folklorist Lydia Cabrera, Cubans commonly and interchangeably used to refer to "all the religious practices or beliefs of African origin."[168] Men suspected of being ñáñigos or brujos were considered to be murders, criminals, devil worshippers, and kidnappers. Cabrera herself admitted to having once imagined in deathly fear that "a black hand ... was taking out my heart" upon hearing references to past (fabricated) murders committed by ñáñigos. In fact, these terms were commonly used to refer to many activities, including musicking and dancing, that were deemed by some to be socially useless, backward, dangerous, or simply African. For instance, in the year after the reauthorization of comparsas the editors of *Adelante* warned again of the dangers in allowing the "lumpen-proletariat" from the surrounding barrios of the city (such as Caraguao) to *arrollar* (parade) behind the city's sanctioned comparsas during carnival, even going so far as to draw equivalences between arrollando, morphine addiction, brujería, and ñañiguismo.[169]

In spite of attempted interventions by the Department of Tourism, Salvador García Agüero, and Fernando Ortíz, the Cuban listener's musical topography of brujería and ñañiguismo continued undeterred into the 1940s and was even presented in the United States, namely through reports in the newsprint media. Winthrop Sargeant, who became *Life* magazine's senior music writer in 1945, published an exposé-style article on the Cuban popular music industry. Titling the article "Cuba's Tin Pan Alley," Sargeant uncovered for his readers Havana's violent, seedy, and seething "underworld of African Cuba" from which Cuban music's most internationally popular styles—such as the rhumba, *son*, and conga—originated. Cuban music's melodies, Sargeant clarifies, "echo the sultry songs that were brought to Cuba from Latin and Moorish Spain," while "its rhythms are descended from the tom-tom beats of the African jungle."[170] This, and Sargeant's survey of Havana's Tin Pan Alley, consisting of "brothels, taxi-dance halls, and clandestine voodoo lodges" and populated by "bullet-scarred, marijuana-smoking characters," could be passed off as journalistic sensationalism if it were not for its consistency with the Cuban nation's evolution toward progress and modernity and its persistent threats from brujos and ñañiguismo. "Seventy percent of the Cuban population," Sargeant states, "is African, and much of the male portion of that percentage is affiliated with a secret organization known to Cubans as Los Nañigos." During carnival celebrations, he continues, "the streets of Havana stream with joyous throngs of fantastically costumed Negroes, prancing and dancing to drumming and chanting *that sounds as though* it comes straight from the heart of Africa."[171]

In stressing that Cuban music rivals the nation's main exports of sugar, tobacco, and rum, Sargeant is careful to put his American readers and potential record buyers at ease by claiming that in the course of preparing (or depathologizing) the record for export, the music is "toned down for the tourist trade." It is significant that Sargeant mentions Chano Pozo, a "big, well dressed Cuban Negro," as an example of a Cuban musician who achieved fame as a dancer and "player of the big African conga drum," and as someone who escaped certain death on at least two occasions as a result of the industry's materialistic and violent ethos. At the time of this article's publication in *Life* magazine on October 6, 1947, Pozo had already traveled to New York City to continue his career as a composer, musician, and dancer (see chapter 4). Moreover, by 1947 American buyers of Cuban music records had doubtless already listened to his songs, some of which in fact contained prayers, melodies, and rhythms from the Congo, Santería, and Abakuá repertories. These include Orquesta Casino de la Playa's "Muna sangafimba," recorded in 1940.[172] Pozo himself was an initiate of the Abakuá order Muñanga Efó located in Pueblo Nuevo, one of Havana's outlying barrios.[173] The reality is that many of these prayers, regardless of the supposed "toning down" of the associated music, resounded in the homes of Cuban music record buyers throughout the United States and beyond.

But these and other prayers and rhythms of Cuba's "African population" resounded in homes from records produced, marketed, and distributed not only by Victor and Decca but also by DISC and Ethnic Folkways Library. In 1947, six years after collecting his field recordings in Cuba, Harold Courlander, in collaboration with Moe Asch, the owner and founder of DISC Records, released *Music of the Cults of Cuba*. The album consisted of three ten-inch records, containing twelve of Courlander's field recordings, along with a booklet that provided the listener with information on the music's background, including names, descriptions, and images of instruments.[174] As an independently owned company, DISC Records attempted to produce records for an impressive variety of markets, such as traditional and contemporary jazz, folk, spoken word, blues, calypso, and classical (including contemporary and opera), doing so by releasing records in diverse formats, including live jazz performances, which was an innovative format at the time.[175] Another album format was the field recording, which DISC Records began to produce for the "ethnic" music market. Courlander agreed to license a select number of his field recordings from Cuba, Haiti, and Ethiopia to Asch, who began to promote the company's new Ethnic Series in March 1947: "New York—Disc records has inaugurated a new Ethnic Series, which will feature albums of authentic folk music from Haiti, Cuba, Russia, Ethiopia and other musically 'neglected' points. All recording will be done 'on location.'"[176]

Although this advertisement, and the DISC Ethnic Series itself, grouped these records under the category of "ethnic" music, Courlander's use of the term "cult" in the title of the Cuban music album signaled that he heard and intended audiences to listen to the music on these records as more than simply authentic Cuban folk from neglected places. In fact, his use of the term was informed by the Cuban notions of ñañiguismo and brujo, and traces back to his correspondence with Fernando Ortiz in 1940, when Courlander was preparing his applications for funding to travel to Cuba. In a letter to Herskovits Courlander mentions that he had "spoken to Fernando Ortiz about the Cuban nanigo and brujo stuff, and he's madly in love with the idea of recording some of it."[177] In his application to the ACLS, Courlander stated that he would be "paying particular attention to the various cults. Nanigo and brujo music will be an outstanding objective, though songs and rhythms of the popular social dances, worksongs, etc., will be included."[178] In publishing excerpts from his diary written while in Cuba, we see that Courlander used the term "cult" extensively to refer to the Lucumí, Abakuá, Arará, and Congo, and to qualify their activities as such (e.g., "cult activities," "cult life," "cult feasts," and "cult business"). He even includes an explanation of the meaning of the term to "most white Cubans": "The word 'cult' is synonymous with 'savagery' and 'crime.' Their knowledge of cults comes entirely from news and columns and gossip. Journalistic reports tell of ritual murders by the Kimbisa people [of the Congo] in various parts of the island, of all the horrible remnants of cult feasts found by the police, and of the disappearance of children ('obviously' stolen for cult use), usually white. The chief delight seems to be recounting the objects seized by police raids, as though each one of them were prima facie evidence of debauchery and degeneration."[179]

Unlike Sargeant, Courlander recognized the sensationalism and racism underpinning the uses of "ñañigo" and "brujo" in Cuban society and in fact addressed this in the album's booklet. "Ñañigo," he explained, is a "term that is not respectful and is much resented" by members of the Abakuá "secret society." He continued, "In addition to suffering as scapegoats for social ills arising out of acute poverty, the cults are ridiculed by the 'Castilians,' who both loathe and, I think, fear, cult activities. Add to these factors the secret character of many of the rituals and you have a not too receptive ear to the idea of recording cult music."[180] Thus, in addressing the social deviancy articulated to the Lucumí, Abakuá, Arará, and Congo, Courlander reveals his motivation in denoting these groups as "cults," for in addition to their secrecy and social marginalization, their music as well existed within "neglected points" of Cuba's social and historical topography.[181] This cult music was not, according to Courlander, folk music, since the latter could consist of "considerable hybridization," such as in conga, rhumba, son, or the music of *guahiros* (or white peasants); rather, cult music of the Lucumí, Abakuá, Arará, and Congo was "true Afro-Cuban, even African, music."

The titles of the sides, as they appear in the booklet, all include the term "cult" preceded by its ethnic affiliation, but not all of these are labeled correctly, beginning with the first side (1512-A), which is a song from the Congo, not the Carabali (or Abakuá) repertory. The second cut on the flip side of this record (1512-B) is mislabeled a Kimbisa cult song; it is the *canto* (song) "Adádará mádá ó" for the Orisha Osain accompanied by the *toque kurukuru bede* of the Santería or Lucumí repertory. Nor are the sides ordered chronologically according to when and where Courlander made the recordings. For instance, Courlander made the two Carabali sides 1513-A (b) and 1514-A (c) on records two and three, respectively, at the same session in Guanabacoa. The original unedited recordings of these sides (251.8 and 251.6, respectively) were 4:36 and 5:11 in length; they were shortened to one minute each for the album. This was Courlander's second recording session of the trip, but unfortunately he did not document it in his diary.

Of course, such factual data had no real or immediate bearing on how audiences listened to the recorded music on this album. But we do know what Courlander heard, for example, in the Abakuá music as it was performed at an initiation ceremony that he attended in Guanabacoa and detailed in his diary.[182] To Courlander, the drumming was "simple but African," while the melodies "sounded hybrid."[183] In actuality, the antiphonal responses are sung in two- and three-part harmony, as heard on the album's Abakuá sides. But he also heard these "hybrid"-sounding melodies as "Carabali" and "African" as well, even after realizing that the singing at the ceremony was being done by white as well as black members of the lodge: "Something bothered me a little, and I sensed it only vaguely. It later came to me *with a shock* that many of the spectators and *ocobíos* [ritual brothers] were white. White men singing Carabali songs. When I closed my eyes there was no way of distinguishing who was white and who black. The white *ocobíos* were as completely 'African' as the Negroes. Their singing gestures and postures, too, were African. I have a great admiration and respect for those white 'brothers' who have *somehow leaped the great gap* between the *guahiro* or Castilian attitude of mind and that of the direct and legitimate heirs of Africa."[184]

Ivor Miller has documented the fundamental role that admission of non-Africans into Abakuá society, beginning with Spanish creoles in the 1860s, played in strengthening and helping defend the brotherhood from Spanish colonial authorities.[185] Miller even quotes Courlander's passage above, arguing that his shock in encountering white *ocobíos* was a result of his North American understanding of race as a primary marker of identity, whereas Abakuá identity since the nineteenth century had been based, Miller argues, on practices of ritual kinship with West Africa, regardless of the racial makeup of members.

Courlander's shock was a symptom, however, of much more than a North American racial logic, pertaining particularly to dispositions of listening to music that transcended national boundaries. First, his understanding of the Abakuá as a cult (and not merely a racial category prescribed by North American attitudes) was directly shaped by Cuban society's notions of ñañiguismo and brujo, notions that were circulated in the United States not only with the release of *Music of the Cults of Cuba* but also with Winthrop Sargeant's *Life* magazine article, both of which were published in 1947. Second, his shock signaled his momentarily lost anchorage subjectively in the general and audio spatial level of modernity. In addition to being shocked, his lost orientation is also revealed in the unresolvable contradiction in his hearing Abakuá melodies as, on the one hand, "hybrid sounding," a characteristic of folk music (according to Courlander's booklet), and, on the other, "cult," "Carabli," and "African." They (white bodies) who were "straight ahead" of Courlander's attention did not accord with that (African music) to which he was disposed to hearing. Even when he closed his eyes, he could not help but try to listen for "who was white and who black." Finally, he regained his orientation in modernity by reasoning that the white ocobíos had "somehow leaped the great gap" separating their modern selves from ñañiguismo and African exclusivity. How they did it, or why black ocobíos allowed it, apparently remained a mystery to Courlander. What is clear is that his reaction speaks to the question of whiteness, which was as much the unraced default of modern Cuban identity as it was for modern American identity. With this in mind, Courlander's affective reaction to this instance of bodies sounding and moving exemplifies precisely what German philosopher Günther Stern Anders theorized about the truth of listening to music, wherein musical situations put a stop to worldly time and space (i.e., the subject's anchorage in identity).[186] In other words, the white ocobíos leaped no such gap; it was Courlander who, in failing as a listener in "smooth space" to be "in the music" and thus free from the subject/object divide, instead leaped "the great gap" from this musical situation's absence of racialized subjectivities back to his self-defined whiteness and anchorage in modernity.

Howard Taubman, music critic for the *New York Times*, reviewed two albums from DISC's Ethnic Series, *Folk Music of Haiti* and *Music of the Cults of Cuba*, in November 1947.[187] Readers were told that the recordings on both albums were made "on the spot" with "non-professional performers." In indicating where the recordings on the Cuban album were made, Taubman noted the distance from Havana of both Guanabacoa and Matanzas Province: Guanabacoa is "a half hour from Havana's Prado," the central avenue down which the publicly sanctioned comparsas parade during carnival; and Matanzas is "several hours east of Havana." Taubman ended his review by telling his readers and potential record buyers, "If you went traveling in search of just such music, the chances are that you would have great difficulty in getting to hear an honest version of it. Disc has made it available for home and study." Taubman's emphasis on demarcating distance, along with the quality of the music and the recorded music's distinction from Cuban popular music (produced in the modern studio), compels the listener to listen to the music on the album in a temporally and spatially defined framework. Moreover, such indexical cues enabled the listener to handle the album itself as having been transported from that distant past and place to the listener's modern present (or home).

Soon after Moe Asch's DISC Record Company fell into bankruptcy in the spring of 1948, Folkways Records and Service was established, as was the 33-1/3 long-playing (LP) record format.[188] By December 1949, Courlander and Asch came to an agreement to rerelease the *Music of the Cults of Cuba* album as a twelve-inch LP on the new corporation's record label, Ethnic Folkways Library.[189] With the new LP format, the rereleased album, retitled *Cult Music of Cuba*, contained twenty-two minutes and thirty-three seconds of recorded music, about ten minutes more than the DISC album of three ten-inch 78-RPM discs. Courlander replaced four tracks on the original album with six new and longer tracks, including "Elube Chango" (labeled "Song to Chango") and toque Ilé (labeled "Lucumi Drums"). The new booklet contained much of the same information found in the DISC booklet, including Courlander's explanation of the difference between folk music, popular music, and "pure African music," and his retelling of his observation of white members participating in the Abakuá initiation ceremony. He does not, however, mention his "shock" at seeing white ocobíos singing, dancing, and becoming African.

Folkways Records sold anywhere between four and forty-six copies of *Cult Music of Cuba* every six months through the 1950s, according to its business statements.[190] In addition to record sales, Courlander's recordings and his narrative explaining their significance reached the homes of radio listeners as well. For instance, Courlander served as the featured commentator for one episode of the *Adventures in Music* radio program, which aired on WNYC in New York City through the 1950s.[191] His script includes the main themes found on the album and LP booklets, such as Cuban recordings a little off the beaten path, city music, highly urbanized styles, highly developed West African musical traditions remaining strong in the interior of the island, and the idea that where cult activity goes on you may hear true Afro-Cuban music or even pure African music. The term "cult" remained a consistent theme as Courlander played excerpts of, for example, drumming of the "Lucumi cult" (toque Ilé). He also played two recorded versions of a *canto* (song) for the Orisha Osain, one from both the album (1512-B [b]) and LP (side A, track 2) (i.e., "Osain adádará mádá o") and another recorded by Herskovits in Bahia and released on *Afro-Bahian Religious Songs from Brazil* by the Library of Congress's Music Division in 1947. He played Herskovits's field recording as evidence of the "antiquity of this type of music." Then, in concluding the program, he stated, "I am going to play you another recordings [*sic*]. . . . This one is also a Lucumi piece, but *musically it is a hybrid*. You will notice that other influences have entered. And I think you will notice also that it is a *good bit closer to what we call modern Cuban music* than anything else I have played for you."

The script's playlist indicates that Courlander in fact played a "Carabali Cult Song," not a "Lucumi piece," a Freudian slip, as it were. Or was it? Courlander's experience at the Abakuá initiation ceremony was indeed disorienting. His "shock" in observing and listening to white ocobíos becoming African was not unlike the "shake" experienced by Demaison upon observing and listening to Gilberto Valdés's musicians similarly becoming Egyptian, Somalian, Makua, Dahomey, Yoruba, and Mandinga in Havana, while he was simultaneously being transported to Africa.[192] Nor were these effects different from the *Washington Afro-American*'s description of Dunham's recordings as "chillingly weird." They are not different in that all of these suggest a momentary state of subjective dislocation induced by listening to music. This application of Koffka's theory of directional listening and subjective localization might seem metaphorical if it was not a contemporaneous discourse of listening, albeit a specialized one, or directly implicated in Waterman's theory of metronome sense, which similarly theorizes those musical events in which a listener's orientation is momentarily dislocated without being completely destroyed.

All of these examples, including statements by Herskovits from the previous chapter, thus give way to an expanded conception of listening disposed to articulating subjectivity to distance through sound:

> It is, of course, interesting to hear them [i.e., Herskovits's field recordings] once more *and at this distance from the music* the correspondence between these [African] songs and the Suriname music of the bush comes out very strikingly.—Herskovits to Hornbostel, March 6, 1932

> It is a *good bit closer to what we call modern Cuban music* than anything else I have played for you.—Courlander, "Adventures in Music," no date

Both, Africans and Spanish, *brought to a geographic zone (space) and evolving into a distinct society (time)* dialectically shaped a different nationality.—Arredondo, "El arte negro a contrapelo," 1937

The left-right localization of sound depends upon the time-difference with which the sound wave strikes the two ears, *localization occurring towards the side whose ear is struck first.*—Koffka, "Perception," 1922

Again, putting these observations (regarding subjectivity in observing and listening to sound and movement) into proximity is intended to gesture beyond the metaphorical. We might also add to this list Waterman's laboratory worksheet. We should be reminded, however, of the unresolvable contradictions that occasionally emerged resulting from these same acts of locating and naming music. For Courlander, the harmonic singing of the "Abakuá cult" was an example of hybridity, a characteristic of Cuban folk and popular music, or "modern Cuban music," but not cult music. When sung by white ocobíos, however, it transformed them into Africans. For Salvador García Agüero, Fernando Ortiz, and Gilberto Valdés, the batá sounded the essences of the modern Cuban, both black and white, Western music's melodic and harmonic language, the Lucumí language, and Cuba's African ancestral purity, all in one.

These are anything but trivial or nonsensical errors; nor can they be reduced to what Freud called parapraxis, since, in all of their not-accidental inexactness, they in fact exhibit what always occurred in listening to music and observing dance as black and of African origins in modernity. Whenever an observer and listener phenomenally puts themselves into proximity of bodies racialized as black musicking and dancing, not only does that music and dance become black and African, the bodies of those musicking and dancing become distanced temporally and spatially from the observer and listener. Without distancing the racialized musician and dancer, the arbitrary essence of the listener's and observer's subjectivity reveals itself and thus threatens his or her contingent anchorage in the world. But what of the racialized musicians and dancers themselves? Did they, in turn, desire the freedom from such anxieties surrounding one's subjective contingency in the world? We turn to the next chapter for insight.

3 /

Embodying Africa against Racial Oppression, Ignorance, and Colonialism

It seemed that Africa was a never-never land and that when they pictured my childhood on the edge of the jungle, they saw me as they did when they viewed one of the films in which I have acted. They knew and were proud that it was their father who moved across the screen; yet he was also *another—a stranger who behaved differently and for different reasons* than did the man who sat at the head of their table at home. —MODUPE PARIS, *I Was a Savage*, 1957

Modupe Paris of French Guinea was one of a number of West Africans who from the 1920s through the 1940s actively engaged in various capacities with Americans' perceptions of Africa and Africans. Whether for film companies, white private dinner parties, black women's clubs, black colleges, or pan-African political organizations, these West Africans materialized for their audiences this never-never land by staging its unifying discursive properties, not least of which were those demarcating the edge of the jungle from the metropolis and the African native or ancestor from the modern American Negro. In addition to materializing the African native and jungle on stage, many also lectured on African music and black music's African origins. In spite of their intentions, however, whether artistic, economic, or political, the political economies of race in colonial West Africa and the United States as well as Cuba always already determined their bodies as black, regulating the rhythms of their racialized subjectivities according to society's distinct social, cultural, and historical dispositions. Because of their locally situated histories, political economies of race made embodying the raced body, particularly the bodies of black Others—as with a West African man's performance of the Negro slave, an Afro-Cuban woman's performance of the American Negro mother, or Afro-Cuban and American Negro men's performances of the African native—potentially destabilizing occurrences in the subjectivities of performers and audience members alike.

It has been posited thus far that the logic of black music's and dance's African origins depended on a temporalizing bush and anthropological field in which or in proximity to which black musicians and dancers were placed, the results being the materialization of modernity's primitive pasts serving as a bulwark of the metropolis's modern present. Imminent in these materializations under this logic were bodies raced as black and white. This chapter expands on the analysis of these actions and reactions by privileging this logic's performances by musicians and dancers, who as modernity's raced black others were, borrowing from M. M. Bakhtin, "shot through with *chronotopic values*."[1] A historicist analysis of these performers as raced black bodies becoming this logic's key figures (e.g., the African native, the Negro slave, and the modern American Negro) and the performances themselves will reveal three fundamental aspects of the logic of black music's and dance's African origins.

The first fundamental aspect is that these performances and lectures functioned as mechanisms of knowledge (re)production, the scientific legitimacy of which, however, was unrecognized by scientifically and politically sanctioned sources. Just as there were anthropologists, comparative musicologists, educators, journalists, and city officials invested in realizing the practical social and political outcomes of discovering and explaining black music's and dance's history from Africa to the New World, so there were musicians, dancers, political activists, and their audiences who rationalized this history in performance to affect social and political outcomes as well. The fact that their performances, unlike the activities of their academic contemporaries (whether black or white), necessitated that they embody raced black bodies in this logic's prescribed temporal and spatial practices meant that they and their audiences assumed well-regulated raced and gendered objectivities and norms of behavior. This was especially the case with Modupe Paris, Paul Robeson, and others who portrayed the African native in films. Because of its very social nature, however, the body's docility as well as its utility and submissiveness makes its investments in the political economies of race, gender, and sexuality an empowering and unsettling proposition. Drawing from Michel Foucault's theorization of the disciplined body, the black body here is thought of not merely as an oppressed ontology but also as a political technology in the logic of black music's and dance's African origins, put into action as such not only by the performers themselves but also by their sponsors and audience members, which included American Negro women's clubs and colleges, Afro-Cuban civic and research organizations, and African anticolonial groups.[2]

In drawing from Judith Butler's theorization of the sexed body, we are reminded that a number of regulatory regimes are operative in setting the limits to a body's intelligibility, such that individuals are compelled to assume sexed bodies along with raced ones.[3] Thus, in the logic of black music's and dance's African origins, the chronotopes of the African pasts and modern presents—the jungle and metropolis, primitive native and modern citizen, anthropological field and scientific laboratory, savage drum and melody-producing instruments, syncopation and rhythm, frenzied ritual dance and artistic choreography, and so on—operate to race and sex the body's flows. Butler's application of the notion of performativity, wherein such socially regulatory norms accrue power through their compulsory appropriation by raced and sexed bodies, alerts us to the dissimulation of these norms and the disavowal of their historicity in the assumption and materialization of the black male and female body. But performativity also takes into account the subject's intentions emanating from within the process of its body's raced and sexed inscriptions, such that each act of embodying a raced male or female body is never a perfect imitation nor a finished event but rather one of "a thousand" raced and sexed bodies.[4]

Thus the second aspect of this historicist analysis of this logic's performances lies in the interrelationship between society's performativity of race and gender and the performances themselves, for this interrelationship compels us to recognize how the performer's and audience's participation constituted *particular* investments in the political economies of race and gender in Chicago, Havana, New York City, and elsewhere. Such attention to this logic's performances as occurring in pure and empty time (i.e., at the disjunction between the past and future) allows us to keep in check the seductions of Origin and Authenticity against which these performers and their sponsors pursued their artistic, economic, and political goals. By demystifying claims of origin and authenticity, we are better able to gauge why these performers invested their racial and gendered capital in performing this historical period's logic of black music's and dance's African origins, reasons that sometimes exceeded but were never completely detached from society's laws of raced and sexed bodies.

That West African musicians and dancers staged their own versions of this historical narrative in order to address what Asadata Dafora of Sierra Leone characterized in 1945 as a "state of almost complete ignorance concerning African dancing and music" in the United States prompts further critical consideration of the privileging of this logic's anthropological and comparative musicological renderings.[5] Some Cuban musicians and historians, similarly, engaged the practical social effects of the Negro spiritual, thereby contributing to what Frank Andre Guridy characterized as a cross-national forging of racial understandings and diaspora making "beyond the realm of Afro-Cuban religion and folklore."[6] Thus, for example, in the 1930s, Modupe Paris and Cubans Zoila Gálvez and Enrique Andreu staked their own claims on both the dominant narrative of the spiritual in regard to its African origins and the power in securing self-reliance and resistance, while from 1943 through the early postwar period the African Academy of Arts and Research (AAAR) sponsored Dafora's own interventions in the historical narrative of the origins of the spiritual, jazz, rumba, conga, and calypso to gain political support from black and white Americans for the decolonization of Africa. Not unlike Franz Boas, Melville J. Herskovits, Fernando Ortiz, Salvador García Agüero, and Havana's Department of Tourism, these African and Cuban performers hoped that by programming their performances and lectures, a renewed knowledge of the shared cultural contributions of Africans and New World Negroes would emerge among their audiences and have a practical impact on reversing the effects of such ignorance, namely, racism and racial terror in Cuba and the United States, and European colonialism in Africa.

But herein lay the ontological dilemma for these performers and their black audience members, since their capacity as knowledge (re)producers was fundamentally complicated by their essentialized status not merely as entertainers but as black Others either descended or directly from the edge of the jungle of that never-never land. To further theorize this dilemma, we turn to Butler's notion of abject beings, in this instance, materialized in the African native or savage, as those who cannot enjoy the status of the modern subject and thus live under the sign of the "unlivable" or jungle. This abject status is secured not only by the circumscription of the normative subjectivity par excellence—modernity's white, heterosexual, middle-class male—but also racial uplift's promise of survival, progress, and independence as promulgated by modern American Negroes, Afro-Cubans, and Africans alike.[7] Here, Butler's psychoanalytical explanation of the abject designation as those who "may not reenter the field of the [modern] social without threatening . . . the dissolution of the [normative] subject itself" invites comparison with Gestalt psychology's notion of the listener's subjective assurance within modernity's auditory spatial level when applied to the performance of black music's and dance's African origins in the metropolis.[8] For in turning to Frantz Fanon's application of Hegel's notion of being-for-others, we get contemporaneous insight into the formation of raced along with spatialized and temporalized subjectivities, and the anxieties experienced therein, between not only blacks and whites but also blacks and their black Others.[9] In the midst of such anxieties, artistic, economic, and political gains were mutually enjoyed by these performers of black Others and their black sponsors, whether they were members of the National Association of Colored Women, the Sociedad de Estudios Afrocubanos, or the African Academy of Arts and Research.

Indeed, Paris, Dafora, and their West African peers contended with this subjective impasse especially when embodying the sounds and movements of black music's and dance's origins, which their American audiences usually identified automatically with the savage and jungle. This was also the case for Chano Pozo, whose instrument, the conga drum, engendered in his Cuban audiences the materializations of the nation's premodern past.[10] Jonathan Sterne has lamented that there is no sonic equivalent of the gaze when enumerating orientations toward sound and listening.[11] In fact, in his own application of Hegel's being-for-others, Jean-Paul Sartre, writing in 1943, stressed that becoming the object of the other's "look" is instigated not only in the "convergence of two ocular globes in my direction" but also "when there is a rustling of branches, or the sound of a footstep followed by silence, or the slight opening of a shutter, or a light movement of a curtain."[12] In this way racialized listening and being heard racially function as integral aspects of the process of intersubjective formation, and in listing these particular examples Sartre further suggests that one's apprehension of sound and movement functioning in the capacity of the "look" affects feelings such as vulnerability, danger, shame, or pride in an aspect of one's being-for-others. Thus in the context of performing *and sounding* the dance and music of black Others, feelings of shame, pride, vulnerability, danger, and pleasure manifested in the performers and audience members as a result, according to Sartre's estimation, of one's recognition that "I *am* as the Other sees [and listens to] me."[13]

In this final assertion by Sartre, the notion that feelings of shame and pride are affected through "the *recognition* of the fact that I *am* indeed that [abject] object which the Other is looking at and judging" opens crucial interpretive avenues into understanding how and why these performers endured embodying Africa and their black Others.[14] Indeed, one's recognition of being seen and heard by others on stage and in the audience unfolded in varying and, oftentimes, contradictory ways. For what purposes did Paris, Dafora, and their West African peers perform the African past of their American Negro contemporaries? What did Gálvez and Andreu's program of Negro spirituals entail in their attempt to persuade Afro-Cubans to harness their collective racial consciousness as they struggled against racial discrimination and for social justice in Cuban society? How did these performances compare with those of Paul Robeson and other American Negroes, who, in turn, collaborated with Cubans and Africans to stake their own claims on a shared racial history originating in Africa and the Caribbean? And, finally, how can we articulate these performances to Black Power in its own significances, organizing principles, and historicism?

In exploring the answers to these questions, race pride, self-determination, anticolonialism, and black nationalism emerge as that which Raymond Williams identified as residual elements of the past that are "still active in the cultural process, not only and often not at all as an element of the past, but as an effective element of the present."[15] Indeed, the analysis of these performers in their varying capacities as raced black bodies shows that Black Power, as Stokely Carmichael himself asserted in 1966, was "not a recent or isolated phenomenon" of the 1960s; rather, it had "grown out of the ferment of agitation and activity by different people and organizations in many black communities over the years."[16] This third aspect of the logic of black music's and dance's African origins—the materializations of this "ferment of agitation" as performance—shows that the black communities Carmichael referred to were not limited to only those located in the United States, and even then they were populated by individuals and organizations of African and Caribbean background. Where black American purveyors of the Double V campaign paralleled the aims of the Allied war effort with those of the Negro community, African and Afro-Cuban men and women performer activists, similarly, staked their own attainment of political freedom and social justice on the ferment of agitation and activity of American Negroes. The programs analyzed in this chapter typically involved American Negro and Caribbean performers under the direction of African male dancers and musicians, whose viewpoints regarding black music and dance of the New World occasionally revealed fissures in the cultural patrimony and racial and political solidarity otherwise evoked in these performances.

"The March of African Music from Africa to the American Continents"

In describing the theme of the African Academy of Arts and Research's (AAAR) second annual African Dances and Modern Rhythms festival, founder and president Kingsley Ozuomba Mbadiwe said it depicts the "march of African music from Africa to the American continents" by showing the influence of African music and dance in jazz, swing, boogie-woogie, tap, and calypso, as well as in the music and dances of Haiti and Brazil.[17] The festival, featuring American, Caribbean, and African performers, took place at Carnegie Hall on April 4 and 6, 1945, just one month before Nazi Germany's surrender to the Allies. In addition to the Allies' advancements against the Axis powers, however, the festival's theme also alluded to demands for the abolishment of both Jim Crow in the United States and colonialism in India, China, the West Indies, and Africa, as had been conveyed at the March on Washington rally at Madison Square Garden in 1942.[18] This militant theme notwithstanding, Mbadiwe stated that the festival's aim was to "broaden the base of understanding of Africa" in the United States, while the academy's larger purpose was to promote "better understanding between Africa and America."[19] With benefactors such as Eleanor Roosevelt, Mary McLeod Bethune, and other American and African political dignitaries, the academy seemed to be well positioned to realize its aims, both political and cultural, from the start of its founding in 1943.

Although knowledge of Africa was indeed limited among most Americans, Mbadiwe's reference to a "base of understanding" of Africa suggests aspects of this knowledge that go beyond its quality and quantity. For the notion of a "base of understanding" suggests that which Michel Foucault theorized as the enunciative field, and Gilles Deleuze and Félix Guattari defined as the plan(e) of organization. Both notions suggest that beyond the quantity and quality of knowledge there is a deeper structure, neither hidden nor visible, neither silent nor audible, that *makes possible* in the first place certain types of statements about, in this instance, Africa and one's status as an African.[20] To be clear, Mbadiwe and his peers were not after changing the understanding of Africa and their identities as Africans in this way. Indeed, the positivist terms that sustained both the colonial situation in Africa and the notion of Africa itself were the very terms by which the members of the AAAR and other West Africans pursued their political and cultural activism in Africa before arriving in the United States.

For instance, at the end of 1938, Mbadiwe, who was of Igbo background, left Lagos, Nigeria, where he was a college student, and traveled to the United States to attend Lincoln University in Pennsylvania.[21] In the years leading to his departure, "a new wave of nationalism," he recalled, "was raging on the West coast of Africa." "A new breed of men and women accepted the credo of nationalism and took the challenge, as its apostles. The battle cry was 'Down with British imperialism, Nigeria must be free.'"[22] Mbadiwe and other West Africans of their respective nation's elite were encouraged by Nigerian nationalist leader Nnamdi Azikiwe, also of Igbo background, to pursue higher education in the United States, where they believed African students could attain the political and economic skills needed back home in order to help realize their nations' independence.[23] In looking toward American Negroes in particular for solutions to their colonial status, West Africans cultivated what Yekutiel Gershoni calls the African American myth, which they perpetuated by idealizing black Americans' political, economic, and cultural accomplishments and well-being while downplaying their miseries in a racist society.[24] Thus they continued the cultural nationalist movement that the previous generation of African intellectual elites started in the late nineteenth century in order to regain a foothold in the colonial political structure and to "refute the assertion based on social Darwinism that blacks were an inferior species of the human race with no claim to civilization or culture."[25]

Once in the United States, however, Mbadiwe encountered, as had Modupe Paris and Asadata Dafora before him, Americans whose impressions of Africans and of Africa were, like those of their European colonial rulers, shaped by social Darwinism, impressions that were indeed disseminated through colonial propaganda as well as by American missionaries and films. "They had regarded us as wild men who ate the roots of trees, and as sleepy-heads," he said.[26] With the exception of some "Africa-conscious" black Americans, inspired by Garveyism, Mbadiwe claimed that he and his peers "further discovered that the majority of the leading members of the Negro race knew nothing about Africa, except in a general, academic sense." To refute the myths of the African native and address the lack of knowledge of Africa in American society, Mbadiwe and other African university students and émigrés worked toward what their peers continued to pursue in West Africa, calling up African history and cultural traditions to prove Africa's contributions to human history, all the while conceiving of this history and their place in it in positivist terms. For instance, as Gershoni notes of the first generation of West African cultural nationalists, "Cultural development was indispensable to political progress. [. . .] The cultural nationalists could not but recognize the vast gaps that separated the Africans from the Europeans."[27]

The cultural nationalism of Mbadiwe's generation of activists, particularly those living in the United States, did not reject European culture either. However, they did not take the notion of an evolutionary gap between African culture and black cultures of the New World as a given. Not unlike their African nationalist contemporaries, Afro-Cuban activists, too, looked toward American Negroes and took advantage of their institutions of higher learning in their pursuit of upward mobility in Cuban society.[28] And even though they remained ever nationalists in response to their nation's neocolonial status under American imperialism, Afro-Cubans did forge a black consciousness based on not only their patriotism but also their interactions with black Americans and Africans.[29] As our first two case studies will show, West African Modupe Paris and Afro-Cubans Zoila Gálvez and her husband Enrique Andreu engaged the vexed social and political situation of black Americans—exemplified by, on the one hand, the growing prestige of the Negro spiritual and, on the other, the racial injustice of the Scottsboro case, and the fascist terrorism of Jim Crow—to gain a foothold in the historical narrative of black Americans' social and political struggles as well as their cultural accomplishments.

For Africans and Afro-Cubans alike, attaining a Western education, including training in operatic singing, though central to the ideology of racial uplift and social mobility, was never quite enough to earn equal access to spaces of prestige, let alone disprove their supposed racial inferiority.[30] Thus for Paris to lecture on, and perform the African origins of, American Negro music, beginning with the spiritual, was as much a demonstration of his African cultural nationalism and racial solidarity with black Americans as it was a recognition of the practical challenges in leading a career as a concert vocal soloist. Gálvez and Andreu similarly looked to the spiritual not to help close any perceived evolutionary gap between Afro-Cuban and black American culture but rather to inspire Afro-Cubans to also work toward their rightful claim for self-determination and social and racial justice. Although Gálvez's solo vocalist career was far more extensive than Paris's, her encounters with African and American Negro musicians, like Paris's, had a formative effect on her racial and gendered consciousness as an Afro-Cuban woman.

As the daughter of José Gálvez, who had served as a colonel in Cuba's liberation army, Zoila Gálvez's musical education was not typical of most Cubans, particularly Afro-Cubans.[31] She began studying the piano in 1905 at the age of six. After completing her degree in piano pedagogy at the Conservatorio Nacional Hubert Blanck in 1917, Gálvez continued her training in voice with Tina Farelli and Arturo Bovi at the Conservatorio Blanck. Her exceptional promise as a soprano led her to Italy in 1920 to study with Giacomo Marino at the Milan Conservatory. While in Milan she debuted at the Teatro Dal Verme singing the parts of Amina in Vincenzo Bellini's *La sonnambula* and Gilda in Giuseppe Verdi's *Rigoletto*. Before her return to Havana, Gálvez traveled through Rome, Paris, Barcelona, London, and, finally, New York City to which she would eventually return in 1923. Meanwhile she continued her opera career in Havana, where she was featured at the Teatro Nacional singing arias by Bellini, Verdi, and Bizet, in addition to "Adieu mon beau rivage" from Giacomo Meyerbeer's *L'Africaine*.[32]

Gálvez also performed the music of Cuban composers, including Eduardo Sánchez de Fuentes's "Linda cubana" (Beautiful Cuban) and Gonzalo Roig's "Para ti" (For you), which she recorded for Columbia in New York City in 1923. She had traveled to New York in January 1923 with the hope of broadening her international success as a soprano in the United States, but high-profile engagements in New York or elsewhere in the country eluded her due to the discriminatory policies of established opera institutions.[33] By 1925 she had traveled to Paris to perform at the Salle Pleyel before returning to Havana in 1926 to perform once again as a soloist at the Teatro Nacional. In attendance at this concert was a group of black American tourists, including Coy Herndon of the *Chicago Defender*.[34] Herndon described Gálvez as the "greatest soprano Cuba has ever developed." He was also impressed with the fact that her accompanying orchestra included black as well as white musicians. He described her voice as "musical and clear as a bell," adding that she appeared "amid thunderous applause and a heavy shower of beautiful flowers thrown from the theater boxes." In addition to this concert, the group also visited Club Atenas, whose members of the Afro-Cuban elite had arranged a reception for the visiting group of Americans. Of their visit to Havana, Herndon wrote that it "will go down in history as the first link in a chain as strong as the Rock of Gibraltar in creating love and co-operation between two great Colored races." Indeed, as Frank Andre Guridy notes, Club Atenas served not only as Havana's most important link to the emerging African American tourist industry but also a "key space of Afro-Cuban and African American interaction in succeeding decades."[35]

Herndon's depiction of this visit signaled a significant development in Gálvez's own engagement with black American culture and women in particular, starting in 1927, when she returned to New York City with her stepmother, Justa Gálvez, this time to perform in black musical revues. She joined *Rang-Tang*, whose show included comedians, a male chorus, solo vocalists (including Gálvez), and dancers.[36] In addition to performing in revues, she continued to give solo concerts, one of which took place at Grace Congregational Church in Harlem. One reviewer, writing for the *Chicago Defender*, considered the concert "one of the most brilliant recitals of the year," in which Gálvez "disclosed a voice of beautiful soprano qualities, which she uses with fine intelligence and judgment. Her singing was remarkable for its pure diction, exceptional tonal qualities and a rare art of interpretation."[37] In addition to performing her regular repertory of arias and Cuban songs, Gálvez sang spirituals, performing these, according to the same reviewer, "with soulful expression." Like her black American vocal colleagues, Gálvez was compelled to sing popular songs and spirituals, even joining black music revues, due to racist practices of opera venues.[38]

Gálvez and her stepmother also established friendships with Beatrice Wilson, among other women of New York City's black American elite whom they would later host in Havana as their guests.[39] While her stepmother decided to stay in New York City, Gálvez returned to Havana in 1929 to continue her performance career, the repertory of which now included spirituals. Her time abroad in Europe and especially forging a career in the United States was indeed formative in her gaining a "broad view," as she would later explain, "in terms of the diffusion and extension of African music and rhythms, both in countries in the Americas as in other places."[40] For example, in 1931 she attended the L'exposition coloniale internationale in Paris, where she claimed to have recognized the music of the Abakuá in the "musical rhythms and melodies of the distinct tribes that were exhibited there . . . , even something that they called *Náncue* which was none other than our *Ñáñigo*."[41] While in New York she attended a performance by the Elkins-Payne Singers, a group of black American singers specializing in spirituals, whose performances, she asserted, "can serve as a historical and chronological index to learn black music and the black presence in music."[42] She even attended a performance of a choir directed by Modupe Paris himself, which she described as a "mass choral of authentic black Africans with their drums and instruments of various types . . . whose playing had a great similarity not only with the music and singing of black North Americans, but also with ours."[43]

Paris's own encounters with black American and other African musicians in the United States also shaped his musical career and outlook on American Negro music's relationship with Africa. His formal training in Western classical music, including voice performance, began with composer Robert Nathaniel Dett at Hampton Institute in Virginia, where he studied from 1922 until 1924 (see figure 3.1).[44] After returning to New York City, where he had first arrived after leaving West Africa, he studied with vocal teachers Clara Novello Davies and Caska Bonds.[45] By 1926 he had begun singing professionally on stage and, soon after, promoted himself in his concert announcements as a "West African baritone."[46] His repertory included pieces by Jules Massenet, Antonín Dvořák, Paolo Tosti, Giacomo Puccini, Carl Bohm, Oley Speaks, and Harry T. Burleigh in addition to spirituals, at around the same time Gálvez began to sing spirituals on her programs.[47] One of Paris's earliest radio performances came the following year. The program, titled *The Negro Achievement Hours*, aired on New York City's WABC, and this particular program included Nigerian drummers from Calabar.[48] By 1929, after a short stay in Richmond, Paris had moved to

FIG. 3.1 Modupe
Paris, 1922, Hampton
University. (Courtesy
of Hampton Univer-
sity Archives)

Chicago, where he continued his singing career and began including African music to his programs.[49]

Paris's addition of African music to his repertory proved to be an effective, if obvious, marketing move. But his self-promotion as a West African baritone, in addition to his including African music in his repertory, cannot be attributed to his efforts to promotion alone. In Chicago, for example, he met and shared an apartment with Robert L. Ephriam, who at the time was the president of the Chicago branch of the Universal Negro Improvement Association.[50] Reports characterized Ephriam as an "orator of ability," which he put on display, for example, in July 1931, when giving speeches denouncing racial segregation in the American armed forces.[51] It was during this time that Paris himself became active in addressing issues of racial segregation, such as by helping to form the Interracial Artists' Club in Elmhurst, Illinois, of which he was elected president.[52]

He had also started to petition organizers of the Chicago World's Fair, which was scheduled to take place in 1933, to help ensure the authentic representation of African music, art, and history.[53] With "A Century of Progress" as the Fair's theme, Paris proposed an African exhibit demonstrating African homes, blacksmith techniques, music, and dance, all of which was to serve as the backdrop for illustrating the "progress made by representatives of the African race on American soil."[54] He continued his concert career; as one reviewer indicated, since arriving in Chicago, he "has been very successful as a concert artist," performing at Orchestra Hall, among other places.[55] Soon, however, he put aside his singing career to deliver lectures on the evolution of spirituals and jazz from their African origins as part of his work advocating for African representation in the Chicago World's Fair. In fact, he had expressed an interest in studying the relationship between the spiritual and the African folk song as early as 1929.[56]

Gálvez's and Paris's addition of spirituals to their solo concert vocal repertories, beginning around 1927, signaled not a new development in the music's history, for its introduction to the vocal concert repertory dates back to the late nineteenth and early twentieth centuries.[57] Whereas Henry T. Burleigh and Roland Hayes were formative in establishing the spiritual within the solo vocal concert tradition, W. E. B. Du Bois, perhaps most notably, had asserted his own version of the spiritual's origin to "primitive African music" in his *The Souls of Black Folk*.[58] Rather, what is unique about their performances of spirituals and, in particular, their programming of lecture-concerts to address the spiritual's African origins and social significance is the fact that they were not Americans, nor were they historians or social scientists. Indeed, each of their iterations of songs such as "Nobody Knows the Trouble I've Seen," "Sometimes I Feel Like a Motherless Child," and "Go Down, Moses" entailed their agency in mobilizing the normative racializing principles of the black American, but as black Others they simultaneously forged the possibility of destabilizing these very same principles as well as those of their own racialized and gendered status as an Afro-Cuban woman and an African man.

Paris's earliest documented performance of spirituals occurred at a benefit concert for the John Brown Memorial Association. Taking place in November 1927 at St. Peter Claver's Hall in Philadelphia, the event featured Paris, "the West African baritone," singing three spirituals and a work song in addition to his operatic repertory.[59] One reviewer of Paris's performance wrote, "Mr. Paris went past all expectations and completely took the audience by storm. He has a commanding appearance on the stage and is genial and polished in his manner. [. . .] As a climax to an otherwise perfect artistic program, Mr. Paris rendered 'Sometimes I Feel like a Motherless Child,' 'Go Down, Moses,' and 'Were You

There?' singing the latter in such a plaintively questioning manner *as to make one think he was really present* when his Lord was crucified."[60] Of Paris's rendition of the work song "Water Boy," the reviewer stated that it "pleased the audience beyond power to express." Paris's choice of spirituals and, in particular, "Water Boy," was in all likelihood inspired by Paul Robeson, who had begun to sing these same songs as early as 1924 to promote Negro music's message of racial dignity, pride, and resistance.[61] Paris's engagement with American Negro music, social activism, and history continued the following May, in 1928, when he participated in the John Brown Memorial Association's sixth annual pilgrimage to Lake Placid, New York, where the grave of John Brown, the abolitionist and leader of the raid on the federal armory at Harper's Ferry, was located.[62] According to one account of the pilgrimage's speakers, James J. Barry, a lawyer from Schenectady, New York, "regarded John Brown as a great emulator of Jesus Christ" and asserted that Christians "who did not recognize the colored people as brothers and equals" were "not Christians but hypocrites."[63]

The symbolism of having an African singer perform spirituals at a pilgrimage honoring a historically controversial figure—one who attempted to overthrow the institution of slavery in the United States through armed insurrection— was indeed provocative and surely not lost on the association's pilgrims, nor on Paris. For based on his performance of "Were You There?" for the association in November, we know that Paris was capable of affecting in his audience a state of being transported to the past, that is, to John Brown's execution, which some allegorized with Jesus Christ's crucifixion. His audience's recognition of him as African also must have played no small role in affecting such imagined metaphysical manifestations. Indeed, for Paris, being an African in the United States enabled him to not only inhabit the discursive space of the black American's past but also shape its narrative in the present.

As noted above, Paris began to include African music on his programs in 1929, a little more than one year after his performance for the John Brown Memorial Association's pilgrimage. In 1931 organizers of the Chicago World's Fair agreed to recognize Paris's African Exhibit Society of the African Student Aid Association to advise in the planning of an African exhibit.[64] Among the fair organizers' many advisors was Melville J. Herskovits, who met with Paris in November 1931 to discuss his group's proposals for the African exhibit. Among Paris's recommendations, according to Herskovits, was to "bring Africans here . . . from the regions from which American Negroes had come to show how their civilization had formed a basis for New World Negro behavior," a recommendation that aligned perfectly with Herskovits's acculturation program.[65] The *Chicago Defender*, similarly, recognized Paris's and the African Student Aid

Association's vision for the fair's planning by inviting them to the newspaper's office. In publishing a group photo, which included Nathan K. McGill, who at the time served as the newspaper's general council and was assistant attorney general of the state of Illinois, the *Chicago Defender* endorsed Paris's recommendation to, as the caption reads, "present Africa's side." Paris's experience advising the fair's organizers, meeting with Herskovits (who had recently returned from Nigeria, Dahomey, and the Gold Coast, where he had researched, among other problems, the spiritual's African origins), and singing spirituals for organizations such as the John Brown Memorial Association were undeniably formative in his decision to program lecture-concerts in which he would render his own theory of the African origins of the spiritual.[66]

One of his first documented lecture-concerts took place in April 1932 at Fullerton Hall in Chicago. For this program he directed the Afro-American Male Jubilee Singers, which consisted of "ten American Negro singers" whom, it was reported, he had trained in African music.[67] In addition to the African repertory, the choir sang "Go Down, Moses," "Swing Low, Sweet Chariot," and other spirituals, while Paris sang "Were You There?" as a solo.[68] The program's first part featured spirituals and was, according to one reviewer, "not in the least a conventionalized concert performance of spirituals but something that seemed entirely spontaneous." Of Paris's lecture on the spiritual's African origins, the same reviewer opined that he "supplied evidence for a plausible theory," the evidence being the song's fundamental importance in various social contexts (work, play, and worship) in Africa. "The Negro brought [song] to America with him, and though the rhythm of a new speech changed the rhythm of the song, though the melody itself changed as well, there is a resemblance that *only the Negro musician could supply*."[69] Paris gave two more lecture-concerts at Fullerton Hall later in April and June to raise funds for the World Fair's African exhibit.[70] At the June event, he was reported to have said that the fair's proposed African exhibit would "give to the world the knowledge that all Africans are not totally ignorant and illiterate, as many Americans especially are inclined to believe."[71] In regard to his lecture, the reviewer wrote, "Paris frequently offered explanations of his material that were as interesting for their psychology as for their content."

Based on these two reports of Paris's lectures, it is likely that he derived his theory of the spiritual's origins in African speech and song from Charles G. Blooah, an anthropologist from Liberia who had graduated from the University of Chicago and conducted fieldwork with George Herzog in Liberia in 1930 to collect proverbs of the Jabo in southeastern Liberia.[72] His claim that "only the Negro musician could supply" the "resemblance" between African song and the spiritual deserves closer scrutiny, however. To begin with, Paris, along with Blooah and several other African university students in Chicago, had organized the African Exhibit Society of the African Student Aid Association to bolster his capacity as an advisor of the World's Fair.[73] Concerned over having the African exhibit's planning handed over to non-Africans, namely black Americans, Paris wrote a letter to the director of exhibits, colonel John Stephen Sewell, on behalf of the association, exhorting him to bring any plans for the exhibit to their society for their approval. Among the society's reasons for its demand was the following: "The primitive native African psychology and the American-Negro psychology are two different things entirely. The African primitive does not understand American Negro psychology, nor does the American Negro understand the primitive native African psychology; *but the African student in Chicago and elsewhere in the States, understand [sic] both*."[74]

Based on this assertion, Paris actually meant that only the African musician in the United States, after having engaged with American Negroes, could supply and thus explain the resemblance between African music and the spiritual. Such an assertion might be attributed to the African avant-garde perspective, according to which Africans perceived black Americans as "not at all superior to Africans but rather foreigners who had lost their African identity."[75] Paris's theory also complements Hornbostel's concept of the psychophysical and anticipates Herskovits's and Waterman's cultural and psychoanalytical theories of African musical retentions in the New World, at least in terms of his utilization of the discourse of psychology to hold up, in this instance, the modern African as the lynchpin in his own origin theory.[76] Moreover, the African Exhibit Society's claim of having unique access to both primitive African and American Negro psychologies by virtue of their Western education and presence in the United States seems elitist but has more to do with, at least in Paris's experience, his having lived in the varying temporal formations of Dubréka, Freetown, and the United States. It throws into sharp relief the discursive wherewithal of psychology, the primitive, and the metropolis in spatializing and temporalizing oneself in a privileged modern present. In the end, Paris's varying perspectives, from black national and pan-African to his elitism and interracial activism, indicate that, for individuals raced as black, living in the political economy of race in the United States in the 1920s and 1930s demanded that one mobilize multiple, even contradictory, ideological perspectives and identities. For Western-educated Africans in particular, appropriating the discourses of the primitive and modern served them strategically in transmuting their individual interests (political, social, and economic) into the interests of all groups raced as black, in ways that were unavailable to or undesirable among black Americans and

Afro-Cubans. In the end the efficacy of the performativity of being black and African lay not in the discourse of the primitive and modern itself but in its recognition and authorization in American society, of which Paris made use to advance his musical career and social status among concert audiences, anthropologists, and local municipal authorities.[77]

Indeed, Paris's social capital, materialized in his identities as royalty as well as an African baritone and advisor to the Chicago World's Fair organizers, brought him and his wife, pianist Vivian J. Neale, recognition in the press as sanctioned knowledge brokers.[78] Eugene Stinson, music critic for the *Chicago Daily News*, for example, interviewed Neale in 1932 regarding the place of music in black American society and culture. At least three black newspapers—the *Afro-American*, the *Pittsburgh Courier*, and the *Atlanta Daily World*—printed a report of Stinson's article written by the Associated Negro Press, titling the ANP article "Wife of African Prince Thinks Spirituals Best," "Rates Negro Music Best for Negroes," and "Negro Music Best for Negroes?," respectively.[79] While the ANP article highlighted Stinson's charge that the "Negro in the United States should guard most jealously that kind of music which the general public ascribes to him," it also quoted one of Neale's statements: "Musically . . . the Negro feels and has been made to feel that the Aryan forms must be studied, understood, and employed."[80] Stinson recognized that, in spite of the regional and social differences among northern and southern black Americans, there is a "certain vigor in the Negro's characteristics which forces him to be viewed as a Negro rather than as an American." And, in addressing Neale's concern over the pressure to assimilate "Aryan" music, he suggests that because the "Negro possesses a musical talent which the Aryan could never imitate, [it] should certainly be preserved by the race through whom it has been developed."

Although he does not explicitly identify African music as the source of the spiritual, Stinson does characterize it as a "birthright" of the Negro and thus an invaluable source of cultural and racial self-esteem. What is most instructive of this article, however, is the reference to European music as "Aryan," which situates Stinson's interview with Neale and the ANP report within the context of the steady rise to power of the Nazi Party in Germany. Clearly, the circulation of Nazi propaganda concerning white racial superiority within the political economy of race in the United States compelled music critics, anthropologists, musicians, and others to hold up Negro music as viable and necessary for not only social but nationalist purposes as well. Thus, for instance, as Herskovits increasingly pointed to the practical social benefits in scientifically proving the African origins of the spiritual and Negro music of the New World in general, Stinson argued for American Negro valuation of their music as a show of nationalism couched, however, in race pride, but he did so without avowing American society's own regime of racial superiority and terror.

In this regard, the lecture-concert "Los 'Spirituals negro songs' y su acción étnico-social" (The 'Negro spiritual songs' and their ethnic-social action) presented by Zoila Gálvez and her husband, poet, writer, and journalist Enrique Andreu, at the Club Atenas in Havana in March 1937 is particularly instructive.[81] Occurring five days after Gilberto Valdés's concert at the same location in honor of visiting French dignitaries, including M. André Demaison, and two months before Fernando Ortiz's lecture-concert "The Sacred Music of the Yoruba Negroes in Cuba," Andreu and Gálvez's event addressed the African presence in Cuban society but from a very different perspective ontologically (see chapter 2). While Gálvez's performance was presented (like Ortiz's lecture-concert of Santería drumming, singing, and dance) as an authoritative rendering of the Negro spiritual, Andreu's lecture focused on the spiritual's contemporary social significance in mobilizing a collective racial consciousness among American Negroes in their struggle to attain social equality:

> The Negro Spiritual Songs can be taken as a sociological index of the life and state of consciousness of the black American. The content of these simple songs of *seemingly relative importance* is always transcendental and symptomatic for those of us who study social phenomena. Because, today, the Negro Spiritual Song is no longer the only tool that the black [individual] of the United States utilizes to move public opinion and the opinion of his coracials in favor of their true collective interests. [. . .] At this moment, the book, press, poetry, theater, and all sorts of modes of diffusion that you can imagine are also utilized with proven success to realize the constructive campaign of human interest and of ethnic dignity, from which the black American is determined to eliminate from his path anything that can in any way denigrate, depress, or twist the course of his principles and ideal demands. Today, already, in a drama titled *The Stowaways*, the repugnant tragedy of Scottsboro is presented on stage, presented to the world in all of its bareness.[82]

Nowhere does Andreu address or mention the origins of the spiritual, whether African or European. Nor is the music's religiosity its preeminent aspect, for the spiritual, Andreu stressed, had "converted into a vehicle of social action to move the [black American] masses and *orient them* not only spiritually but also with a view toward [historical] materiality."[83] His most significant claim, however, was in regard to the spiritual's relative importance beyond the United States, for in Andreu's opinion, Afro-Cubans had a stake in the present and future social status of American Negroes. Indeed, it was the ongoing Scotts-boro case, due to the "Jim Crow racist machinery," as Frank Andre Guridy notes, that "produced a massive international solidarity campaign to free" the nine young black men accused of allegedly raping a white woman in Alabama.[84]

Thus, whereas Ortiz advocated the celebration of the "cryptic traditions" of Afro-Cubans' Yoruba ancestors as new sources of "art for the glory of the national music of Cuba," Andreu held up the importance that black American church leaders had gained as "sociological leaders" of the masses, conceiving the spirituals as an allegory for Afro-Cubans to rally around their own collective racial consciousness to address racism and racial oppression in Cuban society, and not merely for Cuban nationalist aims.[85] Andreu went further and contrasted Cuban popular musicians from Negro spiritual performers: the latter "are not vulgar caricatures, who sacrifice embarrassment and personal and collective prestige to win a handful of cents, putting on display and ridiculing their own families, race, and country. . . . Those black American artists, with an elevated concept of his labor, very far from all defeatist tendency, and with a healthy constructive critique, practice their art, when they sing Spirituals, like a true ministry."[86] His perspective here, in spite of its elitism in line with Adornian neo-Marxist criticism of popular culture, might best be read in the context of the heated debate that had been traversing Havana society in the previous months regarding the city's reauthorization of *comparsas* and the question of Africa's presence in Cuban music. His position is also seemingly in line with Alberto Arredondo's Comtean view of the necessity of Cuban society's progress, leaving behind its African and Spanish pasts. But by virtue of speaking to the racist trappings of performing music when racialized as black in an unjust society, whether Cuban or American, his concern in regard to black pride and race consciousness contrasts starkly with Arredondo's as well as Ortiz's and García Agüero's nationalist sentiments. Furthermore, his interpretation, along with Gálvez's performance of "Oh, Mary Don't You Weep," addressed the unique role of black women in resisting racial terror, a topic, of course, which never was broached by Arredondo, Ortiz, or García Agüero.

For the concert portion of the evening, Gálvez sang ten spirituals, accompanied on piano by Pedro García Arango. Although reviews of this performance were apparently not published, we do know that, based on her performance of spirituals in Harlem, she sang them with "soulful expression," which suggests that Gálvez could successfully assume the voice of a woman singer of spirituals by generating those sonic and embodied qualities long considered by American Negroes and others as the essence of the spiritual and the blues.[87] Furthermore, before each of her renderings, Andreu provided the audience with a synopsis of the song's biblical content, adding his social justice interpretations of these religious themes. Thus, whether or not her Cuban audience members were fluent English speakers, we can assume that Gálvez performed each song again with soulful expression, knowing that her sonic and physical gestures—the grain of her voice, her upper body movements, and her facial expressions—along with Andreu's prefatory remarks in Spanish, had the potential to affectively signal a maximum of desires or feelings in her audience members and for them to articulate these to their racialized subjectivities and experiences as well as to those, in solidarity, of their American Negro contemporaries. Thus, her performance of "Oh, Mary Don't You Weep," in affecting in sound and movement the desire to console a woman whose son, as interpreted by Andreu, has been lynched, enabled the potential for Gálvez as well as the women in her audience to assume the subjectivity of an American Negro woman. In fact, it is likely that Beatrice Wilson (who had sailed to Havana with Justa Gálvez in December 1936) and Helen Cooper were in the audience. (According to one report, Wilson planned to visit Cuba for four months before leaving for the Bahamas and Haiti.[88]) Such renderings of solidarity across cultural difference, born from feelings of protest and resistance against an unbearable life living in a society that was unjust and violent toward its black citizens, along with Wilson's and Cooper's presence, surely unfolded into the recognition of themselves as the American Negro mother of a lynched child. Gálvez's renderings of "Nobody Knows the Trouble I've Seen" and "Bye and Bye" further conveyed to her audience Andreu's discussion of the moral and material injustices that burden American Negro men and women, the valor with which they resist these but, as Andreu suggested, "with their teeth clinched with anger," and their determination to protest their oppressed status regardless of the potentially violent consequences.[89] This occasion of Negro spiritual performance by Afro-Cuban women and men in solidarity with their Negro American contemporaries is what bell hooks would identify as a truer feminist act of solidarity, in which both women and men together act against the oppressive work of sexism and racism.[90]

In addition to being a performer, Gálvez was also a founding member of the Sociedad de Estudios Afrocubanos, of which Fernando Ortiz served as the first president. In March 1938, Gálvez delivered a report to the association, which was later published as an article titled "Una melodía negra" (A black melody) in *Estudios Afrocubanos*. She was inspired to present this report after discussing with Ortiz his correspondence with American folklorist Eleanor Hague, who had published *Latin American Music: Past and Present* four years earlier. Their correspondence concerned Hague's transcriptions of two melodies, the first, known as "Xangó," from Brazil, and the other a hymn as sung by whites in the mountains of Tennessee. Upon playing these two melodies, as transcribed by Hague, on the piano, along with a third melody originating from the Africans "imported" to Cuba and transcribed by Gálvez herself, she concluded that all three melodies shared a common African origin. To substantiate her conclusion, she pointed to her many encounters with African and American Negro music, in particular those with the African music of the Calabar in Paris and the spirituals in New York City mentioned above. In addition to these encounters, she also discussed her recognizing "in some of the melodic and rhythmic music" in the jungle scenes in the film *Sanders of the River* (1935), starring Paul Robeson, none other than Gilberto Valdés's "Ilé-nko Ilé-nbe." She finished by mentioning the melodic and rhythmic familiarity that Beatrice Wilson and Helen Cooper had heard in Valdés's music at his concert at Havana's national amphitheater in 1937.

Gálvez's claims of hearing resemblances in the music of varying black cultures in Paris, New York City, and Havana were no more ideologically driven than the claims Herskovits repeatedly made when listening for the origins of the spiritual in his Suriname and West African field recordings. The fact that Gálvez heard such resemblances in music performed at exhibits, concerts, and on film (as opposed to in the anthropological field and the modern laboratory) also differs little from claims of either primitive African music sounding from discs made in recording studios in New York City or music of the African unconscious sounding from field recordings analyzed in the laboratory. What distinguishes Gálvez's, Andreu's, and Paris's assertions, however, was their agency in taking the floor and stage to disseminate and perform their knowledge of the spiritual and its historical and social significance in ways unique to their lived raced and gendered experiences.

Although their reasons for disseminating and performing the spiritual were as strategic or even contrived as those of anthropologists, educators, public officials, and music critics, their programs necessitated their assumption of the bodies of black Others to perform their collective histories of slavery and ongoing racial and sexist oppression. Whereas Herskovits and Ortiz planned for their scientific studies to inspire race pride among American Negroes and Afro-Cubans, as well as change the hearts and minds of Americans and Cubans in regard to matters of racial equality, Paris, Andreu, and Gálvez made race pride and feminism a question of praxis—and not just a goal of social scientific activity—by virtue of their embodying the histories of oppression not only of their raced and gendered bodies but also those of black Others. Moreover, their lecture-concerts not only coincided historically with Hornbostel's and Herskovits's research and scholarship on the spiritual's origins, but they predated John Hammond's first

From Spirituals to Swing concert at Carnegie Hall in 1938. Like Hammond's concert, however, their performances, as well as those of Paul Robeson, Chano Pozo, and others, were full of contradictions, as Antonio Gramsci noted of the historicism of the philosophy of praxis itself.[91] The following section will suggest that such performances of the African native necessitated the making palpable, visible, audible, and tangible the native and Africa if these performers and their audiences were going to transform this knowledge into a principle of action offering the possibility of other modes of being and experience.

Embodying the African Native

After the critical and financial debacle of the Chicago World's Fair's *Epic of a Race* pageant, which was intended to demonstrate the progress American Negroes had made over the previous one hundred years, fair organizers approved a second pageant for its second season.[92] On August 25, 1934, at Chicago's Soldier Field, a company of three thousand performers put on *O, Sing a New Song*, which was described as an "Afro-American pageant" dramatizing the "story of the Negro in music from early times in Africa until the present day" and depicting the "path of progress of the colored race from Africa to the post-slavery civilization in America."[93] Attended by an integrated audience of over forty thousand people, the pageant, written by Nobble Sissle and Onah Spencer, was organized into three acts—Africa, Plantation, and Freedom—each lasting about one hour. The pageant's composers included Will Marion Cook, W. C. Handy, William Grant Still, and Major N. Clark Smith, and its narrator was Richard B. Harrison, who had gained fame performing in the Broadway show *The Green Pastures*. The first act featured what was described as an "African ballet," choreographed by Modupe Paris, Katherine Dunham, Hazel Thompson Davis, and Sammy Dyer. Reports of this act described the stage, which covered the entire playing field, as including huts, camp fires, and native women doing daily tasks while native men prepared for the hunt and warfare. As for the act's music and dance, according to one article, "Dominant in the life of the natives was the tom tom, the lugubrious accompaniment to their dances and their worship. Its tremulous rhythms pervaded all their comings and goings. Until the coming of the white man, their chief enemy had been the beasts of the jungle."[94] Portuguese slavers and slave or ghost ships closed the first act, and act 2 followed, featuring slaves in the South working cotton fields and singing plantation songs or spirituals, including "Nobody Knows the Trouble I've Seen" and "Go Down, Moses." Act 3 closed the pageant, highlighting emancipation and the promise of a "new day with Booker T. Washington and the gift of song which the Negro was to give to the world."[95] This final act, in addition to representing American Negro participation in World War I and modern industrial life, featured performances by jazz pianist Earl Hines, Noble Sissle's orchestra, soprano Abbie Mitchell, and dancers Irene Castle and Bill "Bojangles" Robinson.

According to newsprint accounts, *O, Sing a New Song* was an artistic and commercial success, receiving much applause throughout the performance and wide coverage in both white and black newspapers. One report noted that Bill Robinson's tapping, which was amplified and could be heard throughout the stadium, attracted the most enthusiastic applause. But in addition to documenting the performance and the audience's reactions to the action and music on the field, these reporters also reiterated representational markers, that is, those established impressions of the bodies, objects, sounds, movements, and feelings that brought primitive Africa to life, in this instance, inside the city's main sporting venue. The beat of the tom-toms, dominant and lugubrious, and its rhythms, tremulous and pervading, constituted the sonic accompaniment to the depiction of, according to William G. Nunn of the *Pittsburgh Courier*, the "jungle superstitions, fear, conquest, joy and trust" of a "downtrodden group."[96] Nunn continues: "And it was from these tom-toms that modern music received its rhythms." Even those who were critical of the pageant's depiction of "jungle life" as "idealized," resulting in a "bright-colored meaningless fairyland," still heard "some suggestion . . . of those primitive musical traits" during the first act, while, in terms of dance, Modupe Paris was, according to one report, "among the cast of principals, so that some suitable example of authentic African dancing might give concrete evidence of the high quality of the Negro's aboriginal heritage."[97]

As in his performances at the John Brown Memorial Association's events in 1927 and 1928, Paris's performance of the African native, as captured and published by the *Chicago Daily Tribune*, authenticated the music and dance of the American Negro past, in this case its African past. Such representational performances—depicting either the African native's confrontations or collusion with white moderns as a stand-alone story or the evolution of the native's music and dance into modern black music—not only circulated in films and print as well as staged productions but also encompassed audience members themselves. For example, the effects presumably evoked among the audience's black moderns by Africans performing the native, savage, or black American's ancestor seemed indeed to constitute what Frantz Fanon theorized as their overwhelming desire to disavow the black Other, lest he or she be identified with the savage by their fellow audience members, whether black or white.[98] As the following report written by the *Chicago Daily Tribune* columnist June Provines demonstrates, the process in which black and white audience members became aware of each other's "look" generated key moments of the performance. As Kwesi Kuntu and his group of Ashanti drummers and dancers took the stage at a nightclub in the South Side of Chicago, Provines writes,

> High laughter broke out from the Negros, well groomed, modish and sophisticated, *sitting about the room*. The laughter subsided as the drums began to throb and the dancers began to whirl, but it broke out intermittently. Meantime *they watched*, with a tolerant air, the antics of these strange black men. . . . Whether the laughter was because they thought it was intended for a humorous performance, or whether it expressed derision and *covered a dislike of the whole business*, a better informed person could tell you. [. . .] More interesting still was *watching the Negro patrons* of the south side night club where the party was held *watch the black men from the continent that bred their ancestors.*[99]

Likewise, in those instances in which black American reviewers exclaimed that performances such as *O, Sing a New Song* "made me proud that I'm a Negro," they did so not in spite of this anxiety (generated as much from other audience members as the black Others on the stage) but rather as an equally integral component of the larger performance of modern citizens going to, occupying, and exiting the city's premiere sporting venue: "We saw Negro history unfold itself. Much of it was not pretty. But it was *terrifyingly true*, and *as we walked away from Soldier Field tonight*, we felt that we had been taught an all-important lesson in race pride."[100] Thus, not unlike Havana's temporal and spatial practices as pertaining to Cubans racialized as black, Chicago's historical and spatial demarcations also functioned fundamentally to orient moderns racialized as black in the American metropolis and away from their ancestors' rural and savage pasts. What performances of the African origins of black music and dance did in particular was to lend the audience's anchoring in modernity's metropolis a normative viewpoint from which they could experience a believably terrifying and primitive African past that was temporally and spatially distant enough yet an ever-present source of feelings of shame, pride, fear, and pleasure, depending on who was looking. No one was more aware of the immediate impact of such performances on modern audiences than African performers, knowing that their performances had the potential but no guarantee to subvert that which had evoked deriding laughter in, for instance, Kuntu's audience. What was clear was that Kuntu, Paris, and other Africans mastered traversing the temporal and spatial distance separating the primitive from the modern.

Although Asadata Dafora was no less active in presenting African music and dance in the United States, his cultural and social background differed from Modupe Paris's. Paris grew up in a village in Dubréka in what was then French Guinea, where his maternal grandfather served as a tribal chief.[101] His mother's family was Susu; his father's was Yoruba. Paris traveled with his father throughout West Africa, where "he learned many dialects, customs and much about the terrain and folklore of the visited tribesmen."[102] He was sent to Freetown, Sierra Leone, where he attended the church missionary school and later attended the boys' high school in Lagos, Nigeria.[103] Dafora (whose full name was Austin Dafora Horton), in contrast, was born in Freetown into a prominent Krio family of predominantly Yoruba background.[104] His uncle James Africanus B. Horton was a physician who had graduated from the University of Edinburgh in the 1860s and became an influential leader of the African avant-gardist movement, whose members supported African political representation in the British colonial administration of Sierra Leone.[105] As he came of age, Dafora carried on his family's African nationalist outlook by immersing himself in the cultures of the various ethnic groups that populated and surrounded Freetown. He traveled throughout West Africa, as did Paris, attending folk dance festivals and learning the music and dance repertories of various ethnic groups. He and his siblings were also taught Western classical music, including voice, by their stepmother, who had studied piano in England.[106] Dafora's Western music education in all likelihood continued while he was a student at Wesleyan high school in Freetown.

Dafora reportedly traveled to Milan, Italy, in 1910 to study operatic singing.[107] In spite of the lack of documentation, Marcia Heard suggests that Dafora might have toured Europe as a member of La Scala Opera House's productions of *Aida* and *L'Africaine*, and apparently performed in nightclubs and taught African dance. By 1918, he had returned to West Africa, where he would eventually sail from Dakar to Baltimore, arriving in the United States in November 1918.[108] No documentation exists of his activities in the United States until 1930, when he was reported to have sung French and Italian songs at the third annual Native African Union of America meeting, which took place in Harlem.[109] Speakers at the event included Nigerian and Liberian officers of the association, whose mission was to forge "closer cooperation between Africans abroad and those in Africa." Dafora also sang music for tenor at a political function in Harlem featuring assemblyman Francis E. Rivers.[110] Soon after, Dafora abandoned his operatic repertory, as Paris had done, and dedicated his performance career to presenting African dance dramas, beginning with *Zoonga* in 1933, followed by *Kyunkor* in 1934, and, eventually, dramatizations of the African origins and evolution of American Negro and Caribbean music and dance.[111]

One of Dafora's earliest performances of the African native occurred in February 1939, less than two months after John Hammond's *From Spirituals to Swing* concert at Carnegie Hall. The Labor Club of the democratic socialist American Labor Party of New York produced the concert *Negro Music Past and Present*, and enlisted Carlton Moss and Albert Moss to write and direct the program and compose the music.[112] The Labor Club's press release described the program as a "historical survey of the origin and development of Negro music from the African period to the present day."[113] It also characterized the music as having sprung from the "conflicts that arose out of the Negro's necessary attempt to cope with the problems of social injustice, and not out of an abject humility and sense of resignation." While it stresses the history of struggle against the racial oppression of black Americans, as told in the music, the press release does not describe the significance or content of the program's African music. Instead, newspaper announcements merely reiterated the description of the program as tracing Negro music from the "African period" to the present day.[114] Like the *O, Sing a New Song*'s narrative this program followed the conventional historical and spatial trajectory of the music's evolution, beginning with Africa as act 1. It is in this portion of the program that Dafora and his group performed "Festival Song" and "Song of Joy." Olin Downes's review of this performance is especially instructive in terms of understanding what Bakhtin described as the representational importance of the chronotope, that is, the making of historical time and events palpable, visible, and concrete, and causing them to take on flesh or materialize time in space through sound and movement.[115] Thus "the Labor Party . . . squeezed the cozy precincts of the Labor Stage with a *bird's-eye view of the long story* of 'Negro Music: Past and Present.' [. . .] The voice of Carlton Moss (who conceived the show) issued from the darkness to *link the pictures into a sustained narrative*. Asadata Dafora and his group *went back to Africa* for songs and dances that set the tempo and the temperature of the evening. Then the stories *jumped the centuries*."[116]

The use of Africans to not only play the part of the American Negro's ancestor but also to consult with directors of plays and films on the authenticity of their representations of the African past and jungle was by 1939 a common occurrence. One of Paris's earliest performance in this regard was in the pageant *Ethiopia Lifts as She Climbs*, which took place in the Grand Ballroom of Chicago's Palmer House Hotel in July 1933, more than a year before the *O, Sing a New Song* pageant. Written by Sallie W. Stewart, who had stepped down earlier that year as president of the National Association of Colored Women (NACW), *Ethiopia Lifts as She Climbs*, according to one report, "depicted many of the sterling qualities (and their number is legion) of the Negro woman."[117] Paris arranged the first act, titled "In the Jungles of Africa," for which he prepared an "African jungle dance" accompanied by "weird music distinctively African in nature and making and practice." His performance's effect on the reporter was not unlike that of Gilberto Valdés's musicians on M. André Demaison in Havana: "For once, *we all were carried* to the crude and primitive life of the jungle . . . of Africa—and the impression was lasting" (my emphasis). The remaining three acts—"The Deep South," "In the Wake of Freedom," and "In the Midst of Civilization"—completed the narrative. What was unique about this production, however, was its central theme of the "African Mother," "Slave Mother," "Emancipated Mother," and "Modern Mother," dramatizing the woman's steadfast resilience in the face of her separation from her children, symbolized in the singing of "Nobody Knows the Trouble I've Seen"; abject poverty, sung to "Sometimes I Feel Like a Mother's Child"; and, eventually, redemption, symbolized by the return of the mother's daughter from a "great conservatory of Music." This version of the African origins narrative as told by Stewart is clearly shaped by the principles of American Negro women clubs such as the NACW and the soon-to-be-formed National Council of Negro Women, wherein racial uplift and education were the most valued strategies toward black women's resistance to racial and gendered oppression and their struggle for group survival.[118] The title itself, *Ethiopia Lifts as She Climbs*, was drawn from the NACW's motto "Lifting as We Climb."

Paris also put on one-act performances of the history of the Negro at private dinner parties, such as one hosted by banker and art collector Walter S. Brewster in April 1934. As reported by one of the guests, columnist June Provines (who had also reported on Kwesi Kuntu's nightclub performance), Brewster ushered his guests into his private art gallery, where "before the high, white Adam mantel, squatting beside a native drum, was a young African. He looked like a figure of Malvina Hoffman's from the Hall of Races at the Field museum as he waited there, motionless, for the guests to be seated."[119] Introduced by Brewster as a "native of the west coast of Africa," Paris gave a "short outline of the history of music in Africa," which included playing "native music," following this with performances of "examples of later developments in Negro music." As with his performance of "In the Jungles of Africa" in Stewart's pageant, Paris embodied the African native in sound ("the sound of an African drum, portentous, rhythmic and monotonous" and "the native beating out his savage rhythms"), but in "squatting beside a native drum . . . *motionless*" at the start of the performance he affected a rather unique kind of demarcation of the past, one that remained etched or frozen in Provines's memory. Her association of Paris's motionless body with those statues of raced others sculpted by Malvina Hoffman and presented in the exhibition *The Races of Man* in Chicago's Field Museum that year speaks in no uncertain terms to the regulatory laws of bodies raced as black and temporalized to the historical past. Against this demarcation of the American Negro past was the white dinner guests' modern present, the subjective assurances of which were anchored by the "wide, skylighted room, hung with a Pruna and a Picasso, a Matisse and a Ferat; a room bespeaking cultivated and sophisticated taste in every ornament and piece of furniture." Paris further affected the spatial and temporal delineations of the Negro's evolution at the moment when the "rhythm of the drum stopped and the African prince, in beautiful soft English, began the tale of his next number," which was a spiritual accompanied on piano by Vivian J. Neale.

The performance of the African native or savage was, of course, not limited to Africans. Whether in pageants, ballets, or films, black Americans also participated in these portrayals but rarely without controversy, unlike Africans, whose authenticity within the logic of black dance music's African origins was taken for granted. In two editorials titled "Mother Africa" and published in the *New York Amsterdam News* in 1933, the writers debated the legitimacy of African music and dance as performed by American Negroes and West Indians.[120] As one writer cited the authenticity of Dafora's performances based on his members' assumed African background (in fact, most were black American), the other writer claimed that as descendants of Africans, American Negroes and West Indians had a legitimate cultural claim to perform African music and dance. But their debate actually concerned the motivation behind such performances, such as whether it was to commercialize the name of Africa or to raise funds for the legal defense of the Scottsboro defendants. Indeed, the economic and political stakes for black Americans seemed to be particularly high when it came to their involvement in the embodiment of the African native on stage and film, as was the case in Paul Robeson's portrayal of Bozambo in the 1935 film *Sanders of the River*.

The main complaint of the film's critics was not its representation of African natives—the camera crew, as it was reported, filmed "native Houssa soldiers," "Acholi natives," among other African groups in Nairobi, Kampala, Gulu, and Stanleyville—but rather the film's "propaganda justifying British imperialism," as the *Afro-American* noted.[121] This *Afro-American* review quoted extensively from British antifascist activist Nancy Cunard's stinging criticism of the film, which was produced by London Film Productions, and included the following:

"Sanders [the "paternal" British administrator] is the iron hand in the velvet glove, with . . . his 'affection' for these 'black children.' Lucky man, he finds a real white man's n——r in the person of Bosambo, played by Paul Robeson." Another review printed in the *New York Amsterdam News* also noted the film's inherent propaganda of "white rulership" as the "salvation of Africa," but in addressing Robeson's apparent culpability, this reviewer states, "He finds himself caught every time in the struggle between commercialism and white propaganda, on the one hand, and true art, on the other."[122]

In addition to British colonial propaganda and Robeson's stereotypical portrayal of Bozambo, the African native ally of the local colonial officers, the film's narrative hinges on the chronotopic sounds, images, and movements of the African native and jungle. Scenes containing dialogue between the main characters alternate with other scenes of African women singing and dancing, men preparing for battle, and drummers relaying messages through the jungle, as well as white Europeans dancing to jazz music at a party "on the coast at a Government House" (as the film indicates in captions), all of which mobilize the audience into and back from the jungle. Just as the juxtaposition of this jazz dance party with tribal dancing, drumming, and singing was suggestive enough of the evolution of modern jazz from its African primitive origins, the superimposition of Robeson's Africanized black body (filmed in a London studio) over footage of African boat rowers (filmed on the Congo River) was keenly indicative of the American Negro's liminal status as both modern and primitive (figure 3.2). On the one hand, the chronotopic value of the black body affected in some viewers the believability of Robeson's transference (on)to the African jungle—"Robeson's singing of the African war-songs, spear in hand, in the midst of his African warriors, is unforgettable."[123] On the other hand, his status internationally as an artist, political activist, and intellectual destabilized the veracity not of his portrayal of an African tribal chief but of the filmmaker's intentions, as indicated in one review titled "Africans Believe Paul Robeson Was Tricked in British Film" published in the *Chicago Defender*.[124]

Robeson himself fired back at his critics, saying, "To expect the Negro artist to reject every role with which he is not ideologically in agreement . . . is to expect the Negro artist *under our present scheme of things* to give up his work entirely—unless, of course, he is to confine himself solely to the Left theatre."[125] He had in fact established himself as a political activist performing spirituals as a solo concert vocalist to effect a sense of dignity and pride among American Negroes. Yet while he accused the film's director, Zoltan Korda, of adding the "imperialist angle . . . during the last five days of shooting," he also expressed his eagerness to work with Korda on producing films on the lives of Emperor

FIG. 3.2 Paul Robeson as Bozambo superimposed over African boat rowers. From *Sanders of the River* (London Film Productions, 1935).

Menelik II of Ethiopia and Henri Christophe of Haiti, to which Katherine Dunham hoped to contribute her ballet of Christophe, which she was choreographing while conducting fieldwork in Haiti at that time.[126] We will recall, too, that for Zoila Gálvez the jungle scenes in *Sanders of the River* contained resemblances to the music of Gilberto Váldez. In the end, Robeson's retort to his critics suggests most poignantly what he, as well as Paris, Dafora, and Kuntu, knew to be requisite under the political economy (or "present scheme") of race when performing the African native—a body raced as black and shot through with chronotopic values of the African past. Whereas Frantz Fanon in 1952 would advocate disalienation as a way out of this racialized impasse, Robeson and his African contemporaries seemed to believe that breaking away entirely from this political economy of race would in fact be detrimental to its subversion.

As *Sanders of the River* was premiering in London in April 1935, Modupe Paris moved from Chicago to Los Angeles, where he continued to lecture on African history and perform African music and dance, including a stage production he titled *Zunguru*, which was described as "revealing incidents from daily life" "on the edge of the jungle."[127] After Italy invaded Ethiopia in October 1935, Paris began to address the Ethiopian situation in his lectures.[128] It is likely that he chose to move his family to Los Angeles ultimately to get work in the city's film industry, which is in fact what he did beginning in 1936, when he was hired as a "technical advisor" for Metro-Goldwyn-Mayer's *Tarzan Escapes*.[129] Instead of superimposing the main actors (filmed in the modern studio) onto scenes with African natives (filmed in the African jungle), this film's production took place in the Santa Monica mountains (just west of downtown Los Angeles) and included black American extras, reportedly from "Los Angeles's Harlem, Central avenue," for the film's jungle scenes.[130] Reports of the film's production mentioned Paris's role as "African technical expert" charged with writing "African songs and to authenticate several primitive dances and hunts in the picture."[131] Following his work on *Tarzan Escapes*, Paris, now known in Hollywood as "an authentic authority on things African," received requests from other studios to advise the filming of the "native portions" of films such as *White Hunter* (Twentieth Century Fox, 1936) and *Jungle Jim* (Universal Pictures, 1937).[132] In spite of Paris's reported criticism of films that present "Africa as a land of savages and as an uneducated country," he in fact took roles in films such as *Darkest Africa* (Republic Pictures, 1936), *South of Suez* (Warner Brothers, 1940), *Sundown* (United Artist, 1941), and *Nabonga* (PRC Pictures, 1944), in which he portrayed the conventional African native in accordance with the African jungle's chronotopic elements.[133]

Bodies raced as black becoming African natives—whether filmed in a London studio and superimposed onto film of their African contemporaries, or taught to be African natives by a "real" African in the mountains of Santa Monica—materialized in Havana nightclubs as well, affecting many of the feelings and impressions generated by Paris's, Robeson's, Kuntu's, and Dafora's performances in sports venues, nightclubs, ballrooms, and homes in Chicago and New York City, as well as in films. Chano Pozo, for example, portrayed a native African hunter in the ballet *Conga Pantera*, which was directed by David Lichine of Colonel W. de Basil's Ballet Russe. This ballet occurred only after eighteen members of the Ballet Russe had gone on strike on March 20, 1941, the day the company was scheduled to open a five-day engagement at Havana's Pro-Arte Auditorium.[134] Stranded in Havana, the ballet's remaining nonstriking members, including choreographer David Lichine and dancers Tatiana Leskova and Olga Philippoff, scrambled for work, programming additional performances and recitals in Havana, Matanzas, Cienfuegos, and Santiago de Cuba. For his part, Lichine engaged the management at Havana's newly opened Tropicana nightclub with his idea to produce a short ballet titled *Conga Pantera* for which he would cast "coloured people and one artist [Leskova] from the ballet."[135] The plot consisted of a "panther [portrayed by Leskova] being chased through the African jungle" by the hunter, portrayed by Pozo.[136] The first performance took place on April 18, and was followed by four more performances.[137]

As Lichine conducted rehearsals for his Afro-Cuban ballet with Pozo, Leskova, and other performers at the Tropicana located in Buena Vista, just west of the city, Harold Courlander had arrived in Havana to begin collecting his field recordings. As discussed in chapter 2, Courlander traveled to Guanabacoa, just east of the city of Havana, and rural Jovellanos, in Matanzas, to record Afro-Cuban cult music in remote and out-of-the-way places. It is important to establish these coinciding activities not as fortuitous or coincidence but rather as equally generated by the capacity of performing bodies raced as black to materialize the distant African past, in these instances, for a Russian ballet choreographer and an American folklorist. This, in addition to the fact that records of Pozo's popular songs appeared in Courlander's (and later Waterman's) field recordings. Indeed, by 1941, Pozo had gained local, national, and international recognition as a composer of Cuban popular songs. Not surprisingly, he accepted the lead offered to him by Lichine, the internationally known Russian ballet choreographer, as a unique opportunity to further recognition of his work as a dancer and a composer, regardless of the nature of his role in the ballet.[138] Reviews of the first two performances deemed the ballet a success, noting that the audience frequently interrupted the performance with ovations. As one reviewer noted, the "Tropicana's audience was left pleasantly surprised with that magnificent spectacle accomplished by Lichine who has miraculously given an artistic status to something primitive."[139] Similarly, another reviewer characterized the "jungle ballet" as being "in tune with the modern currents in dance and the spirit of the times."[140]

Such allusions to Igor Stravinsky's and Vaslav Nijinsky's *Le Sacre du printemps* notwithstanding, the Tropicana's six-acre lot in Buena Vista surrounded by tropical gardens, as well as descriptions of the ballet's scenery and action, including its use of Afro-Cuban drummers and dancers, effectively situate *Conga Pantera* in the same body of work as that of the anthropological and comparative musicological enterprise discussed in the previous two chapters, not to mention as well the films, historical pageants, and performances (both private and in nightclubs and sporting venues) discussed above.[141] The black performers in *Conga Pantera*, since they "carry in their blood the original rhythms" of their African ancestors, were directed to climb onto trees surrounding the stage, where they perched themselves (becoming simian) and provided the ballet's music on their "bongoces" (bongos and conga drums); while the native African hunter (Pozo) danced "in a ritual style" before chasing after the panther (Leskova) as other black dancers, "unspoiled by academic and theatrical dance," completed the performance.[142] These bodies raced as black, as those in *Sanders of the River; O, Sing a New Song; Cult Music of Cuba*; and so on, were shot through with Africa's and the African native's movements, sounds, surroundings, and even blood plasma—all intensities distributed by the temporalizing and spatializing principles of the African past and circulating in and out of the bodies (societies) of modernity's raced others.

There is no doubt that—like Paris, who differentiated the "stranger" from that "never-never land" onscreen from his other self, "who sat at the head of the dinner table" at his home—Pozo, Robeson, Dafora, Kuntu, and Gálvez slipped back to their other selves (husband, wife, mother, father, etc.) when crossing the threshold into their homes, leaving behind those potentially abject beings of the African native and Negro American slave to be embodied another day. This is not to say that these same raced intensities did not circulate in their homes, given that newspapers, magazines, 78-RPM discs, sheet music, and people themselves, including anthropologists, comparative musicologists, and newspaper reporters, crossed over these same thresholds. In an interview at his home with Arturo Ramírez of Havana's *Carteles* magazine, Pozo was photographed posing with his wife and conga drum (figure 3.3). He was also photographed playing his drum seated in front of a wall covered with sheet music of his songs and "medallions of Santa Barbara and La Virgen del Cobre."[143] Ramírez's descriptions of these objects, but in particular the conga drum, demonstrate the potential one's intentions have in destabilizing the normative laws of the performativity of race and the materialization of the African jungle. In this instance, the conga drum is emptied of its intense chronotopic value as the sound of the African jungle in its becoming a table and piano: "We sat down facing each other, separated by a drum, which serves us as a table. For him, it serves as a piano. [. . .] 'In here is encased everything'—he tells us, with a tone which appears to us as honest pride— . . . 'I sing the motive and I 'put it' into the rhythm.'"[144]

At that very moment the conga drum was not only the instrument of the African jungle sounding lugubrious, tremulous, pervading, throbbing, weird, portentous, monotonous, and savage rhythms, though Pozo, Paris, Dafora, and Kuntu were intimately familiar with the jungle drum's affect in an audience's "look" preceding their articulation of these chronotopes to their racialized bodies. Indeed, Pozo's "tone" of "honest pride" transmitted to Ramírez's "look," and his facial expression of said pride photographed *from his home* and transmitted to *Cartele*'s readers points back to the broader field of embodying Africa's pres-

FIG. 3.3 Chano Pozo with his wife and conga drum at home in Havana. From Arturo Ramírez, interview for *Carteles*, June 14, 1942.

ence in the modern present. What Brent Hayes Edwards describes as *décalage*, or that something which serves to fill a gap or gaps in the formations of the African diaspora, is applicable to such presencings whether asserted in a jungle ballet, comparsas, and lecture-concerts in Havana; historical pageants, commemorations, and private performances in Chicago and New York; or on film in studios and sets in London and Hollywood.[145] All such assertions rested on becomings of the African, becomings that actuated regardless of the degree of contrivance. Yet, although each of these becomings of the African (ancestor, mother, native, savage, slave, or hunter) entailed a confluence of diverse forces (Chicago World's Fair, South Side nightclub, American Labor Party, National Association of Colored Women, London Film Productions, Ballet Russe) centered on the African, each performance as a unique reiteration of this logic's temporalizing and spatializing principles generated nevertheless distinct recognitions of, for example, the Negro's African heritage, the struggles with social injustice, the qualities of the Negro woman, and solidarity with the Scottsboro defendants, along with deriding laughter and comparisons with statues in the Hall of Races as well as accusations of commercialism and colonial propaganda.

Performances of the African native gave black Americans, Afro-Cubans, and Africans occasions to occupy the positivist viewpoint of the progress they and the immediately preceding generations had made. The performances and lectures of black music's evolution from its African origins served a similar purpose, though in both cases the African native and his music generated varying and contradictory recognitions of the present social and political conditions of African, American Negro, and Afro-Cuban men and women. While such performances were indeed shot through with chronotopic values of the African past, enabling audiences and performers alike to witness their ancestors from centuries past graphically and narratively, as well as sonically, they also enabled other temporal and spatial materializations, such as the transference of Africa's *present* conditions under European colonialism onto the *past* history of slavery and its legacies of oppression as embodied in the everyday lives of New World Negroes.

This particular development of the temporal and spatial principles of the logic of black dance's and music's African origins remained squarely within the positivist viewpoint of history, yet it sometimes coalesced with an African exceptionalism that inverted modernity's trajectory of progress and, at other times, with modernist and humanist viewpoints whose anticommercialism and attribution of artistic authenticity to dancers' movements (as opposed to their racialized bodies exclusively) led to their celebration of African music and dance as valued aspects of the present. Other viewpoints, however, including those of American liberalism, progressivism, and racial uplift, anchored these performances back within the fold of the logic's temporal and spatial principles even as purveyors of these viewpoints expressed their support for the decolonization of Africa.

Black Power as Residual (and Contested)

In his 1971 essay "From Black Power Back to Pan-Africanism," Stokely Carmichael urged Africans, American Negroes, and all black peoples to understand slavery and colonialism not as separate entities nor in nationalist terms but rather as constituting one history bounded by the shared struggle against racism and imperialism.[146] "African Nationalism finds its highest aspiration in Pan-Africanism. So too Black Power really means African Power," he exclaimed. He admitted to have had "fallen victim in this chronic ailment of inferiority complex" in referencing the anxiety he had felt toward pan-Africanism as a political philosophy. "It is usual procedure for advocates of Pan-Africanism to assure Africans of the diaspora that Pan-Africanism does not mean returning to Africa. [...] Those suffering from chronic inferiority complexes *observe the continent* superficially and conclude that Africa is fated for eternal doom. Pan-Africanists know better. Mother Africa is ours, we are proud of her and to her glorious reconstruction we pledge our lives."[147] Here, again, we have psychoanalytical discourse in diagnosing the anxiety generated from taking the positivist viewpoint on Africa. There, too, in Carmichael's reasoning is modernity's topographical coordinates of time and space wherein the idea of "returning to Africa" means going back in time, leaving one's subjective anchorage in the modern present. What is key in Carmichael's remarks, however, is the shift he proposes in observing the continent as sharing not only in one's own present in Western time but also as mother and a woman. By historicizing Carmichael's advocacy of "Mother Africa" and "her glorious reconstruction," in addition to his own proposed historicization of the Black Power movement, we are better able to critically gauge the humanist, African exceptionalist, and male viewpoints that Asadata Dafora, K. O. Mbadiwe, and the African Academy of Arts and Research took toward music and dance while advocating for African decolonization in the United States during World War II.

Indeed, Dafora's performances of African music and dance, which the AAAR sponsored, while including the representation of the African native man and woman, helped advance what African male university students in the United States had discovered before the start of the war, that is, that their struggle for freedom from colonial rule was linked with the struggle for democracy and equality of American Negroes. The fact that World War II was a global conflict, in turn, induced interest among more American Negroes in the plight of other oppressed groups, thus enabling black leaders such as those affiliated with the March on Washington movement to articulate their struggles to similarly oppressed groups in Latin America and Asia as well as Africa.[148] As Hollis R. Lynch states, these African university students were "academically able and well-prepared, all were already fiercely nationalistic," and "from among them came the founders and leaders of two major African nationalist organizations in the United States," the African Student Association and the AAAR.[149] Absent among these African students and activists, according to Lynch, were African women, whose viewpoints would have added unique insight to black women's own histories of struggle and survival as embodied, for example, in Sallie W. Stewart's *Ethiopia Lifts as She Climbs* and Zoila Gálvez's performances of spirituals. In addition to the founders of these organizations, which included A. A. Nwafor Orizu, Mbonu Ojike, and Mbadiwe, other students from this group—such as Abdul Disu and Julius Okala, both of whom had served as research assistants to Melville J. Herskovits and Richard A. Waterman from 1941 through 1943—were also active in raising awareness of the oppressive colonial conditions of Africans. In March 1939, for example, while students at Lincoln University, Disu, with Kwame Nkrumah, led a discussion on the lack of civil liberties among Africans under colonial rule.[150] For his part, Okala joined the AAAR and served on its festival-organizing committees.[151]

To publicly announce and celebrate the founding of the AAAR, organizers led by Mbadiwe chose Carnegie Hall as the site of the dedication ceremony and contracted Asadata Dafora to produce the celebration's program, which he titled "African Dance Festival." With the festival scheduled for December 13, 1943, the AAAR and Dafora sent out joint press releases on November 14 (one day after its offices officially opened on 55 West Forty-Second Street in New York City) to black and white newspapers across the country promoting the founding of the organization and its upcoming event.[152] The press release described the AAAR as a "new organization devoted to spreading information about that continent which is practically unknown to most Americans, where so many of our soldiers are now fighting and perhaps witnessing, in some villages, similar festivities to those that will be seen on the Carnegie Hall stage."[153] In regard to such festivities, the press release noted that the "theme of African courtship and wedding festivities will be the connecting link between the various dances, songs and music interludes that will make up the program." One newspaper article noted Mbadiwe's choice of a dance festival for the program's theme. "The strongest link between the two parts of the world was their respective cultures [citing as] proof, the fact that Negro artists in this country instinctively adapt themselves to African rhythms and art forms."[154]

Mbadiwe's emphasis on African music, dance, and drama was indeed a politically shrewd move, in spite of African music's discursive trappings discussed thus far, one which he had decided to pursue earlier that year, as a result of having lived and studied in the United States since 1939. Although Mbadiwe had a strong black nationalist perspective regarding European colonial rule in Africa and race relations in the United States, he understood the need to couch his black nationalism within the rhetoric of mutual understanding and cooperation in the pursuit of liberty, given the political economy of race itself in the United States. For example, in his two-part essay titled "Africa in the War of Destiny," which he published in the National Urban League's *Opportunity: A Journal of Negro Life* in 1942, he stated his unequivocal support for the Allied war effort against the Axis powers, all the while using the theme of freedom as a lynchpin in attempting to draw support from black and white Americans for the complete and immediate dismantling of colonial rule in Africa. Outraged by British prime minister Winston Churchill's declaration that the Atlantic

Charter's goal of the restoration of self-government did not apply to the colonies under the British empire, Mbadiwe reminded or edified his American readers about the sacrifices Africans had made in World War I and were making in the current conflict in spite of Britain's ongoing "colonial totalitarian practices" in West Africa.[155] The United States, however, "does not fall short in its interpretation of the Charter," he pronounced, though he did lament America's policy of noninterference in regard to its British ally's unwavering commitment to colonialism.[156] Then, attempting to woo his American Negro readers, Mbadiwe mentioned the recent riots in the Bahamas by "1,400 native laborers working on an American project because of extremely low wages." Indeed, it had only been slightly more than a year since president Franklin Roosevelt had issued Executive Order 8802 outlawing discriminatory practices in the nation's defense industry. In the second part of his essay, Mbadiwe was much more explicit in drawing connections between the challenges that faced black Americans and Africans and included taxation without representation, denial of equal opportunity, and segregation.[157] He declared that before the United States can become a spokesman for justice and liberty, it "must solve the Negro problem within her own gates."

Mbadiwe concluded his essay by outlining the five reasons why he believed Africa had entered the war: (1) to free itself from the clutches of imperialism and pave the way for a united free Africa; (2) to defend liberty; (3) to counter the West's "materialistic, exploitative, and acquisitive mentality" with the civilizing capacity of the African soul and its human values; (4) to support President Roosevelt's Four Freedoms (freedom of speech, freedom of religion, freedom from want, and freedom from fear); and (5) to preserve African cultural customs and social institutions while purging those foreign elements that have "sapped [Africa of] her manhood" and given it a "dual personality." Soon after publishing his essay, Mbadiwe decided to adopt reasons three and five as the most politically prudent methods of garnering support among the American public, particularly those on the political Left, to pressure the American government to demand its British ally decolonize Africa. His plans to pursue an African cultural and humanist, rather than an explicitly militant, platform paid off early when he secured the sponsorship of First Lady Eleanor Roosevelt and the president of the National Council of Negro Women, Mary McLeod Bethune, both of whom were the guests of honor at the "African Dance Festival."[158] It is indeed ironic that Mbadiwe attained the support of two of the country's most influential feminists given that his, as well as Dafora's, perspective was exclusively male, as signaled by his indictment of colonialism's emasculation of African culture and society. Yet what Bethune, Mbadiwe, and Dafora shared, besides their struggle against discrimination and racial terror, was a belief in Africans' inherent humanism, a characteristic that Filomina Chioma Steady and Patricia Hill Collins marked as particularly crucial in African and Black feminist thought.[159]

Immediately after Roosevelt and Bethune accepted their invitations to the festival, the AAAR's organizers made sure to include both names and even to quote from Roosevelt's acceptance letter in the announcements published in the newspapers and in its letter to patrons.[160] The statement "A Great Tribute to a Great Ally!," included in the letter to the AAAR's patrons and on posters, stressed further the immediate bonds they attempted to forge with the American public in wartime. Mbadiwe's welcoming remarks regarding the academy's aim to "dissipate the curious misconceptions" that Americans and Africans have of each other, and the realization that the world is getting smaller, set the tone for the "African Dance Festival."[161] According to reviews, Dafora's production consisted mostly of the music and dances from his dance dramas *Kykunkor* (1934) and *Zunguru* (1938), which were widely known to New York's dance audiences and to critics such as John Martin and Edwin Denby. *Kykunkor* in particular had maintained its popularity throughout the 1930s.[162] Dafora's Shologa Aloba Dance Group had most recently performed these dances at the Festival of Music and Fine Arts hosted by Fisk University in April 1943. According to the festival's program, Dafora's presentation had consisted of fifteen dances and drum solos, with an intermission.[163] The program notes, which Dafora presumably wrote, identified each dance's ethnic affiliation, including Temne ("The Stick Dance" and "Wedding Dance"), Yoruba ("The Dance of Love"), Kru ("Battu, the Challenge Dance"), Susu ("The Bell Dance"), and Sudanese ("The Dance of Appreciation" and "Spear Dance"). He also claimed that the rhythms in "African Drum Rhythms" performed by Norman Coker included some from which modern swing rhythms were derived, and that the "Primitive Conga" (called an African "creole dance" in Africa) and "Rhumba" (from Sierra Leone) are the origins of their Latin American derivations. Both Martin's and Denby's reviews of the "African Dance Festival" performance were not only positive but also lacking in the discourse of African primitivism, or those temporal and spatial principles of the logic of black music's African origins. Denby's two reviews are especially remarkable for the detailed attention he gives to the choreographed and bodily movements of the dancers.[164]

For example, Denby characterized West African dance, as represented by Dafora's company, as "highly interesting," "graceful," "gentle," and a "completely civilized art." In describing the general characteristics of the dancers' movements, he states that the "torso is bent forward slightly, the chest is open and the shoulders, relaxed [and] it is in the arms chiefly that the dance ornamentation takes place." His descriptions of the dancers' movements also demonstrated his keen awareness of their musical qualities: the "feet keep a rather steady rhythm of strong and light beats"; "the feet kept beating sharply a syncopated rhythm of steps and sole-taps"; "the arms performed the dance variations, creating a secondary rhythm." And, finally, he described Dafora's dancing as displaying a "sense of courtesy toward his partner and toward his audience." Perhaps Denby's most revealing comments in regard to Dafora's and his company's dancing are those in which he intentionally diminishes or altogether dismantles the temporal and spatial distances separating primitive Africa from the modern metropolis.[165]

In this first example, there is no doubt that Denby's attention to the dancers' postures and movements derived from his modernist theory of dance, which he apparently applied whether he was reviewing ballet, modern dance, or, in this case, African dance: "And in the end one noticed that the exactness of the posture, the firmness of the rhythm gave to the dance both dignity and force; that the peculiarities of the style could not be 'savage' or accidental, but were the outcome of a consistent and highly cultivated dance tradition." In addressing the musical qualities and resemblances to the blues in Dafora's dancing, he sidesteps the kind of evolutionary thinking that otherwise typified the performance of black dance music's African origins: "The way [Dafora] phrased the rhythmic patterns in these movements and so heightened the meaning of the dance resembled the way a blues singer phrases her song and heightens its meaning against the steady beat of the orchestra." Lastly, as he denies any semblance of exoticism in Dafora's program, he does express a desire for Dafora to "bring over across the ocean a small company of real West African dancers to add to his well-trained American pupils, and then show us more of the extraordinary wonders West African dancing holds."[166]

Denby's interpretive and analytical outlook seemed to coalesce perfectly with the academy's intention to use African music and dance to diminish the cultural and historical gulf that most Americans perceived separated them from Africans. John Martin, in fact, came to this conclusion: "There can be no question that the elemental qualities in both cultures find a meeting place here, for neither [dance] movement, song nor rhythmic pulse require translation. The academy, accordingly, could scarcely have chosen a more persuasive medium for initiating its program of mutual understanding."[167] Denby's dance criticism, however, allowed him to do more than analyze African dance within the same theoretical parameters he applied to ballet and modern dance. As he noted in his essay "Dance Criticism" published in 1948, the essence of dance, as movement "in space and in time, has no specific terminology to describe it by," thus inviting "the lively critic to invent most of the language and logic of his subject."[168] It is because of dance's elusiveness and ephemeralness, as exemplified by Dafora and his dancers, that Denby fixed his critical "look" onto their bodies' movements and past their racialized status, knowing that the discourses of the African savage and raced body, as well as Dafora's own claims of cultural authenticity, were, in the end, inadequate or irrelevant to his task as dance critic, which was to convey to his readers dance's essential meanings in its movements (smooth space).

During the program's intermission, both guests of honor, Roosevelt and Bethune, spoke to express their gratitude for the academy's work in forging the spirit of goodwill and brotherhood among Americans and the "millions of Africans across the waters."[169] After proclaiming her pride in "feeling that the royal blood of Africa runs through my own veins," Bethune expressed her support for the academy by stating that Americans have a role to play in addressing the "problems that are confronting the Africans" and congratulated the academy's African members for "endeavoring to pull themselves up and to join more firmly not only with America, but with the [modern] countries of the world." For her part, Roosevelt blamed ignorance as the source of prejudice, impressing upon the audience the urgency for Americans to know more "about the world that we are going to live in" in the postwar era. "We are men who tolerate other men's beliefs. We don't just tolerate—we accept," she continued, alluding to the president's Four Freedoms. Contrast this with Roosevelt's column, "My Day," in which she wrote about attending the "African Dance Festival," sharing with her readers across the country that "it had slipped" her "mind that [drums] are really the oldest language in the world, until I saw the people actually talking to each other on the drums on the stage last night."[170] She also described her impression of parts of the performance as "looking like an old Egyptian picture. The color and rhythm of the evening remains with me as a very vivid impression." Her thoughts about the source of prejudice, however, or any mention of the academy's goals of mutual understanding between Americans and Africans are absent in this entry.

It is clear that the academy and Dafora's program succeeded in presenting African dance, music, and drama as a cultural bridge for their audience to reconfigure, if at least momentarily, their perception of Africans as sharing in the present challenges facing other nations at war. Bethune's and Roosevelt's reflections also show, however, the ideological thrust that the political economy of race and positivist thinking maintained, in that the notions of "royal blood of Africa runs through my own veins," "pulling themselves up," "the oldest language in the world," and "looking like an old Egyptian picture" reconstituted the chronotopic values in the "color and rhythm" of the evening's performance. Such notions do not discount Bethune's and Roosevelt's own activism for social justice and racial equality nationally and internationally. By 1943, Bethune, whose parents had been slaves in South Carolina, had accumulated over thirty years of work as an advocate and spokeswoman in education, service organizations, and government for the oppressed and disenfranchised, particularly among American Negro women.[171] Her political activism was highlighted by her appointment by President Roosevelt in 1937 to organize and direct the Federal Council on Negro Affairs, a position that she eventually used to pressure Roosevelt to sign the executive order on fair hiring in the nation's defense industry. She was also a leader in Negro women's clubs, serving as president of the National Association of Colored Women from 1924 to 1928 and founding the National Council of Negro Women in 1935. But Bethune's primary contributions were in education, through which she began attaining the promises of uplift from a young age. We can thus attribute her public pronouncement approving the AAAR's work and identifying as a proud descendent of Dafora's own ancestors to the premium uplift placed on education, social commitment, and dignity of race.

Eleanor Roosevelt had also been very active as an advocate and spokeswoman for the poor and other oppressed groups, including women and American Negroes, during the Depression and World War II.[172] Her progressive and feminist politics not only informed her activism but also prompted her criticisms, particularly after the end of the war, of what she regarded as the Democratic Party's complacency in regard to securing women's and American Negroes' civil rights. During the Roosevelt presidency, however, she maneuvered adroitly between her roles as First Lady and activist. Thus, perhaps, she decided not to broach the question of ignorance as the source of prejudice in her "My Day" entry of December 15, 1943. After attending the academy's festival in April 1946, however, she did mention its work on bettering race relations, and followed this by stating that Africa would be a "vast market in the future for our products."[173] In the end, both Bethune and Roosevelt saw and heard the performance by Dafora's dance group primarily in historicist terms, not representing the African savage past but the ancestral and ancient pasts nonetheless.

For his part, Dafora expressed his own critiques of the flawed perceptions Americans had of Africa and Africans, tying these to the barbarism he attributed to American racial terror even before beginning his association with the AAAR. A program for a performance of *Kykunkor* (probably dating from the late 1930s) included his biographical notes, which stressed his "deep knowledge" of the "rich heritage of art and culture among the native Africans," and gave information of his singing and dance activities in Europe, in addition to his service with the British Army during World War I (figure 3.4).[174] He is then quoted as saying he disliked American jazz but that he "resents what he calls the frequent distortion of spirituals, those musical expressions of the soul of American Negroes," after which comes the following description: "Quiet and composed, and very well-dressed off-stage, [Dafora] listens to dressing-room visitors who express their enthusiasm for his work and their amazement at the revelation that Africa may not be so 'barbaric.' 'Barbarism?' he murmurs, 'but there are lynchings in this country. And voodooism? But that is a real religion, practiced as any other religion is practiced.'"

Dafora's critiques of jazz and inauthentic spirituals, and his accusations of African acts of barbarism and savage religions brilliantly and succinctly indict, as Paul Gilroy would do decades later, modernity's ambivalence and, in this case, the place of Africans within it.[175] Specifically, Dafora's critique brings to the fore how modernity frames the complicity of rationality and progress with its practices of white supremacist terror and Western materialism. Whereas the perception of Africa as savage and barbarous fed modernity's fantasy of Western civilization's progress (and thus its complicity in distancing Africa in time and space), the racial terrors practiced contemporaneously on Jewish and black bodies in Europe and the United States, respectively, were no fantasy but were in fact public spectacles put on display as matters of social ritual and the popular theater of power. This is precisely the reality of racial terror that threatened Mieczyslaw Kolinski's life as an exile in hiding in Belgium, and that Andreu and Gálvez conveyed through the spiritual to their audience at the Club Atenas in Havana in 1937.[176] Dafora, accordingly, identified the undistorted spiritual as the musical expression "of the soul of American Negroes," the wording of which suggests he had read and interpreted Du Bois's *The Souls of Black Folk* accordingly.

But Dafora's critique of modernity's contradictions does not stop here. For his rejection of jazz speaks to his own African nationalist perspective in the face of a music perceived to simultaneously embody American Negro progress and American cultural imperialism. Dafora's musical director, Nigerian Effiom Odok, announcing in his own press release his participation in the "African Dance Festival," also rejected jazz's status along similar lines: "He [Odok] has never played in jazz orchestras, despite offers, being somewhat scornful of such comparatively primitive rhythms and tone effects on the drums."[177] Odok, like Dafora's critique of barbarism, flips the notion of primitive on its head as an act of not only African exceptionalism but also rejection of modernity's standards

FIG. 3.4 Asadata Dafora pictured on the program cover for *Kykunkor*, ca. 1939. From *Kykunkor*, program, n.d., Asadata Dafora Papers.

of musical progress. Whereas Modupe Paris had adroitly performed across temporal and spatial distances in the late 1920s and early 1930s, Dafora and Odok aimed to reconfigure the temporal and spatial terms of modernity altogether for reasons specific to the postwar context.

For instance, during and immediately following the war, the AAAR and Dafora organized several more festivals of African dance, music, and drama. These included *African Tribal Operetta*, which took place in New York City's YMHA in May 1944; the aforementioned *African Dances and Modern Rhythms* ("The March of African Music from Africa to the American Continents"), which took place in Carnegie Hall in April 1945; and the *African Dance and Music Festival*, which took place at the Norfolk USO Auditorium in Virginia in December 1945.[178] The festivals of April and December 1945 are significant for several reasons. Both featured a diverse cast of over thirty African, American Negro, and Caribbean performers, the program of which revived the narrative of the African origins of American Negro music, only this production included a section dedicated to music and dance of the Caribbean and Latin America. Also, the performances in April took place less than a week before the death of President Roosevelt and almost three weeks before the start of the United Nations' Conference on International Organization (UNCIO), which met in San Francisco. However, by the time the performances in December took place, the war had ended and the UNCIO's charter, despite intense lobbying by African, American Negro, and other anticolonial organizations, had failed to guarantee a plan for the decolonization of Africa.[179] In their efforts to lobby American government representatives at the UNCIO as well as in American and international newspapers, and as the likelihood of a charter supporting decolonization faded, activists including Azikiwe, Ojike, Mbadiwe, and others became increasingly militant in their protests. Mbadiwe, for example, on behalf of the AAAR, sent a telegram to the American delegation, warning that any compromise on the issue of decolonization would falsify the purpose of fighting the war. "Our choice is either total freedom or a Third World War," he asserted.[180] At the April meeting, L. D. Reddick, who served on the AAAR's board of directors and who was the curator of the Schomburg Collection of Negro Literature, presented a posthumous award to Felix Eboué, former governor-general of French Equatorial Africa, and included a similar warning that "there can be no durable peace until the colonial question is settled and settled right."[181]

With the Truman administration's complicity in the demise of both the Atlantic Charter's promise of decolonization and Roosevelt's Four Freedoms, the AAAR's rhetoric of goodwill nevertheless continued, as did their efforts to increase understanding among Africans and Americans through dance and music. Furthermore, by including dance and music from the Caribbean and Latin America, they were able to "emphasize the interrelation between African music and dancing and similar forms in the Western Hemisphere," and not only the United States.[182] Whereas the American Negro producers of *Ethiopia Lifts as She Climbs* and *O, Sing a New Song* represented the African origins of Negro music, Dafora and the AAAR took a decidedly hemispheric view on brokering cultural understanding of Africa, a decision that we can attribute in no small measure to the increasing foment among colonized peoples for freedom from colonial rule in the aftermath of World War II and the UNCIO meeting. In addition to African and American Negro musicians and dancers, the casts now included Afro-Cubans, Haitians, and Trinidadians. Lastly, by sending the festival on tour, beginning in Norfolk in December, the AAAR endeavored to take its cultural activism to audiences throughout the United States, starting in the Jim Crow South.[183]

Part 1 of the AAAR's program, "Africa," featured Dafora's *Festival at Battalakor*, consisting of eleven dance and song numbers, many of which were taken from *Kykunkor*. Set in the seventeenth century in West Africa, *Festival at Battalakor* dramatizes the appearance of slavers interrupting a festival celebration in a village.[184] After the village surrenders several of their people to the slavers, the captives "mournfully [sing] nostalgic songs of their homeland as they are carried, in the galley of the slave ship, to unknown destinations and a fearful future." Dafora's aim with this first part of the program was to present "a colorful background for the other artists and [for the audience to see] the ripples of the subtle African drums correspond closely to the rhythms manifested in American music."[185] The cast consisted of over twenty singers and dancers, most of whom were American Negroes, including Alma Sutton (who would appear in a Broadway production of *Show Boat* the following year). The April program included drummer Abdul Assen, who was well known among dance critics as the "medicine man" in *Kykunkor*, a role he first played for the premiere in 1934.[186]

Part 2, "Western Hemisphere—The Caribbean," featured four song-and-dance numbers titled "Brazil," "Trinidad (Calypso)," "Haiti," and "Cuba," the "scenes" of which, according to one review, "[shifted] quickly through the centuries giving glimpses of the African slave trade through the Caribbean and thence to America."[187] Afro-Cubans Princess Orelia and Pedro performed both the "Brazil" and "Cuba" pieces. Orelia and Pedro had started their careers performing "African drums and dance" numbers as well as rhumba and conga in black revues throughout the United States in the 1930s.[188] The calypso pieces were performed by Duke of Iron and Macbeth, both of whom began their careers and formed their styles in New York City rather than in Trinidad in the early 1940s.[189] Part 2 concluded with Josephine Premice performing Haitian music and dance. Born in Brooklyn of Haitian parents, Premice began her dance career performing interpretive versions of Haitian dances, including on the AAAR's "African Dance Festival" program in 1943, before making her Broadway debut in 1945 in *Blue Holiday*.[190]

After an intermission, part 3, "Good Will," featured a number of speakers, including Rev. James H. Robinson of New York City; Ralph P. Bridgeman, president of Hampton Institute; and Mbadiwe. According to a review of the Norfolk performances, Mbadiwe "pointed out that the festival was intended to show the progress of African culture and is being presented periodically as a means of furthering good will between America and Africa."[191] Part 4, "Western Hemisphere—The United States," featured stride pianist Maurice Rocco, dancer Bill Robinson, and jazz pianist and composer Mary Lou Williams in the April shows, and stride pianist Luckey Roberts accompanying dancers in the December show. Robinson, who had been featured in *O, Sing a New Song*, tapped in the AAAR's April program "to the accompaniment of seven native African drums, and spoke a spurious African tongue to the delight of the crowd," according to one report.[192] A finale, featuring the entire company, concluded the program.

Although the AAAR was apparently unable to continue sponsoring Dafora's tour, the troupe continued performing across the country, eventually under the management of Natural Concert and Artists Corporation of New York City. From 1946 through 1948, they performed at various black colleges, including Clark College in Atlanta, the Hampton Institute's Arts of the Theatre Festival, and Tuskegee Institute.[193] His troupe also performed at public venues in Kansas City, Saint Louis, Flint, Waco, and Richmond.[194] During this time, Mbadiwe decided to return to Lagos, Nigeria, arriving in May 1948, after visiting London, Freetown, Monrovia, and Accra, where he had attempted to establish branches of the AAAR and raise funds for the AAAR in New York City.[195] Dafora, however, stayed in the United States, where he continued his performance career advocating for African freedom from colonial rule. His performances toward this end were occasionally recognized, as one reviewer writing for the *Call* of Kansas City noted: "Mr. Dafora's efforts to acquaint American Negroes with the culture of the land of their forefathers have been hailed in many quarters as of great significance and quite in line with the new nationalistic movement among Negroes in various parts of the country in which pride of race and achievement are being stressed with pointed emphasis."[196]

In October 1947, as the House Un-American Activities Committee opened hearings investigating communist activity in Hollywood, Dafora premiered a new dance drama titled *Batanga (African Freedom Rings)* at the Kaufman Hall in Harlem.[197] This dance drama's narrative once again dramatized the history of African music from Africa to the Western hemisphere in which slaves "bring their music, rhythms, and traditions to the various islands on which they land and determine to free themselves from the yoke of brutal masters."[198] While the content of *Batanga* seemed rather innocuous in regard to the growing panic surrounding communism—indeed, Dafora and Mbadiwe never expressed communist or socialist leanings in their programs or writings—he at least considered, if not actually participated in, another play that condemned Western capitalist imperialism in Vietnam, India, French and British West Africa, South Africa, French Morocco, Puerto Rico, Cuba, and the United States. The untitled script of this play, which is included in Dafora's collection at the Archives and Rare Books Division of the Schomburg Center for Research in Black Culture, probably dates from 1950, based on historical references to the American Youth for a Free World (which was eventually red baited in 1952), Bao Dai's installment by France as South Vietnam's head of state in 1949, and the World Federation of Democratic Youth meeting in Budapest in 1949. In the play's Africa section, which dramatizes France and the United States plotting military action to control the continent's natural resources, the script contains the following instructions: "drums start low" and "dancer starts behind screen."

We do not know if this play was ever mounted or, if so, whether Dafora played the African dancer behind the screen. What it indicates, however, are the political shifts that had occurred within the seven years since Dafora had programmed the AAAR's first "African Dance Festival" in 1943 and the seventeen years since Modupe Paris performed the African native in *Ethiopia Lifts as She Climbs* in 1933. In these three performances, the African native or dancer served particular social and political purposes: to celebrate black women's survival, to promote and foster better relations and understanding between Africans and Americans, and to condemn European and American imperialism in Africa. Yet the struggle for freedom and mutual understanding of blacks in the Western Hemisphere and Africa was more urgent than ever given the added oppressive emergences of McCarthyism and the Cold War.

"Modern man, the ordinary everyday citizen, feels that he requires to know his past in order to understand his present."[199] This is how C. L. R. James, the Trinidadian historian and social theorist who lived and worked in the United States from 1938 to 1956, theorized the necessity of popular art, particularly film, in the early and mid-twentieth century, of which he wrote, "No age has been so conscious of the permeation of the historical past in the actual present." James attributes this overwhelming necessity of having to know the past to the everyday individual's "desperate struggle against the constantly increasing social forces . . . in the midst of the cruelties and pretenses of modern society." Indeed, as everyday citizens of society in modernity, Modupe Paris, Zoila Gálvez, Asadata Dafora, Paul Robeson, Kwesi Kuntu, Chano Pozo, and so many others lived and carried out this need to know and perform the past of their racialized and gendered selves in order to not only understand but also survive their present under modernity's pressures of racism, sexism, and colonialism. Their actions on and off stage, as well as on film, were sometimes in line with divisive social and political forces. Most other times, however, they served to energize local, national, and international political movements against similarly oppressive and divisive forces. Their interventions as either performers or lecturers were both politically innovative and epistemologically bold. Innovative, because their work anticipated, for instance, the United Nation's Educational, Scientific, and Cultural Organization's rationale, published in 1945, for the "diffusion of culture, and the education of humanity for justice and liberty and peace" to prevent prejudice and war, which spring from ignorance.[200] And bold by virtue of their occupying the historicist perspective in order to instruct their audiences, the impact of which was aided and complicated by their sponsors' and audiences' worldviews, which were shaped by nationalism, racial uplift, and modernism. The African past for others, however, constituted a temporality from which one had to continuously strive to expel himself or herself in order to move toward an authentic consciousness and freedom. What follows are analyses of such strivings within projects that otherwise seemed deeply entrenched in the logic of black music's and dance's African origins.

4 /

Disalienating Movement and Sound from
the Pathologies of Freedom and Time

The discovery of the existence of a Negro civilization in the fifteenth century confers no
patent of humanity on me. Like it or not, the past can in no way guide me in the present
moment. —FRANTZ FANON, *Black Skin, White Masks,* 1967

Thus far we have explored how practices of analyzing, listening to, and embodying music and dance as black and of African origins operated as particularly intensive modes of temporalizing and spacializing individuals, along with
their musicking and dancing, to distant times and places. In his concluding
chapter in *Black Skin, White Masks,* Frantz Fanon identified the notion of scientific objectivity (analyzing) and the racialized body (embodying) as mechanisms
of alienating individuals, black and white, from their present situations, doing
so, however, without taking into account these mechanisms' rectifying capacities in the context of performance. Even in one of the few passages in which
he addresses music, Fanon reiterates his singular theoretical concern, ontology's racial strictures, by relating the following incident: "A few years ago, the
Lyon Association of Overseas Students of France asked me to reply to an article
that made jazz music literally an eruption of cannibalism in the modern world.
Knowing exactly what I was doing, I rejected the premises of the Association's
representative, and I asked the defender of European purity that he get rid of a
spasm that had nothing of cultural [significance]. Some men want to swell the
world of their being."[1]

Fanon goes on to refer to a "German philosopher [who] had described this process [i.e., swelling the world of one's being] under the notion of the pathology of freedom." That philosopher was Günther Stern Anders, whose "The Pathology of Freedom: An Essay on Non-Identification" (1936) theorizes the self in its "freedom" of identification to be in fact indeterminate, contingent, and thus unfree.[2] Stern, who changed his surname to Anders while working as an editor in Berlin in the early 1930s, conceived of human freedom in its basic ontological form as humanity's "a priori separation from the world." As such, humanity is condemned, Stern argued, to create its relationship to the world, the symptoms of which he identified in the nihilist, the "historical man," and most acutely in one's "desire to render the world congruent with oneself."[3] According to Stern, the nihilist "reaches a pathological extreme in so far as he . . . does not realise his freedom in practice, in the constitution of *his* world." Whereas historical man "escapes from the strangeness of the world" by taking possession of his life in the world, by uniting not only with his own past but with the pasts of other persons as well.[4] The latter's "freedom" of identification reveals itself to be pathological, however, because "man must comply with and answer to the claim to identity" that other subjectivities place on him.[5] Fanon thus understood the "defender of European purity" and individuals who want to "swell the world of their being" in general as exhibiting and exerting such pathological symptoms of humanity's ontological freedom. What, then, did Fanon prescribe for humanity in order to achieve disalienation from freedom's pathologies?

After declaring that he "did not have to take up a position on behalf of black music against white music but rather to help my brother to give up an attitude in which there was nothing beneficial," Fanon attributed the pathological condition exhibited in the association's request of him to answer for jazz to the problem of *temporalité* (temporality), for which he offers the following solution: "Those Negroes and Whites will have been disalienated who have refused to be let shut away in the Tower given as the Past. For many other Negroes, disalienation will arise in other ways through the refusal to take the present scheme of things as definitive."[6] In other words, Fanon proposed disalienation as a strategy for individuals, regardless of race, to engage the world without allowing it to subsume one's presence (or being) under the long shadows of modernity's temporal schemas. In this sense, he was drawing from psychoanalytically and phenomenologically defined conditions of being based on conceptions of logical or original time (temporalities of the present) differentiated from chronological time (temporality). In taking into account how race factors directly in the ontological straightjackets that are schemas of chronological time (e.g., Christianity, evolution, modern civilization, colonialism, and capitalism), Fanon theorized the way for racialized black individuals in particular to take action not only in but *upon* the present in order to achieve nonalienated freedom from the pathologies of society's political economy of race and its contingencies in the form of the performativities of race and historical time.

In spite of his lack of attention to performance, Fanon's recourse to action in order to take hold of one's freedom of identification in the present actually constitutes one of the most explicit and radical challenges to the temporalizing and spatializing practices given to the black body, Africa, and, with that, the logic of black music's and dance's African origins. In rejoining Fanon's disalienation with Stern's theorizations of "the fact of human action," "authentic listening," and "being in music," we are led back to dance-music as smooth spaces of identification wherein disalienation may be enacted (as was the case during moments of Katherine Dunham's fieldwork) against this logic's and its practices' many pathological manifestations.[8] As Stern concluded, there is nothing more suspect than philosophical anthropology's demand for a "moment's pause to pose questions of 'authentic' definition," this coming six decades before Christopher Small's call to conceive of music and dance as action or movement and not merely as abstract entities conceived in the notion of "the work."[9] As Veit Erlmann concludes regarding Stern's theory of "authentic listening," time stops when the truest manifestation of one's being in the world materializes, this occurring as a result of our well-intentioned actions, as when being in music: "It is in the plenitude of presence, in a realm beyond the threshold of sensory immediacy," says Erlmann, "but also well below the arrogance of reason, that musical situations put a stop to time."[10]

Whereas the previous chapters looked at analyzing, listening, and embodying as this logic's constitutive practices, this chapter explores seemingly fleeting actions taken by Katherine Dunham, Duke Ellington, and Harry Smith that resisted these practices and, in doing so, brought this logic's temporalizing and spatializing practices to bear upon itself. Their actions included taking possession of key conceptual devices, such as the authentic, origin, progress, and linearity, in order to recuperate moments of their own authentic (disalienated) selves in performance, devices that otherwise were given to things and others as a matter of course not only for the propping up of the logic (*décalage*) but also in constricting their everyday lives.[11] Dunham and Ellington took action in this regard under the cover of the New Negro ideal of self-identification, a strategy that, as we will see, often landed them in what Stern described as the pathology of the "historical man," or what Fanon rejected wholesale as the taking of a position on behalf of Negro dance and music.[12] Whereas Smith, in his early abstract or nonobjective films, desired to cut off the dominant representational devices otherwise necessary for the practices of the logic of black music's and dance's African origins to materialize. Rather than identifying the results of such actions (disalienation achieved or not), this chapter seeks to measure their reverberations connecting to and shaking up in varying directions the political economies of race and gender as well as history and capitalism.

It is difficult to compartmentalize Katherine Dunham's work as anthropologist, recording artist, dancer, educator, and entrepreneur, especially when considering what her work entailed in producing *Heat Wave: From Haiti to Harlem* (ca. 1943), *Tropical Revue* (1943–1945), and *Bal Nègre* (1946–1947), as well as in establishing her Dunham School of Dance and Theatre in 1945. During this period she reiterated her imperative to synthesize her anthropological training and dancing to create serious Negro dance, a challenge that she described as a "problem" and "paradoxical."[13] Like Paul Robeson, Duke Ellington, Zora Neale Hurston, and many more of her contemporaries, Dunham was faced with reconciling her New Negro ideals and principles with the strictures of race, gender, and sex with the entertainment industry's capitalist system, from which she procured financial backing for her artistic and educational ventures. As she had done in her proposals to the Rosenwald Foundation, she resorted to anthropology's primitivist discourse in her production proposals written for potential financial backers and in her promotional publications, which we can interpret as one of her tactical actions in her maneuvering in and around the economic flows traversing the anthropological and entertainment fields. Yet what we see in *Heat Wave*'s script is a bitingly satirical portrayal of the anthropologist as scientist and anthropology as a science set within the context of jazz's concurrent traditionalist-modernist debate. Although Dunham did use her anthropological training, as Susan Manning notes, to subvert the "critical conundrum of natural talent versus derivative artistry that white critics had scripted for African-American choreographers," her ideas for *Heat Wave* reveal an underlying irreverence toward that which had projected upon her an alienated double consciousness as Negro woman anthropologist and artist.[14] Drawing from VèVè A. Clark's method of analyzing Dunham's choreographies, this analysis takes a proposal-to-performance-to-proposal (and so on) approach to consider how Dunham maneuvered through the field of dance entertainment to realize Negro dance's universal properties, her acts of which did provoke disalienations of dance and music, no matter how fleeting, from the ontological straightjackets of anthropology as science.[15]

Duke Ellington's *Liberian Suite*, commissioned for the centennial anniversary of Liberia in 1947, reintroduces the significance of West African politics into this analysis of freedom and the logic of black music's and dance's African origins. The fact that American abolitionists and slaveholders, with the assistance of the American government, founded Liberia in 1822 as a settler colony for freed black Americans complicates the historical pageant's and acculturation theory's unidirectional narratives of Africa as origin, particularly since these black American settlers, as Claude A. Clegg III notes, constructed an ethnic minority-dominant society "marred by many of the same exclusionary, oppressive characteristics common to modern colonial regimes."[16] Moreover, the League of Nations commission report of 1930 that documented forced labor practices by Americo-Liberian government officials exposes Ellington to charges of complicity in the government's ongoing propaganda efforts to improve its reputation internationally and among its own native populations.[17] In fact, the analysis of Ellington's *Liberian Suite* and the circumstances surrounding its commission and reception indicate that Ellington shrewdly registered his critique of the world's second black-ruled republic's official historical narrative by referencing Franklin Roosevelt's Four Freedoms and, most significantly, a fifth freedom that he tactically left undefined. As both Kevin Gaines and Eric Porter note, jazz critics' formalist concerns in Ellington's music and the economic and historiographical strictures of the jazz canon have obscured or altogether erased the freedom he took in using musical formulas, European-derived or otherwise, as platforms to strike a balance between his New Negro ideals and aesthetic convictions.[18] Yet there seems to be no place for *Liberian Suite* in Gaines's paradigm for his analysis of *Black, Brown and Beige* (1943), Ellington's most recognized tone parallel of the history of the American Negro: "I am concerned here with his self-conscious construction of historically situated narratives of African-American group consciousness as part of a progressive, antiracist agenda during World War II."[19] If Liberia poses a narrative of black American complicity in colonialist oppression in Africa, one so contradictory that it compelled most black intellectuals in the 1930s and 1940s to deflect blame for Liberia's precarious international standing onto capitalist imperialism, then what does Ellington's *Liberian Suite* do to the jazz canon's dominant historical narrative, which in overlooking this piece has perhaps implicated itself in perpetuating this historical amnesia? Moreover, Ellington's consternation over the economic contingencies of tactics used by civil rights organizations, in regard specifically to his and his musicians' livelihoods, places further doubt as to the notion of American Negro group identity and Ellington's contributions to it.

Finally, Harry Smith, along with other American avant-garde filmmakers of the 1940s, created films that manipulated space, time, and motion in response to the stark reality of the postwar nuclear age.[20] Smith, who was identified with the nonobjective school of abstract film design in San Francisco, employed abstract images, color, and movement "as an experience in itself apart from their power to express thoughts or ideas."[21] He tested, however, the realization of his images, colors, and movements as nonobjective films of the late 1940s by showing these while playing records of "Guarachi guaro" and "Manteca," songs cocomposed by Chano Pozo and Dizzy Gillespie and recorded by Gillespie's big band, as well as having jazz musicians improvise to his films. Smith incorporated "Guarachi guaro" as his *Film No. 2*'s soundtrack and based the production of *Film No. 4* on his abstract painting *Manteca*, thereby attempting to translate these cubop recordings into images, and vice versa, in order to transcend the boundaries between sound and image as well as the linear unities in film and music. These films are indeed striking in their capacity to disrupt the delineation between image and sound, particularly when compared to the reception of Pozo and Gillespie's music among jazz critics, which largely unfolded within the analytical, listening, and embodying practices of black music's and dance's African origins.

Taking into consideration Antonin Artaud's and Gilles Deleuze's caution, however, regarding abstract film's inability to provoke "critical and conscious thought and the unconscious in thought," we might conclude that Smith's abstract films obscured rather than overcame the temporal and spatial strictures that compelled individuals such as Pozo, Gillespie, Ellington, and Dunham, not to mention Paul Robeson, to operate strategically within the material world's racialized and gendered scheme of things.[22] Indeed, Smith's unconventional lifestyle, along with his abstract films, constituted his own attempts at disalienation from the macropolitics of American capitalist society and the Cold War, actions that were accessible to him due in no small measure to the privileges of whiteness. In the end, by juxtaposing the work of Smith, Ellington, and Dunham within the frameworks of Fanon's and Stern's notions of disalienation and the pathology of humanity's freedom in the world, we uncover micropolitical flows of artistic and political actions wherein the logic of black music's and dance's African origins, along with wartime and Cold War American capitalist society, implicate modernity to be utterly indeterminate, yet hegemonically constitutive of self nonetheless.[23]

"Cool Scientist or Sultry Performer?"

As discussed in chapter 1, Katherine Dunham formally left graduate school in the fall of 1937 after feeling disillusioned about what she perceived to be Melville Herskovits's and Robert Redfield's doubts that she had the intellectual capacity to conduct the scientific work of an anthropologist beyond the study of primitive dance. This, in addition to her busy professional dancing career, factored into her leaving the program at the University of Chicago. From 1938 through the end of the war, Dunham devoted much of her work to directing her dance company and creating choreographies, many of which were drawn from the dances she had studied in the Caribbean. At first her company performed mostly in Chicago, but by 1940 they toured regularly throughout the country, adding to its repertory choreographies of Cuban and Brazilian dances, in addition to those of Haiti and Martinique, as well as black American dances.[24] While dance critics and journalists praised her choreographies and her company's performances for their uniqueness and artistry, most also stressed her anthropological training, citing her research of native dances for the authenticity they anticipated in her choreographies.[25]

Indeed, Dunham worked toward developing dance choreographies centered on the artistic techniques and social functions of the dances she had studied, participated in, and filmed in the anthropological field. Her synthesis of her artistic and anthropological work materialized in her Dunham Technique, of which much has been written, but her work in its entirety, particularly in regard to her belief in dance's universal properties, has best been described as a "philosophical meditation on how individuals can achieve some degree of equilibrium within larger community formations . . . , locating dance as a primary means of stimulating self- and communal discovery."[26] Whereas Dunham valued her anthropological training as key to demonstrating the "links between social activism, self-awareness, and self-actualization," it was her desire to ultimately realize in her dance schools the universal principles of the dances she had studied in the anthropological field, the first permanent school of which she opened in New York City in 1945. Yet, for most of her artistic aims that she pursued in her choreographies leading up to and following her school's opening, Dunham proved to be willing to compromise these in large part for the financial viability of her school.

Like Asadata Dafora, Dunham choreographed dances from the Caribbean and Latin America in her productions to broker cultural understanding— not, however, of Africa, nor for that matter of the origins of American Negro dances, but rather of these dance's universal qualities. Dunham thus registered the notion of Negro dance in a different temporality than that put forth by Dafora, a difference of temporality, however, that did not take hold with most audiences and spectators. In addition, the everyday rhythms of a woman director of an all-black dance company proved to consistently challenge Dunham's realization of her philosophical ideals and aesthetic principles. She portrayed, for example, the sultry dancer in Broadway and Hollywood film productions, beginning with *Cabin in the Sky* (1941) and followed by appearances in *Carnival of Rhythm* (1941), a short produced by United Artists, and *Stormy Weather* (1943), produced by 20th Century Fox.[27] Critics tended to interpret her performances in these productions through the combined lenses of race and sex. Dunham and her company also confronted discrimination wherever they performed, for example, at hotels that refused them accommodations in cities such as San Francisco.[28] But if Dunham really intended to put forth dance's universal properties regardless of race, style, and so forth, then why do the notions "zombies," "deep in the jungle," and "the Other World of the tropics" appear in her promotional material, not to mention her choreographies?[29] In situating her script for *Heat Wave* (1943) in this context, her use of satire to criticize what she had always considered to be anthropology's major problematic, that is, its scientific prerogative to put individual human action into its temporal and spatial place, seems to further confuse the matter.

Heat Wave's caricature of the anthropologist and his mishandling of the program's jazz sequence calls forth both the emerging traditionalist-modernist debate surrounding jazz music—wherein swing music marked either jazz's decadence and decline or its progress—and the confluence of anthropology and comparative musicology in this debate. A close look at the script's contents lends important insight into Dunham's response to not only the tenets of this debate but also the events organized by some of its purveyors, such as John Hammond's *From Spirituals to Swing* concert at Carnegie Hall in 1938 and Rudi Blesh's jazz lecture series at the San Francisco Museum of Modern Art in 1943. It also invokes comparison to the uses of satire by some of her contemporaries in their own responses to anthropology's and society's handling of issues concerning race and racism. Her eventual transformations of the script, however, leading to the production of *Tropical Revue* will shed further insight into her maneuverings in and around the economic flows of the entertainment industry, maneuverings that involved taking another approach to resolving her apparent vexed relationship with anthropology.

Dunham's original conception for *Heat Wave* was a humorous and dance-filled revue in two acts titled "The Tropics" and the "Blues to Boogie-Woogie." The script calls for a "milquetoast actor" to play an anthropologist who serves as the revue's emcee.[30] Most of the revue's musical and dance numbers are introduced by the emcee, whose lines are filled with plays on words intended to belittle the anthropologist and anthropology as a white patriarchal and exoticizing field of inquiry. Examples include the emcee's instructions to "define anthropology as Study of Man," followed by "Now on field trip to broaden Anthropology to include the Study of Woman"; the stage instruction that the "Voodoo pantomime of terror frightens M.C. who scurries across stage, stops and introduces [Nanigo Priest] as sister-anthropologist"; and a description of the song "Apology to Anthropology" as an "Afro-Egyptian-Mayan-Persian-West Indian mélange, mixing styles and locales into a World's Fair phantasmagoria consisting of excavators, snake charmers, priests, belly-dancers, houris—running wild during the annual convention of the Society of Anthropology." These sardonic moments of anthropological bumblings alternate with serious dance numbers, including the Caribbean-inspired "Afro-Rumba-Jive," "Nanigo Priest," and "Shore Excursion," and featured performers that were to include boogie-woogie piano duo Albert Ammons and Pete Johnson, singer-guitarist Josh White, the Original Dixieland Band, and Puerto Rican singer Bobby Capo.

These and other elements of the script point to not one particular anthropologist or jazz historian as a target of its satire but in fact a number of events that factored in the growing traditionalist-modernist divide in jazz discourse and the formation of a jazz historical narrative. To begin with, *Heat Wave's* subtitle, *From Haiti to Harlem*, references the historical impulse in Hammond's *From Spirituals to Swing* concerts of 1938 and 1939, signifying on the concerts' construction of the "history of jazz rooted in the African American experience" in several ways.[31] For instance, its proposed featured musicians, Ammons and Johnson, had performed on Hammond's program in 1938, representing in both cases boogie-woogie music as one representative of authentic preswing hot jazz music. But whereas, according to the program, Hammond's concert began with "African Tribal Music: From Scientific Recordings Made by the H. E. Tracy Expedition to the West Coast of Africa," part 1 of Dunham's script, "The Tropics," called for a hodgepodge of dance and musical numbers described as South Pacific native pantomime, a native Mayan chant, and a plaintive Haitian song, in effect satirizing anthropology's and jazz criticism's obsessions with the scientific pursuit of musical origins and its authentic iterations.[32] Finally, Dunham's bumbling emcee might have been a satirical dig at Hammond's own inauspicious performance as the emcee for the concert in 1938.[33] The specious erudite portrayed by *Heat Wave's* emcee was, it seems, less a personal attack on Hammond or, for that matter, on Blesh, than an attack of anthropology's claims of scientific rigor as implied nevertheless in Hammond's use of field recordings, which went off apparently with little explanation, either in his introductory remarks or the concert's program, as to the recordings' relationship to the program's music.

Certain details in part 2 of *Heat Wave's* script suggest that it was drafted around spring 1943. For one, this section of the script lists, among other featured performers, the Original Dixieland Band, whose members are described as "jazz musicians, aged 60 to 77, each of whom have actually played in one of the famous Dixieland bands. They were once mustered by the San Francisco Museum of Modern Art for a single performance—and will be recruited for this show." Dunham's troupe performed at San Francisco's Golden Gate Theater and the Mark Hopkins Hotel in April and May 1943.[34] At the time, Rudi Blesh was giving a series of lectures on hot jazz at the San Francisco Museum of Art that culminated in a concert at the Geary Theater on May 9 featuring veteran New Orleans jazz musicians Willie "Bunk" Johnson, Kid Ory, Papa Mutt Carey, Bertha Gonzales (or Gonsoulin), and others.[35] Based on the script's reference to this concert and on the presence of her company in San Francisco at the time, it is very likely that Dunham attended the concert and perhaps even one or more of Blesh's lectures earlier in April. Blesh eventually edited his lectures at the San Francisco Museum of Art into his book *Shining Trumpets: A History of Jazz* (1946), one of a growing stream of books that put forth jazz's historical roots and evolution. According to John Gennari, Blesh's was the first of these books, however, to base its claims of the African origins of jazz on contemporary anthropological and comparative musicological scholarship, namely that of Melville Herskovits, Mieczyslaw Kolinski, and Richard Waterman.[36]

Hammond's and Blesh's use of field recordings played on the very same listening practices (analyzed in the previous chapters) that accounted for listeners' reifying their anchorage in the modern present. Whether in the concert hall, laboratory, or home, listeners of either black bodies performing the African native or recordings of black music made in the field or studio in Cuba, the United States, or elsewhere heard that music as of the distant past, unchanged. The fact that field recordings contained music performed by the listener's temporal contemporaries, as with Hammond's audience and musicians, went very simply unnoticed due to the epistemological power of the Western philosophies of history. With this in mind, we should interpret the significance of Blesh's use of Herskovits's and Waterman's scholarship not only in terms of its innovation in jazz scholarship but also as another instance in which science was tapped to address, in Blesh's words, the "position of the Negro in this democracy and . . . our white attitude toward the art of this black minority."[37] Accordingly, Blesh believed that a "thorough treatment of jazz as music not only deals with the American Negro but goes all the way back to Africa." In addition to receiving assistance from Herskovits, Blesh got access from Waterman to the field recordings at the Laboratory of Comparative Musicology at Northwestern University. What is more, he drew from Waterman's Gestalt-based interpretation of extended offbeat accentuation as a characteristic of African and American Negro music, to include (he noted) ragtime and boogie-woogie, for his lectures in April 1943.[38]

The confluence of such intellectual production and public musical events, centered on addressing the presence of Africa in society, politics, and history, had similarly been occurring as curated by Modupe Paris, Asadata Dafora, and K. O. Mbadiwe in the United States, and Zoila Gálvez, Salvador García Agüero, Fernando Ortiz, Gilberto Valdés, and others in Cuba. Dunham's *Heat Wave* belongs to this artistic and intellectual production across constituencies and national boundaries, but only tangentially, for it distinguishes itself by questioning in satirical form anthropology's epistemological tenets with respect to origins and authenticity, which was also fueling the traditionalist-modernist debate in jazz. To be clear, the historical narrative of part 2 of the script is similar to the narrative constructed in Blesh's *Shining Trumpets* as well as in Hammond's *From Spirituals to Swing* concerts. For instance, part 2 includes allusions to pre-jazz dance styles, "Plantation Dances" ("Darktown Strutters' Ball," "Ballin de Jack," and "Cake Walk") and "Barrelhouse—A Florida Swamp Shimmy," which Dunham's company had been performing since 1940 and 1938, respectively.[39] According to Dunham herself, she began exploring the rural roots of black urban dance forms soon after returning from her field trip to the Caribbean in 1936. Unlike Hammond and Blesh, however, she pursued the roots of American Negro and Caribbean dances not to use these to constrict her dancers and musicians to authentic imitations but rather to create new pieces or creative translations of these sources—translations, that is, with which she hoped to provoke individuals to achieve their own equilibrium between self- and communal identification. Furthermore, for Hammond's and Blesh's narratives, the blues served as the essence linking jazz's authentic incarnations, yet part 2 of Dunham's script called for Josh White to represent the blues. In light of the conventionally regarded lines drawn by Blesh and other jazz traditionalists, on the one hand, and jazz modernists such as Leonard Feather and Barry Ulanov, on the other, White fell decisively through the cracks, which is precisely where Dunham located this debate's and anthropology's shared shortcomings.[40]

As already mentioned, *Heat Wave*'s script rather mercilessly lampoons the anthropologist turned jazz historian serving as the revue's emcee. To introduce Josh White, the proposed opening act of part 2, the script instructs the emcee to describe the "music of jazz with complete incoherence; he only learned of the existence of jazz at 5 P.M. the day previous and is agog at his discovery. Quick in research, he has already found a clinical case."[41] Putting aside the hyperbolic reference to the emcee's supposed amateur status (Blesh and

Hammond were serious, if ideologically driven and paternalistic researchers of black American music) and focusing on the words "incoherence" and especially "clinical case" points to additional logical peculiarities in the traditionalist-modernist debate. Specifically, characterizing White as a "clinical case" of the "early American blues" implies a pathology of sorts in White's music, the em-cee's diagnosis of which contributes to the incoherence in his description of jazz. Indeed, in his discussion of "postclassic" or contemporary blues in *Shining Trumpets*, Blesh characterizes White's approach to the blues as exhibiting "intellectual sophistication," using the "blues for their social significance."[42] But, he continues, "There is a measure of artificiality in this, although the singer's sincerity is not to be questioned. Such singing may be, in some degree, effective as propaganda, but it remains to be seen whether it is more so than the stark power of the pure folk blues, the grim drama of Ma Rainey, Bessie Smith, or 'Chippie' Hill." After further criticizing White's singing as lacking in deep conviction, Blesh settles on categorizing his blues style as "revivalist."[43]

Blesh's rhetoric indeed exhibits the kind of subjective judgments based on the observation method characteristic at the time of conventional psychological and anthropological practice. But his notion of authentic blues does the same kind of temporal violence to White's and, for that matter, folk blues musicians' place in modern society as that committed by, for example, Herskovits toward Trinidadian calypso singers (see chapter 2). What we have here, in other words, are examples of what Fanon accused the Lyon Association's representative of committing, the jazz historian and anthropologist "swelling" or temporalizing the world with their being. Blesh's desire to define the boundaries of authentic and artificial (folk and sophisticated) blues contradicted his prefatory stated goal of studying jazz music "thoroughly" in order to question the "position of the Negro in this democracy" and "our white attitude toward the art of this black minority." For the outcomes of White's music and performances in the early 1940s, particularly his duo performances with blues musician Lead Belly and white Broadway star Libby Holman in New York City, helped bolster at least white progressive attitudes toward black American folk music and against segregationist practices if even at a micropolitical level.[44] It is through White's presence in her script against the backdrop of jazz's traditionalist-modernist debate that Dunham intended to restore his music without concern about questions of origins or authenticity, folk or urbanity, but rather in terms of the communal and humanistic aspects of the blues; her outlook in this instance as pertaining to the blues joined those of Ralph Ellison and Albert Murray.[45]

As for the introduction of Ammons and Johnson and the boogie-woogie dance routine "Barrelhouse—A Florida Swamp Shimmy," the script instructs the emcee to give an "incomprehensible explanation of boogie-woogie, the jargon of the hepcats flows out of his elbow." Unlike his assessment of Josh White, Blesh did consider Ammons's and Johnson's music as authentic representations of barrelhouse boogie-woogie piano music.[46] What is significant here is the script's instruction for the emcee to be "incomprehensible" by using jive or the "jargon of the hepcats." This is not simply a case of irony in that a "hep cat" in fact is aware, competent, and has the ability to perceive quickly, but rather another dig at the expense of the anthropologist turn jazz historian feigning to have a command of the language of urban black youth.[47] In this way, Dunham's sardonic tone delves into the kind of satirical social commentary that writers George S. Schuyler and Dan Burley had contributed since the 1920s in their editorials, articles, stories, novels, and other published work. As Jeffrey B. Ferguson explains, Schuyler used satire as an antiracist weapon to oppose the tenets of New Negro and white supremacist ideologies, encouraging a nonmoralistic "balance of reason and play as the proper response to an empirical world much more complicated than any of the interpretations invented to explain it."[48]

As for Dan Burley, his work on various areas of black American culture and society came primarily in his editorials and articles. In addition to his work as a writer, Burley was a barrelhouse and blues pianist whom Blesh helped record on the Circle label in 1946.[49] Perhaps best known as the author of *The Harlem Handbook of Jive* (1944), Burley also wrote a social gossip column, "Back Door Stuff," for the *New York Amsterdam News* from 1935 through the 1940s. His satirical piece "Anthropologists Study Meaning of 'Conk'" from 1947 is particularly relevant here.[50] This piece, worded mostly in Burley's customary jive style of writing, casts a bewildering and sarcastic eye toward the "assorted probers" at "Columbia, NYU, CCNY and other founts of knowledge in these parts" who are teaching jive (or the "meaning of such words as 'conk,' 'solid,' and 'alreet')," "food habits of the North American Negro," the various grades of Negro hair, and other stereotyped aspects of black American rural and urban cultures. In identifying the anthropological "probers" by name, Burley targets Ruth Benedict, Gene Weltfish, Ralph Linton, and Margaret Mead, all of whom (in addition to Melville Herskovits) were associated with Columbia University and the Franz Boas school of anthropology. The piece ends with a stark assessment of anthropology's alienation from the day-to-day survival of those whom it claims to study: "Anthropology is a heluva subject in that all you gotta do is to look out the window at the nearest zoot suit or drape shape and write what you think is on his mind as he dodges streetcars, police, his gal's old man, crumbling walls of rotten tenements, jumps out of windows in the middle of the night to keep from being burned up, and runs like hell all the time to get out of the dangerous shadow of his own color!"

Burley's unraveling of social science's pretensions by situating it in the language and world of the dispossessed further reveals a perspective of suspicion, if not complete indifference toward, claims of scientific research on black American culture, society, and history.[51] One of Burley's readers, Ollie Okala, whose husband, Julius Okala, had worked as Richard Waterman's informant at Northwestern University starting in 1941, wrote to the columnist, thanking him for addressing topics that are "concerned with the very core of our lives." She described his satirical entry on anthropologists as outstanding and a masterpiece, and disclosed that it made her husband, an anthropologist himself, "do some thinking!"[52] These insights provide yet more examples of anthropology's problematic standing among both its practitioners and its subjects of research, which Dunham experienced and encountered herself while conducting research in Jamaica and Haiti (see chapter 1).

Following her success in the Broadway show *Cabin in the Sky*, Dunham began to lecture and write about the tricky place her anthropological training and dance research occupied in her dancing and choreographies, attempting, it seemed, to close the gap that separated, as we have seen, anthropology from the day-to-day life of black Americans. Meanwhile, she criticized reporters for exaggerating the distinctions between her training "in the awesome science of anthropology" and her success in the "popular art of Broadway dancing," rather than recognizing the "synthesis between them," which her former professors refused to recognize as well.[53] But even her producer, Sol Hurok, could not resist referring to her "split personality": "She is," he stated in his memoir, "a quite superb combination of exoticism and intellectuality."[54] In fact, it seems that Dunham began to foster this dilemma in her production's programs and in her press releases in order to create a liminal space between the authentic and interpretive for her choreographies, particularly her Caribbean and Latin American dances, to reside. What we read, then, in the reception of Dunham's performances of *Heat Wave*, *Tropical Revue*, and *Bal nègre* are reviews that are as much the writer's reiteration of Dunham's promotional material as their own impressions of the company's performances. In terms of publicity, Dunham's tactic worked, but in regard to her universalist philosophy of Negro dance, it on occasion backfired, sometimes even in ways that raised questions about the ethics of her representations of black dance music of the Caribbean.

The Dunham troupe premiered *Heat Wave: From Haiti to Harlem*, produced by Sol Hurok, at the Chez Paree nightclub in Chicago in June 1943 and then took the revue to New York City, where it premiered in September and ran for eight successful weeks at the Martin Beck Theatre on Broadway.[55] Also in July the film *Stormy Weather*, staring Lena Horne, Bill Robinson, Cab Calloway, and Katherine Dunham, premiered in New York City to very positive reviews.[56] Riding the wave of *Stormy Weather*'s popularity, *Heat Wave* also garnered positive reviews, but little mention was made of the revue's satirical underpinnings. Will Davidson, writing for the *Chicago Daily Tribune*, described the "tropical motif" of the first part as a "gay, kaleidoscopic concert of native movements decorated with humor and exuberance," and the second part as "jive in its glory—insolent Barrel House, the imaginative and delightful Honky Tonk Train."[57] Davidson described Jack Marshall, who played the emcee for the Chicago production, as a "crowd pleaser for sure, with his rubber face and his speedy, sure delivery. He's good fun, and a safe bet for Chez Paree fame." According to another article, Mead Lux Lewis, whom Blesh wrote about extensively and who also performed at Hammond's first *From Spirituals to Swing* concert, was the featured boogie-woogie pianist for the troupe's tour of the West Coast that summer.[58]

Then for the revue's opening on Broadway's Martin Beck Theatre, Hurok and Dunham decided to change the revue's title to *Tropical Revue*.[59] In his attempt to further fashion the production for Broadway audiences, Hurok had Dunham drop the role of the emcee and, with that, the revue's satirical undoing of anthropology's and jazz criticism's power of representation. As Hurok explained, "It did not take me long to discover the public was more interested in sizzling scenery than it was in anthropology, at least in the theatre. Since the *Tropical Revue* was fairly highly budgeted, it was necessary for us, in order to attract the public, to emphasize sex over anthropology."[60] Indeed, the company's weekly operating costs were on average $13,500, and thus Dunham, according to Hurok, supported his proposed changes to the program and its overall theme.[61] The program now shifted focus to its variety of Haitian, Cuban, Brazilian, and American Negro dance numbers, and Hurok and Dunham hired popular musical acts performing in various nightclubs throughout the city to boost the program's featured entertainment. They included the Leonard Ware Trio, who also provided the music for the blues and boogie-woogie portions of the program; Bobby Capo, who was listed in the original script as a featured vocalist but joined the cast in October to sing "Callate" and "Choro" during part 1's Latin American music and dance portion; and the Original Dixieland Band, which was also listed in the original script but joined the cast for its opening in Philadelphia in January 1944.[62] Through the end of the revue's run in May 1945, Hurok and Dunham continued to revise the program, replacing, for example, Dunham's Haitian dance–inspired "Rites de Passage" with her ballet in three parts, *L'ag'ya*, which her troupe had originally premiered in 1938 (see figures 1.3 and 1.4).[63]

John Martin, for one, was critical of the revue's Broadway production, suggesting that Dunham had "sacrificed" commentary and integrity to "conform to what Broadway expects the Negro dance to be."[64] Indeed, as Dunham's company took *Tropical Revue* on tour, both black and white newspapers ran advertisements and reviews in which the revue's intended exotic and sexual themes were highlighted, while her anthropological credentials were also foregrounded. Examples of titles of reviews included "Katherine Dunham Learned Voodoo from Natives" and "Dunham Revue Is Altered, but It Still Sizzles." The articles themselves reprinted highly exoticized stories of Dunham's activities in the field with the "secretive peoples of the West Indies," her participation in "voodoo ceremonies" and "uninhibited African-born dances," and her having "black magic spells" performed "over her in graveyards." And the dancing and music itself were described as being "from African primitive to boogie woogie," "music that spills from jungle drums, from the Dixieland Jazz band," " 'L'Ag'ya,' the voodoo number from French Martinique," and "a musical heatwave from the south of the equator to north of jive!"[65]

Dunham's *Tropical Revue* excited in most critics the practice of seeing, hearing, and feeling the exotic and erotic from bodies racialized as black. But what if we disalienated Dunham's and her dancers' movements from such practices (or machines), attempting to conceive for example, *L'Ag'ya* not as an object of anthropological study or an artistic interpretation of primitive black dance but rather as flows of movement and sound? In the previous two chapters such practices and their effects—as generated, for example, in observing comparsas on the streets of Havana, listening to the "chillingly weird" numbers on Dunham's Decca records, or in performing the African native and American Negro ancestor by Modupe Paris—were attributed to the conceptual equipment at hand, listening in the subjective assurance of modernity, and the performativity of race of these occasions. Only by reconstituting the temporal and spatial distances disavowed in the exoticism and eroticism of l'ag'ya, as performed either by Martinicans or Dunham's troupe can we then attribute the perceived distances in historical time and geographic space to modernity's practices of observing, listening, and embodying in order to finally get at the flows of movement and sound coming from the bodies depicted in figures 1.3 and 1.4, bodily moving in sound that modernist dance critics Edwin Denby and John Martin indeed attempted to capture in writing.

Yet, even though Dunham's work as scientist and artist prioritized movement in sound, she simultaneously operated accordingly to maximize her profitability from modernity's racial, gendered, and capitalist machines. To wit, one reporter simply congratulated Dunham for turning "an anthropological fellowship into irresistible box office."[66] Indeed, the changes Hurok and Dunham made to *Tropical Revue* enabled it to run for fifty-seven weeks and make a net profit of over $250,000, a large portion of which Dunham used to open her Dunham School of Dance and Theatre in Manhattan in September 1945.[67] Although hers was not the first interracial dance school, the Dunham School certainly distinguished itself by virtue of its far-reaching and innovative curricula and degree programs—which it prominently listed on its advertisements (figure 4.1)—not to mention the fact that the director was a black American woman.[68] For by 1946 the school (which was also called the Katherine Dunham School of Arts and Research) included a Department of Cultural Studies and an Institute for Caribbean Research, along with the Dunham School of Dance and Theater. Employing a faculty of over twenty instructors, the school offered elementary, master graduate, and professional certificates in the fields of dance, drama, and primitive cultures.[69] While the aim of the school's curricula was to foster a "new way of doing art [and] of looking at peoples and cultures," its connection with Dunham's professional company, according to Dunham herself, served as a "model to the student as well as an incentive for those who otherwise might be inclined to doubt a career in the performing arts, particularly in the social structure existing in America."[70]

In addition to the opening of Dunham's school, her new production, a musical drama titled *Carib Song*, played at the Adelphi Theater on Broadway on September 25, after premiering on August 30 in New Haven, Connecticut.[71] World War II had just ended on August 15, and Dunham's performance and teaching careers seemed to be flourishing. *Carib Song* closed after only eight weeks, however, and Dunham had to soon mount another production to generate additional revenue to keep her school open. She began to solicit potential producers as early as January 1946.[72] Eventually, she secured Nelson Gross and Daniel Melnick to produce *Bal nègre* and began rehearsals in August, but not before writing several drafts of the script.[73] Following the revue format, which she felt had been the most successful for her company, Dunham proposed that *Bal nègre* be produced at a larger scale than *Tropical Revue*. It was to be set in three acts, and many of the dance numbers (e.g., "Nanigo," "Choro," "Haitian Roadside," "Shango," and "L'ag'ya") had been performed in *Tropical Revue*, *Heat Wave*, and even earlier productions. According to one report, Dunham had set a goal of grossing $1.5 million from *Bal nègre* to help fund her school.[74] Thus, along with proposing "expert staging," "expert costuming," and original music, she planned for the revue to feature virtuoso musicians, native drummers

FIG. 4.1 Dunham School of Dance and Theatre advertisement. From the *New York Amsterdam News*, January 12, 1946, 19.

and instrumentalists, and additional featured groups. One of the featured musicians was to be "Cuban drum virtuoso" Chano Pozo, whom she proposed to feature in the second part of "Haitian Roadside." As mentioned in previous chapters, Pozo had achieved national and international recognition by 1941 as a percussionist, composer, and stage entertainer. It should be no surprise, therefore, that Dunham planned to feature him playing multiple conga drums as he "furnishe[d] the accompaniment for 'Primitive Rhythms B,'" the choreography for which consisted of a "pas de quatre, pas de deux, ensemble variations, etc."[75] A revised version of the script indicates that Dunham eventually replaced two featured musicians, Pozo and Bobby Capo, with another, Gilberto Valdés, whom Dunham hired as the orchestra director. In addition to directing, Valdés con-

gap b/w
Dunham intervention + audience
interest

tributed several of his compositions, including "Ilé-nku Ilé-nbe," which was featured as the revue's overture.[76]

After premiering to very positive reviews on September 13, 1946, at the Schubert Theatre in Philadelphia, *Bal nègre* opened in New Haven before playing at the Belasco Theatre in New York City for six weeks in November and December. Predictably, reviewers writing for both black and white newspapers and periodicals characterized Dunham as a scientific researcher of primitive dance and a sultry dancer of film and the Broadway stage—the "Dunham schizophrenia," as John Martin put it.[77] These same writers described the dancing, accordingly, as flashy, undulating, highly sexed, and orgiastic, while they characterized the dance numbers as interpretive or authentic. In either case, they regarded the dances as primitive or modern, referring to the former as a "frenzied jubilee of uninhibited tropical passions," and to the latter as "jive."[78] Other reviewers noted that parts 1 and 2 of the three-part revue featured songs sung mostly in Spanish and whose setting was exclusively the West Indies. The part 3, on the other hand, evoked nostalgic commentary on the golden age of 1920s jazz.[79]

Rarely did reviewers assess the social significance of the actual dancing and music of Dunham's productions. One rare example was Dan Burley, who in his "Back Door Stuff" column dating back to 1943 made the following telling assessment: "Katherine Dunham is today to dancing what Duke Ellington has been to swing music. The importance of what she is doing cannot be minimized. That is why she has been accepted so widely as the ultimate in Negro dancers and choreographers. What she doesn't do is more important, in a sense, than what she does, for Katherine Dunham and her dancers never seem to overexert themselves as might be expected. Instead, their art is so subtle and expressive that even the twitch of a shoulder or the wink of an eye can speak volumes."[80] Burley's assertion that the dancers "never seem to overexert themselves as might be expected" represents an intentional foil to the exoticized and eroticized reportage of almost all of the other critics, much of which derived from Dunham's own promotional material. For what Burley achieves here is not unlike Edwin Denby's assessment of Asadata Dafora's company, a kind of meditation on their bodies' most subtle movements that enabled a critique of the capacity of exoticism and eroticism to temporalize and spatialize individuals out of their present situations. Indeed, Burley does not attribute such powerfully subtle movements to any one category of dance, whether West Indian or American Negro, primitive or modern, authentic or interpretive. Rather, it seems as though he was able to listen past the sonic signifiers employed by Dunham's musicians, including the "native" drummers, to accompany these varying

DISALIENATING MOVEMENT AND SOUND / 191

dances while at the same time analyze their movements past the textual signifiers in the programs, not to mention their racialized and sexed bodies. Denby himself commented on the "provocative and yet discreet" and modest character of Dunham's dancing and the overall "pelvic litheness" of her dancers in her production, demonstrating in no uncertain terms his modernist predilections for abstracting meaning from movement and not the racialized body itself.[81]

However, Burley does not say much about the musicality of Dunham's movements (as Denby did of Dafora's dancers) except to equate her with Duke Ellington in terms of their importance to Negro dance and music, respectively. As jazz historians today readily credit Ellington for helping to develop jazz as an art form, dance scholars similarly credit Dunham for having established Negro dance as a black self-represented modern art form.[82] Burley's and Denby's assessments thus represent two rare examples whereby Dunham's and her dancers' self-identificatory aspirations in movement were recognized. For most other critics, audiences, and even her promoters at the time, Dunham's work continued to provoke mixed and contradictory reactions. For instance, by the time of its New York premiere, Dunham's producers Gross and Melnick promoted *Bal nègre* as "A Musical Revue of Caribbean Exotica."[83] Previously, in New Haven, they had promoted the production as a "torrid, sexy attraction," to which Dunham objected and about which she complained publicly, threatening to walk out if her promoters did not change their advertising style.[84] An article published in the *Chicago Defender* quoted Dunham stating, "I hate this kind of advertising. My show is a serious and artistic study of native Negro dances. The only thing torrid and sexy about the revue is the dirty minds of those customers who come to see sex." Perhaps Dunham's public rebuke of her producers' advertising methods was a promotional tactic itself given that *Tropical Revue* and *Bal nègre* did indeed feature dances such as "Barrel House" whose intentions were in part erotic.[85]

But the most damning criticism of Dunham came from Ezra Goodman, a film critic who happened to write a review of *Bal nègre* for the January 1947 volume of *Dance* magazine. While we can attribute his opinion that Dunham was "an inferior dancer" for "not using her body in a vital, creative pattern of movements" to a flawed or narrow application of modern dance aesthetics (compare with Denby's modernist assessments of Dunham's and Dafora's dancing), Goodman's accusation that Dunham was "exploiting the ethnic of a people" was in fact a fair question.[86] In citing her credentials as an anthropologist, author, and educator, he asserts that Dunham has the obligation to be the "custodian of a minority people's folkways." "In a world troubled by suspicion, ignorance and intolerance," he continues, "her role as a dancer-sociologist could constitute her a true ambassador of the arts." Instead, he concludes, "Miss Dunham has seen fit to ... dish up an ethnic without ethic, to turn her material into voodoo-jungle frenzies in Hollywood's best Technicolor tradition." Goodman's review provoked impassioned letters to the editor of *Dance* magazine condemning his accusations and defending Dunham's "transformations" of her "raw material" as her "privilege as an artist."[87] It was Goodman's article, furthermore, that compelled Dorathi Bock Pierre, the administrative director of the Katherine Dunham School of Arts and Research, to write the article "Katherine Dunham: Cool Scientist or Sultry Performer?" for the May volume of *Dance*, for which she interviewed Dunham.[88] In the article, Pierre affirms that Dunham is both a "torrid, sultry performer" and a "cool, analytical scientist," but, more importantly, she is, quoting Dunham, "only interested in dance as an education, as a means of knowing peoples, and I want students who want to learn and have a desire to develop peoples and tastes."

Goodman's critique and the letters to the editor raise what at first appears to constitute the two opposing types of theater in Gilles Deleuze's philosophy of performance, the theater of representation and the theater of presence.[89] The latter attends to the escaping of institutionalized representation namely by depending on the purposeful disruptions to this kind of representation generated in the actions of repetition and variations themselves. Key to the ethics of Deleuze's theater of presence is the subtraction of not merely representations of power but also actual representation itself *as power*, the actions of which bring the performers and audiences closer to the real. In short, it is difference generated in the act of repetition, according to Deleuze, wherein the "real" or, better yet, perception of sameness resides. Dunham's most successful actions toward creating a theater of presence, wherein her company exposed anthropology's and jazz criticism's power to represent as power itself, took hold in their earliest performances of *Heat Wave: From Haiti to Harlem*, before she and Hurok replaced anthropological satire with sex. But even then, the sameness desired by Goodman and most other spectators of Dunham's productions resided not in the minority people's ethnic or folkways to be represented on stage but rather in their desiring of sameness or authenticity itself. Dunham was correct when she located the sex attributed to her productions in none other than "the dirty minds of those customers who come to see sex." Goodman, it seemed, went to see the ethnic of a minority people and thus did not see and hear Dunham's re-presentings of *her own experiences* in the world, re-presentations in which she actively muddled the distinctions between her scientist and performer selves. She, as did Pearl Primus and Zora Neale Hurston, found such tactics not only useful but necessary as an American Negro woman.

But not all of Dunham's spectators fell into representation's epistemological straitjacket as did Goodman. Richard A. Long, a black student at Temple University, was inspired to represent the affectivity of Dunham's performance in *Bal nègre* in a poem he titled "Dance Movements":

Shorn of the impedimenta of time and place,
Rhythm is abstracted, color-inlaid,
Fused with pulse-urgency.
The jungle path is thick and dark.
Passion alone is the swift spark
That can send light racing across
Thick, vine-entangled fern, and moss.
Passion, long compressed, is now free
Sweeping a sirocco through me.
Subtle the speech of forms now still, now wind-gyrated,
Subtle the beat of the drum,
Subtle the path the dancer insinuates before my eye.[90]

The poem's references to Africa are indeed subtle; moreover, we can observe Long's sense of equilibrium and freedom in his own temporal present. We need only read the first line to be convinced that what Long was expressing at the moment is what Fanon intended to capture with his notion of disalienation. Long's poem, therefore, joins Dunham's, Burley's, and the Okalas' recognitions of the dislodgments of racialized subjects, whether within the domains of anthropology or entertainment, and it is these recognitions that embody the kinds of action that Fanon theorized as having the capacity to rectify one's presence in modernity's present. As we will see in the next section, the pervasive and pernicious dislodgments of the racialized subject's present condition also swelled from the very histories and agents of freedom themselves.

Freedom from the Pathology of Freedom

As discussed in chapter 3, the decolonization movement led by African activists in the United States intensified after delegates to the United Nations Conference on International Organization in 1945 failed to guarantee a plan for the decolonization of Africa. In addition to Asadata Dafora and the African Academy of Arts and Research, other activists and organizations worked continuously to raise awareness of European colonialism in Africa by linking decolonization to the domestic struggle for civil rights. Among these organizations was the Council on African Affairs, whose rallies calling for the liberation of the "oppressed people of Africa and other imperialist-dominated lands" received the support of Eleanor Roosevelt, Albert Einstein, Leonard Bernstein, black American ministers, and other public figures.[91] But the joint actions taken to realize decolonization and civil rights were not always successful, due in no small measure to the emergence of Cold War politics.[92] In the months leading up to the House Un-American Activities Committee's opening hearings in October 1947, Paul Robeson, W. E. B. Du Bois, and other black activists publically denounced government proposals to outlaw the Communist Party as a fascist measure threatening American Negroes and other minorities, while they also held rallies in support of African decolonization.[93] Then the annual "Negro Freedom Rally" at Madison Square Garden took place on June 16 and was to include Nigerian nationalist leader Nnamdi Azikiwe. However, Azikiwe pulled out after members of the Universal Africa Nationalist Movement protested the rally, accusing it of being "communist dominated."[94] The African Academy of Arts and Research, which had sponsored the rally in past years, also disavowed any involvement with the 1947 rally. According to one report, organizers of the "Negro Freedom Rally" in turn denounced the African protesters' "black nationalism" and accused them of protesting the rally's inclusion of white speakers.[95]

Whereas the strain in the coalition among American Negro civil rights and African anticolonial activists emerged in part from the divisive forces of domestic Cold War politics, Liberia's centennial of July 26, 1947, entailed a renewed yet no less ambivalent articulation of African and black American cooperation to a shared history steeped in slavery, freedom, nation building, and modernity. The week before the "Negro Freedom Rally," on June 7, the National Committee for the American Celebration of Liberia's Centennial, representatives of the Liberian government, and the Liberian Centennial Commission met in Washington, DC, to plan for the West African republic's centennial celebration.[96] The three-person American committee consisted of William Dawson, a black Democratic congressman from Illinois; Perry Howard of the National Republican Committee of Mississippi; and Frank Stanley, president of the Negro Newspaper Publishers Association. An executive committee for the centennial's American organization included Mary McLeod Bethune, Charles S. Johnson, and Rayford Logan, while in the preceding weeks, invitations to join a committee at large had been offered to Marian Anderson, W. E. B. Du Bois, Alain Locke, Lionel Hampton, George Schuyler, Duke Ellington, and other black leaders in politics, education, and entertainment.

In addition to discussing plans for the celebrations in both countries, the American committee announced three commissions, for composers Duke Ellington and James E. Dorsey and poet Melvin G. Tolson, whose works celebrating the centennial were to be premiered and broadcast live on July 26.[97] Ellington accepted the commission at a public ceremony, where he was photographed with Moss H. Kendrix (executive secretary of the National Committee), Ruth Spencer (president of the Baker's Dozen Youth Center in Washington, DC), and Willis Conover (wwdc radio announcer), but he would not premiere his new composition, *Liberian Suite*, until December.

Into his third decade as an orchestra leader, composer, and recording artist, Ellington continued to maneuver strategically in and around the paradoxical strictures of the jazz industry, especially in regard to critics' identifications of his music with "jungle jazz," swing, modern jazz, or, in Rudi Blesh's opinion, "ridiculous and pretentious," "hollow and stagy" jazz.[98] Ellington instead staked his and his music's identity on the stability implied in the New Negro ideal of self-identification such that his and his musicians' aesthetic principles of creating "authentic Negro music" were inspired not by prescribed definitions of swing or jazz but rather by, as he stated, "our lives, and the lives of those about us, and those that went before us."[99] Ellington's understanding of American Negro history indeed carried a deep significance in his formulation of his ideals and principles, as his following statement from 1932 further attests: "The music of my race is something more than the 'American idiom.' It is the result of our transplantation to American soil, and was our reaction in the plantation days to the tyranny we endured. What we could not say openly we expressed in music, and what we know as 'Jazz' is something more than just dance music."[100] Africa, on the other hand, seemed to occupy an elusive, even contradictory place in his formulations of his ideals and principles. At various times in his career Ellington proclaimed, "Jazz had its origin in Africa" (1931), "Even the Negroid element in jazz turns out to be less African than American" (1947), or "After writing African music for 35 years, here I am at last in Africa!" (1966).[101] In reality, he knew who is audience was, whether he was performing or giving interviews, such that we can attribute the inconsistencies of these statements, respectively, to inquiries about his music's evolution, to his music's legitimization among music educators, and to his presence in Senegal at the invitation of president Léopold Sédar Senghor. His engagements with African history in his actual music showed similar instances of ambivalence, if strategically so.

From as early as 1930 Ellington planned to compose a multimovement piece narrating the "history of the Negro," beginning in Africa. According to one early report, the music was to take the "Negro from Egypt, going with him to savage Africa, and from there to the sorrow and slavery of Dixie, and finally 'home to Harlem.'"[102] By 1933 he conceived of the piece as a suite in five parts, titled "Africa," "The Slave Ship," "The Plantation," "Harlem," and a finale.[103] As

Brian Priestley and Alan Cohen suggest, his plans for a "negro suite" in five parts eventually materialized as *Black, Brown and Beige*, which Ellington described as a "tone parallel" of the history of the Negro in the United States, but not after reportedly admitting in 1941 that he was "having trouble in representing the Negro American as he is today, what he wants, what he's got, what he's tried to get and didn't, how he is going to get it."[104]

The Ellington orchestra premiered *Black, Brown and Beige* in Carnegie Hall on January 23, 1943. Besides forming a prominent part of Ellington's oeuvre, *Black, Brown and Beige*, including his earliest plans for the work, joined Sallie W. Stewart's *Ethiopia Lifts as She Climbs* (1933), *O, Sing a New Song* (1934), and the many other pageant-like performances of American Negro history in which Modupe Paris, Katherine Dunham, Asadata Dafora, and others participated. It is important to note that the first part of the "Brown" section of the tone parallel included what Ellington described as a dedication to the "700 Negroes who came from Haiti to save Savannah, Georgia during the Revolutionary War, so we call it 'The West Indian influence.'" He marked this "West Indian influence" by using a *tresillo*, or "Latin" rhythm, for this section's rhythmic and melodic phrasing.[105] The Carnegie Hall concert's program notes added that this "West Indian influence" was an "important one to the whole Negro character."[106] Whereas Ellington's inclusion of Haiti lent his tone parallel of Negro history a hemispheric dimension, the absence of Africa suggests otherwise. Indeed, performances of the African slave and the native savage, as we saw in the previous chapter, entailed difficult ideological, political, and social consequences, particularly for black Americans such as Paul Robeson, which might explain why Ellington chose to leave Africa out of *Black, Brown and Beige*'s programmatic narrative. Would representing Liberian history in music pose similar challenges to Ellington's ideals and principles as those confronted by Robeson and others?

Liberia, the sole republic of West Africa, held a precarious, complex, and conflicted place in the thinking of most American Negro and non–Liberian African intellectuals and political leaders. In his memoir *Music Is My Mistress* (1973), Ellington states that the "moods and rhythms" of the five movements in his *Liberian Suite* "were related to what I knew of the Liberian past and present."[107] What he knew of Liberia at the time of his commission was in no doubt shaped by the propaganda generated by the National Committee for the American Celebration of Liberia's Centennial as well as by the Liberian government itself. It is also very likely that he had come across what Alain Locke, George Schuyler, and others had written about Liberia in the early 1930s, perhaps even what Marcus Garvey and W. E. B. Du Bois had also written in the 1920s—

all of whom attempted to grapple with Liberia's social and political standing within the context of European colonialism and American imperialism.

"By an irony too tragic to dwell on, a small black republic, itself founded in 1847 under anti-slavery auspices as an asylum from American slavery, has just been pilloried in the stocks of world opinion as an internationally indicted slave-holder and oppressor of labor."[108] This is how Locke began his essay "Slavery in the Modern Manner" (1931), in which he commented on the findings of the League of Nations' International Commission on Forced Labor in Liberia published in 1930. After years of rumors, complaints, and investigations concerning the forced export of native Liberian laborers to the Spanish island of Fernando Po, the League of Nations, with the approval of the Liberian government, commissioned a three-man committee to investigate any such practices. The committee, consisting of sociologist Charles S. Johnson, British medical doctor Cuthbert Christy, and former Liberian president Arthur Barclay, did indeed find that some government elected officials and appointees under the administration of president Charles D. B. King, with the collusion of some native chiefs, had forced laborers to work on government projects and had plotted with the Firestone Company to forcibly export laborers. Among the elected officials who were indicted was senator (and future president) W. V. S. Tubman.[109] For his part, George Schuyler went on assignment to Liberia in early 1931 for the *New York Evening Post*, and the articles and editorials he wrote there were also published in the *Washington Post*, the *Afro-American*, the *Pittsburgh Courier*, the *Philadelphia Tribune*, and other newspapers, both black and white, across the United States.[110] Schuyler reported on slave labor, sex slaves, native children who had been pawned, and the tributes exacted of natives, attributing these practices to Liberian officials in Monrovia, and he complained that, first, these officials were blocking reforms mandated by the International Commission, and, second, the largely black American missionaries in Liberia remained "silent on Liberian outrages."

Marcus Garvey, in 1924, had already criticized what he called the Americo-Liberian oligarchy in Monrovia for its exploitation of native Liberians and obstruction of his plans to realize Liberia as the black Zion, whereas Du Bois, even after traveling to Liberia beginning in 1923, perpetuated what many black Americans believed and what Ibrahim Sundiata described as a "mythic Africa visualized from the Diaspora and projected back onto the continental reality."[111] Writing in 1924, Du Bois praised the virtues of both city life in Monrovia and native life of the bush. Liberia, in symbolizing the whole of Africa, was for Du Bois the "Spiritual Frontier of human kind," where "life is slow . . . life slows down . . . a civilization without coal, without noise," all the while ignoring the nation's caste system, which marked Americo-Liberians as the politically dominant ethnic minority in Monrovia, who exerted their power over the nation's native populations which included the Vai, Kpelle, Gola, Grebo, Kru, and others.[112] By the time the International Commission report and Schuyler's articles were published in 1930 and 1931, Du Bois as well as Locke, Azikiwe, and others were careful to attribute Liberia's troubled situation not merely to government corruption but also to economic imperialism, which, they all argued, affected much of the world, not only Africa and not only the colonial world. The United States, too, practiced forced labor within its territories as well as in Liberia by virtue of the role that the Firestone Company played in Liberia's forced labor practices. Economic freedom was linked directly to personal freedom, and thus colonialism and imperialism, not to mention Jim Crowism, were in their view merely clandestine modern forms of slavery. They argued all of this as bulwarks against the racist exploitation of the Liberian situation as proof of the inability of the "black man's incapacity for self-government," an argument that had also been used in rationalizing the American occupation of Haiti starting in 1915.[113]

Liberia represented yet another African past for some black Americans and Americo-Liberians alike, a past whose consummation in the resettlement in West Africa of freed American and African slaves beginning in the early nineteenth century was invoked and celebrated in the discourse of the nation's centennial. The discursive formation of this more distant yet equally troubled past, centering on the notion of a common ancestry of black Americans and Americo-Liberians, can be attributed to the "mythic Africa" upheld among some black Americans as well as to the Liberian government's ongoing efforts to repair and reconstitute its image following the 1930 and 1931 reports. Ellington's press agent and adherent to jazz's progressive and modernist purview, Leonard Feather, wrote the program notes for the Carnegie Hall concert in which *Liberian Suite* premiered. Both his and Ellington's descriptions of the suite, along with contemporaneous Liberian and American reports surrounding the centennial, and the wording of his commission itself suggest that all parties were in concert with representing the Americo-Liberian elite—and not Liberia's native populations—as the brethren of black Americans, and Liberia as the beacon of colonized nations in and beyond Africa aspiring to democratic self-rule.

In its official commission, dated June 7, 1947, the National Committee for the American Celebration of Liberia's Centennial made clear its rationale for choosing Ellington to compose a musical tribute to the centenary. The commission celebrates Ellington as a "composer and proponent of modern musical development" whose musical works "embrace the toils and struggles of mankind." The commission mandated that Ellington "prepare a musical score *depicting the inception and national growth* of this member of the World Family of Nations."[114] In the days leading up to the premiere of *Liberian Suite*, newspapers published excerpts of the concert's press release, which described the piece, accordingly, as a "serious study with themes *depicting the growth and development* of the small West African republic."[115] At least one report included the following brief historical fact of Liberia's founding—it was "first settled as a colony by American Negroes in 1822."[116] Thus, Ellington's commissioned composition was to be a modernist work representing the nation's progress from its founding by freed American slaves to its current status as a modern African republic. At the time of the premiere of his *Black, Brown and Beige*, Ellington characterized his band as the "only serious exponents of Negro music."[117] We might thus situate *Liberian Suite* as a product of his aesthetic principles based not on European models of composition, an inference made from his other extended compositions that he had always disavowed, but rather on his and his musicians' commitment to self-identification based on their lived experiences as Negro men.[118] But Ellington's convictions, musical or otherwise, were often ironic by design, which was as much an expression of his New Negro ideals and aesthetic principles as his putting into action his belief that what he was unable to say openly could be expressed in music.

In the program for the Carnegie Hall concerts of December 26 and 27, Leonard Feather quotes Ellington's own explanation of *Liberian Suite*'s intentions, in which he creates through a use of subtle irony the rhetorical space to simultaneously celebrate Liberia's centennial and disavow the nation's official historical narrative of freedom, national unity, and progress:

> This is the spirit in which the republic of Liberia was founded. In this work we salute a group of people who decided to go to Africa and set up a government. They sailed away, with little more than hope to spur them on, and the land they had bought and paid for had to be fought for, inch by inch, as hostile tribes were encountered. But in 1847 they established themselves and were recognized by the major powers of the world as a nation. So today, on the occasion of the one hundredth anniversary of the foundation of Liberia, we interpret the event musically in a gay spirit of celebration.[119]

The spirit in which Liberia was founded and developed was in fact one of hope and hostilities, beneficence and aggression, international recognition and condemnation. As the Monrovia newspaper the *Liberian Age* retold the story in the months leading up to the centenary, the black colonists who founded Liberia were sponsored by the American Colonization Society, and up until the time of the presidency of Hilary R. M. Johnson (1884–1891), American-born Liberians filled the chief executive chair.[120] The American Colonization Society was formed in the United States in 1816 by a group of abolitionists and proponents of slavery in order to resettle free blacks in Africa; as Claude A. Clegg III explains, however, this unlikely coalition of Americans pursued resettlement for freed blacks for divergent beliefs, including that blacks could not attain true liberty in a white dominated society, and that free blacks posed a threat to the regime of slavery in slave states.[121]

The "group of people" that Ellington referred to as establishing the nation of Liberia were eighty-eight free American blacks who, under the auspices of agents of the American Colonization Society and, by extension, the American government, purchased by force from a native chief Cape Mesurado (current-day Monrovia) on the West African coast in 1822. For the next few decades, the black American colonists who continued to receive freed blacks from the United States battled malaria, extreme weather conditions, and so-called hostile tribes, namely, the Dei and Gola, as they established by force additional settlements along the coast. All the while the black American colonists differentiated themselves in language, religion, dress, and social organization, which Clegg III and Yekutiel Gershoni argue served as their rationale for claiming racial and cultural superiority over neighboring native African populations, whom they regarded as heathens and uncivilized. Thus, their shared sense of community and citizenship rested on a sense of a providential purpose in the civilizing experiment they were undertaking, a worldview that drove the black American colonists toward declaring their independence in 1847.[122] Over the next one hundred years, the *Liberian Age* proclaimed, "there is not recorded one revolution within her borders, administrations have thru the ages peacefully assumed the reins of government. . . . Liberia has been very fortunate to have leaders for the moment and they have been all God fearing men receiving the respect of the international world."[123] In reality, between 1884 and 1946, native chiefs did not have representation in the legislature, a policy that was initiated by the nation's first president born in Liberia, Hilary R. M. Johnson, but reversed by president William V. S. Tubman in time for the nation's centenary.[124]

Returning to the concert program notes, the following paragraph gives more insight into Ellington's conception of *Liberian Suite* and, in so doing, further indication as to his wishes for perhaps not the Liberian nation but instead its native populations, who had suffered under the tyranny of Americo-Liberian domination: "The work comprises five dances—parallel, says Duke, with the four freedoms '*and the fifth that we hope for.*' The five parts are punctuated by a device borrowed from Billy Strayhorn, linking the movements together" (my emphasis).[125] Here we see that Ellington reaffirms the shared demands of civil rights and freedom from colonial oppression that K. O. Mbadiwe and many other African and black American leaders had invoked as well. His reference to Franklin Roosevelt's Four Freedoms (freedom of speech, religion, from want, and from fear) is his most forthright reflection on Liberia's one-hundred-year history, about which the official Liberian narrative also commented, including in regard to the recently guaranteed rights granted to its native citizens. In anticipation of the arrival of foreign dignitaries and visitors to Monrovia to participate in centenary celebrations, the *Liberian Age* published two articles, "We Welcome You—Meet Our President" and "The Tubman Administration 1944–1947," in which were listed all of President Tubman's recent legislative accomplishments, including guaranteeing all citizens the right to employment, securing congressional seats for "three Representatives purely natives from the hinterland," and women's suffrage.[126] It is important to note, however, that these articles, while praising President Tubman's progressive policies, also congratulated the nation for "having all but completely conquered the jungle wilderness" and referred to native Liberians as the "uncivilized element," indicating that the Americo-Liberian ontological worldview of the nineteenth century as modern civilization's purveyors in Africa remained unbroken.

So, then, how free did Ellington believe Liberia's native populations to really be? What was the fifth freedom that he hoped for? Did the answers to these questions have anything to do with Strayhorn's musical device or devices linking together the suite's five parts? In programmatically reading the music of *Liberian Suite* as performed at its premiere Carnegie Hall concerts, and its reception, several possible answers to these questions emerge.[127] The roughly thirty-minute suite opened with the slow ballad "I Like the Sunrise" sung by Al Hibbler, the protagonist of which expresses hope for a bright, new tomorrow in the face of the nighttime's dreariness. In his introduction to the *Liberian Suite* at the December 27 concert, Ellington, from the stage, described it as starting with "the spirit in which this small group of people set out to establish a government in Africa." The song text clearly narrates the kind of hope and struggle experienced by the founders of Liberia, former slaves, but since the lyrics do not contain specific historical references, nor even mention of Liberia, it can also describe any oppressed group's hopes for a better future, including Liberia's native populations who remained under the political and ideological yoke of the dominant Americo-Liberian minority. The piece is in *aaba* thirty-two-bar song form. After Hibbler's first verse, the music transitions into a har-monically unstable and dissonant eight-bar interlude featuring Harry Carney's baritone saxophone solo, the first seven bars of which are based on a pentatonic scale. The dreariness of the "nighttime" is then invoked by particular features in the second verse's arrangement, the first two sections of which are led by Car-ney while the orchestra emphasizes every other beat with drawn-out half-note chords. Sonny Greer, meanwhile, strikes every quarter-beat on the floor tom, accentuating the feeling of drudgery not unlike that conveyed in the use of the floor toms in "Work Song" from *Black, Brown and Beige*.

Recalling Ellington's enumeration of the suite's first four dances with Roosevelt's Four Freedoms, "Dance No. 1" is supposed to express the freedom of speech. Read programmatically, however, nothing explicit occurs in any of these instrumental dances to suggest the Four Freedoms. Furthermore, the concert's program notes describe this first dance as the "building of a nation" and as having, "says Ellington, a sexual beat," notions that hardly represent the theme of freedom of speech. Rather than only seeking to read such pro-grammatic explanations into the music, we might instead take into account Ellington's overarching definition of jazz as the "freedom of musical speech" unrestrained by musical form to convey the feelings, thoughts, and experiences of a people.[128] He expressed his preference for dissonance, for instance, as one musical device that he believed represented the "Negro's life": "Dissonance is our way of life in America. We are something apart yet an integral part."[129] The devices he attributed to his arranger, Billy Strayhorn—dissonant chords along with pentatonic, octatonic, and whole-tone scales—are indeed the most recur-ring characteristics of *Liberian Suite* and thus link its otherwise stylistically and structurally distinct movements. As such, the dissonance Ellington attributed to the Negro experience of belonging yet not belonging in the United States can similarly be attributed to the native situation of marginality and disenfranchise-ment in Liberia. It is, it seems, Ellington's own career-long resistance to the domi-nant contingencies of jazz critics, the popular music industry, and the United States' political economy of race, including black civil rights organizations, that suggests what he hoped for as the fifth freedom, that is, the freedom from free-dom's pathologies, materialized in the context of Liberia as neocolonialism. Such a fifth freedom in the context of Liberian history pertained to the pathology of freedom and time that determined Americo-Liberian and native relations, which Ellington began gesturing toward in the lyrics of and musical devices used in "I Like the Sunrise."

"Dance No. 1" follows, with Oscar Pettiford's and Junior Raglin's bass line descending down a whole-tone scale before settling on a peddle G, at which point the trumpet and saxophone sections play mostly consecutive inversions of a G^7 chord with varying harmonic extensions drawn from the octatonic descending scale played by the trombones. Greer resumes striking every quarter-beat on the floor tom but at a faster tempo compared to the tempo set for "I Like the Sunrise." Screaming tone clusters played by the trumpet and saxophone sections follow over Greer's incessant quarter-note beats on the floor tom, conveying a sense of laborious work, as in "building a nation." After additional whole-tone and octatonic scalar passages, played first by Jimmy Hamilton on the clarinet, followed by other sections of the orchestra, the main section of the dance in ternary form begins, featuring Al Sears's tenor saxophone over a moderate swing beat executed by Greer and Elaine Jones on timpani, this perhaps being the "sexual beat" referred to as such by Ellington. The A and B sections hover over F minor and B-flat minor chords, respectively, thus lending this dance a harmonically static quality, which may be read to counteract the sense of progress otherwise implicit in the notion of "building a nation."

"Dance No. 2," which Ellington described as expressing a "gayer mood," is in cut time and features clarinetist Hamilton and vibraphonist (and trombonist) Tyree Glenn. The piece is built on two disjointed sections, the first of which is again harmonically static, with the exception of its first two iterations, which include a harmonic and melodic passage built on whole-tone scales. The B section, based on an altered sixteen-bar blues form, is less tonally unpredictable. After Glenn's extended vibraphone solo, based on the B section's altered sixteen-bar blues form, the orchestra returns to repeat the B section before playing the outro.

"Dance No. 3" follows, contrasting dramatically in style, which Ellington described as a "sort of Afromantique." His description's allusion to blackness and romanticism seems to be borne out in the bass's habanera rhythmic ostinato and the tango-like arpeggiated figures played on the violin by Ray Nance. In fact, in an earlier handwritten draft of this movement, its title was given as "Rhumba, Dance No. 3," further indicating that Ellington, as he had done in the "Brown" of *Black, Brown and Beige*, intended to incorporate the sounds of the Caribbean and Latin America into this tone parallel of Liberian history. Yet no Caribbean or Latin American nation, with the exception of Haiti, factored in Liberian history. In the decades leading up to the colonization of Liberia, Haiti seemed to be the most promising nation to which some freed black Americans aspired to emigrate and, in fact, American abolitionists succeeded in sending freed blacks to both Haiti and Liberia during the 1820s and 1830s. Moreover, black American political leaders and pan-Africanists rose to both Haiti's and Liberia's defense in the late 1920s and 1930s, when the former black republic was under American occupation, while the latter was in danger of falling under foreign occupation as well.[130] Thus, the fact that "rhumba," the habanera rhythm, and tango are not typically associated with Haitian music did not take away from the more immediate necessity, at least in Ellington's estimation, of situating Liberian history within a broader Negro history that transcended the structural boundaries of the modern nation-state. In other words, Ellington seemed to be paralleling his music's freedom from conventional jazz or classical musical forms with the freedom from neocolonialism's contingencies of official national narratives, not to mention of colonialism and imperialism as well, a gesture indeed toward a fifth freedom from the contingencies of another's subjective formations in the world.

The concert program describes "Dance No. 4" as a "galloping affair" and quotes Ellington further characterizing this dance as being "full of the velocity of celebration." After fifteen repetitions of a two-bar ostinato phrase, played in a bright tempo, drummer Greer and timpanist Jones perform solos, which are interspersed with orchestral interludes characterized by simple melodic themes that are harmonized in block chords for the saxophone section. "Dance No. 5" features, according to the program, "an exotic bass figure" along with a signature Ellingtonian wah-wah trombone solo played by Tyree Glenn. For a finale, this dance is set in a seemingly misplaced moderate tempo, with relatively sparse orchestrated material. The "exotic bass figure," which Ellington doubles on the piano, stresses the tonic, fourth, raised fourth, and fifth of F minor, while rhythmically it is very reminiscent of contemporaneous cubop patterns such as the bass figure in Chano Pozo and Dizzy Gillespie's "Manteca," which was recorded the same month as *Liberian Suite*'s premiere. The bass figure's exotic quality is amplified by the music's harmonically unstable and dissonant character. Indeed, this final dance's harmonic language moves slowly, starting in F minor, to the not so tonally distant but nevertheless dissonant chords F major, D-flat^7, A-flat^7, and C^7, which include flat and raised fifths, flat ninths, and sharped sevenths, ninths, and elevenths.

Jazz critics at the time of its premiere paid relatively little attention to the *Liberian Suite* compared to the wide critical reception *Black, Brown and Beige* had received. The newspapers that did publish reports on the piece's premiere nevertheless represented a diverse range of black newsprint media, including mainstream black newspapers (e.g., the *New York Amsterdam News* and the *New Journal and Guide*), leftist black newspapers (e.g., the *People's Voice*), and African anticolonial newspapers (e.g., the *African*). In addition to reporting on Ellington's commission and the premiere concert, these newspapers also covered a luncheon honoring Ellington and hosted by the National Committee for the American

Celebration that took place on the afternoon of December 26.[131] Guest speakers at the gathering included Mary McLeod Bethune; Channing H. Tobias, director of the Phelps-Stokes Fund (an American philanthropic organization that had supported American involvement in instituting Liberian reforms following the 1930 report and during the crisis of Liberian independence); and former Liberian president Charles D. B. King.[132]

After seventeen years the League of Nations' report of forced labor in Liberia was, according to the *Liberian Age*, "still green in the minds of Liberians."[133] For King in particular his resignation from the presidency following the report's implication of his administration in the scandal was also a source of embarrassment, though he remained within Monrovia's circle of oligarchic power.[134] Thus he attended both Ellington's luncheon and the premiere concert as an official representative of the government with the title "First Minister Plenipotentiary of Liberia." The concert, unfortunately, occurred on the same day that a snowstorm hit New York City, which significantly delayed the concert's start. Although the event had sold out, reports indicate that only half of the seats were filled. Apart from these logistical challenges, writers complained that the orchestra's performance was marred by "insufficient rehearsal" and "sadly lacking in fire and technical execution," while others praised *Liberian Suite* as adding "another lustrous page to his considerable record of achievements" and being "perhaps the best work from the Ellington pen."[135] The program allotted time during the second half of the concert for King to deliver a speech in which he presented Ellington with an award on behalf of the Liberian government. In addition to thanking him for his piece, which he described as a "sensitive musical picture of the life and pulse of the Liberian Republic," King proclaimed that Ellington's "soul was in Africa."[136]

Once again, Africa's multitemporal and -spatial dimensions allowed for the primitive past to coexist alongside the modern present and the future, lending, in King's case, the ability to extol the nation's "remarkable progress" while not having "lost sight of the grass roots of the sacred rites of the jungle." King was not the only audience member to invoke Africa's temporal and spatial distance in situating the sound of *Liberian Suite*. The *New York Amsterdam News* identified the predominant characteristics of the five dances as the "jungle beat and exoticism of primitive emotions."[137] The same reviewer also complained that the fifth dance's use of "wow-wow blues [took] the suite from its locale and [placed] it in a medium of early American rag-time with all its banal tricks." The finale, the reviewer suggests, should have instead concluded with a "note of triumph," "a chant of exultation and jubilation . . . denoting a new day of freedom and progress for all races and nationalities."

These assessments of Ellington's *Liberian Suite* reiterated the kinds of temporal and spatial hypotheses about sound and racialized musicians that as a matter of course observers (both black and white) in Cuba, Africa, and the United States articulated to the notions of progress, the jungle, primitive emotions, and the nation. To be sure, Ellington as well often followed the same logic in reflecting on the history and nature of jazz music. But in relating this final anticlimactic movement, "Dance No. 5," to a "fifth [freedom] that we hope for," Ellington staked his relationship to the world via Liberian and African American history on a different logic. None of the anxieties, shame, or even pride having materialized in the embodiments of the African native and black Other explored in the previous chapter pertained to Ellington's formulation in this regard. Nor could charges of ethical transgression have been made against his participation in the centennial events so long, again, as his formulation of a fifth freedom was concerned, for it bespoke his judgment on the forestalled promise of real political and social progress—that which "we hope for"—for all oppressed people, black Americans and native Liberians alike. Even so, it is not enough to explain the *New York Amsterdam News*'s critique of the fifth dance by claiming that Ellington intentionally reserved such musical tropes of triumph in the pursuit of progress because of Liberia's history of oppression of its native peoples.

Instead, bringing to bear Günther Anders Sterns's notion of human action on Ellington's *assertion* of a fifth freedom restores its phenomenological independence beyond the legitimating limits of philosophical anthropology and epochal or historicist analysis.[138] In other words, his assertion of a fifth freedom (as understood here) has no obvious homologous relationship with the canonical structures of jazz historicism or Ellington's biography, a fact that helps explain the *Liberian Suite*'s relative obscurity in either canon. Opposed to the universals or generalizing of jazz criticism, white supremacy, New Negro ideology, acculturation theory, African origins, and so forth is, borrowing from Sterns, the "fact of human action." Ellington's proposal of a fifth freedom suggests a commentary on what he had always experienced and knew he would continue to experience as the impingement of another's freedom of being upon his own self-identities, whether such swellings of another's being in the world irrupted from the jazz industry, New Negro ideology, Africa, progress and modernity, or even American Negro civil rights organizations. His will to obtain freedom from the pathology of, for example, the will of the National Association for the Advancement of Colored People (NAACP) to freedom is indeed highly paradoxical, yet such a pathology emerged in fairly mundane ways.

Up until 1951, Ellington had maintained a long record of financial and political support for the work of the NAACP, the Council on African Affairs, and other civil rights and anticolonial organizations. His standing with the NAACP and with many black Americans soured, however, after a series of incidents occurring at two of his concerts brought to the fore, from Ellington's perspective, the impingements of both segregation and the NAACP's tactic of boycotting segregated public venues on his performances and livelihood. First, after J. M. Tinsley, the president of the Richmond branch of the NAACP, announced plans to boycott an Ellington orchestra concert that was to take place in January 1951 at the segregated venue the Mosque, Ellington decided to cancel the concert, expressing nevertheless his anger over the local branch's targeting of concerts featuring black musicians but not white musicians.[139] Indeed, earlier that month, not only did the Richmond branch of the NAACP boycott Marian Anderson's concert at the same segregated location, but Ellington's orchestra performed at a NAACP benefit concert at the Metropolitan Opera House, an event that reportedly raised fourteen thousand dollars for the civil rights organization's national office.

Then, later that year, Ellington's orchestra, along with Sarah Vaughan and Nat King Cole, were booked to perform at the Atlanta Municipal Auditorium. Shortly before the performance was to begin, the concert's black promoter, J. Neal Montgomery, in placating the demands of white policemen, announced to black ticket holders that they needed to enter the auditorium through a side entrance.[140] In order not to lose the five thousand dollars guaranteed to the musicians, Neal decided not to cancel the concert, but he as well as Ellington, Vaughan, and Cole felt indignant, not merely over the fact of segregation—Ellington and other jazz performers regularly but grudgingly accepted performances at segregated venues—but at the indeterminate way in which the city-owned auditorium's Jim Crow policy was doled out. According to reports, the last-minute decision to implement segregated access points to the venue was made after more black ticket holders than expected, four thousand in total, arrived at the venue. Only four hundred black ticket holders decided not to go in. After these and surely many more similar incidents of segregation and humiliation, Ellington lashed out to Otis Thompson, an *Afro-American* reporter, stating that the fight for integration was a "silly thing," that "nothing can be done" about Jim Crow, and that "we ain't ready yet." His inflammatory remarks were published widely and, unsurprisingly, were met with anger and disapproval from many readers.[141] Some editorial writers, however, did come to his defense, blaming, as had Ellington, both the indeterminate enforcement of Jim Crow and the NAACP's ill-conceived boycotting strategy, which affected black entertainers only. One editor concluded simply, "Like everybody else, Duke Ellington has to live in order to continue his artistic endeavors which indirectly benefit all of us."[142]

Whereas others have explained such conflicts as a result of the NAACP's transitions in ideology, tactics, and strategy over time, what Ellington's action did in attributing the fifth dance of the *Liberian Suite* to a fifth freedom "we hope for" is invite analytical attention to the self's subjective contingency as it rubs up against identification formations more desirous of power or simply more pathological.[143] Conceived of in this way, actions such as Ellington's discussed above suggest his desire of being emptied of others' determinations of the past, which Frantz Fanon and Katherine Dunham similarly hoped to attain for their own subjectivities in the present. Not unlike the pathology of freedom and time that Fanon detected in the request made by the Lyon Association of Overseas Students of France, Ellington—who indeed willingly took the position of authentic Negro music against European music and even jazz—did so, but without never experiencing at times feelings of consternation. Given the heavy investment demanded by identification formulations in the past, a bet that Fanon outright refused to take for its conferring "no patent of humanity on me," what if any cultural conventions were actually available for avowing the loss of spatialized and temporalized identities? Or was modernity's inability to once and for all grieve the contingency of its normative subjectivities (white, male, and straight) preempting the ontological promise of disalienation for all?

Movement and Sound in Nonobjective Time and Space

According to a report published in 1949, avant-garde film production in the United States had experienced an "unexpected outburst of concern and activity" due in part to the spread of film use and techniques during the war and the formation of film interest groups following the war.[144] Frank Stauffacher and Richard Foster led one of these groups, the Art in Cinema Society, which, with the sponsorship of the San Francisco Museum of Art, organized a series of avant-garde film showings starting in 1946.[145] Just three years earlier the San Francisco Museum of Art had sponsored Rudi Blesh's hot jazz lecture series, and it hosted the United Nations Conference on International Organization in 1945. From 1946 to 1954 the Art in Cinema film series featured experimental films by foreign filmmakers such as German émigré Oskar Fischinger as well as American filmmakers Maya Deren, John Whitney, James Whitney, Harry Smith, and many others. One of the technical and aesthetic concerns characterizing avant-garde filmmakers in the United States at this time was the manipulation of space and time by the use of "abstract images, colour and rhythm, as an experience in itself apart from their power to express thoughts or ideas."[146] Some of these filmmakers paired dance and music with various filmic techniques in their explorations into the fundamental nature of space and time. Harry Smith, in particular, pursued such experimentation in filmmaking and music in order to address his metaphysical questions concerning forces of the spiritual and physical worlds. In his films of the late 1940s, Smith indeed shattered linear unities of time and space, though in still adhering to binary logics of various sorts he never fully extricated himself from modernity's pathologies of identification.

In a letter written in 1950 to Hilla von Rebay, his patron and the artistic director of the Museum of Non-Objective Painting (later known as the Solomon R. Guggenheim Museum) in New York City, Smith explained the aim of his films in the following way: "To me, the soul is expressed in the relations that exists between the rhythm of the physical world and the rhythm of the spiritual world. In worldly life the limits imposed by the material state keep us from comprehending the ultimate physical unit or the ultimate spiritual unit, however our intuitive perception of the ever changing relation between the two clarifies them both. My films so far have been examinations of these forces."[147] In articulating the materialization of the human soul to what he believed to be the interrelated "rhythms" of the spiritual and physical worlds, Smith suggests in interesting ways the musical significances in his technical and aesthetic imperatives. In this regard, he continues, "these films are made up of visual percussions in strict time like music, and must be thought of by the mental sequences that integrate strongly rhythmic auditory sensations, for example, and not the ones used for stationary art." Although Smith claimed that his films were best shown silent, the fact is that by 1948 he began regularly incorporating live bebop and recorded cubop music into his film showings, even including in one of his films a painting that he created, the content of which represents the notes and rhythms of Chano Pozo and Dizzy Gillespie's "Manteca." Why, then, did Smith use bebop and cubop over other genres of music when choosing to show his films with music? His metaphysical conviction in the intuitive capacity of humans to create nonobjective art, his earlier activities and training as an anthropologist and comparative musicologist, and his drug use offer not only possible answers to this question but also insight into how binary logics of objectivity and nonobjectivity, of intuitive and learned, or even of space and time itself structured his understanding of the multiplicities of nature and everyday life.[148]

Before his first film showing in 1947, Smith had conducted extensive field recordings, along with musical transcriptions, on the Lummi and Salish reservations in the Pacific Northwest before matriculating at the University of Washington, where he studied anthropology from 1942 until 1944. He had also started to collect records of American folk music and had begun to use 35-millimeter film as a medium for his paintings. One of his more consequential early biographical events was his first experience smoking marijuana in 1944 in Berkeley, where he attended a Woody Guthrie concert, after which he decided to discontinue his formal training at the University of Washington and move to Berkeley and eventually to San Francisco.[149] From a young age and continuing throughout his career, Smith pursued what Rani Singh described as an "alchemical synthesis of the arts and sciences, which culminated in the melding of music, anthropology, linguistics, ethnology, film, occultism, design, and the plastic arts."[150] In pursuing his alchemical and metaphysical interests, however, Smith still conveyed (as did Rudi Blesh and other jazz critics at the time) commonly held understandings concerning race and folk music, such as that of the illiterate but intuitive and genius black musician. It is striking indeed to read in Smith's letters to Rebay, for instance, of his disdain for the very material world whose political economy of race, as analyzed thus far in the preceding three chapters, dictated the logical terms by which he and others racialized musicians as vehicles bearing human universal qualities that were increasingly endangered by a modernizing and oppressive world. Whereas he intended his films to transcend the temporal and spatial strictures generative of objective narratives, emotions, and formal structures, his conviction in what he and others considered to be the metaphysical, nonobjective, and intuitive qualities immanent in bebop musicians betrayed, as we will see, his rejection of the mechanizations of the macropolitical or material world. Such contradictions were, in fact, immanent in his initial uses of recorded music to accompany his films.

Smith's first contributions to the Art in Cinema series were his *Film No. 2*, *Film No. 3*, and *Film No. 4*. Scheduled for October 24, 1947, this showing's program included the film *Horror Dream* by Sidney Peterson and Hy Hirsch, with an original score by John Cage. The program lists Smith's films as "color animations," though he used this technique of hand painting designs in each of the frames only for *Film No. 2* and *Film No. 3*, and for *Film No. 1*, which he completed in 1946 but did not premiere until the Art in Cinema series showing of February 11, 1949.[151] Up until 1948, Smith's film showings were silent. According to his own account, he first realized that music could be put to his films after attending a Dizzy Gillespie concert in July 1948, when Gillespie's big band premiered at the Trianon Ballroom in San Francisco.[152] Smith recounted, "I had gone there very high, and I literally saw all kinds of colored flashes. It was at that point that I realized music could be put to my films."[153]

Ralph J. Gleason's review of Gillespie's San Francisco concert in *Down Beat* magazine gives important insight into the reception he and bebop music were garnering at the time, including the controversy surrounding Gillespie's stage antics as well as critical praise of his band's technical virtuosity and sonic power.[154] It also enables an ideologically broader context in which to analyze Smith's decision to incorporate bebop and cubop music into his films. Gleason listed Gillespie's "specials" of the night's performance as "Manteca," "Second Balcony Jump," "Good Bait," and "Things to Come," reporting that "by the time Dizzy got through playing Manteca and seated himself on top of the piano to play Second Balcony Jump the crowd was absolutely wild." Gillespie's big band had recorded "Manteca" for RCA Victor in December 1947, the cocomposer of which, Chano Pozo, was also the band's conga player. Indeed, much of the excitement over Gillespie's big band was centered on Pozo's stage presence and seamless integration of his conga playing with Teddy Stewart's drumming, about which Gleason stated, "[Pozo] and Stewart have so many rhythmic patterns worked out between them that they seem almost to act as one man many times." Gleason also dispelled jazz critics' charges of Gillespie's music being "without form" by noting that members of the audience sang along with the arrangements, which "couldn't be done if there weren't some definite pattern."

However positive Gleason was of the Gillespie band's performance, much of his review was intended to counteract the damning criticisms of Gillespie's and bebop's associations with "Mohammedanism," psychoanalysis, abstract art, drug use (heroin and cocaine, in addition to marijuana), elitism, cultism, and so on, which writers typically identified as evidence of the moral decay of modern life as well as of the decadence of jazz itself.[155] In other words, in rejecting or defending bebop, writers such as Gleason, Leonard Feather, John Hammond, Barry Ulanov, Ralph Ellison, and others were perpetuating the traditionalist-modernist debate that had started a decade earlier and that Katherine Dunham, Duke Ellington, and Dizzy Gillespie had satirized or else utilized, if only rhetorically, to further their professional careers. As for the not so subtle racial implications of bebop's associations, Harry Smith's decision to use Gillespie's records and live jazz musicians with his films owed as much to white American liberalism in all of its contradictions in regard to race relations and racial politics as to the impact of his drug-induced experience at Gillespie's concert. For Smith, along with his white liberal jazz critic contemporaries, shared a desire for a metaphysical (or magical) essence in black culture (whether urban or rural, modern or traditional) that, when engaged seriously and properly, carried the potential to counteract the morally corruptive aspects of modernity, including the threat of nuclear annihilation, totalitarianism, mass culture, and, of course, racism.[156]

To put music to his films, Smith chose two methods. The first involved simultaneously playing a film and a 78-RPM disc, the time constraints of which seemed to counteract his aesthetic desire for his films to aid the viewer in transcending the limits imposed by the material world toward one's full realization of the soul. He went as far as to "cut down [*Film No. 2*] to match" the length of "Guarachi guaro" (3:12).[157] Moreover, since he had already painted designs on the film, there was no intentional synchronization between the visual and the sonic contents of the film and record. In fact, in a letter to Rebay, he stated that the "rhythm of my films will automatically synchronize with any music having the same general speed. They are best silent, however."[158] Many listeners of cubop music like "Guarachi guaro" at the time characterized the music's temporal aspects as repetitive, formless, or primitive.[159] Gleason, as noted above, attempted to dispel the notion that bebop was also formless. Unlike Gillespie's bebop music, which is in fact structured in conventional song forms, "Guarachi guaro" and most of "Manteca" are indeed based on short repeating or cyclic figures typical of much, but not all, Afro-Cuban music at the time, much to the chagrin of even Gillespie's arranger, Walter "Gil" Fuller: "If you listen to 'Guarachi guaro,' it will *drive you nuts* because it does the same thing all over again because it just keeps going and repeats itself ad infinitum. And it never got off the ground like it should have because it wasn't structured. It wasn't structured in terms of something with form. The form was lacking."[160] Duke Ellington similarly complained that the "most desperately unmodern thing in the world is the repetition of one chord. The idea is to make it sound that way—but not to do it."[161] As for some in Gillespie's audiences, watching Pozo play the conga drum evoked materializations of the native savage not unlike that which had occurred with his performance in *Conga Pantera* in 1941. At a Gillespie concert in Paris in February 1948, French jazz critic and historian André Hodier recorded one woman's reaction to Pozo accordingly: "'A real cannibal,' said one brave lady sitting next to me, with a little shiver of horror at the idea she could meet him at the corner of the jungle."[162]

It is important to also compare how Fuller and Ellington listened to cubop music with how M. André Demaison listened to the Gilberto Valdés orchestra's performance of "Tambó" and "Sangre africana," in that all three auditory experiences seemed to be overwhelmed with those sonic chronotopes typically associated with the primitive or African past to different effects. For Fuller and Ellington, the result was psychologically pathological (insanity or desperation), whereas for Demaison, it was ontologically transformative. In all three instances, however, the sounding of musical modernism's chronotopes, as in seventh chords with ninths, thirteenths, and sharped elevenths, remained as the ground of their subjective assurance in the modern present. Gillespie and Smith, however, heard in these sounds redeeming qualities in the face of modernity's or the material world's failures and shortcomings. For Gillespie, as for Fernando

Ortiz, Salvador García Agüero, and Richard Waterman, Afro-Cuban music and the black Other retained the material and metaphysical culture of the African past, which in Gillespie's case included "our drums," which he lamented had been taken away from slaves in the United States.[163] In this way, Gillespie's and Pozo's music, as captured in their recordings of "Guarachi guaro" and "Manteca" and performed on stage, entailed the same listening and embodying practices that spatialized and temporalized Kwesi Kuntu, the white *ocobíos* of the Abakuá, and Jamaican Maroons, for instance, to African pasts and Kuntu's black American audiences, Harold Courlander, and Katherine Dunham in their modern presents. Accordingly, as he had done in Havana before relocating to New York City in 1947, Pozo maneuvered within these practices as he pursued the expansion of his professional career into the jazz industry. Smith's engagement with Gillespie's and Pozo's recorded music unfolded within yet another distinct spatialized and temporalized modern present.

Since Gillespie's big band recorded "Guarachi guaro" in December 1948, the earliest Smith could have edited his *Film No. 2* was March 1949, when the recording was released for sale.[164] Just one year later, Smith explained the content of the film to Rebay as "an investigation of the rhythmic organization of man's mind. Just as the atom is a small model of the solar system, in that both consist of a central force with circling points around it, the mind of man is miniature of a greater mind."[165] Out of this description, cyclic phenomena in proportional relationship to each other emerge as the film's organizational basis. This exact type of phenomena—that is, the cyclic clave pattern and its aggregate patterns as sounded from the congas, saxophone section, trumpet solo, chorus call-and-response, and so on—function as the temporal and sonic structures of "Guarachi guaro." It is important to make this comparison without regard to harmonic language, as these linearly conceived musical phenomena functioned as modern aurality's pathologizing basis upon which Fuller, Ellington, and others measured sanity and progress in order to distinguish bebop from cubop music. Rather, it seems that Smith listened to "Guarachi guaro" in atomistic terms (i.e., sonic cyclicities having proportional relationships) and thus chose it to give sound to his film's visual representations of the rhythmic relationships that he perceived linking the metaphysical and material worlds.

As he continues his explanation of *Film No. 2* to Rebay, other types of temporalities and temporal relationships emerge also in contradistinction to the linear unity of modern music, or bebop in particular:

> This film is like the diary of the earth's path around the sun during the two years I worked on it. I feel that certain forces effecting us originate

in the sun. It is possible to partially explore these by comparison of creativity among musicians playing, unconsciously, at different angles to the sun, and also at night when the forces must pass through the earth and be changed in quality for that reason. In making this film I suppressed sensory impulses from my body, as much as possible, and tried to record actual daily changes in the brain. The film divides itself into two general sections. This is partly due to my being able to induce a more perfect trance state as time went on, but is perhaps also because the sun's changing position in the Galaxy changes the strength of energy coming from other sections of the universe.

In this instance, Smith articulates a perception of time and space to music so radically distinct from but no less temporalizing or spatializing than that posited by Fuller, Gillespie, Ellington, and many others. Both sounds and images as captured and represented in the synchronization of "Guarachi guaro" and *Film No. 2* emanate from multiple locations and temporalities, whether the calendrical cycle encompassing the film's production, forces originating in the sun, one cycle of the Earth's rotation, the transition from a worldly to a transcendental mental state, or the sun's position in the universe as perceived from Earth. On the one hand, Smith's temporalization and spatialization of the forces determining the origin and meaning of his films follow a universal and not human evolutionary time scheme. On the other hand, such cyclic relationships in universal time still required dualisms, the Earth and sun, playing consciously and unconsciously, day and night, body and mind, optical and auditory, and so on. What reigned over all of these was a logic of distance measured in time and space.

In his *Film No. 4*, Smith abandoned his hand-painting technique in favor of film photography using an actual camera. The film begins with Smith panning the camera over his *Manteca* painting, each stroke of which he described as representing a "certain note on the record. [. . .] The main theme in there, which is [sings the main theme of the A section], are the curved lines up there. Each note of the painting is on there" (figure 4.2).[166] With his painting of the recording of "Manteca," Smith again subverts the mechanisms of power, this time to represent as embodied in Western musical notation a technology that he in fact used earlier in his career as an anthropologist. Musical notation's graphical system, in addition to its exclusive scientific legitimacy in ordering the linear unity of music, also entailed a signifying regime of complexity and progress (e.g., in the form of chords with harmonic extensions), all of which Smith reconfigured in his use of curved lines, circles, and hornlike shapes in blues, reds,

FIG. 4.2 Harry Smith, *Manteca*, ca. 1951, gouache and mixed media on board, approx. 16 x 20 in. Courtesy Harry Smith Archives.

greens, and yellows. The painting appears for only ten seconds, during which time the camera pans both up and down and chaotically in circles primarily across the central region of the painting. The remaining portion of the film portrays in black and white grills and circles whose movements are engendered by the camera's own movements.

Smith's forging of the temporal and spatial significances in his films were no less determined by binary logics of time and space than those Dunham choreographed for *Heat Wave* and its revisions or those Ellington composed in *Black, Brown and Beige* and *Liberian Suite*. Whereas Dunham's and Ellington's temporal and spatial representations were of the orders of chronology, evolution, progress (whether oppressed or realized), and geography, Smith's representations were of the orders of basic or pseudo astronomy and physics. Regardless of the scientific veracity, or lack thereof, of his explanations, his renderings of astronomy and physics were clearly not equipped discursively or logically to enable racializations of Gillespie, Pozo, "Guarachi guaro," or "Manteca." His desire, however, to produce nonobjective films whose function it was to enable the viewer to comprehend or experience the forces binding the spiritual to the physical world was, according to his own admission, complicated by the everyday contingencies of museum culture as generated, in fact, by the pathologies of his own subjective identifications.

Like his previous three films, *Film No. 4* was intended, it appears, to be shown not exclusively with the recording of "Manteca" but rather with any recording, or even accompanied by improvising musicians. Indeed, for his showing at the Art in Cinema series of May 12, 1950, Smith titled films 1 through 4 "A Strange Dream," "Message from the Sun," "Interwoven," and "Fast Track" (respectively, in their numerical succession), all under the main title *Five Instruments with Optical Solo*. As he explained, "The titles . . . were added for the museum audience. Originally they were not titled and I still feel that giving specific titles is destructive because it tensions them to specific emotions, and for these particular films are as out of place as a chemist naming his experiments according to the colour they produce, rather than the purpose. But, for an audience as at the museum who represent as a really stupid element who are prejudiced against accepting *anything* unless they are first told what it is, titles are of some value."[167] Thus the contingencies in showing his films to the museum's film series audiences, or else Smith's concern over his films' nonobjective functions (as opposed to film's subjectively held emotional effectuations), led to the kind of pathologizing or swelling of the world with one's being that Sterns and Fanon theorized as occurring in one's acts of spatializing and temporalizing.

This was particularly evident in Smith's explication of the jazz musicians who participated in the showing of his *Five Instruments with Optical Solo.*

This showing's program describes, for example, Smith's films, or "optical solo," as serving as the "sixth instrument in a be-bop jam session. . . . This is the first presentation anywhere of a performance in which the optical images will be tried, not as visualization of the music, but as a basis for its departure."[168] Another version of the program explains that the musicians improvise based on their interpretation of the "measured rhythmic designs" composed by Smith. "Each frame itself is considered as a separate composition, altering gradually from frame to frame."[169] In addition, a short article published in *Down Beat* described the "shape and color of the designs" on the films as suggesting "all the harmonic possibilities and the progression of the music."[170] The musicians who performed Smith's *Five Instruments with Optical Solo* were Atlee Chapman (trombone, bass trumpet), Henry Noyd (trumpet), Kermit Scott (tenor saxophone), Robert Warren (bass), Warren Thompson (drums), and Stanley Willis (piano), all local San Francisco jazz musicians. Of these six musicians, Kermit Scott was the most widely known at the time for having played at Minton's Playhouse in New York City with Dizzy Gillespie, who credited Scott with helping to develop bebop in the late 1930s.[171] In fact, Scott and Willis gave a short talk on bebop music before the start of the Art in Cinema program. As for Smith's general impressions of their improvised music, these shed light, if not on the specific musical qualities of their playing, then on his attitudes toward popular music's "vulgar" "striving for effect" and "objectivity." For example, he proclaimed that the musicians who have played his films "are now intuitively creating a new kind of music that will not be accepted by the public probably for 50 years. They are all really poor, sometimes hungry, because they would rather express what they call 'soul' in their playing than hurt themselves by changing it to fit the backward standards of today's listeners."[172] He continued by characterizing the creators of spirituals, ragtime, jazz, blues, boogie-woogie, swing, and bebop as "intuitive, but uneducated geniuses who died without getting any money or recognition. . . . But now . . . a great change, unsuspected, to the world is about to occur in music."

In his excitement about what we can perhaps interpret as a precursor to avant-garde jazz, Smith further expresses his resolve to compare his recordings of the film/jam sessions "with each other and with the films . . . to make a start toward an investigation of intuitive creation. By investigating these observable forces which effect man, but which are scorned by pedantic science, it will be possible for us soon to realize the final stages of man's development."[173] Like Katherine Dunham, Smith had grown skeptical of anthropology's scientific imperative in spite or because of his earlier formal training in anthropology. Both Smith and Dunham, it is clear, desired to engage with the universal qualities of movement in time and space rather than New World Negro culture's "objective" elements as Melville Herskovits, Richard Waterman, and Mieczyslaw Kolinski continued to promulgate. Yet, at the same time, Smith considered such a study of intuitive creation and its generating forces to potentially bring about, in his words, "the final stages of man's development." In this instance, Smith, or the "fabulous alchemical magician painter-filmmaker," as Allen Ginsberg described him, reverted to a temporality that, in conjunction with his racializing identifications of Willis and the other "intuitively genius" jazz musicians, intersected dangerously with the evolutionary temporalities of anthropology, comparative musicology, and jazz's traditionalist-modernist debate.[174]

To conclude, the ideals of avant-garde film of the 1940s raise questions regarding art's potential as a nonrepresentational space. Could Pozo, Gillespie, Ellington, or Dunham have created nonobjective music and dance had they desired to do so as disalienating expressions of their selves in the world? More to the point, did they have access ontologically to such a space, or were avant-garde artists' ideals of abstract and nonobjective expression a prerogative of the temporal and spatial privileges that came with (or determined) one's status as a racially unmarked or white modern body? That critics associated avant-garde jazz musicians of the 1960s with black nationalist thought, regardless of the actual politics of individual musicians such as John Coltrane, lends provocative insight into likely answers to these questions.[175] Smith, it seems, had no recourse to avow the nonobjective experimentalism of his film's jazz musicians without shutting them away as he did (in Fanon's words) "in the Tower given as the Past." Smith's representation of them as "intuitive" and in the racialized lineage of the "creators of the spirituals" was as much constitutive of his own normative whiteness as it was constitutive of their racial otherness. Indeed, as Matthew Frye Jacobson argues, in the political economy of race in the United States during World War II and the Cold War, the biracial logic of black-white solidified such that whiteness, which now unified previously differentiated white ethnics under the newly conceived category of Caucasian, rendered race "something possessed only by 'other' [i.e., black] peoples."[176] But Judith Butler reminds us that such racial boundaries must be continuously reiterated precisely because of the anxiety their inherent tenuous status generates, regardless of the kinds of historical developments that Jacobson cites.[177]

To understand further the theoretical implications of this notion of normative whiteness as the social field of the racially unmarked, we turn to the peculiarities of capitalist democracy in modernity. Gilles Deleuze and Félix

Guattari's analysis of capitalistic schizophrenia suggests that conditions such as alienation and disalienation never completely "come into being" (as Fanon asserted) due to capitalism's "twofold movement of deterritorializing flows on the one hand [smooth space], and their violent and artificial reterritorialization on the other [striated space]."[178] Indeed, American capitalism at the start of the Cold War touted individual freedom regardless of race, nationality, or gender as a matter of economic progress and international order at the same time that its political economies of race, gender, and sexuality worked to inhibit the full realization of freedom by recoding oppressed identities and rechanneling them as racially inferior and sexually subservient or deviant. Such a regime, as the next chapter will further explore, was predicated on maintaining white heterosexual male privilege in spheres of human activity—whether political or economic, sexual or familial, academic or artistic—and across national boundaries. Even not so subtle intimations of avant-gardism in Cuban popular music of the 1940s and early 1950s were mowed over by capitalism's reterritorializing machines. In focusing on the national, international, and transnational movements of the mambo, the final chapter will explore how such strictures of capitalism and Cold War politics intensified while at the same time obscured the practices of the logic of black music's and dance's African origins into the 1950s.

Desiring Africa, or
Western Civilization's Discontents

Black rhythm vitalizes, rejuvenates, liberates the primitive that we carry inside, makes one forget, returns a bit of savage happiness. Anguish—existentialist?—receives black rhythm's baptism of oblivion. The "Mambo" takes the triumph of pure rhythm to a level higher than rhythmic euphoria, than the drums which until yesterday were hidden in the orchestra. Even if Pérez Prado hadn't invented it, the "Mambo" would still have been. Because it is in the excitement of our time which for ample reason overlooks the primitive of yesterday, for what civilization promises is atomic war with its possible destruction of all organized life. —JUAN LISCANO, 1951

Venezuelan poet and folklorist Juan Liscano made this statement in response to a survey conducted by Carlos Dorante of the Caracas newspaper *El Nacio-nal* regarding the mambo music of Dámaso Pérez Prado.[1] In reflecting on Pérez Prado, who in 1951 was the most profitable mambo musician internationally, Liscano imparts his perspective, drawing from Spenglerian historicism, Carpentierian *lo real maravilloso*, and especially Sartrean existentialism to explain black rhythm's capacity to remove one's excuses (laws, rules, or ideals) to not realize her or his freedom, happiness, and human essence.[2] As the previous four chapters have shown, Western civilization had fashioned many laws, rules, and ideals— among them, scientific observation, nation, history, and nonobjectivity—to assuage, silence, and interrupt modern man's and woman's desires in sounding and moving. It is the mambo, according to Liscano, that liberates the modern's recognition of the primitive or savage essence within. Furthermore, the mambo is

fundamentally of the modern present, as is folklore in general, and thus constitutes a uniquely Latin American magical path toward the modern's reconciliation with her or his primitive essence. Elsewhere, Liscano defined folklore as
a living dynamic, continuously in the process of renovation, transformation,
and mutation, and that which conditions the creation of "true culture."[3] The
creator of "true culture" was the "cultured man . . . who in general are always
those human groups more in touch with the earth, closer to the communal
knowledge which has much magical knowledge," as opposed to the urban and
college-educated "cultured man." In short, the mambo, according to Liscano,
reveals that only the modern's inhibitions separate her or him from her or his
primitive essence. It is not this primitive essence that is the source of the modern's anxiety but rather the arbitrariness of the modern's inhibitions, the same
uncertainty in fact that keeps the modern from annihilating "all organized
life" itself.[4]

During World War II and through the early 1950s black music and dance
continued to be temporalized and spatialized in accordance with modernity's
arbitrarily racialized and gendered laws, rules, and ideals as exemplified in
the work of Asadata Dafora, Katherine Dunham, Melville J. Herskovits, Fernando Ortiz, Chano Pozo, Richard Waterman, and others. This was a time of
particularly intense and urgent concern over the meanings of war and Western civilization's sanity and morality such that modernity's uncertain future
seemed to affect dispositions toward black music and dance. To be sure, writers
of black culture internationally held on to modernity's temporal and spatial
frameworks, though certain rhetorical shifts in the conceptualization of black
ontology suggested otherwise. For example, intellectuals from throughout the
Americas established the Instituto Internacional de Estudios Afroamericanos (International Institute of Afroamerican Studies; IIEA) in Mexico City
in 1943, publishing three issues of its journal *Afroamérica* in 1945 and 1946. Its
members were internationally diverse (Melville J. Herskovits, Alain Locke, Fernando
Ortiz, Jean Price-Mars, Arthur Ramos, Aimé Cesaire, Eric Williams, W. E. B.
Du Bois, Charles S. Johnson, Alfred Métraux, Miguel Covarrubias, and Juan
Liscano, among others) but all men, and its stated aim was the "study of black
populations of America, in their biological and cultural aspects, and of their influences in American nations."[5] Although Afroamerican, *afroamericano*, and
afroamericaine were by no means new appellations for black populations, their
appearance in the early 1940s to denote a specified area in New World Negro
studies expressed the recognition of black populations as consisting of active
subjectivities of the modern nation and not merely descendants of their Af-

rican ancestors. Moreover, Afroamerican studies implied severing the Americas from the epistemological domain of Old World historiography.[6] Yet, like UNESCO's 1950 and 1952 statements on race and racial difference, the IIEA held on to modernity's premise of defining race scientifically.

At the time of the IIEA's founding in Mexico City, Alioune Diop and other African students living in Nazi-occupied Paris, along with some French intellectuals, were similarly in the throes of rethinking Africa's place in the world, a shift that was fundamentally induced, according to Diop, by the "suffering of a Europe that was questioning itself on its essence and the authenticity of its values."[7] Their efforts eventually led to the publication of *Présence Africaine*'s first volume in 1947. As the title suggests, the journal's aim was to "define the African essence and hasten its insertion into the modern world" as well as "examine the terms of this integration of the black man in Western civilization."[8] Like the African Academy of Art and Research, the editors of *Présence Africaine*, all men as well, supported the liberation of Africa from European colonialism, yet the war and its aftermath seemed to have an effect in their worldview beyond African decolonization. Latin American philosophers as well increasingly felt the urgency to initiate the formation of a philosophy proper to their respective nations; as Mexican philosopher Samuel Ramos wrote in 1943, "If the current catastrophe does not destroy European civilization, it is very probable that its creative activities, in the area of thought, will suffer a long-lasting collapse."[9] The war also helped reshape literary models. After having worked in Paris throughout much of the 1930s, Western classical music critic Alejo Carpentier of Cuba, while visiting Haiti in 1943, took the European literary form magical realism and formulated his notion of *lo real maravilloso americano* based on his observations of the magical in modern Latin American culture and society.[10]

The ten years following the end of World War II were particularly anxious years internationally: the United States revealed the mass destructive power of the atomic bomb over Japan in 1945; the French Indochina eight-year war started in 1946; three years later the Soviet Union announced their own nuclear capabilities; less than a year after this North Korea invaded South Korea; and in 1954 the Secretary of State of the United States, John Foster Dulles, officially announced the doctrine of "massive retaliation," later to be coined "mutually assured destruction," or MAD. It is thus significant that the seemingly unrelated emergences of Afroamerican studies, negritude, lo real maravilloso, and mambo, among other developments in the 1940s, should coincide around a subjectively threatened and thus reconfiguring modern ontology as a result of Western civilization's crises. But as Juan Liscano's comments above about the mambo demonstrate, Western civilization's racial and gendered desiring machines stubbornly kept modernity's primitive African anchored in its otherwise reformulating ontology, the existence of which was threatened by its own devices.

To wit, as Jean-Paul Sartre revealed in his "Orphée noir" (Black Orpheus), "We [Europeans] are feeling our dignity crumble under *les regards* [the look] of the Americans and the Soviets. . . . At least we were hoping to retrieve a little of our grandeur in the domesticated eyes of the Africans. But there are no more domesticated eyes; these are *les regards* savage and free which sit in judgment of our land."[11] In his foreword to the first volume of *Présence Africaine*, André Gide similarly expressed a skepticism regarding Western civilization's values, asking "Do we return to barbarism? We have come very close to it in the last years."[12] Like Liscano, Gide believed that "partaking with an elementary and savage energy [such as in black music] regenerates our dwindling forces." What was in Asadata Dafora's case the performance of Africa as point of origin of New World Negro music and dance was in these instances black music's promise of the reconstitution of modernity's subjective assurance to claim a new kind of modern present. By no means, however, were Western civilization's machines (e.g., capitalism, Catholicism, psychology, and nationalism) dead, for as other respondents to *El Nacional*'s survey opined: the mambo, "like all Afro-Cuban music is . . . intolerable" and "decadence, hysterics, and extreme lewdness are the diapason for this class of music" (Marcos Castillo, painter); "what I like least is its name" (Luis Felipe Urbaneja, minister of justice); and it is a "product for Yankee tourism that invades Cuba," "it has no cultural value" (Raúl Ramos Calles, psychiatrist).

This final chapter explores how in mambo dance-music the subjective assurance of the metropolis's modern present, along with its constitutive machines, came under assault, such that mambo musicians, dancers, and listeners, as Liscano recognized, apprehended that Western civilization's motives and values could not guarantee their survival. It analyzes such ontological assaults and phenomenological apprehensions in the mambo's varying trajectories in its sounds; movements; neurosis; psychosis; immorality; mortal sinfulness; urban essence; American, Mexican, and Cuban provenance; blackness; modernism; and, lastly, savage and primitive power. In other words, this analysis begins (in the absence of an origin) with the mambo's multiple starting points as sound and movement and then follows its manifestations in, for instance, records; American, Cuban, and Mexican television; the Peruvian and Venezuelan Catholic Church; and Mexican film, using the events, affects, forces, and intensities or simply the desires and pleasures it entailed to further get at understanding the practical necessity for the logic of black dance's and music's African origins.

For the "organized life" that Liscano named as that which was threatened under nuclear technology was, this chapter argues, the nation's modern family, or what Gilles Deleuze and Félix Guattari refer to as capitalism's "Oedipal triangle" (daddy-mommy-child).[13]

Whether or not Liscano speculated correctly that the mambo would have materialized in spite of Dámaso Pérez Prado, his reference to an "excitement" characteristic of the modern present gestures toward the kind of desire that Deleuze and Guattari distinguish from the negative desire as "lack" (in the sexual sense), the former on which, they state, capitalism thrives and psychoanalysis, the church, nationalism, and even capitalism in turn expend much energy to regulate.[14] Indeed, it was capitalism's "awesome schizophrenic accumulation of energy or charge, against which it [brought] all its vast powers of repression to bear," that made possible mambo's equally viable threats to and revitalization of Western civilization's hold on time and space. Only, as this chapter will show, it was the Oedipal family's integrity—most urgently expressed in terms of the nation's cultural and racial patrimony (Cuban, American, and Mexican included)—that capitalism's excess threatened through the mambo.

To its detractors, the mambo unleashed instinctive feelings and actions that overwhelmed Western civilization's mechanisms set up to keep modern man's and woman's instincts in check. Whereas for its supporters, the mambo's generative force of overwhelming pleasure in the face of the madness of the atomic age, or simply in the Latin American metropolis's fantastical realism, failed from the start to expose modernity's social machines as the dictatorial mechanisms they were set up to be. In both cases Western civilization was reaching another breaking point if not for the lasting horror the primitive signified in modernity's absence. Sigmund Freud, in his *Civilization and Its Discontents* (1930), had already critiqued Western civilization's promises of the "prevention of suffering" in which he made the same contention that Gide would rhetorically flirt with seventeen years later regarding returning to barbarism.[15] Freud admitted that his contention is "so astonishing that we must dwell upon it. This contention holds that what we call our civilization is largely responsible for our misery, and that we should be much happier *if we gave it up and returned to primitive conditions*. I call this contention astonishing because, in whatever way we may define the concept of civilization, it is a certain fact that all the things with which we seek to protect ourselves against the threats that emanate from the sources of suffering are part of that very civilization."[16]

Freud, by looking back to modernity's primitive past, goes far to critique the dictatorial machines of Western civilization before stopping in his tracks when addressing "primitive peoples who exist to-day": "careful researches have shown that their instinctual life is by no means to be envied for its freedom. It is subject to restrictions of a different kind but perhaps of greater severity than those attaching to modern civilized man."[17] Indeed, in their respective critiques of Western civilization, Spengler, Freud, Diop, Gide, Sartre, and Liscano, not to mention Frantz Fanon, among others, expressed a kind of anguish set forth by Sartre himself over modernity's insufficient effectiveness in guaranteeing freedom in the present. Is this why modernity could not make do without its primitive and racial Other? Even in Latin American reconfigurations of the modern present—such as with José Vasconcelos's *raza cósmica* (cosmic race) or Alejo Carpentier's lo real maravilloso—Hispano-centrism and the African primitive still held sway. As such, and as Deleuze and Guattari argue, the laws, rules, and ideals to which modern citizens have made themselves subject under capitalism's schizophrenia have been severe in their own right, for how could the rendering of mambo musicians, dancers, and listeners as mad, excommunicated, unpatriotic, and savage in one instance, and as the materialization of Western civilization's promise of freedom in another not be considered oppressive?

Many commentators of mambo music and dance indeed could not make do with Western civilization's African past or its notion of reason without also naming modernity's abject excesses of neurosis, psychosis, or simply madness. The mambo's earliest recordings were particularly rife in emitting an intense vertigo of sounds and movements, which were coded early on in its reception in Havana as excessively improvisational or unorderly. As capitalism continued to realize the full extent of mambo's profitability, nationalism and psychology were simultaneously and jointly unleashed to reaffirm the racial and gendered coordinates of modernity's subjective assurance in the un-raced family to keep orderly the metropolis's hierarchically racialized and gendered social landscape. It was only a matter of time before Western civilization, after mambo showed an immunity to nationalism's and psychology's policing machines, enlisted religion and capitalism itself to contain mambo in its social and international dissemination.

Thus, in addition to television programs produced in Havana and Los Angeles, the Catholic Church in Peru and Venezuela and Mexican filmmakers exerted their power to recode mambo's desires as Western civilization's excesses, that is, sinful, foreign, and even pleasurable. And because of the premium that efficiency carried within capitalism, these machines targeted one person, Dámaso Pérez Prado. The fact that the engines of these industries were capitalism and modern technology is proof of where the mambo's madness truly emanated—not in its sounds and movements nor in its African origins but in modernity and capitalism itself. Pérez Prado's compositional philosophy and his music in fact suggest his triumph (if momentarily) over that which existentialism, the cosmic race, and lo real maravilloso failed to escape, modernity's temporal dependence on the primitive. It seems as though the madder modernity revealed itself to be in mambo dance-music, the more it needed to be "silenced."[18]

Logic's dualisms, whether primitive and modern, white and nonwhite, cultural and biological, national and foreign, moral and immoral, real and magical, sane and mad, or dance and music, are indeed deeply flawed yet enduring inventions of Western civilization, which in its most precarious states has tended to enable its contradictory nature to emerge most stridently. Hence, the contradictory representations of mambo's social effects in the Mexican films *Ritmos del Caribe* (Rhythms from the Caribbean, 1950) and *Del can can al mambo* (From the can can to the mambo, 1951). Whereas the Cuban mambo woman dancer morally corrupts the Mexican married male doctor, destroying the patriarchal pillar of the modern Mexican family and threatening the nation's integrity in the process, mambo dance and music also enmeshes itself within Mexico's technological marvels, promising in the process to replace positivism's oppressive forces in the nation's rural states with energy, individuality, and happiness. It is as if mambo was poised to accelerate the coming of Vasconcelos's *quinta raza* (fifth race), or cosmic race, if not, however, for the Mexican film industry's racially erasing nationalist project. What is in fact happening here is Western civilization's redirection and recoding of its decrepit, yet still violent, impulses onto its Others, the gendered and raced objects to its Cartesian- and Euclidean-centered subjectivities. For black music and dance it is space-time that serves modernity's sublimations particularly effectively, thanks to time's naturalness.

Mambo Madness

In recalling his experiences as a mambo dancer in the 1940s and 1950s, Pedro Aguilar, known also as "Cuban Pete," described his dancing in ways that tended as much to its policed formulations as to its affectively produced movements. He did the latter even when naming readily perceived dance movements, leaving implicit the infinite number of other movements that occurred not only throughout his body but among other bodies present and in dialogue with his.[19] For instance, in proclaiming, "The best thing that ever happened to me was the clave, and the people taught me that. Cuba did not push the clave like the Puerto Ricans did here [in New York City]," he gave form (i.e., national, geographic, and kinesthetic) to the perceived basic movement of dancing mambo, in which its co-occurring (micro) movements remain implicit.[20] In other instances he located the original impulses of his movements in the movements and sounds of musicians on stage. As he recalled, "I used to watch Arsenio [Rodríguez]. In watching him, there was something that he was giving away, when he leaned back and you would think he was looking at the ceiling and his hands [on the *tres*] were going crazy. I loved to watch him." On yet another occasion, Cuban Pete reiterated "he made me crazy," referring again to watching and listening to Arsenio Rodríguez while dancing.[21] What Cuban Pete demonstrates in this instance is a perception of dance-music that associates flows of sound and speeds of movement beyond what is namable or quantifiable, as is the case with his reference to "clave." In short, what he names "crazy" were simply actions and desires that exceeded any possibility of ordering if not for the proper rhetorical and discursive equipment at hand.

How certain flows of sound and speeds of movement obtained meaning and how they were perceived in the first place while other sounds and movements were not can be understood by conceiving of mambo dance-music as constitutive of smooth and striated spaces.[22] Simply put, sound and movement in smooth space grow and flow amorphously at varying speeds, while in striated space selected sounds and movements are organized into coordinates to be used for society's varying machines. Both kinds of spaces, however, often happen simultaneously, one passing into the other. Thus, as with Pierre Boulez's explanation of smooth and striated space in music (as interpreted by Deleuze and Guattari), one musicks or dances without counting in smooth space-time, whereas one counts in order to play, dance, and name in striated space-time. Reflecting back on Cuban Pete's comments, "pushing the clave," as in giving form to and advocating one (perceived) fundamental dance movement over others, is a materialization of dance, not to mention music, as striated space, while the same can be said for the capturing of manifold sounds and movements under one word ("crazy"), all of which function toward articulating dance and music to social and historical structures. At the same time, his reference to Rodríguez's movements on stage approaches haptic perception whereby his senses, in this case, optical and audible as well as tactile (with respect to his dance partner), fulfill cross-sensual functions. Watching his movements (leaning back, playing his instrument) giving way to hearing (musical) sounds coming from the stage flowed into Cuban Pete's bodily movements, all of which approaches smooth space-time or "dance-music" conceived here as operating on a different plane than the striated binary dance and music, or "dance music."

The application of these analytical models (movement, flow, speed, smooth and striated spaces, haptic perception, and dance-music) to the analysis of mambo goes far to avoid long-worn questions of its origins, evolution, and authenticity, which nevertheless, beginning as early as 1948, served to striate mambo's emergences in existing Cuban dance music genres—*danzón* and *guaracha*—into nationalist and historicist renderings. Rather, in paying keen attention to the mambo's striations on records and in television, film, and newspaper reports, we see that these very representations were incapable of completely containing this dance-music's excesses. We have already taken stock of Katherine Dunham's fieldwork and ethnographic publications in regard to the importance of her participation and haptic perception in decentering anthropology's dominant spatial and temporal striations, such as those that located "bush" Negroes in the Negro American's ancestral past (see chapter 1). Similarly, listening practices directed toward mapping the concert hall, modern amphitheater, and comparative musicological laboratory as modern aurality's spatial centers and temporal presents functioned by intensely striating music and dance according to racial, historical, political, economic, and scientific imperatives (see chapter 2). With mambo, however, the emergence of new or else disavowed chronotopes of modernity's metropolis, incited by capitalism's intense investments in mambo dance and music, dangerously threatened to reconfigure the societal parameters that regulated the normative modern's subjective assurance within the family, which was already under the strain of war and the nuclear threat of annihilation (see chapter 3). As we will see, however, Western civilization's machines, operating within the heterogeneous flows of modern society, worked fiercely to keep capitalism's own madness turned back onto its psychologically pathologized gendered and racial Others.

By the time Cuban Pete had begun dancing professionally, two articles on the mambo had appeared in periodicals published in Havana. *Bohemia* published the first, Manuel Cuéllar Vizcaíno's "La revolución del mambo" (The mambo revolution) on May 30, 1948, and *Inventario* published the second, Odilio Urfé's "La verdad sobre el mambo" (The truth about the mambo) in June 1948. Whereas Urfé wrote his article in response to Cuéllar Vizcaíno's, revealing much about the concerns Cuban writers had in regard to the changes danzón had been undergoing, their attempts to explain such changes let slip much of what exceeded their chosen discourses. One of the more revealing excerpts in this regard is Cuéllar Vizcaíno's application of the phrase *a la diabla* (carelessly, any old how) to describe how musicians play during the newly added finale section of the danzón as performed by *charangas*.[23] He says that the flutist, violinists, pianist, and *timbal* and *güiro* players "are authorized to do whatever they feel like ... in a way that establishes what we would call a capricious and informal conversation."[24] The bassist and conga player, meanwhile, "quarrel rhythmically as if to try to put the house back in order." Meanwhile, the dancers, he continues, "are doing their own thing," including a step he calls *diablo* (devil), which occurs as the final of a sequence of four steps "in which the point of the foot barely touches the floor" or, in other cases, which the dancer stresses by "shaking" his or her body. He finishes by saying that those "who are able to overcome these sensations undertake elegant steps, but those who remain at the mercy of the bewitching strains, principally the women, have to give off yells as safety valves of security." This, Cuéllar Vizcaíno concludes, is mambo.

Urfé's greatest objection to Cuéllar Vizcaíno's article was not his description of mambo as it flowed among musicians and dancers during the final section of the danzón but rather his claim that the word "mambo" does not appear in any reference sources, including Fernando Ortiz's *Glosario de afronegrismos* (1924), and that it was first used, according to one of his sources, Obdulio Morales, spontaneously as an onomatopoeia by a dancer and caught on thereafter among other dancers. After listing its uses in Haitian Vodun, among Cuban rumba musicians, in Palo religious music, and Cuban popular music, Urfé states that the "popular musical phenomenon known as mambo has always existed" under different names dating back to the "origins of our music."[25] "Improvisation" over a "persistent rhythm," "theme and variations," or a musician's embellishment of written music are the phenomena that, for Urfé, connected music making by slaves during the colonial period, *orquestas típicas* of the mid-nineteenth century, charangas of the early twentieth century, and contemporary groups like Antonio Arcaño's. He also challenged Cuéllar Vizcaíno's claim that Arcaño and his musicians "created" this style of playing; rather, according to Urfé, Arcaño's was one among many groups who "'ordered' the mambo's presence, development, and completion." Since then, charanga musicians, he laments, have standardized and simplified mambo, eschewing improvisation and playing instead one rhythmic ostinato—that is, the mambo rhythm—from the beginning of the finale until its end.[26]

In spite of their differing claims about the mambo's etymology and creator, both writers in effect reiterate Cuban music's dominant historicist narrative that ten years earlier Salvador García Agüero, Alberto Arredondo, and Fernando Ortiz enlisted in their own dialectically conceived and positivist renderings of the African presence in Cuban society. What we have here in essence is what Deleuze and Guattari distinguish as the point system of history from the line system of becoming.[27] These renderings of Cuban music history (comparsa, danzón, and mambo) structure its temporal and spatial axes in such a way that history is made subordinate to points of musical or terpsichorean action in the present. It is not so much that the comparsa, danzón, and mambo are forced into this dominant historical narrative as that the historical narrative itself is made to disavow dance-music's immanence as movement, sound, touch, and speed, thereby clearing the path so that selected connections can be made between current actions and their (perceived) resonances in the past. This punctual system of history is at its most racially intense when Cuéllar Vizcaíno details the evolution of Cuba's national dance, the danzón: "That fine style of danzón [dancing] came to be monotonous and it went disappearing in the final section because the African influence emerged in it, since African rhythms emphasized *contratiempos* [offbeat phrasings], the dance couples, who . . . instantly felt the strong beat, needed, in order to maintain their equilibrium, to sway their body and make contortions in search of the *contratiempo*; so that the *sandunga* [syncopated rhythmic groove] was strengthened in that third part of the danzón."[28] He later mentions that the inclusion of the conga drum, which plays only in the final part, lent the "characteristic rhythm" that eventually won out over the others a further assurance or "major solidity."[29]

The layers of Cuban history in Cuéllar Vizcaíno's and Urfé's narratives are many but not new. Both connect the mambo to the nation's lineages, whether of the national dance, danzón, or in uses of improvisation starting with slaves during the colonial era. In each case, they invoke Africa's presence as the cause of the disappearance of that "fine style" of danzón dancing and the source of both *contratiempo* and the "primitive" and "rough sounding" conga drum, all of which function here as heavy striations of mambo dance music.[30] What is especially significant is their perception of dancers needing to maintain their "equilibrium," "overcoming" the "bewitching strains," and contorting their bodies "in search of the contratiempo" of the mambo, in addition to their description of a genuine mambo as "ordered anarchy." Once again, subjective assurance, especially for women dancers, according to Cuéllar Vizcaíno, is at stake not so much with respect to locating mambo in a distant African past, being transported back to Africa, or even hearing the threat of disorder of a bygone stage to the nation's subjective assurance in the modern present. Rather, their portrayals of maintaining bodily equilibrium within an ordered sounding anarchy seem to speak more to the current lot of Cubans, the youth as well as their families, in the pathological conditions of the modern present. Indeed, because of mambo music's (perceived) anarchical and bewitching effects, Cuban society's patriarchal and racialized norms and its capitalism did not have to answer for such displays of "revolution" by its youth.

Both articles in fact describe mambo as a revolution of the Cuban youth. Their realization of freedom and liberation in sound and movement was mambo's essence. Mambo "lit within the youth" innovations in dance, which for some dancers "reflected the front occupied by the forces [i.e., the United States and Soviet Union] allied at that moment in history." "No definite tunes or melodies," writes Urfé. "The heat of the 'mambo' makes the couple separate in order to . . . execute the varied figures and steps that the dance calls for," writes Cuéllar Vizcaíno.[31] It is as dance-music—conceived as indivisible sound, movement, speed, and flow—whereby we can grasp the mambo's excesses leaking out of not only historicism's but also capitalism's machines. For just as Cuéllar Vizcaíno, in counting mambo dancing into sequences of four steps, changed the mambo's fundamental nature from dance-music (smooth space) to dance (striated space), the RCA Victor record company produced heavily striated renderings of mambo as music recorded by Cuban big bands and charangas.

For example, the title "Rarezas" (Oddities), recorded by Orquesta Maravilla de Arcaño in Havana in April 1940, suggestively describes the contents of the record in terms of not its musical novelty per se but rather the record's truncations of mambo dance-music into a hypermetrically divided sound commodity. If displacing the musicians from the dancehall to the recording studio was not striating enough, the approximately three-minute-and-thirty-second playback time of a 78-RPM disc dictated that the danzón's final section would begin at about halfway from the start of the recording. The division of the remaining playback time into sequences of violins and cello executing ostinatos in contratiempo, refrains, piano and flute solos, and breaks represent, on the one hand, the sonic parts of the 78-RPM disc as commodity and, on the other, sonic representations of previous dance music events. In "Rarezas" a sixteen-second portion of the flute solo perhaps best exhibits the otherwise nonmetric or nondivisible conditions that were identified as favorable for the execution of mambo by dancers and musicians alike. The timbal's cross-rhythms ("rhythm against rhythm"), a flute's A-natural sounding either a major seven of the dominant five chord or a sharp four in the home key of E-flat ("no definite tunes or melodies"), the strings' contratiempo, and so on, all seem to contribute to an "ordered anarchy." During such moments, Arcaño stated, dancers become "infected," they "create steps and they contort in plain communion with us in the new rhythm." As such, mambo dance-music was not the sum of dance plus music but rather, borrowing from Deleuze and Guattari's line systems of becoming, "mutant abstract lines that have detached themselves from the task of representing a world [disalienation], precisely because they assemble a new type of reality that history can only recontain or relocate in punctual systems."[32] Even within Arcaño's deployment of striating or pathologizing discourse ("infected," "contort") emerges a smoothing objectification ("communion") of dance-music.

The theorization of music as the deterritorializing art form par excellence—capable of unhinging even the most hackneyed "refrains" toward new creations and realities—is especially applicable to dance-music such as mambo, whose own hackneyed elements, namely, the standardization of its contratiempo into a "mambo rhythm," were simultaneously in the service of capitalism's social and international dissemination of mambo. Its emergence in cities across the Americas certainly signaled not so much new realities of mambo dance music as the increasing intensity of its desiring-production capability, the reactionary forces against which reveal themselves in the schizophrenic-induced discourse that appeared in reports about mambo. Urfé, for example, condemned mambo dancing's "infringement on our folklore," charging that its choreography in the danzón as performed by Cuban youth is a "prostituted and crude copy . . . of the dances of the North Americans."[33] Of course, he made this claim only by separating mambo dancing from the music, whose historical coordinates Urfé securely plotted within Cuban music history. Two years later, in 1950, Juan S. Ramos, writing for the Havana daily newspaper *Diario de la marina*, proclaimed that a "new form . . . has arrived to revolutionize choreography: the mambo. *It was not born on our ground*, though its author [Pérez Prado] is from Matanzas. He has come from outside, bringing with him players from other places, especially from Mexico."[34] Such attempts to deny young mambo dancers and musicians the immanence of their affectively produced movements and sounds were themselves generated from a fierce nationalist and historicist asceticism that was certainly not unique to Cuban intellectuals and writers (as we will see later in this chapter). Driving the mambo's intensifying schizophrenia—that is, its simultaneous decodings as affect and recodings as Cuban, North American, and Mexican or simply pathological—were modern society's capitalist machines, including its recording and dance studio industries.

Ramos in fact assessed the mambo's "dislocated nature, in its music and lyric," as constituting its "marvelous virtue," describing it as international, hybrid, and profitable. Dámaso Pérez Prado had become, in Ramos's estimation, an "important investment in the Cuban and American exchanges" (i.e., financial investment markets). Indeed, mambo's profitability fueled its circulation, freeing desires among the youth, while at the same time wreaking havoc on the codes of Cuban nationalism and historicism. Alejo Carpentier similarly recognized mambo's provenance in modernity and capitalism, though his modernist and neo-Marxist convictions ultimately overtook his criticism. It was not a "pure outbreak of popular inspiration," Carpentier clarified, but rather the "product of what has always been called 'modern life.' "[35] After identifying the mambo's lineage with the past dance music styles of the waltz and saraband, which he explains had similarly been perceived as frenetic, immoral, and diabolical, Carpentier predicts that mambo will "act as an enema on Cuban dance music, obliging it to take new paths." He specifically condemns guaracha for its monotony, triviality, stupidity, and having invaded the world of Cuban urban dance music, resulting in its decadence throughout the decade. Mambo, on the other hand, displays some "very dignified characteristics," he states. They include its "modern harmonies," instrumental and melodic "inventiveness," and a "rare sense of variation that breaks from the bored mechanism of repetition and refrains that contributed to bounding certain Antillean dance genres," all of which has led to mambo overtaking the "audacities of the players of North American jazz."[36] This final nationalistic utterance aside, Carpentier deploys a modernist perspective hardly shaped by his theory of lo real maravilloso wherein he put forth a Latin American realism made unique by the magic inherent in Latin American culture, geography, and history.[37] Rather, he writes in this instance in his music critic voice, from a perspective that is rather conventionally neo-Marxist, modernist, and difficult to apply, with rare exception, to most mambo records made before 1949.

Until 1949, most mambos and guarachas as recorded by big bands, Cuban or otherwise, were rather formulaic, exhibiting diatonic harmonies with little or no harmonic extensions and no variation in instrumentation or musical form. Julio Cueva y su Orquesta's "Figurina del solar" (Costume designer of the Solar), for example, made in February 1944 in Havana, is one of the earliest recorded guarachas that includes what had become the standard contratiempo ostinato marking the mambo rhythm. It does not, however, feature "modern harmonies" or inventive instrumentation. But lead vocalist Orlando "Cascarita" Guerra's phrasing of the melody does lend this and his many other recorded guarachas a more varied and nuanced sense of contratiempo. Two years later, in October 1946, the Cueva orchestra recorded Bebo Valdés's "La rareza del siglo" (The oddity of the century), which did feature the modernist characteristics that Carpentier would later list. The record starts with the standard two-measure mambo rhythm arranged for the saxophone section and piano with double bass and percussion accompaniment. The phrase's harmonies descend chromatically from A minor to A-flat major then resolve to the tonic G chord, each chord of which includes ninths and thirteenths. After two iterations of this phrase, the trumpet section enters with a counter melody, the first two notes of which imply an A half-diminished seventh chord. The sounding of an E-flat note in the accompanying A minor chord essentially adds a flat five (or enharmonic sharp eleventh) to the chord's other two extensions (ninth and thirteenth), resulting in an especially dissonant or "modern" sounding mambo. A resolving four-measure phrase follows with a melody that moves through the circle of fifths (i.e., A minor, D^7, G, and so on). This introductory material also serves as the musical accompaniment for much of the sung verses, which thus extends the modernist inflections throughout much of the recording.

The Cueva orchestra's recording of "Rareza del siglo" is indeed an oddity as well. The RCA Victor label lists it as a "montuno-beguine," suggesting a sort of hybrid between Cuban and Martinican dance music. Its musical contents, however, belie the label's implication. Regardless, the song's recordings by other orchestras, such as Venezuela's Luis Alfonso Larrain y su Orquesta, as well as its use in the Mexican film *Ritmos del Caribe* suggest that other record companies, musicians, and film producers considered it profitable. The Larrain orchestra's record was made in 1948 and features the Cuban singer Celia Cruz. For Cuban musician Humberto Cané, this recording of "Rareza del siglo" was the "first mambo I heard with the name 'mambo.' I was living in Mexico City."[38] Such flows of mambo records internationally only begin to scratch the surface of capitalist society's voracious coding and decoding machines. Even women's fashion designs in the United States evoked the mambo, as was the case in the marketing of a Ceil Chapman evening gown made of organdy material that, according to the advertisement, "goes with mambo rhythm though it has an old-time flavor."[39] Entertainment at academic gatherings in addition to radio programs featured mambo dance and records, respectively.[40] Besides the recording industry, perhaps no other industry profited more from mambo in the United States than the ballroom and dance studio industry.

In New York City, for instance, dance studios began to advertise lessons in mambo dancing as early as 1948, the same year in which Cuéllar Vizcaíno and Urfé published their articles in Havana.[41] By the following year, dance studios in Chicago and Los Angeles had followed suit.[42] From Arthur Murray and Fred Astaire to Don Pallini and Dale Studios, mambo's profitability fueled the dance industry, the instructors of which, not unlike record company A&R personnel, scouted mambo dancers in performances. As Cuban Pete recalls, "Arthur Murray and his wife and his crew used to be steady customers of the Palladium [Ballroom] especially on Wednesday because I was dancing. And every time I danced for a show or on the side they will be sitting there and . . . they were counting to see if they can get the basics. I stopped for the moment, stepped to their table, and I said to him, 'If you ask me, I'll show you.' I got the job."[43] During the time the Arthur Murray dance studio employed Cuban Pete as an instructor in the early 1950s, the studio's advertisements promised potential customers, "Because there is only this one master step to learn [regardless

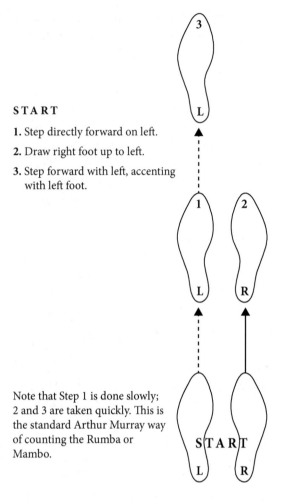

FIG. 5.1 The mambo, Arthur Murray's basic steps and turn. From Mrs. Arthur Murray, "What the Heck Is the Mambo?" *Down Beat*, December 1, 1954, 2.

START

1. Step directly forward on left.

2. Draw right foot up to left.

3. Step forward with left, accenting with left foot.

Note that Step 1 is done slowly; 2 and 3 are taken quickly. This is the standard Arthur Murray way of counting the Rumba or Mambo.

of the style of music], you need fewer lessons and thus save time and money."[44] Kathryn Murray even published an article titled "What the Heck Is the Mambo?" in *Down Beat* that included a drawing of numbered footprints representing the "standard Arthur Murray way of counting the Rumba or Mambo" (figure 5.1).[45] At least two other articles published in *Dance Magazine* and *Life* provided readers with instructions on how to count and execute the mambo's "basic step" (figure 5.2).[46] In addition to teaching such striated renderings of mambo as dance, studio directors also marketed new ballroom dances. Marie Phillips and John Phillips, directors of the Phillips School of Social Dancing in Manhattan, for example, introduced the "rumbop" in 1949 as part of their floorshow at the China Doll nightclub.[47]

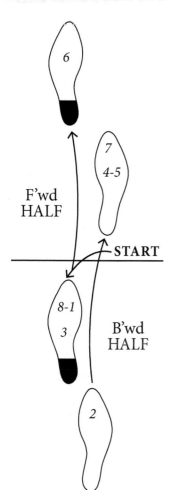

FIG. 5.2 The mambo, Don Byrnes and Alice Swanson's basic step. From Don Byrnes and Alice Swanson, "Mambo: A Vest Pocket Analysis," *Dance Magazine* 25, no. 10 (October 1951): 29.

It is worth noting that American jazz critics reacted to mambo's emergence in the United States in ways similar to Cuban music critics' reactions. For instance, Michael Levin reviewed Machito and His Afro-Cubans' concert at Town Hall in February 1948. Levin began his review by saying the orchestra is "one of the most important influences in jazz today."[48] After citing the consternation of "jazz purists" over jazz "losing its birthright," Levin suggested that the Machito orchestra's music offsets both jazz purists and other critics who complain that "jazz is getting sterile, too intellectualized, lacks feeling and emotion." "A casual glance on the floor of the Palladium ballroom," he advised, "will show a partnership in mutual excitement between dancers and musicians

not seen since the early big band days of the middle thirties." To wit, the fol-
lowing year Mercury Records hired jazz concert promoter Norman Granz
to supervise the company's bebop jazz catalogue. Granz set out to emphasize
"Afro-Cuban bop," producing for its first disc "No Noise" (parts 1 and 2), featuring Flip Phillips on the first side and Charlie Parker on the second side with
Machito and His Afro-Cubans serving as the backing band.[49] Later that year
Granz produced "Mango Mangue" and "Okey Dokie," also featuring Charlie
Parker backed by the Machito orchestra, which received an enthusiastic review
in *Down Beat*.[50] Jazz's traditionalist-modernist debate seemed now to be over-
shadowed by jazz big band's declining commercial viability. Indeed, writers like
Levin and Nat Hentoff, who advised jazz groups that "night clubs and dance
halls require the bands they book to have at least some Pan-Americana in their
repertoire," seemed to suggest that mambo's profitability, not to mention its
musical qualities, would help save bebop's own commercial decline, the imminent death of which one *Newsweek* article announced in 1950 under the title
"Good-by, Bebop."[51]

As mambo's dissemination traversed multiple areas of capitalist society,
Western civilization's disciplinary machines reacted accordingly. In 1951 Havana's magazine *Bohemia* reported that television station CMQ-TV, which
had only recently begun broadcasting, ran afoul among some viewers and
sponsors when several women dancers, including Mexican film personality
Tongolele, "animated by the epileptic rhythm of the mambo contorted their
bodies in front of the cameras, barefoot and seminude."[52] The notion of the
mambo rhythm as "epileptic" and animating the almost nude female body to
contort recalls both Urfé's lamenting of the Cuban youth's "complete erasure"
of danzón dancing's "elegance" with those "wild forms" of dancing, and Cuéllar Vizcaíno's description of Cuban young women having to yell to help secure
their subjective assurance while dancing mambo "a lo diabla." It is perhaps not
coincidental that such striations of mambo as psychologically and somatically
pathological began to be diagnosed during the introduction of television in
Cuba and its growing presence in middle-class homes throughout the United
States. In fact, as mambo sounded and moved in domestic and public places
through an increasing number of machines—record disc players, radio, print
media, television, and film—the more strident, noisy, and pathological it and
the metropolis seemed to become.

Urfé distinguished the "strong" and "sweet sound" produced in some danzones
by the "orquesta típica" from the "strident" mambo. "This is a strident era," Urfé
bemoaned, in which we live: "Stridency, disorder, hullabaloo, and noisy mambos."
Fernando Ortiz, writing in his *Los bailes y el teatro de los negros en el folklore de*

Cuba (Black dance and theater in Cuban folklore, 1951), similarly stated, "We live in a megaphonic and out-of-tune time, noisy and rhythmic, for reasons that cannot be attributed simply to African influences, but rather to the resonances of oto-acoustic technologies and the rhythms and cacophonies of machines," of which he named "neighboring radios which regularly annoy us" and "record players which are used to sell in multitudes cheap and noisy music."[53] He follows this statement by clarifying that mambo, "that beautiful and most difficult effect in vogue," exemplifies the "rhythmic complexity in Afro-Cuban music." Ortiz's explanation is especially significant not for his attribution of mambo's rhythmic qualities to Afro-Cuban and African influences but rather for his attribution of the disruptions of modernity's subjective assurance, including within the modern urban family ("neighboring radios which regularly annoy us"), to the spread of "otoacoustic" technology in the metropolis. Although Urfé and Ortiz seemed to perceive the mambo in rather different ways—as "controlled anarchy" (Urfé) and as rhythmically characteristic of Afro-Cuban folklore (Ortiz)—both Cuban writers agreed with their colleague Alejo Carpentier that it was ultimately a product of modern life in all its strident, noisy, and dissonant excitement. Musicians in New York City as well, such as Pupi Campo, expressed concern about his "mambo blasting colleagues": "Something has to be done about loud music. . . . We have to consider other people who maybe aren't so fanatic."[54]

Whether in Havana or New York City, string- and flute-based charangas or big bands, mambo or the growing volume of radios and record players, modern "organized life" in Western civilization's metropolis was becoming noisier, more amplified, and thus increasingly troubling, disorienting, and in need of silencing. What had been a state of ideal health (national and familial) sounded and enacted in the danzón, for example, was now with the mambo in need of noise control.[55] Thus, capitalism's repressive machines were set into action to recontain mambo's strident sounds and epileptic movements into socially ordered and desire-controlled actions. Dance instructors' and record companies' striations of mambo dance and music were effective manifestations of capitalism's ability to simultaneously profit from but also control sound and movement. But a more explicit inscription of capitalism's capacity to limit its own excesses is evident in the syndicated television episode of *Confidential File* titled "Mambo," which aired in the United States in January 1956.[56] The series, which initially aired locally in Los Angeles beginning in 1953, presented journalistic exposés on various types of social ills and deviants, including shoplifters, prostitutes, child molesters, and con men.[57] By May 1955 organizations in Los Angeles, from women's clubs to the Parent Teacher Association to and the city council to the Emmys, recognized the series for its "cultural" programming. It went into national syndication later that year, airing episodes on barbiturate addicts, phony charities, childhood mental illness, the effects of LSD, and "mambo dance addicts." National newspapers noted that the series "has been endorsed by lawmakers on both state and national levels" for attempting to "shock the public into doing something about grave evils which are flourishing in this country."[58]

The synopsis for the "Mambo" episode reads, "A Mambo dance addict, Manuel Politas, relates how the dance has affected his daily routine. Then actor Cesar Romero discusses his early dance background and how he decided to quit dancing for acting. Then Dr. Sidney Prince, a clinical psychologist, discusses the problem of addiction to things other than drugs and alcohol."[59] In the opening monologue host Paul Coates admits that this particular program is an exposé not of any grave social issue but rather of "mambo addicts" who are a "problem to themselves." Specifically, thirty-five-year old "Manny" Politas, like the few hundred other mambo addicts in New York, Los Angeles, Chicago, and Miami, does not work, eat, or sleep and has no interests in life except mambo and sex. As the camera shows Manny dancing mambo at a dance club, Coats says, "That's what gets them, the rhythm" and adds that the dance is a "frenzied, off-beat shuffle." Coats continues his narration, "One thing I noticed in making the rounds was the surprisingly low number of Latins among the mambo addicts," adding, "Manny's only source of income is teaching mambo dancing," at which point the camera shows Manny, who is (according to Coats) of Greek descent, teaching two middle-aged white women. Then Manny gives his biography, noting that he has tried to stop dancing but "can't kick the habit." "It's going to take a miracle to kick." "I wish I would have never heard of the mambo." Cesar Romero is then featured as a successful actor who was once a dancer but stopped because he felt he was "wasting his time." "What kind of future is there in the mambo?" Romero asks. In the final segment of the program, clinical psychologist Sydney Prince states that he approves of dancing, adding, "People need some outlet from work." The problem arises, he explains, when people "grow up unwanted and unloved" and as a result, as in Manny's case, are incapable of accepting their limitations and moving on to another profession, as Romero did.

Confidential File accomplishes its style of realism entertainment (or protoreality TV) by concluding the episode with the clinical psychologist's Oedipal-based diagnosis of Manny's addiction to mambo dancing. In fact, such diagnoses, including those exhibited in Cuéllar Vizcaíno's and Urfé's reports, were in the service of capitalism's keeping its internal desire-producing limit in check. The Venezuelan psychiatrist Raúl Ramos Calles, who answered *El Nacional*'s survey, did condemn the mambo as a product to boost Yankee tourism but did so as a critique of American imperialism and not of capitalism itself. In other words, the pathologizing of Manny and mambo in general under the regimes of Oedipal psychoanalysis, nationalism, and race enabled the continued disavowing of capitalism's extraction of profits from mambo bodies, on the one hand, and its extraction of surplus value from those same bodies as workers, on the other. In Manny's case, he became a mambo dance addict and thus an unproductive worker not because of the mambo's rhythm but because capitalism exceeded its limit in its desiring-production.

We can trace the terms of mambo's psychological-induced pathologizing back to psychology's own originations as traced by Michel Foucault in his *History of Madness*. For instance, the fact of mambo's capacity to encompass a space in which reasonable men and women could dance as an "outlet from work," as Sydney Prince recommended, and "get rid of their inhibitions," as Jess Stearn of the *New York Daily News* suggested in his article "Touch of Jungle Madness" (1951), recalls the emergence of the asylum as a concealed space to allow madness to express itself freely.[60] "The Broadway home of the mambo is the Palladium, a dance hall at 53rd St., but the craze is spreading to other halls, and there is no telling where it may stop," adds Stearn. "The feverish intensity of the dancers is contagious," all of which point to the long histories of not only madness's removal from society into confinement but also the confinement of contagion embodied by the leper and those suffering from venereal diseases.[61] The symptoms as observed by Stearn in Manhattan had already been noticed in the racialized and gendered bodies in Havana: "Arms, legs, hips and heads are thrown around with rhythmical abandon," or "a lo diabla," all of which are animated by the "epileptic" rhythm of the mambo or are constitutive of its "anarchical" and "bewitching" effects. We saw how such implications of witchcraft, sacrilege, and social disorder, or *brujería* and *ñañiguismo*, served the Cuban historicist's dialectical construction of Cuba's African past and Winthrop Sargeant's racialization of the Cuban popular music industry (see chapter 2). In this instance, the mambo's pathological implications have as much to do with the logic of black music's and dance's African origins as with Europe's own histories of witchcraft, sorcery, divination, and magic, the criminalizing of which contributed to the forging of Western civilization's modern binaries of reason/unreason, sanity/madness, worker/addict, and music/noise.[62]

But what of mambo's racializations? Whereas the black body's chronotopes functioned conjunctively in the performance *and performativity* of black music's and dance's African origins, the mambo body's racial and gendered transgressions seemed to compel the remarking of racial difference and gender comportment in Cuba as well as in the United States. Such transgressions, occurring as a result of capitalism's exceeding its own limits upon the Greek American addict, might even have contributed to the consolidation of whiteness in the United States that Matthew Frye Jacobson traces to the 1940s.[63] For instance, seven years after Sargeant's article "Cuba's Tin Pan Alley" appeared in *Life*, the same magazine published "Uncle Sambo, Mad for Mambo," the title of which signals a neurosis over racial mixing—Uncle Sam (un-raced) becoming the miscegenized Uncle "Sambo" (raced)—as a result of mambo's dangerously transgressive broad appeal, namely among white American women.[64] The article depicts in pictorial form the mambo's dissemination in almost all areas of American social life—white women of all ages and white students taking dance lessons at Manhattan's Palladium Ballroom and in a Portland, Oregon, high school, respectively; sheet music covers of hit pop songs and standards in "mambo rhythm"; Broadway producer George Abbott scouting Cuban mambo dancers; Palladium mambo dancers Millie Donay, an Italian-American, and Cuban Pete, a Puerto Rican; white children dancing and wearing mambo pajamas; mambo on television and in film; and mambo dancing at Harlem's Savoy Ballroom and San Francisco's Macumba Club. Not so hidden among these pictures are those that suggest mambo madness's most endangering implication to the United States' patriarchal and binary racial social order. Indeed, it was the mambo's encroachment on the racial integrity and capitalist productivity of the American Oedipal family—that is, the un-raced patriarchal family par excellence—that threatened to reconfigure the temporal and spatial foundations of modernity's subjective assurance, in this instance in the United States.

Thus "the mambo is beloved by housewives, teen-agers, light-footed members of all races," declared *Life*.[65] Stearn adds, "Take a typical night at the Palladium. An attractive olive-skinned brunette twists and turns with the gyrational artistry of a strip-teaser. (She's a housewife from the Bronx. Comes here regularly with her mother.) Nearby, a grandmother and an ex-Lindy-hopper are hip-slinging. An elderly man with a long beard studies her movements and tries to imitate them. (His wife is a mambo fan. She's threatened to divorce him unless he learns the steps.)" These are the mambo's most palpable instances in which capitalism pushes forward just short of transgressing (Oedipus) modernity's foundational pillars: an "olive-skinned" housewife, chaperoned by her mother, dances mambo, becoming a striptease dancer with a man not her husband; and a grandfather imitating a grandmother's hip-slinging as she, too, dances with another man, lest his wife divorce him for not learning to dance mambo. Insofar as mambo among the youth in Havana similarly disrupted the Cuban family's normativizing of national forms of elegant (healthy) dancing and mu-sicking, capitalism also held to its relative limits specific to Cuban society.

The able-bodied worker, Manny Politas, however, dramatizes the point at which capitalism breaks past its limits, enabling the emergence of a mambo "addict." This is disalienation achieved indeed, yet one that modernity patholo-gized by necessity less it meant the destruction of capitalism and with it "all organized life." No longer was it enough for capitalist time to use the primitiv-ist discourse of "indolent and childlike" to racialize an unproductive body; it now depended also on psychology's discourse of neurosis.[66] The mambo served as an outlet from not only work but also the anxiety of Western civilization's imminent nuclear destruction, as Juan Liscano observed, yet sometimes to mo-dernity's own detriment.

The Existentialist and Lo Real Maravilloso Turns?

The final image of *Life* magazine's "Uncle Sambo, Mad for Mambo" article de-picts the King of the Mambo, Dámaso Pérez Prado, in midleap as he performs with his orchestra on stage in New Orleans (figure 5.3). The caption claims that Pérez Prado created the mambo dance in 1943 in Cuba and made Mexico "wildly mambo-minded." In September 1954, just three months before *Life* issued its "Uncle Sambo, Mad for Mambo" article, the British jazz trade magazine *Melody Maker* published Ernest Borneman's "Big Mambo Business," in which he pro-claimed that mambo was the biggest thing to hit the American business world since the war, though mambo was still a "minority cult" in Britain.[67] Borne-man's estimated figures included 600,000 records of Pérez Prado's "Que rico el mambo" sold and RCA Victor's mambo disc sales of over six million dollars. He adds that because mambo records were outselling jazz records, record compa-nies were featuring jazz band leaders such as Stan Kenton and Duke Ellington on mambo discs.

His profit-generating music was only one aspect of the process of Pérez Prado's production. As early as 1950 newspapers as well as trade and entertain-ment magazines throughout North and Latin America reported on his perfor-mances as spectacles in which, according to Cuban journalist Juan S. Ramos, "vanguardism has exceeded in all its arbitrary fullness." Pérez Prado, that "dy-namic figure," wrote Ramos, is the "most peculiar, because he directs the mambo more with his feet than with his arms."[68] *Variety*'s review of Pérez Prado's perfor-mance in Pasadena, California, in August 1951 refers to his dancers as "addicts" and credits him with being a "canny showman": "He conducts with his hands,

FIG. 5.3 Dámaso Pérez Prado performing in New Orleans, ca. 1954. From "Uncle Sambo, Mad for Mambo," *Life* 37, no. 25 (December 20, 1954): 19.

head, shoulders and feet, and he just about has to. The arrangements meld a little bit of every kind of rhythm including a jungle beat."[69] Although journalists were keen to report on Pérez Prado's profitability and eccentric mobility on stage, the music's primitive African origins remained indeed always at hand. Baltimore's *Sun* reported on what American tourists could expect upon traveling to Havana to experience mambo: "Almost at the moment of landing they can hear the undertone of jungle beats from Africa. The infectious rhythms which greet visitors of the ancient Afro-Negro dance beats."[70] Because of his profitability and mobility, the mambo's Pérez Prado did the most to propel it sputtering onto a manifold of trajectories in Latin America and the United States, including existentialism's and lo real maravilloso's concurrent and emerging vogues and the Catholic Church's increased efforts to stem the growing threats of capitalism, communism, Protestantism, and atheism.

In February 1949, just eight months after it published Manuel Cuéllar Vizcaíno's article on the mambo's growing popularity among Cuban danzón dancers and musicians, *Bohemia* published a short report on Pérez Prado, naming him the inventor of the mambo, that "new rhythm which has been well received in and outside of Cuba."[71] Pérez Prado began writing arrangements with mambo inflections with Orquesta Casino de la Playa soon after Julio Cueva y su Orquesta popularized the big band style of mambo. Casino de la Playa's recording of Pérez Prado's arrangement of "Consuélate" (Comfort yourself) in June 1945 demonstrates his use of the mambo rhythm, scored for the saxophones in the *montuno* section of this guaracha. By April 1949, Pérez Prado had moved to Mexico City to continue recording with RCA Victor's international division, with whom he had begun to record as the director of his own band in Havana in 1946. Among the recordings he made in Mexico City in 1949 and 1950 were "José," "Que rico el mambo" (How tasty is the mambo), and "Mambo No. 5." Reviews of these records appeared in periodicals across the United States, including the *Atlanta Daily World*, *Down Beat*, the *Chicago Daily Tribune*, and the *New York Amsterdam News*.[72] As the records circulated throughout Latin America on RCA Victor's international label, and as American dance band leaders such as Dave Barbour and Sonny Burke recorded their own versions of Pérez Prado's "Que rico el mambo" (retitled "Mambo Jambo" for the US market), pressure to record Pérez Prado on its domestic Pop label came from trade magazines such as *Down Beat*. In addition, *Down Beat* attempted to sway industry doubts about marketing a Latin American band leader in the United States by urging that "Copies of [Pérez Prado's records] should be posted to all Victor leaders as well as artist and repertoire supervisors and Victor brass in general to prove that it can be done, even by Victor."

In fact, RCA Victor had already begun to market Pérez Prado in the United States as the "South American Stan Kenton," "The Stan Kenton of Cuba," and the "Glenn Miller of Mexico," eventually signing him on its Pop label by August 1950 to "satisfy the tremendous demand for more Perez mambo."[73] By November, Pérez Prado's recording of "Mambo Jambo" was in the top twenty-five for radio plays as well as for record and sheet music sales in the United States.[74]

Meanwhile, in addition to records, Pérez Prado's music circulated in movie theaters throughout Latin America. Produced by the Mexican film company Filmadora Chapultepec and directed by the Mexican Chano Urueta, the film *Al son del mambo* (To the sound of the mambo), costarring Cuban actress and dancer Amalia Aguilar, premiered in Mexico City in October 1950 and featured Pérez Prado performing several mambos, including "José" and "Que rico el mambo."[75] As already discussed, the Caracas newspaper *El Nacional* published its survey of mostly Venezuelan intellectuals and public figures regarding Pérez Prado and the mambo in February 1951. One month earlier, Gabriel García Márquez, who at the time was an art and literature columnist for the Colombian newspaper *El Heraldo* in Barranquilla, published an entry titled "El mambo."[76] In contrast to Cuéllar Vizcaíno's and Urfé's historicist perspectives on the mambo in Cuba, García Márquez gives a realist account of Pérez Prado's and the mambo's significance to, in his words, the "little kid from the street corner." In this way, he shares Juan Liscano's and Alejo Carpentier's conception of the mambo as an urban phenomenon, praising Pérez Prado's "discovery" of "threading all urban noises in a thread of saxophones." García Márquez's realism, however, sets his rendering of the mambo apart from his Venezuelan and Cuban colleagues by his privileging of the voice of the "street corner kid" over those academics who are "ripping off their clothes" over the mambo's vulgarity. "I have a feeling that there will be more than two academics underground before the little kid from the corner is ready to accept that 'Mambo No. 5' is simply a hodgepodge of barbarous chords, arbitrarily cobbled together." He continues, "The maestro Pérez Prado has discovered the definitive key to the heart of all of the little kids who whistle on all the world's street corners."

But García Márquez's ultimate distinguishing insight into the mambo comes in his conclusion, in which, in speculating on the validity of the mambo's criticism as a "silly absurdity," he renders the entire project of music and social criticism (modernist, historicist, or otherwise), along with the desire for mambo itself, as equally absurd. All of this absurdity is, García Márquez concludes, "so natural, so human, that it could even be the best motive for a mambo." His realism in this instance points to existentialism's notion of the absurd, defined by Albert Camus as the "insuperable lack of fit between reason's aspirations [i.e., rules, laws, and ideals] and the world as we find it."[77] All is unattainable, García Márquez suggests, whether it be true happiness desired by the urban youth from listening to mambo records as they feed the jukebox their last nickels, or social and political relevance by academics as they vainly anoint themselves as the bearers of scientific knowledge. In his other entries on mambo published between 1950 and 1951, García Márquez similarly undercuts the criticisms of academics as well as modern society's "laws of moderation and discretion" as absurdly irrelevant to the potential freedom of mambo musicians, dancers, and listeners, whose own desires, he notes, are equally alienating.[78] In short, the mambo's absurdity is modernity's absurdity; this, according to García Márquez, is mambo. Such observations, along with mambo dance-music itself, incited modernity's religious machines—the Catholic Church in this instance—into action.

In anticipation of Pérez Prado's return to New York City on March 25, 1951, the Spanish-language newspaper *La Prensa* began to report on his whereabouts early in the month. On March 6, for instance, the newspaper reported that Pérez Prado had arrived in Lima, Peru, where "his rhythms are causing a furor."[79] In addition to performing on radio and in theaters, Pérez Prado also served as a judge for a mambo dance contest at the Plaza de Acho organized by Lima's radio station El Sol. The contest, depending on the report, attracted anywhere between fifteen thousand and forty thousand spectators, and was condemned, as was Pérez Prado's presence in Lima, by the cardinal of Peru and archbishop of Lima, Juan Gualberto Guevara, for the "furor" the mambo and the singer were causing in the city.[80] In fact, Cardinal Guevara threatened would-be spectators and participants of the contest with denial of absolution if they partook in the contest, which was scheduled to take place during Holy Week. The mambo was, in the cardinal's estimation, a sensual and immoral dance, driving "its practitioners to such wild exuberance in Peru," as *Time* magazine reported, and for this reason the cardinal instructed priests not to grant absolution to anyone who danced it (figure 5.4).[81] Pérez Prado caused a furor of sorts among dance promoters in New York City as well when he failed to arrive in time for his concert at the Manhattan Center on March 25. As *La Prensa* reported, after returning to Mexico City from Lima, he went to the United States embassy to apply for a visa, but the embassy was closed on account of it being Good Friday.[82]

On March 26, the day after Easter Sunday, young members of the Acción Católica (Catholic Action) of Lima protested the appearance of Amalia Aguilar, the Cuban actress and dancer who had costarred with Pérez Prado in *Al son del mambo* and was currently promoting her newest film, *Ritmos del Caribe*,

FIG. 5.4 Peruvian dancers dancing mambo against the prohibition of Cardinal Juan Gualberto Guevara. From "The Mambo in Lima," *Time*, April 9, 1951, 38.

which had premiered in Mexico City in December 1950.[83] The protesters, according to one report, had been encouraged to organize by several priests "who had condemned Aguilar's dances, calling them scandalous."[84] Catholic Action groups were lay committees sanctioned by church leadership to maintain the unity of the church against challenges to its teachings from liberal and socialist initiatives and state law as well as all attempts toward social, cultural, and philosophical reform falling under modernity. Catholic Action groups were officially recognized by Pope Pius X in 1905 as tools to exert the church's influence in the world; they continued to play a vital role in the church's ecclesiastical initiatives throughout Pope Pius XII's papacy in the 1940s and 1950s.[85] The Catholic Action group of Lima, founded in 1935, succeeded in consolidating existing lay associations, including youth and women's groups. According to Jeffrey Klaiber, SJ, the group quickly became an important arm of the church in its work to establish an identity in Peru, lending its lay leadership a sense of belonging and even a militant spirit.[86] Among its activities were holding study groups, teaching religion and catechism, and protesting cultural and social activities that the church deemed indecent or immoral, such as the mambo and its performance by Pérez Prado, Aguilar, and their Peruvian audiences in March 1951.

Catholic evangelization in Latin America at this time was of such concern that Pope Pius XII, in his encyclical *Evangelii praecones* issued on June 2, 1951, singled out missionaries in the "interior of Latin America" for the "dangerous pitfalls to which they are exposed from the open and covert attacks of heretical teaching."[87] Although in this instance Pius XII was warning against the spread of Protestantism in Latin America, he also identified the "prevalence of atheistic materialism" and a "certain so-called Christian creed which is infected by the tenets and errors of communism" as "grave dangers" throughout the world. As Joe Holland points out, Pope Pius XII was equally critical of capitalism and communism for their exploitation of the "dignity of the human person."[88] What is more, he had already acted against the grave danger of the prevalence of atheistic materialism by, for example, banning all of Jean-Paul Sartre's work in 1948.[89] Thus, in the eyes of the Catholic Church, Pérez Prado was a perpetual mortal sinner, for in addition to performing the immoral mambo, his favorite author, as reported by *Newsweek* in September 1950, was Jean-Paul Sartre.[90] By June 1951 the Catholic leadership of Venezuela also issued a notice of excommunication of Pérez Prado and another Cuban mambo dancer and actress, María Antonieta Pons, whose film *La reina del mambo* had premiered in Caracas in February.[91]

In June 1951, García Márquez published another entry in his column titled "El diablo de Pérez Prado" (The devil of Pérez Prado) in which he drew upon the irony in the Catholic Church's decision to excommunicate the "serious and well-dressed Cuban composer, Dámaso Pérez Prado, and the rumbera María Antonieta Pons."[92] He points out that film producers and radio broadcasters can make great use of the phrase that the "group of respectable Catholic ladies and gentlemen of Venezuela" have applied to these entertainers—the "true incarnation of the devil [who] go about personally setting the world ablaze"— for their "thunderous promotion campaigns." It is difficult, García Márquez wrote, to find a better phrase that synthesizes with metaphorical preciseness what Pérez Prado and his "excellent creations" mean to "today's world." We, the unconditional admirers of his "originality, technique, and magic," cannot recognize this characterization given to both without "harboring serious fears for the salvation of our souls," but when read metaphorically, he noted, it becomes an "exaltation of [their] merits" as artists. What García Márquez does here is recognize capitalism's axiomatic dominance over or ability to elude and deterritorialize all codes, even those of religious authority delivering souls to eternal damnation. As *Ebony* reported, Cardinal Guevara's condemnation of the mambo "proved ineffectual as hundreds of good Peruvian Catholics lined up to get into theaters and night clubs where the Prado band performed."[93]

As capitalism's internal Oedipal machine operated to recontain its own excesses in the mambo in the United States, mambo simply overwhelmed the limiting capacity of the Catholic Church in Latin America. As Pérez Prado himself explained to *Ebony*, "Music is frequently a stronger force than religion or politics. 'In Lima,' he says, 'the mambo triumphed because it gave pleasure to the people and made them happy. That is more important than church edicts or laws.'" Indeed, but as García Márquez also recognized, the pleasure Latin American urban youth took from the mambo was as absurd as the consternation and damnation academics and priests attributed to mambo musicking and dancing. All that remained in García Márquez's opinion was for film producers and radio broadcasters as well as mambo musicians, dancers, and audiences alike to celebrate the insurmountable schism that separated themselves from the world, their happiness from reality. Pérez Prado's mambos, it seemed, embodied in movement and sound existentialism's fundamental axiom: "Since God does not exist and we all must die, everything is permissible."[94]

In addition to Sartre being Pérez Prado's favorite author, *Newsweek* reported that his favorite composer was Igor Stravinsky. Pérez Prado described his compositional philosophy and the mambo's significance in an interview with *Time*: "I am a collector of cries and noises, elemental ones like seagulls on the shore, winds through the trees, men at work in a foundry. Mambo is a movement back to nature, by means of rhythms based on such cries and noises, and on simple joys."[95] *Ebony* added that he was an "ardent bebop fan" and grew a "goatee in admiration of his hero, Bop King Dizzy Gillespie."[96] Such comments do not readily suggest Pérez Prado's having an existentialist perspective in regard to either composing or the mambo's social significance. They do, however, reveal his modernist musical convictions, which bear themselves out in his recordings, especially those dating from 1949 and 1950. The most recurring techniques that best convey his compositional convictions, whether attributable to Stravinsky or Gillespie, are his use of dissonant harmonic extensions, the whole-tone scale, and static harmonic progressions.

Two bars into "José," for example, a pyramid stretching almost three octaves commences, starting with the saxophones (G^3, B^3, C-sharp^4, F^4) followed by the trumpets (A^4, C-sharp^5, F^5, A^5, C^6), which creates a G^7 chord with ninths, sharp elevenths, and a natural eleventh. This pyramid occurs twice more, following the first verse, which consists of a sung chant over a static harmonic progression that alternates between the tonic C minor and B-flat major, and at the conclusion in an altered version. We hear similar uses of dissonant melodic passages and chordal voicings in "Macomé" and "Saca la mano," in which another pyramid occurs on the root notes B-flat^2 and B-flat^3 played by the baritone and tenor saxophones, followed by a C^4, D^5, G-flat^5, and A-flat^5 played by the alto saxophones and trumpets. The pitches of the pyramid also spell out a whole-tone scale (with the absence of an E). Other harmonically static compositions include "Mambo No. 5" (i.e., the alternate piano solo version), "Timba, timba," and "Pianola." "Mambo No. 5" features Pérez Prado on piano improvising over a two-chord progression alternating between D minor and C^7. He voices these chords with thirteenths and ninths, while his melodic phrasing includes instances of pentatonicism and tone clusters. He concludes the recording by repeating a tritone several times. His piano solo in "Pianola" features many of these same techniques in addition to what a record reviewer for *Down Beat* characterized as "Gershwinesque phrases," specifically variations of piano passages from *Rhapsody in Blue*.[97]

As we have seen, Gilberto Valdés, Antonio Arcaño y sus Maravillas, and Bebo Valdés had used similar modernist techniques, as did Duke Ellington, Dizzy Gillespie, and other American jazz musicians, all of whom shared the desire to expand the musical possibilities of existing structures, whether tonal, rhythmic, formal, or instrumental. The conditions of their desires for using modernist compositional techniques, however, varied among them, as they had among Claude Debussy, Igor Stravinsky, and others who had helped forge these techniques in their production of late tonal and modern art music. Yet, in many instances, performances of their music entailed intense disruptions of the social order, as had occurred in the Paris premiere of Stravinsky's *Rite of Spring* in 1913, in the heated debates surrounding Valdés's compositions and concerts and the reinstatement of comparsas in Havana in 1936 and 1937, and in the orders of Catholic Church authorities in Peru and Venezuela to deny absolution of dancers of Pérez Prado's music in 1951. Insofar as these modernist techniques had continued to function for less than a century as chronotopes of modern music (e.g., impressionism, jazz, bebop, and mambo) and modernity's auditory limits, their implementation in dance-music retained the potential to reconfigure the modern present's social coordinates and their proximities to primitive pasts and racial Others.

That Pérez Prado was, in his own words, a collector of noises from both nature and the modern world suggests that he conceived of his music dialectically, thus enabling some sort of reconfiguration of at least the sounds, if not also the movements, of the metropolis as the spatial center and temporal present of modernity. But if the mambo was also a *movement back to nature* by means of rhythms based on such noises, as he also claimed, then perhaps he understood nature in these instances to mean something more than the temporal and spatial antithesis of modernity. In fact, we might interpret his reference to nature to be akin to existential naturalism's understanding of nature as the rejection of otherworldly doctrines and the affirmation of an otherwise silenced way of experiencing the world that "undermines *any* locus of fixed identity, either in 'us' or in 'reality.'"[98] Indeed, Pérez Prado said as much when he proclaimed that the pleasure his mambo engendered was more important than church edicts or laws. Thus his mambos' movement "back to nature" literally entailed the production of movement and sound by dancers and musicians with the result of their undermining modernity's loci of space, time, morality, and work as these pertained to their subjectivities. The movement "back" was not so much temporal in historicist terms but rather spatial in subjective terms. We might even programmatically read such movements back to existentialism's human nature in some of his recordings.

The first minute and fifteen seconds of "Kon-Toma," for example, begin with a short mambo-inflected figure played by the saxophones, followed by a thunderous C^7 with sharped ninth and eleventh chord played by the entire orchestra. The conga and bongó are then featured, signifying at first primitive Africa as the tempo increases and the bongó improvises, but then the two drums settle into a moderate tempo and a rather mechanical or "silenced" sounding beat. The saxophones enter, playing a two-bar figure consisting of two sets of tritones, that is, G^4 and A^4 alternating with D-flat^4 and E-flat^4, which are then joined by the trumpets creating a pyramid consisting of E-flat^5, G^5, and B^5. The entire pitch set constitutes a whole-tone scale with the absence of an F. The overall musical effect is certainly not one of any identifiable genre of music, nor is there any semblance of melody or form—only noise and rhythm, but the kind of noise that Jacques Attali theorizes as "silence," as with the silence that mass production compels. "A programmed, anonymous, depersonalized workplace, it imposes a silence, a domination of men by organization."[99] Then this silencing noise is broken by the saxophones' mambo rhythm, the trumpets' counterphrases, Pérez Prado's marquee grunt, and eventually the musicians' shout-sung chant. Everything is possible again in spite of worldly motives and values.

A similarly noise-silencing recording is his "Mambo del ruletero" (Mambo of the taxi driver), which was also featured in the film *Al son del mambo*. It includes both a musically simulated and a real taxi horn. The simulation is executed by the playing of C^{3}s and C^{4}s by the saxophones and A-flat^4 and A^4 by the trombone and trumpets. Pérez Prado also sings a verse from the perspective of the Mexico City working class: "Yo soy el ruletero. Yo soy el chafirete" (I am the taxi driver. I am the chauffer). The finale occurs with screaming trumpets playing C^6 and C-sharp^6, topping off a B-flat chord with sharped sevenths, ninths, sharped ninths, and a flat thirteenth. To be clear, such materializations of noise in "Kon-Toma" and "Mambo del ruletero" emanated not from the capitalist commodification of Pérez Prado's music but rather from the metropolis's mechanisms of noise production and control that he, as well as Odilio Urfé, Fernando Ortiz, and many others, observed and commented on themselves. As such, his own poietic underpinnings as a composer enabled the reterritorialization of these otherwise hackneyed modernist compositional and orchestration techniques in ways that Juan Liscano, Alejo Carpentier, and Gabriel García Márquez heard as the "excitement of our time," "modern life," and the "threading of all urban noises." Indeed, the first half of Pérez Prado's "Kon-Toma" eerily sounds a kind of capitalist-compelled silencing noise, which he surely heard in the seemingly chaotic metropolises of Havana, Mexico City, New York City, Caracas, Lima, and many other cities where he performed, composed, and recorded. The metropolis remained modernity's temporal present and spatial center as modern aurality sharpened its ability to stabilize the modern's subjective assurance amid capitalism's intensifying noise production, displaced as it was upon the music of Pérez Prado.

Still, for others the stridency, violence, and conflict sounding from Pérez Prado's mambos could not be anything but the embodiment of the primitive, savage past. According to *Ebony*, for example, the mambo's "impulses are primitive, its rhythms are frenetic, its pace is frantic. . . . Basically a simple step that traces its ancestry back to the Africans—with the addition of strong Spanish influences."[100] This was the conventional movement "back" in space and time in modernity's historicist terms. But even in the existentialism of Sartre, whose notions of anguish and the absurd enabled Liscano and García Márquez to recognize the mambo's capacity to triumph over modernity's insufficiencies and thus to stake a claim in modernity's spatial center and temporal present, historicism's primitive takes its place. For instance, in writing his response to Albert Camus's *L'Étranger* in 1943, Sartre described the "absurd man" as innocent as "primitive tribesmen before the clergyman comes to teach them Good and Evil, what is permitted and what is forbidden."[101] When it came to negritude, historicism's grasp on Sartre revealed itself most resolutely when in explaining how black music and dance is the materialization of the drowning of human suffering by nature's fecundity, he states the following: "Perhaps it is necessary in order to understand this indissoluble unity of suffering, of eros, and of joy, to have seen the Negroes of Harlem dance frenetically to the rhythm of the blues, which are the most desolate songs of the human race. It is the rhythm, in effect, which cements these multiple aspects of the black soul; it is that which communicates its nietzschean lightness to these heavy dionysian intuitions; it is the rhythm in the tomtom, in jazz, in the throbbing of these poems, which expresses the temporal aspects of the Negro *existence*."[102]

Liscano, too, traversed existential naturalism's notion of nature with modernity's primitive by naming humanity's natural state as that "primitive" we "carry inside" such that the mambo or black rhythm can "return a bit of savage happiness" to modern men and women. For both Sartre and Liscano, then, black music and dance were modernity's antitheses in their dialectical formulation of modern humanity's ultimate redemption. It was, drawing from Frantz Fanon's critique of Sartre's *Black Orpheus*, a "stage preceding any invasion," and as such Sartre and Liscano deny Pérez Prado's mambo and dance-music in general its own "substantive absoluteness."[103] "I am wholly what I am," Fanon proclaimed. "I do not have to look for the universal. No probability has any place inside me. My Negro consciousness does not hold itself out as a lack. It *is*. It is its own follower." Ironically, wherein Carpentier failed to free "African magic" (or nature) from colonial history in *El reino de este mundo*, as David Mikics points out, his analysis of Pérez Prado's mambo, based on his modernist and not lo real maravilloso outlook, posits it as a product of the metropolis's own history as spatial center and temporal present of modernity.[104] We will see that in Mexican films the mambo similarly sounded in heterogeneous and conflicting ways, including as belonging to the redemptive history of modernity's metropolis and to its own immoral excesses. In the end, the pleasure that Pérez Prado recognized in his audiences as having come from dancing to his mambos and having overwhelmed the rules and laws of the church was nevertheless always already set up to be interrupted, assuaged, or silenced by another machine's rules and laws.

Cosmic Mambo Realism

In July 1951, Federico Ortiz, Jr., reporting from Mexico City, published an article titled "El mambo y su influencia malsana" (The mambo and its unhealthy influence) in Los Angeles's Spanish-language newspaper *La Opinion*.[105] As with other critics in other parts of the Americas, Ortiz, Jr. expressed his alarm over the mambo's widespread popularity and its "displacement" of established styles of dance music. He also conceived of the mambo as a "product of the times, of the atomic era, of life that develops dizzily" with origins, though, in the "songs of ancient African tribes, which still constitute foreign melodies that were the origins of North American jazz." Regarding mambo music, he claims that it "has not had nor acquired complete musical form." Rather, it is made up of "sounds and noises from Nature," and even though all of the instrumentalists "imitate African drums," the music "lacks the rhythm these drums carry." As for mambo dancing, it only "entails finding the speed in the execution of a thousand steps invented by many other dancers ... contortionism is the principle factor in [its] execution." He continues, "All of a grand multitude of diverse countries have been down-and-out from the euphoria of the mambo, the influence that this new class of music has exerted on people—so quickly and without difficulty whatsoever—only shows a disastrous result, the lack of knowledge, aesthetics, and hence a bit of culture inferior or equal to those of other countries from where comes the origins of jazz and mambo."

Although Ortiz, Jr.'s concerns over the mambo were similar to some of those expressed in Cuba, the United States, and elsewhere, their implications were unique to Mexico's political economy of race in the early 1950s. Perhaps the Mexican philosopher who contributed the most unique perspective on questions of race was José Vasconcelos. Before publishing his influential work *La raza cósmica* (The cosmic race) in 1925, Vasconcelos had already ardently critiqued the nation's positivist writers and educators for their acceptance of Aguste Comte's and Herbert Spencer's theories of social order, progress, and racial evolution, which he asserted were "never able to contain our aspirations."[106] Another Mexican philosopher, Leopoldo Zea, writing in 1943, suggested that Mexican critics of positivism did not attack its philosophical foundations as much as they attacked those who used positivism to "justify their social and political prerogatives," which, as Vasconcelos pointed out, involved denying Indians and the working class a stake in the formation of Mexican society, politics, and history.[107] As an example, in his *La raza cósmica*, Vasconcelos critiqued the "science of the positivists, influenced directly in one way by the State's politics," for their rejection of love as humanity's true law toward the redemption of all races. Racial "antagonism" or "survival and the triumph of the fittest," he scorned, "was positivism's law." "We have been educated under the humiliating influence of a philosophy designed by our enemies ... with the aim to exalt their own goals and annul ours. In this way we have come to believe in the inferiority of the mestizo, in the un-redemption of the Indian, in the damnation of the Negro, in the irreparable decadence of the Oriental."[108]

In spite of such attacks of Mexican society's normative racial hierarchy and racialized worldview, the reception of black music in Mexico City as exemplified in Ortiz, Jr.'s critique of the mambo's perceived chaotic and underdeveloped characteristics indicates the ideological hold that positivism continued to have on writers through 1951. In addition, in the course of Mexicanizing positivism, which Zea chronicles back to the 1860s, Mexican intellectual Gabina Barreda made allowances for Catholicism's authority in his positivist program in recognition of the nation's predominant Catholic population if only as a matter of avoiding social disorder. As Zea summarized, "Barreda, conscious of Mexican reality, only took from positivism those ideas that did not provoke in the spirit of Mexicans controversy that could be carried to the battlefield."[109] Given the place afforded Catholicism in Mexican positivist thought, it is no surprise that the controversy Pérez Prado and the mambo provoked among Catholic Church authorities in Peru and Venezuela also emerged in Mexico, where it was similarly condemned as immoral and sinful in addition to embodying the worst of modern society. Only in Mexico, its condemnations played itself out allegorically in Mexican films such as *Ritmos del Caribe*, released in December 1950, and *Víctimas del pecado* (Victims of sin), released in February 1951.[110]

Cowritten, directed, and coproduced by Juan José Ortega, *Ritmos del Caribe* stars Amalia Aguilar in the role of Magali, a cabaret dancer, and Mexican actor Rafael Baledón in the role of Dr. Carlos Ávila. The plot, which unfolds in Mexico City and Havana, centers on the descent into immorality and despair by Dr. Ávila as he falls in love with Magali and eventually divorces his wife and leaves his daughter. Magali, however, feigns an affair with another man in the hope that Dr. Ávila return to his wife. Instead, Dr. Ávila becomes a drunk and is barred from practicing medicine. Both Dr. Ávila and Magali eventually initiate their personal spiritual redemption by taking two distinct actions, which leads to Dr. Ávila's reconciliation with his family. For his part Dr. Ávila prays for forgiveness to Christ on the cross in a church as his daughter is in surgery, whereas Magali substitutes mambo dancing for Mexican folkloric dancing. Not unlike in the "Mambo" episode of *Confidential File*, Magali's hysteric mambo dancing in *Ritmos del Caribe* is a contributing factor to her fainting spells at the end of her routines as well as at least circumstantial in Dr. Ávila's self-destruction, unproductivity, and destruction of his family. For its dénouement the film's screenwriters used, on the one hand, national folkloric dancing to resolve Magali's health problems and in the process redeem her spiritually and, on the other, the Catholic Church to reverse Dr. Ávila's fall from modernity's patriarchal grace.

During the unfolding of the plot, several scenes featuring performances by Cuban musicians convey additional aspects of the mambo and Caribbean rhythms that sexually, racially, and morally Other the music and dance. In the opening scene Magali dances mambo barefoot and almost nude. A whole-tone figure is heard from the piano as Magali concludes her routine before fainting and being helped off the stage. She is cared for backstage by Cuban entertainer and actress Rita Montaner, who plays herself. (Montaner was a featured vocalist in Gilberto Valdés's concert at the National Amphitheater in Havana in 1937.) Dr. Ávila admits Magali into the hospital so she can recover with rest. When she is well enough to leave the hospital and return to dancing, he cautions her not to drink alcohol and not to overexert herself while dancing. "Be as tranquil as possible," he advises. Although her illness is attributed to a bad heart and the high altitude of Mexico City, her fainting spells brought on by dancing mambo draw upon that discourse of mental illness that attributes such episodes of hysterics to the woman's bodily constitution made weak by nature.[111]

Magali returns to dancing in a nightclub, in a scene that features her dancing to Pérez Prado's "Qué te pasa, José" as sung by Cuban vocalist Silvestre Méndez.[112] Magali's costume includes embroidered musical staves and notes as part of its design, along with two drums attached to her hips. Black rhythm and jungle drums have literally attached themselves to her body. Meanwhile, after singing the verses, Méndez starts scatting in the style of Dizzy Gillespie, at the conclusion of which he says, "Eso es bebop, el último sensacional del año" (That's bebop, the latest sensation of the year), to which Magali replies, "Bueno, yo quiero mambo!" (Well, I want mambo!). Having returned to Havana for its more favorable altitude and accompanied by Montaner, Magali continues performing in nightclubs. One scene features two numbers sung by Montaner and Puerto Rican singer Daniel Santos. Montaner sings "Rareza del siglo" with an accompanying group dressed in traditional Cuban *guayaberas* (shirts) and straw hats, and Santos follows singing "Negra" accompanied by the Cuban group La Sonora Matancera. He sings the second verse in English as Magali appears on stage to dance. For the third verse, Santos scat sings in the style of Cab Calloway. These two scenes represent mambo as doubly Othered: first, racially as black and, secondly, as non-Mexican. By virtue of having Méndez and Santos imitate jazz scat singing, the mambo is even triply Othered as not only black and non-Mexican but also yet another product of Yankee cultural imperialism. Regardless of their national provenance, jazz and mambo shared the same abject origins in the songs of ancient African tribes, as Ortiz, Jr. asserted.

Although the mambo's coding as racially Other is made very clear in *Ritmos del Caribe*, its otherness ultimately entails its assault on women's integrity not only racially but also nationally and spiritually, the coding of which is accomplished almost as obviously. For instance, the name Magali is the French version of Magdalene, as in Mary Magdalene, who, according to several Gospels, was cured of her demons by Jesus. Mary Magdalene's periodic bouts of insanity and demonic derangement are paralleled by Magali's hysterical and seminude mambo dancing, which ends in her fainting. Mary Magdalene's association with prostitution, which apparently emerged later in the history of the Roman Catholic Church, is similarly inflected in Magali's profession as a nightclub dancer and her adulterous affair with a married man. Magali's eventual spiritual redemption, as with Mary Magdalene's unwavering devotion to Jesus through his crucifixion and resurrection, manifests in the film when, lying on her deathbed, Magali enables Dr. Ávila's reunification with his wife and daughter. In fact, Magali's deathbed scene signifies on Jesus's sacrifice on the cross; she dies for Dr. Ávila's sins so that he may be forgiven and reunited with his family. Having been cured of her mambo demons, and establishing her devotion to the Mexican nation by performing folkloric dances, Magali's spiritual cleansing and redemption is completed in this final scene.

Such Catholic and nationalist imagery was not unique to *Ritmos del Caribe*, for the film *Víctimas del pecado*, which premiered in Mexico City in February 1951, similarly draws on what others have theorized as the La Malinche and the Virgin of Guadalupe dichotomy wherein the fallen woman, in this case Violeta as performed by Cuban actress and dancer Ninón Sevilla, redeems herself by sacrificing her life for the sake of the racial and spiritual integrity of the nation. In this film as well as in *Ritmos del Caribe*, guaracha, rumba, and danzón dancing are contrasted with mariachi and Mexican folkloric dance and music, accordingly distinguishing non-Mexican from Mexican national culture and immoral from moral musicking and dancing. As Pérez Prado's and the mambo's popularity in South America and Mexico provoked questions of Christian morality and national integrity among Catholic Church officials as well as some writers and film producers, their profitability continued to fuel its dissemination in the United States, eventually raising concerns over the psychological well-being, capitalist productivity, and racial integrity of American mambo dancers. In 1951, however, much of Pérez Prado's reception in the United States still focused primarily on the profitability of both his records and performances.

In spite of having been signed to RCA Victor's domestic Pop label in August 1950, Pérez Prado encountered resistance from the American Federation of Musicians (AFM) to perform in the United States with his own musicians, the majority of whom were Mexican nationals. For instance, *Down Beat* reported in December 1950 that Pérez Prado "can't get into the U.S. due to AFM restrictions."[113] At the time, he and his orchestra were performing in Mexico City at the Teatro Margo and Centro Social Monumental.[114] Then he tried joining AFM's Local 802, after arriving in New York City from Mexico City on April 4, 1951, but the local's executive board rejected his application, the reasons for which were not included in the minutes.[115] In any event, Pérez Prado was able to perform, using Local 802 musicians, at the Teatro Puerto Rico and the St. Nicholas Ballroom, where his orchestra shared the program with Machito and His Afro-Cubans and with Tito Puente's orchestra.[116] After returning to Mexico City to record four sides, including "Broadway Mambo," he flew back to New York City in May to record another four sides with Local 802 musicians, including Fats Ford, Tony DeRisi, and Francis Williams.[117] Then he performed two nights in Chicago at the Ashland Auditorium, some of the proceeds of which were donated to the Saint Francis Youth Center, whose director, Fr. Patrick J. McPollin, administered to mentor Mexican youth.[118] He returned once again to Mexico City, where he recorded another four sides in June and July.

In the next four months, Pérez Prado traveled several more times between the United States and Mexico to perform and record. In August he toured California with his Local 802 musicians, performing at the Zenda Ballroom in Los Angeles, the Pasadena Civic Center, and Sweets Ballroom in San Francisco. In September he recorded four sides in New York City, then returned to Mexico City, where he recorded one side. He was back in New York City in October to record four sides, then back to Mexico City to record two sides. Finally, starting in late October his Local 802 orchestra toured the United States, performing in Texas before traveling back to California in November to perform at the Paramount Theater in Los Angeles, in addition to shows throughout the state, including Fresno, Sacramento, Oakland, San Jose, and San Francisco. During these months, some reports mistakenly identified him as a Mexican bandleader, while most credited him as the creator of the mambo.[119] Other reports detailed the amounts of his fees and the percentage of the gross from ticket sales—for example, he was paid $2,000 plus $4,600 or 60 percent of the gross for his two performances at the Zenda Ballroom.[120] Also published were reviews of his records, which often commented on the technical quality of the recordings themselves and identified those he made in Mexico City as being superior in sound quality than those he made in New York City, in addition to acknowledging the superiority of his musicians in Mexico.[121] In short, these reports stressed profitability and musical quality over suggestions of Pérez Prado's music having primitive African origins or being dangerous to the psychological and moral well-being of dancers and society in the United States.

One notable exception is the aforementioned article "Mambo King" published in *Ebony*. In addition to characterizing the mambo's impulses as "primitive," the article also cited Pérez Prado's prediction that "it will sweep the U.S., becoming a Western Hemispheric dance craze" and noted that the musicians whom he had assembled in New York City in April were "Negro, white, Mexican and Cuban."[122] For a black American magazine in particular, the nationwide popularity of a racially integrated band was a notable occurrence, one that, as Ingrid Monson has argued, was especially important to the pro-integration discourse that had been developing within the jazz industry.[123] Pérez Prado's interracial mambo band was indeed the continuation of African as well as liberal white and American Negro efforts during World War II to point to the contradictions inherent in Jim Crow and the war against fascism, though he did not explicitly address issues of racial discrimination in reports published at the time. Nevertheless, as Katherine Dunham, Asadata Dafora, Duke Ellington, and other dancers and musicians encountered throughout the 1940s, Jim Crow policies at establishments such as hotels, restaurants, and nightclubs were as much a Northern phenomenon as a Southern one.

On October 26 the bus carrying Pérez Prado's racially mixed orchestra crashed on the road from Port Arthur to Fort Worth, Texas, killing nineteen-year-old vocalist Delia Romero and hospitalizing several members of the band, including the percussionist, Ramón "Mongo" Santamaría; trumpeter Tony DeRisi; and Pérez Prado himself. According to one report, the bus left Port Arthur at 2:00 AM and drove all night in fog and rain, crashing into a bridge column later that morning. This and other recent bus accidents carrying musicians led to renewed calls for the AFM to better regulate consecutive bookings that compelled musicians to travel overnight.[124] Even though Pérez Prado's booking agency assured *Down Beat* that "all of the dates on the tour were well within the three-hundred-mile limit prescribed by union rules," the impossibility of finding a hotel in Texas that would accept all of the bands' members was reason enough to sleep on the bus on their overnight drive.[125] What is more, this incident forces us to reconsider the extent to which the political economy of race in the United States had by this time inexorably reduced the American "polity to a simple dyad of black and white—a scheme in which the former white races [including Greeks and Italians] vanished into whiteness, and in which, so far as public discussion went, American Indians, Filipinos, Pacific Islanders, and Mexican and Asian immigrants and their children vanished altogether."[126] Whereas Italian Americans Tony DeRisi and Millie Donay (Cuban Pete's mambo dance partner) fell within this consolidating category of whiteness, Pérez Prado and Santamaría did not automatically fall within the black category, as demonstrated in the *Ebony* article, even if Pérez Prado, as the article noted, dressed like a "hep cat."

The political economy of race in Mexico, however, provides an important contrast within the context of mambo in regard to that nation's constructions of whiteness, national identity, and history. As shown above, positivist thinking, along with Catholic values, in Mexico continued to shape the production and reception of culture, including films, dance, and music, through the early 1950s. And, in spite of Vasconcelos's widely read *La raza cósmica*, a dominant whiteness, distinct nevertheless from the United States' formulation of a consolidating whiteness, still resonated in Mexican society.[127] In fact, it was Vasconcelos's outspoken anti-American and anti-British imperialism and fervent Mexican and Latin American pride in *La raza cósmica* that accounted for its continued resonance in the decades following its publication. Furthermore, the mambo's racialized otherness and, at the same time, racial erasure in Mexican films gave the lie and magic to Vasconcelos's prediction of a future "fifth race that would fill the planet," a "cosmic race" that would emanate from Latin America, the "home" of the four great races, the white, red, black, and yellow, and thus initiate the third and final phase of human history, which he called the aesthetic age.[128]

On the same night that Pérez Prado's orchestra performed at the Paramount Theater on November 15 in Los Angeles, *Del can can al mambo* premiered in Mexico City. This was the sixth Mexican-produced film in two years in which Pérez Prado was featured as himself. Written and directed by Mexican Chano Urueta, this comedy was set in a fictional town in rural Mexico called Tomplatibio where Don Susanito Llueve o Truene, the director of the Instituto Pedagógico de Trascedental Policultura Femenina (Pedagogical Institute of Transcendental General Culture for Women), scorns the pressures of modern life on the customs, morals, and traditions of rural Mexico. In his opening narration, Don Susanito declares that he and everyone else in Tomplatibio "consider everything modern as terribly harmful" and "savage," including his nephew Roberto's loud car and corruption of the "language of Cervantes." Don Susanito recites romantic poetry and frequently recalls his youth, the scenes of which depict him as a country bumpkin making his way in Mexico City as he eventually comes around to enjoy the pleasures of modern life at the turn of the twentieth century. Ads promoting the film in Mexico City's *El Universal* and *Excelsior* describe the film's plot as a battle between "two epochs": the happy and picaresque can can of 1900 and the Pan-American Highway and mambo of the 1950s; from can can dancing, car racing at fifteen kilometers per hour, and oil laps to mambo dancing and television.[129] Both newspapers also reported that the film had the highest ticket sales among new films in the first six days of its showing.

Rather than being morally corrupted by the mambo, *Del can can al mambo* depicts Mexico as having always been a modernizing nation capable of assimilating, if not overcoming modernity's innovations and potential threats to its national cultural sovereignty and integrity, but not without an initial sense of suspicion or scandalized amazement. For instance, during one of his recollections as a youth in Mexico City, Don Susanito attends the opera for the first time to watch Jacques Offenbach's *Orphée aux enfers* (*Orpheus in the Underworld*). He looks on in shock, wonder, and eventually pleasure and excitement as women dance the can can to "Galop infernal." He also enters an automobile race by happenstance. His youthful adventures are quaint by modern postwar standards, according to his nephew Roberto, who urges his uncle to modernize. "We are in 1951 and you live in a dream," he says, and adds, "Dress something like a *pachuco*!" Once alone in his office, Don Susanito contemplates his nephew's advice, repeating the phrase "be pachuco, be pachuco!" The school's headmistress, Madam Perfect, enters and overhears the school director. Scandalized, she asks, "What say you, Sir?" "I heard you say pachuco, pachuco! A foreign word!" This last line in Urueta's screenplay is a quote from Mexican writer Octavio Paz's *El laberinto de la soledad* (The labyrinth of solitude), in which Paz theorizes the pachuco or Mexican American youth as alienated from his Mexican identity, culturally conflicted, and an enigma.[130] The pachuco's style of dress, Paz continues, is an exaggeration of current popular styles of dress and, as such, signifies his rebelliousness and sadism. Like the mambo, the pachuco "seems to personify liberty, disorder, the prohibited . . . someone, also, with whom it is only possible to have contact secretly, in the dark."

Wherein Madam Perfect and the institute for ladies embody the currency of Mexican positivism, the mambo, pachuco, and eventually Don Susanito are its modern antitheses. Indeed, Don Susanito dyes his hair and mustache black, as he hesitantly begins to adopt modern forms of behavior, including eventually dancing mambo. Meanwhile, Roberto, who has begun secretly courting Marta, a student at the school, meets with her in the dark of night to share their wishes, one of which is Maria's desire to visit Mexico City with Roberto. He describes Mexico City as extraordinary, modern, "where one breathes the fantastic air of freedom," where "it is very easy to find happiness," and "life is full of happiness, and all one's fears disappear." Before parting ways, Roberto instructs Marta to quietly gather the other girls later in the night in the basement for a surprise. That night, the girls gather in the basement, where they find a television set, something they have never seen before.

The schoolgirls turn on the television to the station XHTV, which is broadcasting from Mexico City a program featuring Pérez Prado's orchestra, and a group of women dancers perform "Mambo latino." At once, the music's percussion-dominated introduction, not to mention the percussionists' blackness, including Pérez Prado, who plays the claves, compel the Mexican national project's racial erasures to emerge in various spots. First, the women dancers not only appear racially as white but are also organized into two groups, blondes and brunettes. Meanwhile, as the scene alternates between camera shots of the performers and the students imitating the dancers on television, we see that all of the students are white, too, but predominantly brunette. None of the women, neither dancers nor students, appears to be mestiza, though most of Pérez Prado's remaining musicians (trumpet players and so on) are mestizo. This is indeed an instance of interracial musicking and dancing, but one that plays itself out differently in ideological terms compared to Pérez Prado's inter-racial group of Negro, white, Mexican, and Cuban musicians in the United States. Instead of subverting the United States' racially dyadic nationalist project, this instance of interraciality reinforces Mexico's Hispano-centric mestizaje ideal. Whereas the Mexican takes pleasure in assimilating the modern yet foreign and racially Other mambo, the national essence is sounded and racially embodied by Pedro Vargas, whose performance (following Pérez Prado's) is transmitted live from Rio de Janeiro. All along, Don Susanito, peering through a window outside of the basement, has been watching his students watch the television program. At first scandalized by the mambo music and dance, he is suddenly impressed with this new technology as Vargas sings "Lisboa antigua" (Old Lisbon), a Portuguese song popular at the time. In fact, founded in 1950, XHTV was one of the first, if not the first, television stations to broadcast in Latin America, followed by Havana's CMQ-TV.

From this point on, Don Susanito resolves to relive his youth, or at least enjoy modernity's innovations, including its most current music and language trends. He asks his nephew to drive him to Mexico City so he can experience modernity anew. They drive on the Pan-American Highway, which had in fact just opened in Mexico in 1950. Once in the capital, Don Susanito marvels at the city's buildings, movement, and lights. "It's like a dream," he declares. Then they both attend the televised program featuring Pérez Prado's orchestra playing two numbers. The first, "Muchachita," which his New York orchestra had recorded in September 1951, features a solo by Mexican dancer Gloria Mestre, whose skimpy clothing and sensuous mambo provoke nervous excitement from Don Susanito. Musically, "Muchachita" is set in two tempos, one a moderately fast tempo, and another a slower danceable tempo, during which Pérez Prado and his *timbalero* Yeyo Tamallo, dressed in their pachuco-like long coats and baggy pants, hop up and down on stage. During the moderately fast section, Pérez Prado utters a phrase in gibberish, while other members of his group repeat an oink-like vocal effect. Before the start of the next number, "Paso baklan," which his Mexico City orchestra recorded in July 1951, the program's host invites members of the audience to come to the stage to dance mambo. Roberto goads his uncle into volunteering, who responds by saying that mambo dancing looks like *el mal de San Vito*, referring to the disorder known as Saint Vitus Dance or Sydenham's Chorea.

This is a rare instance in the context of mambo's reception in Mexico in which the dance is pathologized, in this case as the form of hysteria that British physician Thomas Sydenham diagnosed in the seventeenth century. Sydenham and his contemporaries believed that the body, stricken by this disorder, had in fact "become prey to innumerable penetrations by the spirits, where the good order of the internal organs is replaced by a disorganised space where large areas submit passively to the disordered movements of the spirits."[131] As Foucault points out, it is the density of the body or lack thereof that explains why Sydenham believed that women, "because of their more delicate and fine habit of body," were more often stricken by this disease than men. As we have seen throughout this chapter, white women mambo dancers, whether in New York City, Havana, or Mexico City, exhibited in the eyes of men occurrences of madness, epilepsy, and hysteria given their presumably moral and physical weaknesses. Moreover, as Don Susanito eventually participated and took pleasure in dancing mambo, what once appeared to him to be the embodiment in sound and movement of modernity's immorality was now that which Juan Liscano had prescribed as vitalizing, rejuvenating, and liberating "the primitive that we carry inside," only the "we," it appears in this instance, is reserved for Mexican men (figure 5.5).

What is ultimately significant here is the fact that the female dancing body racialized as white constitutes as important a political technology in the logic of black music's and dance's African origins as does the male and female body racialized as black. The temporalities of the past exerted in the performativity of the body racialized as black coincides with the temporalities of the present and future exerted in the performativity of the body gendered and racialized as female and white. This play in the mambo of temporalities within racializing and gendering technologies or machines helps begin to explain why the mambo could be unmistakably primitive, of African origins, and unhealthy, while at the same time be revitalizing, pleasurable, and modern. In other words, the chronotopic values of society's racialized and gendered bodies were made to exert themselves particularly stridently, yet resolutely, when mambo bodies performed. In the case of Mexican films, Mexico's political economies of race and gender lent these bodies' values a uniquely Mexican history, a history whose Hispano- or Euro-centrism still held sway even in Mexico's post-Revolutionary racial and gendered imaginary. This racial and gendered imaginary, having played itself out res-

F I G. 5.5 Mambo dancing displaying symptoms of *el mal de San Vito* in *Del can can al mambo*, 1951 (Producciones Calderón S.A., 1951).

onantly in *Del can can al mambo*, also appears in a review of the film, published in *El Universal*. The writer (under the pen name El Duende Filmo) sets out to prove the notion that "music marches to the beat of the evolution of a nation's customs."[132] As examples of this supposed axiom, the writer points to Johann Strauss's waltz as a "consequence of the previous century's romanticism." The mambo, he asserts, must therefore be "in accordance with these times of indifference, of relaxation of customs, and the turbulent life that people carry . . . in which sicknesses of the nerves have displaced all of the others, for according to information from a medical authority in the United States, fifty percent of all illnesses are due to nervousness." The writer continues, "The mambo, for me, is something so horrible like its creator [Pérez Prado], who his friends call 'seal face.' It should be included among the things prohibited in the campaign against bothersome noises. Nevertheless, there are some who are crazy for the mambo."

In fact, Mexico's racial imaginary at this time excelled in prohibiting or silencing not merely "bothersome noises" but the black and even brown bodies perpetuating such noises from pathologizing its historical narrative. In *El laberinto de la soledad* Paz praised José Vasconcelos's work to modernize

Mexico's educational system on the heels of the Revolution by democratizing it and through it revalorizing the nation's folkloric traditions, including its music and dance.[133] We see the impact of this work, for instance, in Magali's spiritual and thus racial, gendered, and national redemption through performing Mexican folkloric dancing in *Ritmos del Caribe*. The origins of the nation's traditional literature, for example, were, according to Paz, in its colonial past and in the Indian. But for both Vasconcelos and Paz, Mexico and, indeed, all of Latin America were in their essence Hispanic, white. "Any return to tradition," Paz asserted, "leads us to recognize that we are part of the universal tradition of Spain, the only one who we Hispanic-Americans can accept and carry on." Accordingly, in rendering the universality of Mexico's racial imaginary as fundamentally Hispanic, he notes that Vasconcelos's philosophy of the cosmic race—"that is, of the new American man who will dissolve all of the racial oppositions and the great conflict between East and West"—was nothing other than the "natural consequence and the extreme fruit of Spanish universality."[134]

Chano Urueta, who directed and wrote the screenplay for *Del can can al mambo*, similarly discussed the impact Vasconcelos's work had had on him, saying, "I believed during that time that Vasconcelos was going to give Mexico a general cleansing, but he did not accomplish this and so I completely lost hope, in spite of the fact that I still admire him greatly . . . Vasconcelos had a great influence."[135] The cleansing, of course, was to be of Mexico's pre-Revolutionary political, social, and ideological commitment to positivism, a cleansing that indeed Juan Liscano prescribed with black rhythm and mambo, and Urueta as well applied to his screenplay. Yet Urueta did not recognize Mexican positivism's gendered and racial erasures in his representations of mambo dance and music in his own films.

Indeed, with Deleuze and Guattari's notion of faciality we find yet another political economy or mechanization through which "your average ordinary White Man" exerts its power to determine all others by "degrees of [racial and gendered] deviance in relation to the White-Man face."[136] We thus return to Frantz Fanon's diagnosis of the ontological alienation of racialized men and women as well as to the abject being as theorized by Judith Butler (see chapter 3). Whereas Fanon prescribes disalienation from colonialism's and racism's temporal trappings as the only treatment for alienation, Deleuze and Guattari's prescription is not a treatment as such but rather a mapping of the semiotic power of the "White-Man face," wherein the destiny of human beings, they assert, is to "escape the face, dismantle the face and facializations, to become imperceptible, to become clandestine . . . [by making] *faciality traits* themselves finally elude the organization of the face."[137] What is fundamentally at stake for

Fanon, Butler, and Deleuze and Guattari, and Pérez Prado and García Márquez as well, is not freedom from racialization and gendering as much as recognizing the absoluteness or spatial presence of all races, sexes, cultures, classes, and so on, or, as Antonio Benítez-Rojo observed, spaces liberated "from the memory of the skin color minted by the Plantation."[138]

It is particularly significant that Fanon, Guatarri, Deleuze, and Butler consider film as a crucial space in which correlations between the face (as master signifier) and landscape are forged effectively. Fanon references the Warner Brothers film *Green Pastures* (1936), in which God and his angels are black and, among other things, sing spirituals in heaven, as an ironic cementing (or facialization) of God as a "white man with bright pink cheeks. From black to white is the course of mutation."[139] The power of film in terms of faciality, according to Deleuze and Guattari, derives not from the "individuality of the face" of the actors but from the "efficacy of the ciphering [film] makes possible" "*through* the face of the star and the close-up"—therein, expanding the semiotic surface for the asignifying, asubjective, faceless, or simply abject beings such as a black God while simultaneously closing it off by, in this instance, attributing the existence of a black God to mere irony.[140] Apparently, the threat of Western civilization's self-destruction could never make such a notion signify reality without definitively undoing modernity's system of spatiality and temporality. Thus was the lie and magic of mambo, lo real maravilloso, and la raza cósmica in their materializations in modernity, a lie that Carpentier himself would own up to later in life.[141]

Dance-Music as Rhizome

A line that delimits nothing, that describes no contour, that no longer goes from one point to another but instead passes between points, that is always declining from the horizontal and the vertical and deviating from the diagonal, that is constantly changing direction, a mutant line of this kind that is without outside or inside, form or background, beginning or end and that is as alive as a continuous variation—such a line is truly an abstract line, and describes a smooth space. —GILLES DELEUZE AND FÉLIX GUATTARI, *Thousand Plateaus*, 1987

More than a logic of oppositions or a historical proposition, black music's and dance's African origins were also matters of people performing the past out of the temporal and spatial practices given to them in modernity. By "practice" is meant the kinds of play (analyzing, listening, embodying, disalienating, and desiring) with the past that this book has mapped and, in the process, ended up following a range of individuals who in engaging in black music's and dance's African origins, either implicitly or explicitly and no matter their motivations (scientific, artistic, political, or experiential), were all along forging futures out of the temporal and spatial conditions of their respective placings in modernity. To support this point is to not only extract the evidence from the previous five chapters of the past's subordination to the workings of their present and futures but also highlight the urgency in our own present of how we are researching, understanding, and, most importantly, teaching black music and dance history.

It must first be reiterated that the past as origin to which this book's case studies looked existed in pure and empty time, that is, the past along with the future existing as fractures in the temporal series of capitalist time and Western evolutionary time, under which were subsumed the jungle, native, primitive, slave, nation, bush, city, unconscious mind, ñañigo, disc record, colonialist, nonobjective, and magical. All of these notions operated—when it came to the logic of black music's and dance's African origins—within and around the spatial and temporal axes of Africa as past and modernity as present. The previous chapters show that modernity as spatial and temporal present carried with it the authority to define the historical past and set the spatial parameters of its relationship to this past. Each case study exerted such authority concerning a past, the imperatives for and outcomes of which, I argued, were determined by that person's present or subjective assurance in modernity. Thus the desires of anthropologists and comparative musicologists to make the so-called bush their laboratory for the study of the present's musical past were matters concerning the legitimacy that came with doing scientific work. Although their purpose was to unravel modern society's political economies of race, their desire to do this work under modernity's regimes of truth in the anthropological field and laboratory paradoxically ensured the essence of race's binary logic (the raced and un-raced) its empirical sustenance.

The disc record and lecture-concert, like the bush and laboratory, constituted similar nodes of modern aurality's spatial practice for the confluence of modernity's intensely paradoxical materializations (presencings) of, on the one hand, the African native-primitive-ancestor-national pasts and, on the other, the un-raced present. Enabled by the discursive formations of history, nationalism, and psychology, including its subgenres (Gestalt, behavioral, psychoanalytical), these spatial practices or dispositions of listening in the end merely helped to renew existing paths of temporally and spatially distancing Africa and bodies racialized as black from modernity. "Renew" in that the lecture-concert and disc record exonerated the modern black body from the nation's history of slavery only to hold the vestiges of the African primitive, savage, or black Other over the modern's head, thus renewing whiteness as the un-raced default of the nation's modern or present identity. Also "renew" in that the modern American Negro's African musical past could be located in the unconscious mind of the native African or bush Caribbean musician. Such archaeologies of the Cartesian body and mind racialized as black and temporalized to the past were, in all of their depersonalizing and dehumanizing violence, paradoxically commandeered by university students, political activists, actors, singers, and dancers as "embodiable" technologies for contending with historical ignorance and partaking of knowledge production for the greater purpose of achieving social equality and political independence.

In contrast, artistic creation in its purest form, as this notion was put forth by modernist dance critics and avant-garde filmmakers, struggled to operate in contention with or outside of capitalism's and Western civilization's strictures, the temporalities of which as we know favored and disadvantaged some over others depending on one's temporal and racial status within modernity's axes. But the fact that some artists and writers racialized as black penetrated capitalist time and Western civilization time, revealing to themselves and others their complicity in perpetuating their own temporalized and spatialized status, reminds us that modernity's temporal and spatial axes to Africa were all along recognized, manipulated, mocked, or else utterly rejected as such. If these subversive actions were not enough to evidence that knowledge of time's and race's contrivances have always accompanied its practices, habits, and dispositions, then the interjections of the cosmic and magical only further muddled yet ultimately failed to overthrow capitalism's and Western civilization's hold on time and space.

Why then modernity's need for this logic of black music's and dance's African origins if it was so arbitrary? Precisely so that it could absorb in all of sounds' and movements' malleability capitalism's excesses together with Western civilization's anxieties. Black music and dance, in this case, were not merely products of New World Negro or black Atlantic history but instead formed, from their affective materializations as movement and sound, a historical map *with* time and race. As the previous chapters show, this fact was not at all inconsequential or inevitable. It required that the individuals presented here expend a tremendous amount of energy and incessantly demanded from them repeated declarations of the Negro's reason for being-in-the-world as in the justification and the premise of their racialized existence in modernity. To be clear, what this book is ultimately proposing is that there is a danger in understanding music and dance *in* its social and historical context, a danger much too readily disavowed by music and dance scholars. The danger being these contexts' blockages that transform sound and movement from affective flow to, for example, African and European, black and white, or primitive and modern music and dance such that people are made temporally and spatially distant from each other.

Hence, more than presenting black music's and dance's African origins in their historical and social contexts of the 1930s through the early 1950s, this book grasped dance-music as movement, sound, and affect in spite of its context and as manifested underneath the analyzing, listening to, embodying, disalienating, and desiring that then gave it its logical shape or form. If we truly believe that race, gender, time, and space are social constructs (and they are), then understanding dance-music must begin and always return to conceiving it as sound, movement, and affect, a blank slate as it were, or a smooth space as it is, knowing however that in every instance we attempt to understand or do it, we turn it into some*thing* (e.g., black music or dance) as directed by our own present or temporal and spatial context. This is how black music's and dance's African origins, or music and dance history in general, continue to be actionable in the imagination, that is, by reterritorializing sound and movement as a proposition of logic or simply conceivable and determinable. But as the previous chapters show, this proposition is inherently a double-edged sword.

All of this hinges on the discourse of race, including its most deceptive form, the un-raced, for instance, of Western classical music. It requires time as well. Even without gender and space, the notion "black music's and dance's African origins," or indeed the origin and history of any music, cannot exist as a proposition of logic. But, of course, they all continue to exist. Perhaps origin has succumbed under the weight of critical theory's speculative work, yet it continues to reign as does history as ordered time (royal science) even in the very disciplines that have proclaimed critical theory's authority, such as in musicology and ethnomusicology. Based on what this conclusion is proposing, is it appropriate to conceive of this book as having to do as much with our so-called postracial, postmodern, post–Cold War, post-9/11 present? Yes, so far as black music's and dance's African origins are meaningful to us today, which is to say, we still feel, think about, and act on the reverberations of its racializing and temporalizing imperatives, habits, and practices and as long as we ultimately articulate these resonances to our own present's empty and ordered time.

As for this book's materials, however, they do have an empirical foot in the real historical past, the crucial question being *whose* historical past? Consider Marshall W. Stearns's diagrams of the origins of jazz and the plane of what he labels "Afro-Euro-American Music" in the 1940s (figures C.1 and C.2).[1] Preparing these around 1956 to use in his lectures on the history of jazz, Stearns, following in the footsteps of John Hammond and Rudi Blesh, not to mention Modupe Paris and Asadata Dafora, began to organize formal events on the history of jazz at the Music Inn in Lenox, Massachusetts, beginning in 1950. More than relics of the intellectual history of jazz studies, however, these segmented diagrams or arborescent systems reproduce the kinds of spatial and temporal thinking that undergirded the logic of black music's and dance's African origins and that still function to structure music and dance surveys, whether historical or regional, jazz or classical, African American or Cuban, as taught in university today, especially "Introduction to" classes.

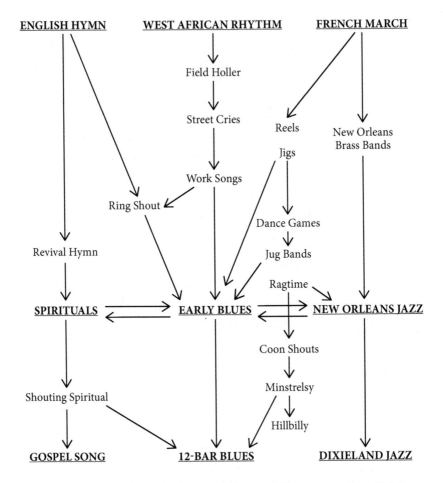

FIG. C.1 "Jazz Origins (The Blues)," prepared by Marshall W. Stearns. From "A Syllabus of Fifteen Lectures on the History of Jazz," ca. 1956. Marshal Winslow Stearns Collection. 1935–1966. Institute of Jazz Studies, Rutgers University Libraries.

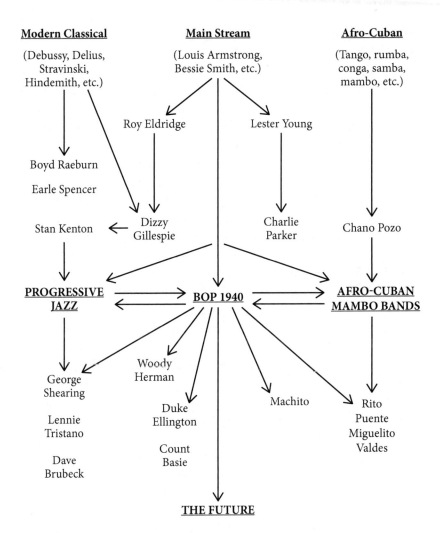

FIG. C.2 "Afro-Euro-American Music, 1940–1950," prepared by Marshall W. Stearns. From "A Syllabus of Fifteen Lectures on the History of Jazz," ca. 1956. Marshal Winslow Stearns Collection. 1935–1966. Institute of Jazz Studies, Rutgers University Libraries.

Of course, the purpose of Stearns's diagrams was and remains heuristic; indeed, following the preestablished paths of his lines or arrows from top to bottom, and diagonal across into adjacent paths, delimits the contours of the English hymn, West African rhythm, French march, modern classical, main stream, and Afro-Cuban through space and time. Still reading these two diagrams heuristically, the spatial representations of these musical developments' time lines clearly indicate how time readily lends itself to be spatialized and contracted as the case may be, that is, according to whose past is being represented. In other words, the logic of each system centers on a central organ or unit around which lower units are organized hierarchically. Thus the paths of jazz's origins, the blues, naturally lead to or circulate around the "early blues," but what this Ptolemaic-like system does besides predetermining the channels of transmission is allot other movement and sound expressions their spatially and temporally distanced and thus subordinate place. Similarly, in his diagram "Afro-Euro-American Music, 1940–1950," Stearns juxtaposes the developments from modern classical, main stream, and Afro-Cuban to progressive jazz, bop, and Afro-Cuban mambo bands, respectively, but contracting time accordingly: the approximately sixty years separating Debussy from progressive jazz is contracted to thirty years separating tango from mambo, which is further contracted to twenty years separating Louis Armstrong from bebop. What accounts for these contractions of time is the fact that the diagram is centered on bebop; it is as if tracing one's genealogy necessitates the contraction of coeval genealogies.

To liberate oneself from these types of spatializing and temporalizing music and dance history is not easy nor perhaps completely achievable or definitively sustainable. This book has nevertheless attempted to do this by excavating new or never considered channels of communication such as those between Modupe Paris, Zoila Gálvez, and Chano Pozo or between Katherine Dunham, Duke Ellington, and Harry Smith. And the paths of communication that have been considered by others, such as those between Melville J. Herskovits, Erich von Hornbostel, Mieczslaw Kolinski, and Richard Waterman, are explored here as centered on not merely the intellectual history of New World Negro studies and comparative musicology but more importantly the turbulent and explosive political economies of race in Europe and the United States at the time. Put simply, these maps that this book produces approach acentered systems, the correspondences of which emanate from a multiplicity of performed occasions instead of being predetermined by a hierarchically defined center rooted in an originating point, whether an individual or repertory of music and dance. Even in the case of the mambo, its origins are located in its executions as sound and movement, whether in the concert hall, reports and editorials, disc record, or film, in Havana, New York City, Lima, Caracas, Mexico City, Chicago, or Los Angeles. The performances scattered throughout the chapters of this book make up the kinds of abstract lines constituting smooth spaces or rhizomes.[2]

This is why black music and dance are powerful because, in exploring the logic of their origins, they reveal themselves to have been not about origins at all or even history as much as quests for freedom in and from modernity's present. Like a rhizome, black music and dance bring into play very different discursive formations while remaining irreducible to any one of these. Such quests for freedom thus pertained to many groups of people beyond any one race, ethnicity, nationality, sex, or profession. In fact, what we have been taking for black music and dance is in its essence about the quest for individual and group freedom, a freedom not of the Hegelian and Comtean traditions but a freedom from all discursive formations, all of one's world's machines, including freedom from itself as discursive formation, hence, dance-music. Sound and movement as music and dance are too easily ordered as presupposing difference, too easily distributed into divisions; this is why this book focused on the phenomenological and ontological nature of these case studies' engagements with and performances of Negro spiritual, Bush-Negro music, Caribbean and modern dance, jazz, mambo, and so forth, and not necessarily on these sounds and movements themselves or, worse, their supposed genealogies. It avoided defining these dance-musics by species or genus characteristics and instead counted them by their affective transformations into "soul," "shakes," "shivers," or "epilepsies," as the case was to be.

In a way, this book does present black music and dance in its origins, but origins of another epistemological order, that of affect, becomings, and nomadic distributions. Yet the problem of dance-music's affects is indeed its own overwhelming power to move people to think, feel, and act in the present. The fact that individuals operating in arenas of discourse and across national boundaries found in Africa a unity and common utility speaks to its ideological potency in meeting their desires to define black music's and dance's racial and historical origins and otherness. These may not be new or innovative notions, but it is necessary nevertheless to reiterate them time and time again if only because the machines of race, history, gender, sexuality, nationality, ethnicity, and geography never quit in making themselves be generators of truth. Indeed, at the moment this paragraph is being written (July 2015), the United States of America and the Republic of Cuba have officially reestablished normalized diplomatic relations and it is one week after President Barack Obama gave the eulogy at the funeral service of Reverend and state senator of South Carolina Clementa C. Pinckney. President Obama's singing of "Amazing Grace" is still evoking thoughtful and deeply emotional commentary from bloggers and others throughout the world. Shortly before commencing the climax of his eulogy by singing "Amazing Grace," the president quoted Reverend Pinckney's observations of history: "Reverend Pinckney once said, 'Across the South we have a deep appreciation of history. We haven't always had a deep appreciation of each other's history,'" which the audience acknowledged with reverent laughter and applause. "What is true in the South is true in America," the president continued. "History can't be a sword to justify injustice or shield against progress but must be a manual for how to avoid repeating the mistakes of the past, how to break the cycle, a roadway toward a better world."

Already, commentaries are placing President Obama's eulogy and singing of "Amazing Grace" into the genealogy or context of African American history. This is important, but it also calls forth once again the distancing that time and race pays forward in the present. The president very clearly is focused on the future of our collective present, but I believe we can take the notion "breaking the cycle" even further to reference not merely the past but also our dependence on history for how we define who we and the Other are, where we and the Other came from, and where we and the Other belong. Whose history? That is the point, I believe, Reverend Pinckney had made, but is there an underlying problem with history's past? Referencing the more than fifty years of hostile relations between the Cuban and American governments, President Obama noted the significance of reestablishing diplomatic relations by saying, "We don't have to be imprisoned by the past. When something isn't working, we can and will change." While the past will always be with us, how we formulate it as history, as with Southern history, Cuban-American history, or music and dance history, might describe the paths of freedom for many while inevitably marginalizing Others. In the end, what I hope readers take from this book is the conviction, if they did not have it already, of putting forth the history of music and dance always as constituting the ground of our present, of our subjective assurances, and always remaining cautious of the illusions of the truth we make origin or history out to be.

Introduction

1 Jones, *Blues People*, x.

2 Johnson, *Book of American Negro Spirituals*, 12.

3 Throughout this book I refer to "historicism" and "historicist" in two interrelated ways: first, in reference to History as determined by modernity's claims of immutable or naturalistic laws; and, second, as the historian's project to understand the human agency necessary to the application or rendering of History as such. Ranjana Khanna's study of the uses of psychoanalysis ethnographically and in terms of its worlding is especially influential in this aspect of the book's methodology, as is Paul Gilroy's commentary on historicality in reference to the differentiating of people temporally and racially. See Khanna, *Dark Continents*; and Gilroy, *Against Race*.

4 From the Asadata Dafora Papers, newspaper clippings, 1934–1962.

5 Jones, *Blues People*, x.

6 See Edwards, *Practice of Diaspora*, 7–15.

7 See Gilroy, *Against Race*, 54–58.

8 See Gilroy, *Against Race*, 31, 67. My use of the notion "un-raced" derives from Judith Butler's formulations of melancholy, unmarked bodies, and normativity wherein whiteness, along with heterosexuality and patriarchal masculinity, becomes the race par excellence whose contingency (or "loss") modernity cannot grieve and thus necessitates and sustains the racialized Other. In fact, Butler considers sexuality, gender, race, class, and other identificatory formulations as forming the same "dynamic map of power in which identities are constituted and/or erased, deployed and/or paralyzed" (Butler, *Bodies That Matter*, 117; see also 170–171, 233–236). Although she considers sexism as the most widespread form of oppression, tracing back to the family and home, bell hooks also sees the interconnectedness of systems of oppression when she says "destroying the cultural basis for [sexist] domination strengthens other liberation struggles" against racism and classism (hooks, *Feminist Theory*, 40–41).

9 It is important to point out, too, that because the terms "Negro" or "*negro*" used to describe and identify music and dance were specific to the historical

period under consideration, and because this book focuses on the ontological and historicist implications in the question of black music's and dance's African origins from the 1930s through the 1950s, it keeps this terminology accordingly for documentary and analytical purposes and turns to contemporary terminology (e.g., African American) when making interpretive observations from a current perspective.

10 Gilles Deleuze and Félix Guattari define their notion of the machine as a "*system of interruptions* or breaks. . . . Every machine, in the first place, is related to a continual material flow . . . that it cuts into." Their theorization of capitalism as a schizophrenic machine is especially important to my analysis of mambo in chapter 5 (see Deleuze and Guattari, *Anti-Oedipus*, 33–36).

11 Whereas Edwards tracks a difference between Africa as diasporic project, the emergence of which he traces to the 1950s, and Africa as incursion into modernity, which he notes was the original rationale for *Présence africaine* (1947), this book focuses on the interstices connecting both diaspora and modernity, namely, constituted in their shared temporal and spatial configuration. See Edwards, "Uses of Diaspora."

12 I use the notion "case study" not in the clinical sense as understood in psychotherapy, psychology, and psychiatry but rather as used more generally in the humanities to mean an individual and events that serve as the focus of my analysis.

13 de Certeau, *Practice of Everyday Life*, 117.

14 Small, *Musicking*, 50.

15 K. H. Miller, *Segregating Sound*, 2.

16 See Sterne, *Audible Past*, 14.

17 Throughout this book, I use Stuart Hall's notion of "articulation" to highlight the processes that enable connections or links of two unlike elements to be made under certain conditions. Hall explains that an articulation "requires particular conditions of existence to appear at all, and so one has to ask, under what circumstances can a connection be forged or made" (Hall, *Cultural Studies 1983*, 121).

18 Deleuze and Guattari, *Thousand Plateaus*, 238–239.

19 Deleuze and Guattari, *Thousand Plateaus*, xvi.

20 Sterne, *Audible Past*, 90–93.

21 Ochoa Gautier, *Aurality*, 3.

22 de Certeau, *Practice of Everyday Life*, 117.

23 This application of practice and space is drawn from Henri Lefebvre's writings on spatial practice and neocapitalism in *Production of Space*, 33–38. Lefebvre's historicist account of the emergence of the modern city separate from the countryside is particularly pertinent to the spatial workings of the logic of black music's and dance's African origins studied here. The conception of this separateness and its perception in terms of distance, according to Lefebvre's estimation, emerged with the spatial practices of town dwellers in Europe and Spanish America beginning in the sixteenth century (*Production of Space*, 268–272). Ana María Ochoa Gautier similarly points to the sixteenth century's significance as the moment of global, capitalist modernity's emergence (Ochoa Gautier, *Aurality*, 10).

24 Deleuze and Guattari, *Thousand Plateaus*, 492–494; see also Ochoa Gautier, *Aurality*, 16–17.

25 Du Bois, *Souls of Black Folk*, 102.

26 See Spengler, *Decline of the West*, 41, 77–78.

27 See Du Bois, *Souls of Black Folk*, 100–103.

28 For an intellectual history of the primitive, see Kuper, *Reinvention of Primitive Society*.

29 Spengler, *Decline of the West*, 231; see also 72.

30 For contemporaneous critiques of Darwinism, see Hofstadter, *Social Darwinism*; Sánchez Reulet, *Contemporary Latin-American Philosophy*; and Zea, *El positivismo en México*. For a critique of primitiveness in Africanist ideology, see Mudimbe, *Invention of Africa*.

31 Fanon, *Black Skin, White Masks*, 12, 17–18, 25–26. Also informative in the critique of the racial implications in Kant's and Hegel's philosophy are Camara, "Falsity of Hegel's Theses"; Kleingeld, "Kant's Second Thoughts on Race"; and Verharen, "New World."

32 See Fanon, *Black Skin, White Masks*, 109–110, 153–154.

33 Du Bois, *Souls of Black Folk*, 102 (my emphasis); see also Sundquist, "Introduction," 10.

34 bell hooks reminds us that Fanon and other important political thinkers often ignored issues of sexist oppression in their own writing (*Feminist Theory*, 41–42).

35 Agawu, *Representing African Music*, 160.

36 Agawu, *Representing African Music*, 165; see also 45, 69–70, 95–96.

37 See hooks, *Feminist Theory*, 113–115.

38 See Krehbiel, *Afro-American Folksongs*, ix, 115–116; Herskovits, *Myth of the Negro Past*, 262.

39 See Modupe, *I Was a Savage*, 91–96.

40 Modupe, *I Was a Savage*, 133–134.

41 Modupe, *I Was a Savage*, 3.

42 For explanations of conceptual equipment and temporality, see Heidegger's *Basic Problems of Phenomenology*.

43 E. P. Thompson, "Time."

44 hooks, *Feminist Theory*, 60.

45 Diawara, *In Search of Africa*, 6.

46 Mudimbe, *Invention of Africa*, 20.

47 My use of "striation" is taken from Gilles Deleuze and Félix Guattari's discussion of striated space (cf. "smooth space") as that which limits or restricts by direction or boundaries anyone or anything in motion. Examples of striating forces include religion, the state, history, philosophy, psychology, and so on (see Deleuze and Guattari, *Thousand Plateaus*, 381–385).

48 See Deleuze and Guattari, *Thousand Plateaus*, 256–257, 406.

49 Deleuze and Guattari, *Thousand Plateaus*, 7.

Chapter 1. African Origins

1 UNESCO, *Race Concept*, 6.
2 UNESCO, *Race Concept*, 7.
3 See Selcer, "Beyond the Cephalic Index," 173–184.
4 UNESCO, *Race Concept*, 11.
5 Melville J. Herskovits to Alfred Métraux, October 22, 1952, Series 35/6, Melville J. Herskovits (1895–1963) Papers.
6 UNESCO, *Race Concept*, 13.
7 Herskovits to Métraux, October 22, 1952.
8 Du Bois, "Africa and the Slave Trade," 630–631; George S. Schuyler, "Views and Reviews," *Pittsburgh Courier*, June 11, 1927, A8; Molesworth, *Works of Alain Locke*, 251.
9 Cf. Jacobson, *Whiteness of a Different Color*, 98–99.
10 UNESCO, *Race Concept*, 10.
11 See Gilroy, *Against Race*, 32–35.
12 Heidegger, *Being and Time*, 476–477; and *Basic Problems of Phenomenology*, 262, 270–274. See also Fabian, *Time and the Other*, 17; and Martin, *Languages of Difference*, 22–24.
13 Du Bois, *Souls of Black Folk*, 199 (my emphasis).
14 As Mudimbe argues, "Time, space, and the (un)conscious of the scientist" constituted the "ideological locus" of scientific practice in Africanist anthropology through the 1980s (*Invention of Africa*, 175).
15 Mudimbe's *Invention of Africa* is particularly pertinent in this regard.
16 The historiographical scholarship on Herskovits's work, particularly of the 1930s, has not adequately addressed the direct impact Nazism had on his work and thinking, particularly in regard to his collaborations with Kolinski.
17 See Cole, "Ruth Landes," 166–185.
18 UNESCO, *Race Concept*, 5.
19 Richard Price and Sally Price state that Herskovits and his wife and coresearcher Frances routinely "Africanized" their informants when doing fieldwork in Suriname and artificially isolated the territory of the "bush" from the outside world. See Price and Price, *Root of Roots*, 21, 46–48.
20 See Spivak, "Translator's Preface," xxiii–xxxv; and Lefebvre, *Production of Space*, 33.
21 Melville J. Herskovits to Fernando Ortiz, June 12, 1946, Melville J. Herskovits (1895–1963) Papers.
22 Herskovits, *Myth of the Negro Past*, 32.
23 Williams Jr., *Rethinking Race*, 27–36.
24 Jackson, "Melville Herskovits," 104–105.
25 Gershenhorn, *Melville J. Herskovits*, 127–128; see also Jackson, "Melville Herskovits," 104–105.
26 Herskovits, "Negro in the New World," 1.
27 See Jacobson, *Whiteness of a Different Color*, 187–199.

28 Robin Moore traces this shift in Ortiz's scholarship. From the 1900s through the early 1920s, Ortiz studied Afro-Cubans from criminology and social Darwinist perspectives and called for the de-Africanization of Cuba, targeting practitioners of Santería as deviant members of Cuban society. See Moore, "Representations," 36.

29 Ortiz, "Relations between Blacks and Whites," 21. This is a published version of a speech Ortiz delivered to Club Atenas, a black and racially mixed middle-class social club, in 1942.

30 Fernando Ortiz to Melville J. Herskovits, January 14, 1929, Series 9/28, Box 17, Folder 15, Melville J. Herskovits (1895–1963) Papers.

31 Presumably, the book that Ortiz refers to is *Los instrumentos de la música afrocubana*, the first volume of which he would not publish until 1952.

32 Ortiz to Herskovits, November 26, 1931.

33 Herskovits to Ortiz, February 2, 1932.

34 Ortiz to Herskovits, November 15, 1934.

35 "Estatutos de la Sociedad de Estudios Afrocubanos," 7 (my emphasis).

36 See Ortiz, " 'Razas Puras' y 'Razas Impuras,' " *Magazine de Hoy*, October 28, 1945, 3.

37 Gershenhorn provides a detailed analysis of this debate as it pertained to Herskovits's research in the early 1920s (*Melville J. Herskovits*, 27–57).

38 Hornbostel, "American Negro Songs," 748–753.

39 Erich M. von Hornbostel to Melville J. Herskovits, May 29, 1927, Series 9/28, Melville J. Herskovits (1895–1963) Papers.

40 Williams Jr., *Rethinking Race*, 4–36.

41 See chapter 2 for a more detailed explanation of Gestalt psychological theory as used by Richard Waterman in his research and scholarship on New World Negro music.

42 Hornbostel, "American Negro Songs," 752.

43 Herskovits to Hornbostel, June 10, 1927.

44 Hornbostel to Herskovits, June 27, 1927.

45 Herskovits to Hornbostel, October 5, 1927.

46 J. W. Johnson, *American Negro Spirituals*, 17; see also Gershenhorn, *Melville J. Herskovits*, 67.

47 Gershenhorn, *Melville J. Herskovits*, 70.

48 Herskovits, "Negro in the New World," 3.

49 Herskovits, "Social History of the Negro," 212.

50 H. Gordon Garbedian, "Dutch Guiana Negroes Keep African Culture: An Expedition to a Little-Known Country Brings Back Objects of an Ancient Art Which Has Persisted in the Jungle of the Western World," *New York Times*, September 23, 1928.

51 "Explorers Return from Dutch Guiana," *New York Times*, September 6, 1928.

52 "Two Scientists Back from Trip to Dark Africa," *Sun* (Kansas), September 7, 1928.

53 "Will Again Visit Negroes of Bush," *New York Times*, June 16, 1929.

54 "Throws New Light on Origin of American Negro," *Philadelphia Tribune*, November 14, 1929, 9.

55 "S. American Slave Rebellion Succeeded," *Afro-American* (Baltimore), November 23, 1929, 7.

56 Price and Price, *Roots of Roots*, 19.

57 Locke, "Apropos of Africa," 263.

58 Herskovits to Hornbostel, November 18, 1929.

59 Roberts, "Possible Survivals," 345, 355.

60 Hornbostel to Herskovits, January 5, 1930.

61 Hornbostel to Herskovits, July 9, 1930.

62 Herskovits to Hornbostel, May 13, 1930.

63 Herskovits, "Social History of the Negro," 244, 246 (my emphasis).

64 For an explanation of the differences between "icon" and "index" in Peircean semiotics, see Turino, "Peircean Thought," 214.

65 Hornbostel to Herskovits, September 20, 1930.

66 Herskovits to Hornbostel, March 6, 1932.

67 Herskovits, "New World Negroes," 258n60.

68 Darnell, *Invisible Genealogies*, 49–50.

69 Khanna, *Dark Continents*, 69. For other critical analyses of the comparative method in early anthropology, see Bowler, *Invention of Progress*, 35, 123; Fabian, *Time and the Other*, 16–27; Kuper, *Reinvention of Primitive Society*, 48–97; and Martin, *Languages of Difference*, 35, 165.

70 Ash, *Gestalt Psychology*, 326.

71 George Herzog to Melville J. Herskovits, April 25, 1933, Series 9/22, Melville J. Herskovits (1895–1963) Papers.

72 Herzog to Herskovits, April 25, 1933.

73 Hornbostel to Herskovits, September 4, 1933.

74 Herzog to Herskovits, April 25, 1933.

75 Herskovits to Herzog, May 18, 1933.

76 See Beckwith, "Kolinski," xvii.

77 Helen H. Roberts to Melville J. Herskovits, April 18, 1934, Series 9/22, Melville J. Herskovits (1895–1963) Papers; Seeger, "Notes and News"; Edward Downes, "Group Mixes Anthropology with Musicology," *New York Times*, August 12, 1956, 95.

78 Seeger, "Notes and News," 2.

79 Besides Hornbostel and Kolinski, Curt Sachs fled to Paris, and Robert Lachmann to Jerusalem (Rice, "Comparative Musicology").

80 Roberts to Herskovits, April 18, 1934.

81 "Nécrologie," 160; Seeger, "Notes and News," 2.

82 As Edward Downes wrote in the *New York Times*, "The American group lost heart, lost funds, lost contact with each other, and World War II did the rest" (Downes, "Group Mixes Anthropology with Musicology," 95).

83 Christensen, "Institutionalization of Comparative Musicology," 205–206.

84 Herskovits to Hornbostel, October 4, 1930.

85 Hornbostel to Herskovits, March 3, 1931.

86 Hornbostel to Herskovits, September 29, 1931.

87 Herskovits to Hornbostel, October 19, 1931.

88 Herskovits to Hornbostel, March 6, 1932.

89 Herskovits to Kolinski, April 5, 1932.

90 Kolinski to Herskovits, October 22, 1932.

91 Herskovits to Kolinski, November 10, 1932.

92 Herskovits to Kolinski, January 30, 1933.

93 See Ash, *Gestalt Psychology*, 39–41.

94 Herskovits and Herskovits, *Suriname Folk-lore*, 517 (my emphasis).

95 Herskovits and Herskovits, *Suriname Folk-lore*, 517.

96 Herskovits and Herskovits, *Suriname Folk-lore*, 498–499, 518.

97 Herskovits and Herskovits, *Suriname Folk-lore*, 520.

98 Herzog to Herskovits, April 30, 1935.

99 Herskovits and Herskovits, *Suriname Folk-lore*, 518. For Herskovits's first use of the term "syncretism," see Herskovits, "African Gods and Catholic Saints." According to Kevin A. Yelvington, Herskovits got the concept of syncretism from Arthur Ramos without crediting the Brazilian anthropologist (see Yelvington, "Invention of Africa," 65).

100 Herskovits to Kolinski, February 10, 1933. Herskovits's student, Richard Waterman, completed his dissertation in 1943, in which he compared Kolinski's analyses with his own comparative musicological study of Herskovits's Trinidadian field recordings of 1939 (see chapter 2). In fact, by 1943 Waterman confirmed that "modern collecting of American Negro songs has begun to outgrow the bias in favor of the Spirituals and is becoming increasingly aware of the rich material to be found in the non-religious songs," and among these were commercial recordings of jazz and swing music, "which show obvious traces of West African musical tradition" (R. Waterman, "African Patterns," 164). Nevertheless, the denial by some of the spiritual's African influences continued to motivate Waterman and others to pursue research on Africanisms in New World Negro music long after the 1930s.

101 Herskovits to Kolinski, April 2, 1934.

102 Kolinski to Herskovits, February 14, 1935.

103 Hornbostel, "American Negro Songs," 750.

104 Herskovits to Kolinski, March 1, 1935.

105 Redfield, Linton, and Herskovits, "Memorandum," 145–148.

106 Herskovits continued to formulate the significance of cultural focus in the acculturative process in his scholarship. In 1948, for example, he stated: "The hypothesis of *cultural focus*, which points the way toward a comprehension of the primary concerns of a people, and, in contact situations, illustrates the carryover of aboriginal modes of custom in unequal degree as the different aspects of culture lie within the focal area or outside it" (Herskovits, "Contribution of Afroamerican Studies," 1–10; see also Herskovits, *Myth of the Negro Past*, 136).

107 Herzog to Herskovits, April 30, 1935; and Herskovits to Herzog, June 11, 1935. The footnote in question remained in the published manuscript (see Herskovits and Herskovits, *Suriname Folk-lore*, 520n1).

108 Herskovits to Herzog, June 11, 1935.
109 Herskovits and Herskovits, *Suriname Folk-lore*, 491.
110 Herskovits to Herzog, April 30, 1935.
111 Roberts to Herskovits, May 3, 1935.
112 Roberts, "Melodic Composition," 82–83.
113 Roberts to Herskovits, June 4, 1935.
114 Herskovits to Kolinski, July 29, 1935.
115 Herzog, Review of *Suriname Folklore*, 505.
116 Kolinski to Herskovits, August 10, 1935.
117 Williams Jr., *Rethinking Race*, 6.
118 Herskovits, "Significance of West Africa," 99.
119 Herskovits, "Significance of West Africa," 100.
120 Herskovits to Herzog, June 11, 1935.
121 Herskovits to Kolinski, November 15, 1937.
122 Herskovits to Boas, August 18, 1938.
123 Herskovits to Smets, August 18, 1938.
124 Herskovits to Leland, December 16, 1938.
125 Herskovits to Flexner, December 31, 1938.
126 Louis Sussdorff, Jr., to Carlton Sprague Smith, October 27, 1939.
127 Addison Hibbard to Herskovits, March 13, 1939.
128 Herskovits to Goldsmith, March 23, 1939.
129 Herskovits to Embree, March 27, 1939.
130 Goldsmith to Herskovits, March 28, 1939; Herskovits to Drury, March 31, 1939.
131 Drury to Herskovits, April 8, 1939.
132 Herskovits to Goldsmith, April 12, 1939.
133 Goldsmith to Herskovits, April 10, 1939.
134 Herskovits to Goldsmith, April 12, 1939.
135 President, Northwestern University, to Charles C. Broy, May 5, 1939; Hibbard to Kolinski, May 5, 1939.
136 Herskovits to Kolinski, May 16, 1939, and May 25, 1939.
137 Sussdorff, Jr., to Smith, October 27, 1939; Immigration Act of 1924, accessed August 19, 2013, http://www-rohan.sdsu.edu/dept/polsciwb/brianl/docs /1924ImmigrationAct.pdf.
138 Louis Sussdorff, Jr., to Scott W. Lucas, January 23, 1940.
139 Herskovits to Kolinski, May 14, 1940.
140 Herskovits to Duggan, April 9, 1941.
141 Hilary Conroy, "Melville Herskovits," *Daily Northwestern*, Evanston, IL, March 13, 1940.
142 Lloyd Wilkins, "Jungle Jive Pans of Roving Savant Monopolized for Anthropologists," *Indianapolis Star*, April 27, 1940.
143 Redfield, Linton, and Herskovits, "Memorandum," 148.
144 See, for example, Fontaine, "Interpretation of Contemporary Negro Thought"; A. Ramos, "Acculturation among the Brazilian Negroes"; Wieschhoff, "Social Significance of Names"; and Znaniecki et al., "Abstracts from the Annual Meeting."

145 See Ramsey, "Politics"; and Osumare, "Katherine Dunham."

146 Osumare, "Katherine Dunham," 613.

147 Aschenbrenner, *Katherine Dunham*, 25–31.

148 Dunham, "Lecture-Demonstration," 508.

149 Herskovits to Dunham, March 23, 1932, Series 7/12, Melville J. Herskovits (1895–1963) Papers.

150 Dunham to Herskovits, June 18, 1933; "Portrait of Mrs. J. G. Coleman Will Be Unveiled at Tea Today," *Chicago Daily Tribune*, April 17, 1933, 17.

151 "Portrait of Mrs. J. G. Coleman," 17.

152 "Portrait of Mrs. J. G. Coleman," 17; John Martin, "The Dance: School Work: Second Symposium at Barnard Advances Movement for Educated Audiences," *New York Times*, June 25, 1933, X5.

153 Dunham to Herskovits, June 18, 1933.

154 Herskovits to Dunham, June 20, 1933.

155 Ogbar marks the beginning and end of the Harlem Renaissance as the antiblack race riots of 1919 and the Great Depression and the Harlem Riots of 1935, respectively ("Introduction," 2).

156 Jackson, "Melville Herskovits," 114; see also Ramsey, "Politics," 201.

157 Yelvington, "Invention of Africa," 70. Jackson also describes Herskovits's successful attempts to derail Du Bois's editorship, as well as the animus Herskovits expressed toward Charles S. Johnson's legitimacy as a social scientist ("Melville Herskovits," 116).

158 Dunham to Herskovits, June 23, 1935.

159 Herskovits briefly commented on the "vitality of the Garvey movement" and sentiments toward Haile Selassie as were shared among some of his informants while conducting fieldwork in Trinidad in 1939. See Trinidad, Field notes, August 10, 1939, Box 15, Folder 82, Melville J. Herskovits and Frances S. Herskovits Papers.

160 Aschenbrenner, *Katherine Dunham*, 44–45. Embree, *Julius Rosenwald Fund*, 33–35. The Julius Rosenwald Fund supported the "advancement of the Negro and the promotion of better race relations" in the United States. True to its philanthropic mission, the fund employed a racially diverse staff and named African Americans and other minorities to its board. In the mid-1930s the fund focused on supporting the following two areas, African American education in rural regions and African American welfare and race relations throughout the country, both of which overlapped particularly in regard to the fund's work in the South. In supporting the arts, for instance, the fund believed it could affect race relations by the demonstration of the intelligence and creativity within the black community. African American fellows included Ralphe Bunche (to conduct dissertation research in Africa) and Marian Anderson (to study and perform in Germany), in addition to W. E. B. DuBois, Langston Hughes, and Richard Wright (see Perkins, *Edwin Rogers Embree*).

161 See Averill, *Day for the Hunter*, 42; and Yelvington, "Invention of Africa," 52–57.

162 Dunham to Herskovits, December 10, 1935. Little is known about Reiser, or Doc Reeser, except that Dunham, in her book *Island Possessed*, explains that he, a

white American marine, had been a ship's pharmacist during the occupation and remained on the island, where he immersed himself in, and was accepted by, the local Vodun culture (Dunham, *Island Possessed*, 18–20).

163   See Averill, *Day for the Hunter*, 42; and Yelvington, "Invention of Africa," 52.

164   Lowenthal, "Ritual Performance," 397.

165   Herskovits, *Life in a Haitian Valley*, 293–294.

166   See García, "Contesting Anthropology." Price-Mars fell out of favor among the Haitian masses beginning in 1934 because of his opposition to the popular president Sténio Vincent's economic policies. In February 1935, four months before Dunham's arrival, the entire Haitian Senate, including Price-Mars, was removed from office by Vincent as a result of a nationwide plebiscite supporting his policies in the face of the nation's worsening economy. He and his fellow ousted senators became "subject to close government surveillance, which extended to their American friends residing in Haiti" (Shannon, *Jean Price-Mars*, 142–154).

167   Dunham to Herskovits, August 25, 1935.

168   Herskovits, *Life in a Haitian Valley*, 322–323; see also Ramsey, "Politics," 208–209.

169   See Ramsey, "Politics," 206–207.

170   Herskovits to Dunham, August 26, 1935.

171   The article published in *Mademoiselle* was reprinted in Clark and Johnson, *Kaiso!*, 267–271.

172   Dunham, "Goombay," 269.

173   Dunham "Goombay," 270–271.

174   Dunham to Herskovits, September 10, 1935. Current dance scholars use the spellings *bele* and *ladja*, respectively. See Cyrille, "Sa Ki Ta Nou."

175   Herskovits to Dunham, October 25, 1935.

176   Dunham to Herskovits, October 27, 1935.

177   See Dunham, "L'ag'ya of Martinique," 204–205.

178   See Cole, "Ruth Landes," 181.

179   Dunham to Herskovits, June 23, 1935.

180   Dunham to Herskovits, November 15, 1935.

181   Boas, "Scientist Explodes Nazi Myth of 'Aryanism,'" *Jewish Exponent*, June 1, 1934, 12; "Franz Boas Again Denounces Theories of Racial Difference," *Pittsburgh Courier*, June 6, 1936, 1. See also "Dr. Boas on the Blacklist," *New York Times*, May 6, 1933, 8; "Christian Clergy Condemn Hitler: Leading Social Scientists Also Sign," *Jewish Exponent*, May 12, 1933, 1.

182   Katherine Dunham, student field notes, Series 107/5, Melville J. Herskovits (1895–1963) Papers, 1906–1963.

183   By "gnostic insight" I am directly referencing V. Y. Mudimbe's use of "gnosis" to capture the breadth and complexity of African knowledge, including its extension into Western epistemological territory. See Mudimbe, *Invention of Africa*, 186.

184   Dunham to Herskovits, November 15, 1935.

185   Dunham to Herskovits, December 28, 1935.

186 Herskovits to Dunham, January 6, 1936.

187 Dunham to Herskovits, January 13, 1936; see also Dunham, *Dance of Haiti*, 1983.

188 Dunham, *Island Possessed*, 198–199.

189 Ogbar, *Black Power*, 11–19.

190 Dunham, *Island Possessed*, 198–199.

191 Dunham, *Island Possessed*, 228.

192 Ramsey, "Politics," 211.

193 See Gilroy, *Against Race*, 144–147.

194 Dunham to Herskovits, June 23, 1935.

195 Katherine Dunham, student field notes. This excerpt appears in Dunham, *Journey to Accompong*, 150.

196 Dunham to Herskovits, October 27, 1935.

197 Dunham to Herskovits, September 10, 1935.

198 Helen H. Roberts to Melville J. Herskovits, April 15, 1935, Series 20/13, Melville J. Herskovits (1895–1963) Papers.

199 Herskovits to Roberts, April 25, 1935.

200 For a critique of racism in the feminist movement in the United States, see hooks, *Feminist Theory*, 50–60.

201 As noted earlier in this chapter, Roberts's fieldwork in Jamaica resulted in three articles, but she had been unsuccessful in finding a university press to publish her work as a book. In addition, at the time of her correspondence with Herskovits, Roberts was serving as the secretary of the American Society for Comparative Musicology and was "left doing all the secretarial and other work" of the society's president, Charles Seeger, and its treasurer, George Herzog, which contributed to her quitting her post and to the eventual dissolution of the society (see Frisbie, "Women and the Society for Ethnomusicology," 250).

202 Roberts to Herskovits, May 3, 1935.

203 Cole, "Ruth Landes," 176–177; see also Price and Price, *Root of Roots*, 84–85.

204 R. Waterman, review of *Journey to Accompong*, 180.

205 Dunham to Herskovits, August 25, 1935; Dunham to Herskovits, September 10, 1935.

206 Herskovits to Dunham, October 24, 1935.

207 Dunham to Herskovits, November 15, 1935.

208 Dunham, "Survival," 87. The *Chicago Daily News*, for example, reported on Dunham's performance of the Vodun loa Damballa, accompanied by Herskovits playing the drum, which took place in June in the Julius Rosenwald Fund's building. "Haitian Voodoo Dance Thrills Savants of Chicago Schools," *Chicago Daily News*, June 5, 1936.

209 Herskovits to Dunham, August 31, 1936.

210 Dunham to Herskovits, September 23, 1936.

211 Herskovits to Dunham, September 29, 1936.

212 Herskovits to Redfield, January 7, 1937.

213 Dunham to Herskovits, April 4, 1937.

214 Dunham to Herskovits, May 5, 1937.

215 Dunham to Herskovits, February 3, 1937. See also Dunham, "Lecture-Demonstration," 508.
216 Herskovits to Dunham, February 9, 1937, and April 10, 1937.
217 Herskovits to Dunham, May 6, 1937.
218 Dunham to Herskovits, August 1, 1937.
219 Dunham, "Plan of Work," Series 7/12, Melville J. Herskovits (1895–1963) Papers.
220 George M. Reynolds to Herskovits, March 28, 1939, Series 20/21, Melville J. Herskovits (1895–1963) Papers.
221 Herskovits to Reynolds, March 31, 1939.
222 Dunham, "Plan of Work."
223 Herskovits, *Myth of the Negro Past*, 270 (my emphasis).
224 Cole, "Ruth Landes," 176–177.
225 Herskovits, *Myth of the Negro Past*, 269.
226 Herskovits, *Myth of the Negro Past*, 270.

Chapter 2. Listening to Africa

1 Ash, *Gestalt Psychology*, ix, 33.
2 Koffka, "Perception," 531.
3 Koffka, "Perception," 553–554.
4 Koffka, "Perception," 570–571; see also Koffka, *Principles of Gestalt Psychology*, 184–185; and Ash, *Gestalt Psychology*, 1–2.
5 Ash, *Gestalt Psychology*, 66–67.
6 Koffka, *Principles of Gestalt Psychology*, 220.
7 See Koffka, "Perception," 576–578, and *Principles of Gestalt Psychology*, 219–221; see also Ash, *Gestalt Psychology*, 188–190.
8 Koffka, *Principles of Gestalt Psychology*, 220–221.
9 See Deleuze and Guattari, *Thousand Plateaus*, 382–385.
10 See Bijsterveld and Pinch, "New Keys," 9.
11 Erlmann, *Reason and Resonance*, 22; see also 307–342.
12 Comte, "General View of Positivism," 741.
13 Bourdieu, *Logic of Practice*, 52–56; see also Sterne, *Audible Past*, 92–93.
14 Bourdieu, *Logic of Practice*, 56.
15 See Fabian, *Time and the Other*, 1–27.
16 Fabian, *Time and the Other*, 26.
17 Becker, *Deep Listeners*, 71.
18 Hegel, "Introduction to the Philosophy of History," 603. See also Hegel, *Philosophy of History*, 91–96.
19 See Grossberg, *Dancing in Spite of Myself*, 96–97.
20 Also known as Regla de Ocha, Santería is the common name for Cuba's religious tradition of *oricha* (deity) worship, the practices of which developed from related practices of West Africa.
21 See Sterne, *Audible Past*, 92–96.

22 The recent publication of Michael Iyanaga's article "On Flogging the Dead Horse, Again" in *Ethnomusicology* is a welcomed reconsideration of Waterman's contributions to the study of black music. It is important to point out, however, that Iyanaga's representation of Waterman's theory of "hot" rhythm, that is, its provenance, and the part the unconscious plays in this theory lacks a critical historiographical perspective, one which I attempt to present in this chapter.

23 "Las comparsas," *Adelante* 2, no. 22 (March 1937): 3.

24 El Curioso Parlanchín, "Las comparsas callejeras de La Habana," *Carteles*, April 4, 1937, 38–39, 41, 59.

25 Moore, *Nationalizing Blackness*, 80–81.

26 El Curioso Parlanchín, "Las comparsas callejeras," 38.

27 El Curioso Parlanchín, "Las comparsas callejeras," 38.

28 See de la Fuente, "Two Dangers, One Solution," 32–33. In an article published in 1942, Duvon C. Corbitt gives a detailed outline of Cuban immigration history, throughout which definitions of whiteness and blackness varied according to religious affiliation, foreign status, and skin color (Corbitt, "Immigration in Cuba"). For instance, in the early nineteenth century, colonial officials marked Mexican Indian and Chinese immigrants to Cuba as "white colonists," a category namely based on a hyperdefinition of skin color (i.e., nonblack) predicated on the fear of black slave revolts. In contrast, records from the 1840s indicate that some Canary Island immigrants regarded immigrants from Catalan as "Catalan Negroes."

29 See Grossberg, *Dancing in Spite of Myself*, 13, 97.

30 See *Las comparsas populares*, 22–28, 31.

31 Fajardo Estrada, *Rita Montaner*, 149.

32 See Departamento de Turismo del Municipio de La Habana, 139–140.

33 García Agüero, "Presencia africana," 127.

34 See García Agüero, "Presencia africana," 118, 121–123.

35 García Agüero, "Presencia africana," 115 (my emphasis).

36 See Comte, "General View of Positivism," 761; Fuller, *History of Philosophy*, 457–500; and Guadarrama González and Rojas Gómez, *El pensamiento filosófico*, 42–46.

37 García Agüero, "Presencia africana," 118.

38 Portell Vilá, "El folklore en Jovellanos," 53; Orovio, *Cuban Music*, 219; Fajardo Estrada, *Rita Montaner*, 125.

39 Orovio, *Cuban Music*, 219.

40 Departamento de Turismo, 139.

41 *Las comparsas populares*, 28 (my emphasis).

42 Gálvez, "Una melodía negra," 26.

43 See Departamento de Turismo, 140–141.

44 "Notas y noticias," 163; Orovio, *Cuban Music*, 180.

45 "Notas y noticias," 163.

46 Orovio, *Cuban Music*, 140–141. Montaner had premiered several of Valdés's compositions (e.g., "Baró" and "Sangre Africana") as early as 1935 in Havana (Fajardo Estrada, *Rita Montaner*, 124).

47 Orovio, *Cuban Music*, 218.

48 Departamento de Turismo, 141.

49 These pitch placements were in fact specific to the unconsecrated drums that were reportedly constructed especially for Valdés's concerts (see Ortiz, *La africanía*, 376–377). Although the tunings of the batá drum heads do correspond to a fixed system, the actual notes vary from one set to another and, more importantly, throughout the course of a performance (see Amira and Cornelius, *Music of Santería*, 20–21).

50 Departamento de Turismo, 141. Of the pieces that his orchestra performed at these concerts, Valdés recorded three—"Tambó," "Sangre africana" (African blood), and "Rumba abierta" (Open rumba)—with RCA Victor in May 1940 (Díaz-Ayala and Florida International University, *Encyclopedic Discography of Cuban Music*). In addition to these recordings, I have obtained a copy of the piano score for "Ilé-nko Ilé-nbe" dated 1937 (courtesy of Robin Moore); this is in addition to its orchestral score dated 1946 and is used as part of Katherine Dunham's *Bal negre* (see chapter 3).

51 Departamento de Turismo, 142 (my emphasis). RCA Victor contracted Gilberto Valdés to record "Tambo" and "Sangre africana," the recordings of which were made on May 6, 1940.

52 Radano, *Lying Up a Nation*, 235–236.

53 García Agüero, "Presencia africana," 127.

54 See Radano, *Lying Up a Nation*, 214, 223.

55 Arredondo, *El negro en Cuba*, 160–163.

56 Arredondo, "El arte negro a contrapelo," 20 (my emphasis).

57 Arredondo, "Eso que llaman afrocubanismo musical," 6.

58 Arredondo, "El arte negro a contrapelo," 6.

59 Arredondo, "Eso que llaman afrocubanismo musical," 5.

60 Arredondo, *El negro en Cuba*, 135.

61 "Notas gráficas," *Carteles*, April 11, 1937, 8. The French dignitaries were in Havana to pay tribute to the memory of the French general and colonizer Pierre Le Moyne D'Iberville (El Curioso Parlanchín, "Las comparsas de 'Los marqueses,' 'Los Guaracheros,' 'Las bolleras,' 'Los modernistas,' 'El barracón,' y 'Los guajiros,' " *Carteles*, April 18, 1937, 28–29, 45, 49). See also Demaison, "Escuchando a Gilberto Valdés," 151–152.

62 El Curioso Parlanchín, "Las comparsas de 'Los marqueses,' " 28.

63 Demaison's article was translated into Spanish and published in *Estudios Afrocubanos* (see Demaison, "Escuchando a Gilberto Valdés").

64 Demaison, "Escuchando a Gilberto Valdés," 154 (my emphasis).

65 See Radano, *Lying Up a Nation*, 76.

66 José L. Franco, "Con André Demaison, novelista y viajero frances," *Carteles*, June 6, 1937, 11, 67.

67 Demaison, "Escuchando a Gilberto Valdés," 153 (my emphasis).

68 For an explanation of equipment, see Heidegger, *Basic Problems of Phenomenology*, 303–305.

69 For a survey of the history and uses of techniques such as the whole-tone scale, octatonicism, and the mystic chord in modernist music, see Morgan, *Twentieth-Century Music*, 44–58.

70 Guadarrama González and Rojas Gómez, *El pensamiento filosófico*, 243.

71 See Ortiz, "La música sagrada," 89–92 (my emphasis).

72 Ortiz, "La música sagrada," 92.

73 Ortiz, "La música sagrada," 89.

74 Ortiz, "La música sagrada," 96.

75 Ortiz, "La música sagrada," 100.

76 Departamento de Turismo, 144.

77 Ortiz, "La música sagrada," 103.

78 Ángel Lázaro, "La academia y los tambores," *Carteles*, June 20, 1937, 11.

79 Attali, *Noise*, 61; Erlmann, *Reason and Resonance*, 24.

80 Heidegger, *Basic Problems of Phenomenology*, 307–308.

81 Waterman eventually published this paper in the journal *Ethnomusicology* in 1963. See R. Waterman, "On Flogging a Dead Horse."

82 R. Waterman, "On Flogging a Dead Horse," 83.

83 The historiographical literature on sound recording technology in the fields of anthropology, folklore, and comparative musicology is large. See, for example, Brady, *Spiral Way*; Shelemay, "Recording Technology"; and Sterne, *Audible Past*, 310–333.

84 Abraham and Hornbostel, "Significance of the Phonograph," 189–190.

85 Abraham and Hornbostel, "Significance of the Phonograph," 195; see also Hornbostel, "African Negro Music," 32–33.

86 Sterne, *Audible Past*, 330.

87 Melville J. Herskovits to Richard A. Waterman, June 17, 1941, Box 16, Folder 2, Melville J. Herskovits (1895–1963) Papers; see also Merriam, "Richard Alan Waterman," 73.

88 Mieczyslaw Kolinski to Melville J. Herskovits, March 24, 1941, Box 12, Folder 1, Melville J. Herskovits (1895–1963) Papers.

89 Herskovits to Waterman, June 17, 1941.

90 R. Waterman, "African Patterns," i.

91 Herskovits to Waterman, August 20, 1941.

92 Herskovits to Waterman, June 17 and August 20, 1941.

93 Robert H. Seashore's chapters in *Fields of Psychology*, published in 1942, in which he summarizes these and other fields and their main theoretical viewpoints, strongly indicate that Waterman received his inspiration to use these concepts from Seashore's instruction.

94 William R. Bascom to Richard A. Waterman, April 9, 1942, Box 6, Folder "Richard Waterman," William R. Bascom Papers.

95 Robert H. Seashore to Herskovits, February 12, 1943, Box 31, Folder 12, Melville J. Herskovits (1895–1963) Papers.

96 Melville J. Herskovits to President Franklyn B. Snyder, June 30, 1944, Box 6, Folder 5, Franklyn Bliss Snyder Papers.

97 Melville J. Herskovits to Mortimer Graves, January 20, 1944, Box 31, Folder 12, Melville J. Herskovits (1895–1963) Papers; Merriam, "Northwestern University Laboratory of Comparative Musicology," 1.

98 N. T. Rider to Melville Herskovits, November 21, 1944, Box 33, Folder 38, Melville J. Herskovits (1895–1963) Papers.

99 Mieczyslaw Kolinski to Melville Herskovits, December 11, 1944. See also Beckwith, "Kolinski," xviii.

100 Edith van den Berghe was the daughter of Fritz van den Berghe and the assistant of linguist and anthropologist Frans M. Olbrechts (Kolinski to Herskovits, December 11, 1944). According to John Beckwith, Kolinski decided to register as a Jew with Nazi officials, and in 1942 he received an order from the Nazi authorities in Belgium to present himself for deportation to a labor camp in northern France. He was warned by another Jewish friend not to appear at his deportation, for the French camp was an interim gathering point for Jews who were eventually to be removed to concentration camps, including Auschwitz and Buchenwald. Kolinski took her advice and went into hiding at the home of the van den Berghes (Beckwith, "Kolinski," xviii).

101 Melville Herskovits to Mieczyslaw Kolinski, December 21, 1944.

102 Beckwith, "Kolinski," xviii.

103 During the summer of 1946, Waterman conducted field recordings in Puerto Rico, sponsored by the Library of Congress' Music Division and the Office of Information for Puerto Rico, located in New York City (Max A. Egloff to Richard Waterman, June 18, 1946, Series 35/6, Box 36, Folder 11, Melville J. Herskovits [1895–1963] Papers. These recordings resulted in the production of *Folk Music of Puerto Rico* (AFS-L18), which was released in 1947. Waterman also traveled to Havana to make his own field recordings, while also supervising the fieldwork of Berta Montero-Sánchez, who was a student of Cuban folklorist Herminio Portel Vilá (Waterman to Egloff, June 24, 1946). Waterman's recorder, however, never functioned properly, and he was thus unable to collect any recordings in Cuba. Waterman planned to return to Havana to conduct field recordings during the summer of 1947, but his application to the ACLS was unsuccessful (Waterman to Herskovits, September 10, 1946).

  Starting in 1946 Montero-Sánchez taught Spanish at Northwestern while studying anthropology with Herskovits. Her proposed research was to study child education for black children in Cuba; in reality, however, she conducted fieldwork on Africanisms in Santería (Berta Montero-Sánchez to Herminio Portel Vilá, March 6, 1946, and Montero-Sánchez to Melville and Frances Herskovits, September 16, 1947, Series 35/6, Box 33, Folder 51, Melville J. Herskovits [1895–1963] Papers).

104 Mortimer Graves to Melville J. Herskovits, January 17, 1944.

105 Melville J. Herskovits to Thomas Moody Campbell, January 22, 1944.

106 Department of State, Music Advisory Committee, Sub-Committee on Non-European Areas, minutes, June 10, 1944, Box 36, Folder 3, Melville J. Herskovits (1895–1963) Papers.

107 *Northwestern University Bulletin* 46, no. 11 (February 11, 1946): 42.

108 See R. Waterman, "African Patterns," 1–3.

109 Melville J. Herskovits to Harold Courlander, July 23, 1939, Box 6, Folder 16, Melville J. Herskovits (1895–1963) Papers.

110 Melville J. Herskovits to George Herzog, October 25, 1939, Box 9, Folder 22, Melville J. Herskovits (1895–1963) Papers.

111 Herskovits and Herskovits, *Trinidad Village*, 3.

112 Herskovits to Courlander, October 3, 1939.

113 R. Waterman, "African Patterns," 7.

114 R. Waterman, "African Influence," 208 (my emphasis).

115 R. Waterman, "African Patterns," 63. Herskovits made his field recordings in Trinidad using a SoundScriber Junior recording machine, Western Electric "saltshaker" microphone, SoundScriber cutting head, steel styli, premium Trimm headphones, and twelve-inch acetate discs. He also used a Kato three-hundred-watt belt-drive gasoline engine to power the recording machine (order form, Sound Specialties Company, May 20, 1939, Box 15, Folder 84, Melville J. Herskovits and Frances S. Herskovits Papers).

116 See R. Waterman, "African Patterns," 89–90.

117 See Seashore, "Convergent Trends in Psychological Theory," 611–613. In his essay "The Uneven Development of Africanist Ethnomusicology," Christopher A. Waterman addresses Waterman's use of acculturation, Gestalt theory, behaviorism, and his own experience as a jazz bassist in fashioning his theory of metronome sense. To better understand the significance of Waterman's work on race and music in the 1940s, a more critical analysis and historical contextualization are needed of, for example, (1) Waterman's thinking in regard to recordings and musical transcription and how these aspects, along with Gestalt theory and acculturation, factored in the development of his metronome sense, beginning with his notion of "hot" rhythm; and (2) the intellectual and disciplinary historical context in which Waterman worked, including Kolinski's effect on Waterman's methods.

118 See R. Waterman, "African Patterns," 2–3, 115; and "African Influence," 211.

119 See R. Waterman, "African Patterns," 85–94.

120 R. Waterman, "African Patterns," 103–104 (my emphasis).

121 See Köhler, *Gestalt Psychology*, 219.

122 R. Waterman, "African Patterns," 94.

123 "List of Papers Read at Annual Meetings," 34. The other two presenters on Waterman's panel were Homer Pearson ("The Pattern of Propaganda in Music") and Karl Geiringer ("The Beginnings of the String Quartet"). Waterman eventually published this paper as an article in the first volume of the *Journal of the American Musicological Society* (see R. Waterman, " 'Hot' Rhythm in Negro Music").

124 Richard A. Waterman to George Herzog, January 3, 1944, and George Herzog to Richard A. Waterman, January 7, 1944, George Herzog Correspondence.

125 R. Waterman to George Herzog, January 3, 1944.

126 R. Waterman, " 'Hot' Rhythm in Negro Music," 24.

127 R. Waterman, " 'Hot' Rhythm in Negro Music," 24 (my emphasis).

128 Field notes, August 20, 1939, Box 15, Folder 82, Melville J. Herskovits and Frances S. Herskovits Papers. Herskovits discusses Shouters ceremonies in Herskovits and Herskovits, *Trinidad Village*, 209–218.

129 Richard A. Waterman to William R. Bascom, October 6, 1944, Box 6, Folder "Richard Waterman," William R. Bascom Papers. Register of scholars, Box 2, Folder "Fulbright," William R. Bascom Papers.

130 "Announcements for 1940–1941," 77; "Alpha Phi Alpha Frat Gives Fellowships," *Chicago Defender*, June 22, 1940, 5.

131 Melville J. Herskovits to Abdul K. Disu, April 13, 1943, Box 27, Folder 31, Melville J. Herskovits (1895–1963) Papers.

132 Richard A. Waterman to Melville J. Herskovits, July 14, 1946, Box 42, Folder 7, Melville J. Herskovits (1895–1963) Papers.

133 Abdul K. Disu to Richard Waterman, May 17, 1943; Melville J. Herskovits to Abdul K. Disu, May 20, 1943; Melville J. Herskovits to Pendleton Herring, April 14, 1944. During the spring of 1944, Herskovits asked Disu to review his *Dahomey, an Ancient West African Kingdom*, "noting similarities and differences between the culture described therein and the Yoruban culture as it is known to you" (Melville J. Herskovits to Abdul K. Disu, March 6, 1944).

134 Julius B. C. Etuka Okala to Melville J. Herskovits, November 26, 1940, and Melville J. Herskovits to Julius B. C. Etuka Okala, December 12, 1940, Box 17, Folder 11, Melville J. Herskovits (1895–1963) Papers. According to an article published in the *Chicago Daily Tribune*, Okala's father was the state advisor to Okosi II, king of Onitsha, Nigeria ("America Still Is Student Heaven," *Chicago Daily Tribune*, January 10, 1943, G7). See also "Talented Ollie Sims Bride of Prince Okala," *Pittsburgh Courier*, April 25, 1942, 10.

135 Julius B. C. Etuka Okala to Melville J. Herskovits, June 9, 1942. See also R. Waterman, "African Patterns," 61–62, 123n1, 142, and 162.

136 The fact that scholars today still quote or reiterate Waterman's claim of taking the concept "hot" rhythm from a linguistic concept of "West African tribesmen" or from West African musical parlance is as much the result of the "shadows" of the anthropological bush as the need for more historiographical research on the early history of American ethnomusicology in the twentieth century. See Iyanaga, "On Flogging the Dead Horse," 179; and Burford, "Mahalia Jackson," 14.

137 Gennari, *Blowin' Hot and Cool*, 34–47, 131–136.

138 See R. Waterman, "African Influence," 211–212.

139 R. Waterman, "'Hot' Rhythm in Negro Music," 26.

140 R. Waterman, "African Influence," 213–214.

141 R. Waterman, "African Patterns," 2–4, 115 (my emphasis).

142 See Freud, *General Psychological Theory*, 116.

143 R. Waterman, "'Hot' Rhythm in Negro Music," 37 (my emphasis).

144 R. Waterman, "'Hot' Rhythm in Negro Music," 29.

145 Herskovits, "Freudian Mechanisms."

146 See Krehbiel, *Afro-American Folksongs*, ix, 23, 115.

147 See Erlmann, *Reason and Resonance*, 60–68.

148 R. Waterman, "African Influence," 210. Eventually, Waterman named Richard Wallaschek, Henry Krehbiel, Newman Ivey White, and George Pullen Jackson among those academics who denied black music's African origins (see R. Waterman, "On Flogging a Dead Horse," 83).

149 See García Agüero, "Presencia africana," 115–118, 125–126. For Freud's explanation of phobia as originating from the dynamics of repression, see *General Psychological Theory*, 128–134.

150 Ranjana Khanna's work on the provincialization and parochialization of psychoanalysis is particularly instructive in this instance (Khanna, *Dark Continents*, 10–12).

151 See R. Waterman, "African Patterns," 166–168.

152 "Melody Hunters," *Time*, December 27, 1937, n.p.

153 "Dunham Cuts Kinship Music of Caribbeans," *Washington Afro-American*, August 23, 1947, 6.

154 Will Davidson, "Recordially Yours," *Chicago Daily Tribune*, March 30, 1947, G15.

155 John Lucas, "Jazz on Records," *Record Changer*, June 1947, 10.

156 Shelemay, "Recording Technology," 281.

157 Harold Courlander, interview by Gary Kenton, May 1989, Series: "Interviews, 1971–1989," Gary Kenton Collection.

158 George Herzog's transcriptions and analyses of Courlander's Haitian field recordings were included in his *Haiti Singing*.

159 Harold Courlander, application to the American Council of Learned Societies, January 31, 1941, Series 35/6, Box 6, Folder 16, Melville J. Herskovits (1895–1963) Papers (my emphasis).

160 Apparently, Courlander confused Zaya's first name for Alfredo in his diary (see Courlander, "Abakwa Meeting in Guanabacoa" and "From the Field").

161 Courlander's and Waterman's recordings are currently kept at the Archives of Traditional Music, Indiana University.

162 See Díaz-Ayala and Florida International University, *Encyclopedic Discography of Cuban Music*.

163 Richard Waterman to Melville Herskovits, June 30, 1948, Series 35/6, Box 42, Folder 7, Melville J. Herskovits (1895–1963) Papers.

164 Richard Waterman, field notes, July 19, 1948, Series 35/6, Box 42, Folder 7, Melville J. Herskovits (1895–1963) Papers.

165 "Toitica la Negra" (Decca 40028) was recorded in New York City on November 8, 1945 (Ruppli, *Decca Labels*, 3:115).

166 "Enlloro" (Decca 50011) was recorded in New York City on July 17, 1942 (Ruppli, *Decca Labels*, 2:792).

167 For information on the enlloro ritual, see Cabrera, *El monte*, 208; and Ortiz, *La africanía*, 386–387.

168 Cabrera, *El monte*, 198; see also 199–201.

169 "A la nación cubana," *Adelante* 3, no. 34 (March 1938): 7–8, 20.

170 Sargeant, "Cuba's Tin Pan Alley," 146.

171 Sargeant, "Cuba's Tin Pan Alley," 151 (my emphasis).

172 Díaz-Ayala and Florida International University, *Encyclopedic Discography of Cuban Music.*

173 I. L. Miller, "Secret Society Goes Public," 176; see also Cabrera, *El monte*, 197.

174 The booklets for both releases (*Music of the Cults of Cuba*, DISC Ethnic Album 131, and *Cult Music of Cuba*, Ethnic Folkways Library P 410) were slightly edited versions of Courlander's article "Musical Instruments of Cuba," which he published with the *Musical Quarterly* in 1942.

175 Olmsted, *Folkways Records*, 41–47, 187–189.

176 *Down Beat* 14, no. 6 (March 12, 1947): 9. DISC's *Folk Music of the Central East— USSR* (DISC Ethnic Album 132) was not recorded by Harold Courlander. He did, however, record the sides in the *Folk Music of Ethiopia* (DISC Ethnic Album 141) album, while he was working for the US Government in Ethiopia during World War II (Goldsmith, *Making People's Music*, 199–200).

177 Harold Courlander to Melville Herskovits, September 10, 1940.

178 Courlander, application to the American Council of Learned Societies, January 31, 1941, Box 6, Folder 16.

179 Courlander, "Abakwa Meeting in Guanabacoa," 462.

180 Courlander, *Music of the Cults of Cuba.*

181 Definitions of "cult" among social scientists during the 1930s and 1940s were anything but consistent. The meanings of "cult" as outlined by Shepherd and Introvigne, for example, do not seem to match exactly with Courlander's uses. Instead, Courlander seems to have drawn from Herskovits's understanding of the term as demonstrated in his article "African Gods and Catholic Saints in New World Negro Belief," in which he traces the fear exhibited toward "fetish cults" in Brazil, Cuba, and Haiti to the threat of revolt that Europeans attributed to African cults during slavery. Courlander also points to the cultural and social practices differentiating the Lucumí, Abakuá, Arará, and Congo as features of cults (see Courlander, "Musical Instruments of Cuba," 228).

182 There is no indication that the Abakuá music on the DISC and Ethnic Folkways Library albums was recorded at this ceremony. Upon close listening, there is no audible chatter or singing from others who are not near the mic, which one tends to hear on recordings made at actual ceremonies. Also, Courlander does not say he made recordings at this ceremony, which is significant, since his diary entry for this event is otherwise very detailed (see Courlander, "Abakua Meeting in Guanabacoa").

183 Courlander, "Abakua Meeting in Guanabacoa," 465.

184 Courlander, "Abakua Meeting in Guanabacoa," 465 (my emphasis).

185 See I. L. Miller, *Voice of the Leopard*, 104–107.

186 See Erlmann, *Reason and Resonance*, 321–339.

187 Howard Taubman, "Records: Mendelssohn's 'Elijah' in Full," *New York Times*, November 30, 1947, X6.

188 See Olmsted, Folkways Records, 61–64.

189 Moe Asch, contract for Harold Courlander, December 15, 1949, contracts for FE 4410, 1949–1950, Moses and Frances Asch Collection.

190 Statements, Folkways Production Files, Cult Music of Cuba, Moses and Frances Asch Collection.

191 No date is given for the program in the script. "Adventures in Music," Folkways Production Files, Cult Music of Cuba, Moses and Frances Asch Collection.

192 See Deleuze and Guattari, *Thousand Plateaus*, 238.

Chapter 3. Embodying Africa

1 Bakhtin, *Dialogic Imagination*, 243. Bakhtin uses the notion of the chronotope (meaning "time-space") as an analytical device in his literary criticism. He regards the chronotope as a formally constitutive category of literature wherein the interrelationship between time and space functions not only in the structuring of the novel's narrative but also in the authorial and interpretive process itself (Bakhtin, *Dialogic Imagination*, 84, 250–258).

2 Foucault, *Discipline and Punish*, 25–26. See also Deleuze and Guattari's discussion of the plan(e) of organization, *Thousand Plateaus*, 265–267.

3 See Butler, *Bodies That Matter*, 9–18, 234.

4 See Deleuze and Guattari, *Thousand Plateaus*, 278–279, and *Anti-Oedipus*, 144–145.

5 "African Arts Head Confers with Governor Darden Prior to Concert Here Dec. 17–18," *Journal and Guide*, December 15, 1945, 29.

6 See Guridy, *Forging Diaspora*, 10–13.

7 See Butler, *Bodies That Matter*, 3; see also Deleuze and Guattari, *Thousand Plateaus*, 292–293.

8 Butler, *Bodies That Matter*, 243n2.

9 See Fanon, *Black Skin, White Masks*, 109–110, 216–222; Hegel, *Phenomenology of Mind*, 104–112.

10 See Garcia, " 'We Both Speak African.' "

11 Sterne, *Audible Past*, 93.

12 Sartre, *Being and Nothingness*, 346.

13 Sartre, *Being and Nothingness*, 302.

14 See Sartre, *Being and Nothingness*, 350.

15 R. Williams, *Marxism and Literature*, 122.

16 Carmichael, "Power and Racism," 21.

17 Mbadiwe, "African Academy of Arts and Research," 17.

18 For a contemporary report of this rally, see James et al., *Fighting Racism*, 213–217.

19 Mbadiwe, "African Academy of Arts and Research," 17.

20 Foucault, *Archaeology of Knowledge*, 111–112; Deleuze and Guattari, *Thousand Plateaus*, 265–266.

21 In 1940 Mbadiwe transferred from Lincoln University to New York University, where he studied business administration. He transferred again to the Business School at Columbia University in 1941 (Lynch, "K. O. Mbadiwe," 185–186).

22 Mbadiwe, *Rebirth of a Nation*, 14.

23 Mbadiwe, "African Academy of Arts and Research," 9.

24 Gershoni, *Africans on African-Americans*, 3.

25 Gershoni, *Africans on African-Americans*, 57.

26 Mbadiwe, "African Academy of Arts and Research," 9.

27 Gershoni, *Africans on African-Americans*, 60.

28 Brock, "Introduction," 12; Guridy, *Forging Diaspora*, 20.

29 Cf. Davis, "Nationalism and Civil Rights," 41.

30 For historical insight into racial uplift and social mobility in Africa, see Gershoni, *Africans on African-Americans*, 112–144; and in Cuba, see Montejo Arrechea, *"Minerva,"* 33–48; and Guridy, *Forging Diaspora*.

31 See Piñeiro Díaz, *Zoila Gálvez*; and Pérez Derrick, "Afro-Cuban Women in Opera," 58–59.

32 "Reseña social," *El mundo*, October 1, 1922, 8.

33 "List or Manifest of Alien Passengers for the United States," December 27, 1922, New York, passenger lists, 1820–1957, accessed October 28, 2014, Ancestry .com; "Movimiento social," *Diario de la Marina*, December 31, 1922, 25; Piñeiro Díaz, *Zoila Gálvez*, 4.

34 "Coy Cogitates," *Chicago Defender*, April 10, 1926, 7.

35 Guridy, *Forging Diaspora*, 58; see also 82–83, 155–156. To Herndon's claim of this meeting being the "first link" to African American and Afro-Cuban cooperation, Marcus Garvey had visited the Club Atenas during his trip to Havana in 1921, though the members of the club ultimately disavowed Garvey's pan-African ideals (see Fernández Robaina, "Marcus Garvey in Cuba," 121).

36 "Jamaica Sees 'Rang-Tang,'" *Brooklyn Daily Eagle*, January 10, 1928, 32.

37 "Music and Drama," *Chicago Defender*, June 2, 1928, A5.

38 For information on the opera careers of African American women in the nineteenth and early twentieth century, see Eidsheim, "Marian Anderson," 648–653.

39 Beatrice Wilson's name appears on various black newspapers' social calendars during this period. For example, Wilson was listed among the guests of parties hosted by Caska Bonds and Countee Cullen (see Bessye J. Bearden, "Tid-Bits of New York Society," *Chicago Defender*, November 24, 1928, 11; "Poet Honored at Elaborate Party," *Pittsburgh Courier*, March 12, 1932, 8). Justa Gálvez was also reported to be among a group of vacationers that included Beatrice Wilson in Sheepshead Bay, New York, in August 1936 ("At the Resorts," *New York Amsterdam News*, August 8, 1936, 9).

40 Gálvez, "Una melodía negra," 25.

41 In all likelihood, Gálvez observed this performance at the Cameroon and Togo pavilion.

42 The director of the Elkins-Payne Singers, William C. Elkins was considered a traditionalist among choir directors specializing in spirituals. Elkins's aim was to preserve the spiritual as it was sung in its original form with simple harmonies and no instrumental accompaniment ("Negro Spiritual Rendition Stirs Up Big Composers War," *Pittsburgh Courier*, October 25, 1924, 11).

43 Gálvez, "Una melodía negra," 25.

44 Paris enrolled under the name of David Benjamin Mudge Paris at Hampton Institute in fall 1922 ("Item of Interest," David Benjamin Mudge Paris, Hampton University Archives). See also Ohman, "Musicians Seeking Progress," 374.

45 "Caska Bonds' Recital," *New York Amsterdam News*, June 9, 1926, 9; "African Baritone in Vocal Offering to New Yorkers," *New York Age*, February 26, 1927; "A New Singer Sings His Song," *Philadelphia Tribune*, November 17, 1927, 5. See also "Clara Novello Davies," *Oxford Music Online*, accessed October 7, 2014, http://www.oxfordmusiconline.com.libproxy.lib.unc.edu/subscriber/;jsessionid=ABA4DB79392FCF72FC7CA2C224E1CBBB.

46 "Side Lights on Society," *New York Amsterdam News*, December 22, 1926, 4.

47 "A New Singer Sings His Song," 5; "African Baritone in Vocal Offering"; "Mr. Mudge Paris, African Baritone," *Virginia Intercollegian* 3 (March 1929): 7.

48 "Listening In: African Artists Go On Air Friday," *Afro-American*, June 23, 1928, 8.

49 "African Baritone," *Afro-American*, September 21, 1929, A8.

50 *1930 United States Federal Census*, accessed October 8, 2014, Ancestry.com; "Garvey Honored on His Birthday," *Afro-American*, August 31, 1929, A5.

51 "U.S. War Dept. in Paris Denies War Mothers' Jim Crow," *Afro-American*, July 18, 1931, 17.

52 "Interracial Artists' Club Unique Group," *Chicago Defender*, October 3, 1931, 7.

53 Ohman, "Musicians Seeking Progress," 374.

54 Untitled document, ca. 1931, Series 35/6, Box 5, Folder 17, Melville J. Herskovits (1895–1963) Papers. See also Reed, "Reinterpretation of Black Strategies," 7.

55 Maude Roberts George, "News of the Music World," *Chicago Defender*, May 16, 1931, 15.

56 "Mr. Mudge Paris, African Baritone," 7.

57 "Spiritual," *Grove Music Online*, accessed October 15, 2014, http://www.oxfordmusiconline.com.libproxy.lib.unc.edu/subscriber/;jsessionid=ABA4DB79392FCF72FC7CA2C224E1CBBB.

58 Du Bois, *Souls of Black Folk*, 233; see also Floyd, Jr. *The Power of Black Music*, 107.

59 "African Baritone Coming," *Philadelphia Tribune*, October 20, 1927, 4; "A New Singer Sings His Song," *Philadelphia Tribune*, November 17, 1927, 5.

60 "A New Singer Sings His Song," 5 (my emphasis).

61 Seniors, "Hypermasculine African American *Übermensch*," 165.

62 "John Brown's Birthday to Be Celebrated May 9th," *Pittsburgh Courier*, April 21, 1928, 2.

63 "Pilgrims to the Grave of John Brown are Increasing as the Years Roll By," *Philadelphia Tribune*, May 24, 1928, 9.

64 Ohman, "Musicians Seeking Progress," 375.

65 Melville J. Herskovits to Howard W. Odum, November 16, 1931, Series 35/6, Box 5, Folder 17, Melville J. Herskovits (1895–1963) Papers.

66 As Ohman documents, Paris's work with organizers of the Chicago World's Fair came to an abrupt end in August 1932 after organizers received complaints from several individuals, accusing Paris of multiple counts of fraud, some in association with Ephriam (see Ohman, "Musicians Seeking Progress," 378–379). None of

these accusations, apparently, was ever pursued in court, nor have I found newspaper reports documenting the veracity of these accusations. As documented in
performance announcements and reviews published in newspapers throughout
his career, Paris claimed to have been, or was reported as being, a "prince," a member of the royal family of Nigeria, and a descendant of African kings; a native of
Lagos, Nigeria, Freetown, Sierra Leone, and Liberia; and a graduate of Oxford
University and New York University. Paris's father was born in Nigeria, and his
mother's Susu ethnic group does encompass the western portions of Sierra Leone
as well as most of southeastern Guinea. In addition, documents indicate that he
did intend to study medicine at Oxford University, but his father refused to pay
for his costs after they had a disagreement ("Items of Interest," David Benjamin
Mudge Paris, Hampton University Archives). According to another document,
Paris began studying mining engineering at New York University before giving
this up for performing music and writing plays and stories ("Mr. Mudge Paris,
African Baritone," 7). At least one reporter expressed his suspicion over Paris's
claims of being an heir apparent to a throne (see Lee Shippey, "The Lee Side o'
L.A.," *Los Angeles Times*, October 31, 1935, A4).

67 "Civic Opera Directors See Signs of Hope," *Chicago Daily Tribune*, April 24,
1932, F1.

68 "African Prince Tells of Birth of Spirituals," *Chicago Daily Tribune*, April 26, 1932,
13.

69 "African Prince Tells," 13 (my emphasis).

70 George, "News of the Music World," *Chicago Defender*, April 30, 1932, 15; George,
"News of the Music World," *Chicago Defender*, June 4, 1932, A3.

71 George, "News of the Music World," *Chicago Defender*, June 4, 1932, A3.

72 Modupe Paris to Colonel John Stephen Sewell, April 3, 1931, Series I, Box 369,
Folder 11817, Century of Progress. See Herzog, "Speech-Melody and Primitive
Music," 454–457; and Herzog and Blooah, *Jabo Proverbs from Liberia*.

73 "The Minutes," April 2, 1931, Series I, Box 369, Folder 11817, Century of Progress.

74 Modupe Paris to Colonel John Stephen Sewell (my emphasis). See also Ohman,
"Musicians Seeking Progress," 376.

75 Gershoni, *Africans on African-Americans*, 68.

76 It is worth noting that by 1932 Herskovits had not published any findings regarding the African origins of the spiritual. Hornbostel, however, had published his
articles "American Negro Songs" and "African Negro Music" in 1926 and 1928,
respectively. It is plausible that at their meeting the year before Herskovits shared
with Paris insight into his and Hornbostel's theories of the origins of the spiritual,
which might have included discussing the characteristics of African music and
their transmission to the New World and retention in the Negro spiritual. While
Paris's assertion that "music is an ingrained part of the Negro nature" is as derivative of stereotypical discourse as Hornbostel's similarly conceived "[the Negro]
is a born musician," his discussion of the interrelationship between language
and melody in the process of musical change does invite speculation that Paris
might have also drawn from Hornbostel's discussion of the relationship between

African tonal languages and melodies (see Hornbostel, "American Negro Songs," 751, and "African Negro Music," 55–59).

77 See Bourdieu, *Logic of Practice*, 110.

78 "Cook County, Illinois Marriage Index, 1930–1960," accessed October 8, 2014, Ancestry.com; "Brilliant Reception for Modupe Paris and Bride," *Chicago Defender*, October 17, 1931, 7.

79 The *Afro-American* and the *Pittsburgh Courier* reprinted the article in their issues of July 16, 1932, and the *Atlanta Daily World* reprinted the article on July 14, 1932.

80 "Wife of African Prince Thinks Spirituals Best," *Afro-American*, July 16, 1932, 18.

81 "Cronica social," *Diario de la Marina*, March 28, 1937, 27.

82 Andreu, "Spirituals negro songs," 90 (my emphasis).

83 Andreu, "Spirituals negro songs," 80.

84 Guridy, *Forging Diaspora*, 145–146.

85 Ortiz, "La música sagrada," 94.

86 Andreu, "Spirituals negro songs," 81–82.

87 See Floyd, Jr., *Power of Black Music*, 203; Radano, *Lying Up a Nation*, 290–291n13.

88 "Society," *New York Amsterdam News*, December 5, 1936, 11, 13.

89 Andreu, "Spirituals negro songs," 85–86.

90 hooks, *Feminist Theory*, 60, 82.

91 See Gramsci, *Prison Notebooks*, 369, 404–405.

92 Meier and Rudwick, "Negro Protest," 164–165; Ohman, "Musicians Seeking Progress," 384–386; Reed, "Reinterpretation of Black Strategies," 9.

93 " 'O, Sing a New Song' Draws 40,000 People," *Philadelphia Tribune*, August 30, 1934, 2; and "5,000 in Cast of Pageant at World's Fair," *Afro-American*, September 1, 1934, 1. From at least the 1910s, American Negro productions of historical pageants were largely deliberate acts of resistance toward their history's misrepresentation in or altogether erasure from white-produced pageants depicting American history (Glassberg, *American Historical Pageantry*, 132–135). To rectify this erasure, W. E. B. Du Bois wrote and produced *The Star of Ethiopia* (1913), which dramatizes the Negro's gifts (iron, civilization, religious faith, humiliation, struggle toward freedom, and freedom) to the world. In doing so, Du Bois fulfills the Hegelian narrative of human history, starting with the African savage's fear of Nature before his initiation of the path toward modernity with the gift of iron. Tom-tom music accompanies the emergence of civilization and religion, and the story moves teleologically from there (Du Bois, "Star of Ethiopia," 305–310).

94 " 'O, Sing a New Song' Draws 40,000 People"; see also "Chorus of 5,000 to Be Heard in Negro Pageant," *Chicago Daily Tribune*, August 5, 1934, SW 4.

95 " 'O, Sing a New Song' Draws 40,000 People"; see also "Chorus of 5,000 to Be Heard in Negro Pageant," *Chicago Daily Tribune*, August 5, 1934, SW 4.

96 William G. Nunn, "65,000 Attend Pageant and East-West Game in Chicago," *Pittsburgh Courier*, September 1, 1934, 1, 4.

97 Eugene Stinson, "O, Sing a New Song," *Chicago Defender*, September 1, 1934, 3.

98 To this point, Fanon invited his readers to attempt the following experiment: "Attend showings of a Tarzan film in the Antilles and in Europe. In the Antilles,

the young Negro identifies himself *de facto* with Tarzan against the Negroes. This is much more difficult because for him in a European theater, for the rest of the audience, which is white, automatically identifies him with the savages on the screen" (Fanon, *Black Skin, White Masks*, 152–153n15). Susan Manning refers to this racially intersubjective process as two-way cross-viewing (see Manning, *Modern Dance, Negro Dance*, 143).

99   June Provines, "Front Views and Profiles," *Chicago Daily Tribune*, April 23, 1934, 17 (my emphasis).

100   Nunn, "65,000 Attend Pageant" (my emphasis).

101   Modupe, *I Was a Savage*, 15, 92–98.

102   Lawrence F. LaMar, "Prince Modupe Paris Carves Niche for Self in Movie Industry," *Chicago Defender*, September 12, 1936, 24. It was because of his father's Yoruba ethnicity that Paris often claimed to be Nigerian. But, as he confirmed in his autobiography, he was born in Dubréka, French Guinea.

103   "Mr. Mudge Paris, African Baritone," 7.

104   Heard, "Asadata Dafora," 65.

105   Gershoni, *Africans on African-Americans*, 74, 116–117; Heard, "Asadata Dafora," 51–53.

106   See Heard, "Asadata Dafora," 59–63. According to one newspaper report, Dafora's father studied at Oxford University, while his mother studied in Paris ("Foremost African Dance Expert to Bring Show Here," *Waco News-Tribune*, March 4, 1947, 5). See also "African Dancers to K.C.," *Call*, October 18, 1946, 8.

107   See Heard, "Asadata Dafora," 63–65, 75–76.

108   "Baltimore, Passenger Lists, 1820–1948 and 1954–1957," accessed October 8, 2014, Ancestry.com. Asadata Dafora is listed under the name Austin Horton. Heard and Dafora's own promotional materials say he arrived in New York City in 1929, though Heard does cite one newspaper report stating that he arrived in 1919 (see Heard, "Asadata Dafora," 73–75).

109   "Native Africans Mark Third Year," *New York Amsterdam News*, February 12, 1930, 19. In an interview published in the *Journal and Guide* of Norfolk, Virginia, Dafora indicated that in "four years of obscurity, he trained a group of dancers, singers and drummers in African techniques" ("African Arts Head Confers with Governor Darden Prior to Concert Here Dec. 17–18," *Journal and Guide*, December 15, 1945).

110   "Manhattan Personals," *New York Age*, March 8, 1930, 2.

111   In spite of *Zoonga*'s African theme, its music was apparently influenced by Western operatic aesthetics (see "St. Marks' M. E. Church," *New York Age*, March 31, 1934, 11). See also "Mother Africa," *New York Amsterdam News*, June 28, 1933, 7; "Author Wants to Use Cast of 'Kykunkor' in Movie," *Plaindealer*, July 6, 1934, 6.

112   *The Labor Club Presents Sunday Evenings of Negro Music Past and Present*, Asadata Dafora Papers, MG 48, Box 1.

113   The Labor Club of the American Labor Party to "Our Friends and Patrons," undated, Asadata Dafora Papers, MG 48, Box 1.

114 See "Programs of the Week," *New York Times*, February 12, 1939, 134; "Negro Music Concert to Be Given Sunday," *New York Times*, February 24, 1939, 21; "Postponed Concert Is Set for Sunday," *New York Amsterdam News*, February 25, 1939, 16; and "Labor Party Sponsors All Sepia Concert," *Afro-American*, March 11, 1939, 11.

115 Bakhtin, *Dialogic Imagination*, 250.

116 Olin Downes, "Negro Music Sung in Tableaux," *New York Times*, February 27, 1939, 10 (my emphasis).

117 C. E. Chapman, "Postscripts," *Plaindealer*, July 28, 1933, 7.

118 See Collins, *Black Feminist Thought*, 132, 149.

119 June Provines, "Front Views and Profiles," *Chicago Daily Tribune*, April 28, 1934, 17.

120 Stabooni, "Mother Africa," *New York Amsterdam News*, June 28, 1933, 7; J. Downer, "Mother Africa," *New York Amsterdam News*, July 12, 1933, 7.

121 "New Wallace Film, 'Kongo Raid,' Ready," *Sun*, March 25, 1934, TM7; "Robeson Film Called Propaganda Justifying British Imperialism," *Afro-American*, July 6, 1935, 9.

122 J. A. Rogers, "Ruminations: 'Sanders of the River' White Propaganda Robeson Restricted Pictorial Magnificence," *New York Amsterdam News*, July 13, 1935, 12.

123 Rogers, J. A., "Ruminations," *New York Amsterdam News*, July 13, 1935, 12. See also Mac Tinée, "Film of White Rule in Africa Is Achievement," *Chicago Daily Tribune*, October 26, 1935, 17.

124 "Africans Believe Paul Robeson Was Tricked in British Film," *Chicago Defender*, October 5, 1935, 24.

125 T. R. Poston, "Robeson to Play King Cristophe in British Production, He Reveals," *New York Amsterdam News*, October 5, 1935, 1 (my emphasis).

126 Melville Herskovits reported to Dunham that he had met with Robeson in Chicago during his stopover on his way to Los Angeles to film *Show Boat* (Melville J. Herskovits to Katherine Dunham, November 11, 1935, and Katherine Dunham to Melville J. Herskovits, December 28, 1935, Series 35/6, Box 7, Folder 12, Melville J. Herskovits [1895–1963] Papers). Neither of these films, however, was produced.

127 "African Prince Bares Injustices Heaped upon Homeland," *Pittsburgh Courier*, April 13, 1935, 2; "Prince Modupe and Natives Entertain Large Audience," *Los Angeles Times*, October 8, 1935, 13; "Jungle Play to Be Given," *Los Angeles Times*, October 26, 1935, A13. See also Patterson, "Prince Modupe."

128 "Social Workers Hear about Ethiopia," *Afro-American*, December 7, 1935, 8.

129 Bernice Patton, "The Sepia Side of Hollywood," *Pittsburgh Courier*, June 20, 1936, A6.

130 "Tarazan Location another Wild, Outdoor Movie Set," *Chicago Daily Tribune*, August 16, 1936, D13.

131 "Tarazan Location another Wild, Outdoor Movie Set," *Chicago Daily Tribune*, August 16, 1936, D13; George Shaffer, "Tarzan Thriller Being Filmed in Mountain Wilds," *Chicago Daily Tribune*, August 18, 1936, 14; "Title Personage Works in Movies," *Los Angeles Times*, September 1, 1936, 14.

132 Lawrence F. LaMar, "Prince Modupe Paris Carves Niche for Self in Movie Industry," *Chicago Defender*, September 12, 1936, 24;

133 "New Firm Plans African Movies," *New York Amsterdam News*, October 31, 1936,
10.

134 "Ballet Russe in Havana," *New York Times*, March 21, 1941, 19; Philippoff, "Enforced
Holiday," 660.

135 Philippoff, "Enforced Holiday," 662.

136 Lowinger and Fox, *Tropicana Nights*, 90–91.

137 "En Tropicana," *Diario de la marina*, April 18, 1941, 9.

138 According to Pozo, he also composed the music for Lichine's ballet, while
Alfredo Brito, who was the director of the Tropicana's house orchestra, arranged
it (Arturo Ramírez, "Compositores cubanos de hoy: 'Chano' Pozo," *Carteles*,
June 14, 1942, 6–7.

139 Kiki Skirving, "Crónica habanera," *Diario de la marina*, April 20, 1941, 5.

140 Francisco Ichaso, "Escenario y pantalla: Un 'ballet' afro de Lichine," *Diario de la
marina*, April 22, 1941, n.p.

141 I am referring here to Deleuze and Guattari's notion of the body as not only a
human or animal body but also a body of work, a social body or collectivity, a
linguistic corpus, and political party, or even an idea (Baugh, "Body," 35–37).

142 Ichaso, "Escenario y pantalla," n.p.

143 Ramírez, "Compositores cubanos de hoy," 6.

144 Ramírez, "Compositores cubanos de hoy," 6.

145 See Edwards, *Practice of Diaspora*, 13–14.

146 See Carmichael, "From Black Power Back to Pan-Africanism," 222–225.

147 Carmichael, "Black Power," 225 (my emphasis).

148 Lynch, "Pan-African Responses," 76, 80n67; see James et al., *Fighting Racism*,
213–217.

149 Lynch, "Pan-African Responses," 70.

150 "Conditions in Africa and Spain Discussed," *Chicago Defender*, March 11, 1939, 4.

151 "Paraphernalia for African Dance Revue Explained at Meeting," *New York Age*,
November 27, 1943, 10. In addition to being colleagues, Okala and Mbadiwe were
apparently close friends. For example, in April 1942, Mbadiwe was best man at
Okala's wedding; Okala married Ollie Sims, a nurse with a masters' degree in
public health from Columbia University ("Talented Ollie Sims Bride of Prince
Okala," *Pittsburgh Courier*, April 25, 1942, 10).

152 Lynch, "K. O. Mbadiwe," 191. For examples of newspaper articles announcing the
founding of the AAAR and the upcoming "African Dance Festival," see "African
Academy Set Up," *New York Times*, November 14, 1943, 50; "Dafora Plans Dance
Festive," *Afro-American*, November 20, 1943, 8; "African Academy Organized
in N.Y.," *Chicago Defender*, November 20, 1943, 8; "To Sponsor African Dance
Program," *New York Amsterdam News*, November 27, 1943, 8B.

153 African Dance Festival, for Release Sunday, November 14th, African Academy
of Arts and Research, African Dance Festival, MGZR. Performing Arts Research
Collections, Dance. Performing Arts Library, New York Public Library.

154 "African Dance Show Planned," newspaper article [uncited], African Academy of Arts and Research, African Dance Festival.

155 See Mbadiwe, "Africa in the War of Destiny," 260–264.

156 In fact, President Roosevelt maintained publically throughout the war that the charter applied to the entire world, including British colonies in Asia and Africa (see Hubbard, *United States*, 8–14).

157 See Mbadiwe, "Africa in the War of Destiny," 298–301, 317.

158 See Mbadiwe, *Rebirth of a Nation*, 17–18; and Lynch, "K. O. Mbadiwe," 191.

159 Steady, "African Feminism," 3–22; and Collins, *Black Feminist Thought*, 40, 151. See also Diawara, *In Search of Africa*, 4.

160 For example, "Dance Festival Praised: Mrs. Roosevelt Commends Project of African Academy," *New York Times*, December 1, 1943, 24; "Support Asked for African Dance Fete," *Afro-American*, December 4, 1943, 10; and African Academy of Arts and Research to patrons, undated, African Academy of Arts and Research, African Dance Festival.

161 "African Dancers in Festival Here," *New York Times*, December 14, 1943, 30.

162 John Martin, "The Dance Novelties," *New York Times*, December 12, 1949, X2. See also Heard, "Asadata Dafora," 79–87, 109. Heard indicates that Dafora continued to recycle and revise the music and dances in *Kykunkor* and *Zunguru* through the 1940s.

163 Festival of Music and Fine Arts, program, Asadata Dafora Papers, MG 48, Box 1.

164 Edwin Denby, "The Dance," *New York Herald Tribune*, December 19, 1943, n.p.; and "A Glimpse of Real African Dancing," *New York Herald Tribune*, December 21, 1943, n.p., African Academy of Arts and Research, African Dance Festival, MGZR. "The Dance" is reprinted as "Asadata Dafora" in Denby, *Dance Writings*, 183–186.

165 Denby, "The Dance," *New York Herald Tribune*, December 19, 1943, n.p.; and "A Glimpse of Real African Dancing," *New York Herald Tribune*, December 21, 1943, n.p., African Academy of Arts and Research, African Dance Festival, MGZR.

166 Denby, "The Dance," *New York Herald Tribune*, December 19, 1943, n.p.; and "A Glimpse of Real African Dancing," *New York Herald Tribune*, December 21, 1943, n.p., African Academy of Arts and Research, African Dance Festival, MGZR.

167 John Martin, "African Dancers in Festival Here," *New York Times*, December 14, 1943, 30.

168 Denby, "Dance Criticism," 83; see also Morris, "Modernism's Role."

169 Roosevelt, "Prejudice Springs from Ignorance," 18–19; and Bethune, "Hands across the Waters," 19.

170 Eleanor Roosevelt, "My Day," December 15, 1943, accessed November 10, 2014, http://www.gwu.edu/~erpapers/myday/displaydoc. cfm?_ y=1943 &_f=md056668.

171 McCluskey, "Introduction," 3–19.

172 Black, "Introduction," 1–16.

173 Eleanor Roosevelt, "My Day," April 20, 1946, accessed November 10, 2014, http://www.gwu.edu/~erpapers/myday/displaydoc.cfm?_ y=1943&_f=md056668.

174 *Kykunkor*, program, n.d., Asadata Dafora Papers, M G 48, Box 1.

175 See Gilroy, *Black Atlantic*, 108–128.

176 The increasing racial tensions and number of lynchings between 1939 and 1945 in the United States are chronicled in James et al., *Fighting Racism*.

177 African Dance Festival, n.d., African Academy of Arts and Research, African Dance Festival, M G Z R.

178 "Asadata Dafora Presents African Tribal Operetta," *Opportunity: Journal of Negro Life* 22, no. 3 (July–September 1944): 129, 147; John Martin, "The Dance," *New York Times*, March 4, 1945, X4.

179 See Sherwood, "No New Deal."

180 Lynch, "Pan-African Responses," 82; see also Sherwood, "No New Deal," 88–89.

181 "Awards to Be Given by African Academy," *New York Times*, April 7, 1945, 12.

182 John Martin, "The Dance," *New York Times*, March 4, 1945, X4.

183 See "African Dance Festival to Play in Norfolk Dec. 17 and 18," *Journal and Guide*, December 8, 1945.

184 African Academy of Arts and Research presents the African Dance and Music Festival, program, December 17 and 18, 1945, African Academy of Arts and Research, African Dance Festival, M G Z R.

185 Rosenberg, "African Rhythm in the West," 26. Rosenberg, who was at the time a student of anthropology at New York University, prepared this essay to provide background information for Dafora's program of April 1945.

186 "African Opera Pleases at Unity Theatre," *New York Age*, May 19, 1934, 4; John Martin, "African Festival at Carnegie Hall," *New York Times*, April 5, 1945, 27.

187 "Dance Festival Shows Progress of Africans," *Journal and Guide*, December 22, 1945, n.p.

188 "George Wiltshire," *The New York Age*, July 20, 1935, 4; "Louis Armstrong Admittedly 'Tops' in Pulling Power in Amusement World," *Atlanta Daily World*, May 3, 1937, 2; "Princess Orelia and Congo Dancers," *Pittsburgh Courier*, June 25, 1938, 21.

189 See Hill and Cowley, "Calypso at Midnight," 6–25; "Dance Festival Shows Progress of Africans," *Journal and Guide*, December 22, 1945, n.p.

190 "Haitian Diplomats Highlight Gay Celebration on Sunday Afternoon," *New York Amsterdam Star-News*, March 27, 1943, 20; "The Theatre," *Wall Street Journal*, May 10, 1945, 6.

191 "Dance Festival Shows Progress of Africans," *Journal and Guide*, December 22, 1945.

192 Martin, "African Festival at Carnegie Hall," 27.

193 "Famous African Dancer Scores High at Clark," *Atlanta Daily World*, January 27, 1946, 3; "Asadata Dafora and African Dance Group to Leave on Coast to Coast Concert Tour," *New York Age*, August 24, 1946, 5.

194 "African Dance Group on Tour," *Chicago Defender*, October 19, 1946, 10; "African Dancer Here in Concert Nov. 17 at Kiel," *Chicago Defender*, November 9, 1946, 19C; "African Dancers in Auditorium in Flint, Feb. 5," *Michigan Chronicle*, January 25, 1947, 16; "African Dance Performance Wins Praise in Waco," *Waco*

Texas News-Tribune, March 7, 194/; "Dafora Group Gives Unusual Presentation," *Richmond News*, April 3, 1948.

195 Mbadiwe, *Rebirth of a Nation*, 22; Lynch, "K. O. Mbadiwe," 200–201. See also *Liberian Age*, April 15, 1948, 7.

196 "African Dancers to K. C.," *Call*, October 18, 1946, 8.

197 See "Dafora Open Concert Series," *People's Voice*, October 4, 1947; and "This Week and After," *New York Times*, October 19, 1947, X6.

198 See programs for *Batanga*, October 1947 and April 1948, Box 1, MG 48, Asadata Dafora Papers.

199 See James, "Popular Art," 248–252.

200 UNESCO, *Basic Texts*, 5.

Chapter 4. Disalienating Movement and Sound

1 Fanon, *Black Skin, White Masks*, 225–226. This is my retranslation of the English version of *Black Skin, White Masks* based on the original French *Peau noire, masques blancs* (217).

2 Anders, "Pathology of Freedom," 280. Anders originally presented this essay as a lecture to the Kant Society in 1929. The French translation of the lecture was later published in 1936. See Erlmann, *Reason and Resonance*, 322, 394n45.

3 Anders, "Pathology of Freedom," 279, 293. See also Wolfe, "From the Archive."

4 Anders, "Pathology of Freedom," 284, 300, 301.

5 Anders, "Pathology of Freedom," 304.

6 A retranslation of this passage is especially crucial given the use of the French future perfect (e.g., *seront désaliénés*) in the original (217), which is not translated as such in the English version (226).

7 For an explanation of Jacques Lacan's definition of logical time and chronological time, see Evans, *Introductory Dictionary*, 205–207. For a definition of original time and Temporality, see Heidegger, *Basic Problems of Phenomenology*, 241, 307.

8 Anders, "Pathology of Freedom," 305–308; Erlmann, *Reason and Resonance*, 316–332.

9 Anders, "Pathology of Freedom," 307; cf. Small, *Musicking*, 9–10. Compare, also, UNESCO's statements on race and racial difference (which were drafted at the same time Fanon wrote and published *Peau noire, masques blancs*), the authors of which depended solely on the natural and social sciences; this entire enterprise fell under both Stern's and Fanon's critique of philosophical anthropology and science as they pertain to human identification (see chapter 1).

10 Erlmann, *Reason and Resonance*, 339.

11 Heidegger, *Basic Problems of Phenomenology*, 160–161, 170–171.

12 I base my understanding of New Negro ideals and aesthetic principles on McKinley Melton's discussion of the role of self-definition in New Negro ideology in his "Speak It into Existence."

13 See Clark, "Afro-Caribbean Dance," 329–330.

14 Manning, *Modern Dance, Negro Dance*, 143.

15   Clark focuses on Dunham's choreographies in *Stormy Weather* (1943), *L'Ag'ya* (1938–1944), *Southland* (1951), and *Tango* (1954) as repositories of Caribbean and African American memory and history. She encourages analyzing Dunham's choreographical work in its historical context and through a critical discourse, focusing on the dialogues between her research, performance, and training of dancers, the ways her repertoire changed over time, and how she articulated difference to class, gender, race, and politics in her works. *Southland* (1951) and *Tango* (1954), she notes, are two rare examples of Dunham choreographies characterized by agitprop. See Clark, "Afro-Caribbean Dance," 323–324, 327.

16   Clegg, *Price of Liberty*, 5.

17   See Sundiata, *Brothers and Strangers*, 133–134.

18   See Gaines, "Duke Ellington," 588; and Porter, *What Is This Thing Called Jazz?* 39.

19   Gaines, "Duke Ellington," 587.

20   For a contemporary overview of avant-garde film production in the United States in the 1940s, see Jacobs, "Avant-Garde Production in America."

21   Jacobs, "Avant-Garde Production in America," 139.

22   Deleuze, *Cinema 2*, 159–167.

23   See Deleuze and Guattari, *Thousand Plateaus*, 208–231.

24   See "Miss Dunham Is Effective in Exotic Dances," *Chicago Daily Tribune*, October 28, 1938, 21; "Dancers Plan Swanky Show," *Los Angeles Times*, September 24, 1941, A10; "Dance Event Wins Praise," *Los Angeles Times*, October 18, 1941, A9.

25   See John Martin, "The Dance: A Negro Art," *New York Times*, February 25, 1940, 114.

26   S. E. Johnson, "Introduction," 5. On the Dunham Technique, see Aschenbrenner, *Katherine Dunham*, 203–232; and especially Rose, "Dunham Technique."

27   Cecil Smith, "Critic Adds 'Cabin in the Sky' to List of Best Musical Shows," *Chicago Daily Tribune*, May 5, 1941, 15; "Notes of Music and Musicians," *Chicago Daily Tribune*, September 14, 1941, G3.

28   "Hotel Refuses Dunham Players," *Chicago Daily Tribune*, January 24, 1942, 7. This particular incident was also reported in the *New York Amsterdam Star-News* and the *Philadelphia Tribune*. See also Manning, *Modern Dance, Negro Dance*, 125.

29   See "Bal Negre" programs, Box 9, Katherine Dunham Papers.

30   "Heat Wave," script, undated, Box 54, Folder 13, Katherine Dunham Papers.

31   For a more detailed analysis of Hammond's *From Spirituals to Swing* concerts and the traditionalist-modernist divide in jazz critical discourse of the 1940s, see Gennari, *Blowin' Hot and Cool*, 43–49, 119–120. To clarify, though Hammond was regarded as a hot jazz purist, his civil rights activism as well as his commercial prerogatives seemed to trump his stylistic allegiances, as was demonstrated by his engagement of black and white swing musicians such as Duke Ellington, Benny Goodman, Cab Calloway, and many others for recording dates and concerts (see Gennari, *Blowin' Hot and Cool*, 26, 34–43).

32   *From Spirituals to Swing*, 1938 program, 7.

33   Gennari, *Blowin' Hot and Cool*, 44.

34 Bill Henry, "By the Way," *Los Angeles Times*, April 12, 1943, A1; "Dance Stylist," *Pittsburgh Courier*, May 22, 1943, 21. Sol Hurok reports that he first met Katherine Dunham while her troupe was performing at the Mark Hopkins Hotel in San Francisco (Hurok, *S. Hurok Presents*, 59).

35 "Sharps and Flats," *Los Angeles Times*, May 9, 1943, C6; "New Orleans Jazz Revived for One Jam," *Down Beat*, June 1, 1943, 23; "Kid Ory Joins Zutty Combo on the Stage," *Down Beat*, June 15, 1943, 2; S. I. Hayakawa, "Second Thoughts: Asleep behind the Piano," *Chicago Defender*, August 31, 1946, 15. See also Blesh, *Shining Trumpets*, 185.

36 Albert Goldberg, "Notes of Music and Musicians," *Chicago Daily Tribune*, August 8, 1943, E3; and Blesh, *Shining Trumpets*, xi. In addition to his lectures, Blesh hosted a jazz radio show, served as president of the San Francisco Hot Jazz Society, and wrote a freelance jazz column for the *San Francisco Chronicle*, all of which contributed to the growing New Orleans jazz revivalist movement on the West Coast (see Gennari, *Blowin' Hot and Cool*, 119–122, 126, 130–137).

37 Blesh, *Shining Trumpets*, x.

38 Blesh, *Shining Trumpets*, 39–40. Blesh's lectures of April 1943 date after Waterman defended his dissertation in February but before he read his paper "'Hot' Rhythm in Negro Music" at the American Musicological Society in December.

39 See Clark and Johnson, *Kaiso!*, 634–636; see also C. V. Hill, "Collaborating with Balanchine," 243, 247n3.

40 Hammond in fact helped promote White's career by securing his recording contract with Columbia Records in addition to performance opportunities (see Wald, *Josh White*).

41 "Heat Wave," script, undated, Box 54, Folder 13, Katherine Dunham Papers.

42 Blesh, *Shining Trumpets*, 142–143.

43 Blesh, *Shining Trumpets*, 142–143.

44 See Wald, *Josh White*, 90–124.

45 See Porter, *This Thing Called Jazz?* 293–299.

46 Blesh, *Shining Trumpets*, 310–311.

47 Burley, *Dan Burley's Jive*, 216.

48 See Ferguson, *Sage of Sugar Hill*, 52–62.

49 Blesh, *Shining Trumpets*, 337.

50 Dan Burley, "Anthropologists Study Meaning of 'Conk,'" *New York Amsterdam News*, January 25, 1947, 19.

51 See Aiello, "Introduction," xx.

52 Dan Burley, "Back Door Stuff," *New York Amsterdam News*, May 31, 1947, 21.

53 See Dunham, "Thesis Turned Broadway," 214–215.

54 Hurok, *S. Hurok Presents*, 58.

55 Will Davidson, "New Café Revues Present Diverting Entertainment," *Chicago Daily Tribune*, June 20, 1943, E7; "Dunham on Broadway," *Los Angeles Tribune*, September 13, 1943, 19; "Katherine Dunham Closes on Broadway," *Los Angeles Tribune*, November 15, 1943, 39.

56 "'Stormy Weather' Rated a 'Sender,'" *Pittsburgh Courier*, July 31, 1943, 20.

57 Davidson, "New Café Revues."

58 "Katherine Dunham Closes on Broadway."

59 See John Martin, "The Dance: Curtain Going Up," *New York Times*, September 19, 1943, X9; John Martin, "Katherine Dunham Gives Dance Revue," *New York Times*, September 20, 1943, 24; *New York Times*, September 23, 1943, 25.

60 See Hurok, *S. Hurok Presents*, 59, 60.

61 Prospectus, "Bal Negre," Exhibit "F" (Sec. 1), summary of gross receipts, 1943–44–45 "Tropical Revue," Box 9, Katherine Dunham Papers.

62 "Dunham Group Turns on Heat," *Afro-American*, September 25, 1943, 10; "Notes from the Field," *New York Times*, October 17, 1943, X5; "Heads Revue," *Jewish Exponent*, December 31, 1943, 15; "Dunham Revue Coming," *Philadelphia Tribune*, January 1, 1944, 13.

63 Hurok, *S. Hurok Presents*, 60. See "The Dance: Holiday Fare," *New York Times*, December 24, 1944, 37; "Dunham Revue Is Altered, but It Still Sizzles," *Chicago Daily Tribune*, January 24, 1945, 13. See also memorandum, "Bal Negre," Exhibit "F" (cont'd), Box 9, Katherine Dunham Papers.

64 John Martin, "The Dance: 'Tropical Revue,'" *New York Times*, September 26, 1943, X2. See also Manning, *Modern Dance, Negro Dance*, 153.

65 "Katherine Dunham Learned Voodoo from Natives," *Philadelphia Tribune*, January 22, 1944, 15; "Katherine Dunham Bringing Dance Troupe," *Chicago Daily Tribune*, April 23, 1944, E2; "Dunham Revue Comes to Cass November 19," *Michigan Chronicle*, November 18, 1944, 14; "New Comedy and Katherine Dunham Here Tomorrow," *Chicago Daily Tribune*, January 21, 1945, E2; "Dunham Revue Is Altered, but It Still Sizzles," *Chicago Daily Tribune*, January 24, 1945, 13; *Michigan Chronicle*, February 3, 1945, 13; and *Michigan Chronicle*, February 17, 1945, 14.

66 "Miss Dunham's Dance Revue Is Brilliant Show," *Chicago Daily Tribune*, May 9, 1944, 15.

67 See memorandum, "Bal Negre," Exhibit "G," Box 9, Katherine Dunham Papers; *New York Amsterdam News*, September 9, 1945, 13; Dunham, "Dunham Schools," 479.

68 Franziska Boas, daughter of Marie Krackowizer and Franz Boas, had opened her progressive dance school in Manhattan in 1933. Allana C. Lindgren details the issues of race, gender, sexuality, and progressive politics that transpired in the founding and operation of the Boas School of Dance (see Lindgren, "Civil Rights Strategies").

69 Dunham, "Katherine Dunham School of Arts and Research," 472–478. According to Aschenbrenner, Columbia University accepted credits from the Dunham School, and classes at the school were accepted for the GI Bill (Aschenbrenner, *Katherine Dunham*, 137).

70 Aschenbrenner, *Katherine Dunham*, 138; Dunham, "Dunham Schools," 480.

71 "'Carib Song' Listed for Sept. 25 Debut," *New York Times*, August 11, 1945, 14.

72 Katherine Dunham to George Abbott, January 22, 1946, Box 7, Katherine Dunham Papers.

73 See memorandum: "Bal Negre" and prospectus: "Bal Negre."
74 "Katherine Dunham Made $891,000 Last Year; Must Go to Work—She's 'Broke'?," *Afro-American*, August 24, 1946, 6.
75 See memorandum: "Bal Negre."
76 See "Bal Negre," draft program, Box 9, Katherine Dunham Papers.
77 John Martin, "The Dance: Dunham," *New York Times*, November 17, 1946, 81.
78 "Katherine Dunham's Ballet Opens Tonite," *Philadelphia Tribune*, September 14, 1946, 11; "Tribune's Own Lee Interviews," *Philadelphia Tribune*, September 24, 1946, 9; "'Bal Negre' Is Exciting Presentation," *Hartford Courant*, September 25, 1946, 17; Miles M. Jefferson, "The Negro on Broadway, 1946–1947," *Phylon (1940–1956)* 8, no. 2 (1947): 146–159.
79 "Pandora's Box Is Opened by Dunham in 'Bal Negre,'" *Washington Afro-American*, September 21, 1946, 13.
80 Dan Burley, "'Dearie' and 'Darling,' That Was Bessye," *New York Amsterdam News*, September 25, 1943, 22.
81 Denby, "Katherine Dunham," 142.
82 For example, see Porter, *This Thing Called Jazz*, 32–39; and Manning, *Modern Dance, Negro Dance*, xx, 142.
83 "Events of the Week," *New York Times*, November 3, 1946, 69; *New York Times*, November 5, 1946, 42.
84 "Katherine Dunham Balks Plugs," *Chicago Defender*, October 12, 1946, 10.
85 See Aschenbrenner, *Katherine Dunham*, 124.
86 Goodman, "Nights Out," 35.
87 John C. Donahue, Jr., "To the editor of 'Dance,'" undated, Box 9, Katherine Dunham Papers; "Readers Write," *Dance*, March 1947, 6.
88 Pierre, "Katherine Dunham." See also Dunham, "Katherine Dunham School of Arts and Research," 473.
89 The following theoretical insights are drawn from Cull, "Introduction."
90 Richard A. Long to Katherine Dunham, September 15, 1946; and "Dance Movement" (poem), Box 9, Katherine Dunham Papers.
91 "Pastors Back Africa Rally," *People's Voice*, April 26, 1947, 6.
92 See Monson, *Freedom Sounds*, 108–111.
93 "We Negro Americans to the President and Congress of the United States," *People's Voice*, April 26, 1947, 7; "Rally with Robeson," *People's Voice*, April 26, 1947, 25.
94 "Lynching Must Stop," *People's Voice*, May 31, 1947, 20; "Smash Dixie Lynch Mobs!" *People's Voice*, June 7, 1947, 20; "Pickets Oppose Rally," *New York Times*, June 1, 1947, 34.
95 "Freedom Rally Hits 'Black Nationalism,'" *People's Voice*, June 7, 1947, 2.
96 "Liberian Celebration," *People's Voice*, June 7, 1947, 2; "Major Wright Special Envoy to Attend Liberia's Centennial," *New Journal and Guide*, June 7, 1947, A14.
97 "3-Man Committee to Plan for Liberian Centennial," *Afro-American*, May 17, 1947, 14; "Dawson Challenges U.S. to Give Tangible Recognition to Liberia,"

New Journal and Guide, June 14, 1947, A1; "Maestro Plans Musical Tribute to Liberia," *Journal and Guide*, June 28, 1947, 19; *Chicago Defender*, June 28, 1947, 2.

98 Blesh, *Shining Trumpets*, 134, 144. John Hammond and many other jazz critics shared Blesh's consternation over Ellington's music, particularly his multimovement works, such as *Black, Brown and Beige* (see Gennari, *Blowin' Hot and Cool*, 53).

99 See Porter, *This Thing Called Jazz*, 35–53.

100 Tucker, "Landmark in Ellington Criticism," 59–60.

101 Tucker, "Ellington Orchestra in Cleveland," 53; Tucker, "Interpretations in Jazz," 257; and Ellington, *Music Is My Mistress*, 337.

102 Tucker, "Two Early Interviews," 45.

103 Tucker, "Wilder Hobson," 98.

104 Tucker, "Interview in Los Angeles," 150; Tucker, "Brian Priestly and Alan Cohen," 186.

105 See Duke Ellington and His Orchestra, *Duke Ellington*, CD 1; Priestley and Cohen: 'Black, Brown & Beige' (1974–1975)," 195.

106 Tucker, "Program," 163.

107 Ellington, *Music Is My Mistress*, 187.

108 Locke, "Slavery in the Modern Manner," 297.

109 See Sundiata, *Brothers and Strangers*, 121–139.

110 Ferguson, *Sage of Sugar Hill*, 19–20. A search of Schuyler's articles and editorials on Liberia in the ProQuest Historical Newspapers database brings up dozens of results.

111 See Sundiata, *Brothers and Strangers*, 61–76.

112 Du Bois, "Little Portraits of Africa," 647.

113 See Locke, "Slavery in the Modern Manner," 298–299; Azikiwe, "In Defense of Liberia,"; Azikiwe, review; and Ferguson, *Sage of Sugar Hill*, 20.

114 "National Committee for the American Celebration of the 100th Anniversary of Liberia June 7, 1947," Series 4 Oversized Graphics, Map Case 2, Drawer 17, Folder 20, Duke Ellington Collection (my emphasis).

115 "Duke Ellington to be Honored in N. Y. Fete," *Atlanta Daily World*, December 17, 1947, 3; "Duke to Receive Honors on Premiere of 'Suite,'" *Afro-American*, December 20, 1947, 6; "Liberian Group Plans Honor for Duke Ellington," *Philadelphia Tribune*, December 23, 1947, 15; "Liberia Honors Duke Ellington," *Cleveland Call and Post*, December 27, 1947, 6B; "Duke Ellington to Receive Liberian Award at Carnegie Hall Concert," *New York Amsterdam News*, December 27, 1947, 3 (my emphasis).

116 "Committee for Liberian Fete to Honor Duke Ellington," *New Journal and Guide*, December 20, 1947, 18.

117 Tucker, "Previews," 156.

118 Tucker, "Previews," 156.

119 "Duke Ellington and His Orchestra," program, Carnegie Hall, December 26–27, 1947, Series 2, Programs, Box 10, Folder 45, Duke Ellington Collection.

120 "Liberia Approaches Her First Centenary," *Liberian Age*, May 15, 1947, 3–4; "How Old Art Thou?" *Liberian Age*, July 15, 1947, 3–4. See also Gershoni, *Black Colonialism*, 18.

121 For a detailed history and analysis of the founding of Liberia, see Clegg, *Price of Liberty*, 29–44.

122 See Clegg, *Price of Liberty*, 103–112; Gershoni, *Black Colonialism*, 21–23.

123 Gershoni, *Black Colonialism*, 26–27.

124 Gershoni, *Black Colonialism*, 26–27; "Liberia Approaches Her First Centenary," 4.

125 "Duke Ellington and His Orchestra," program, Carnegie Hall, December 26–27, 1947.

126 "We Welcome You—Meet Our President," *Liberian Age*, May 30, 1947, 1–2; "The Tubman Administration 1944–1947," *Liberian Age*, July 30, 1947, 3–4. See also "Plaque-Unveiling Ceremonies Commemorating the Centenary of the Republic of Liberia," *Liberian Age*, September 30, 1947, 1–2.

127 The main materials for my analysis of *Liberian Suite* are the score's 1947 manuscript and parts (*Liberian Suite*, Series 1A, Music Manuscripts, Boxes 199 and 200, Duke Ellington Collection). In addition, my analysis draws from the recording of the concerts at Carnegie Hall in December 1947 (Duke Ellington and His Orchestra, *Carnegie Hall Concerts, December 1947*).

128 Tucker, "Interpretations in Jazz," 256–257.

129 Tucker, "Interview in Los Angeles," 150.

130 See Clegg, *Price of Liberty*, 22, 48–51, 75; and Sundiata, *Brothers and Strangers*, 106–107, 177.

131 "Liberian Group Plans Honor for Duke Ellington," *Philadelphia Tribune*, December 23, 1947, 15; "Duke Ellington to Receive Liberian Award at Carnegie Hall Concert," *New York Amsterdam News*, December 27, 1947, 5; "Liberians Honor the Duke at Testimonial," *Atlanta Daily World*, January 9, 1948, 1.

132 See Sundiata, *Brothers and Strangers*, 164, 167, 188.

133 "Liberia Approaches Her First Centenary," *Liberian Age*, May 15, 1947, 3.

134 See Sundiata, *Brothers and Strangers*, 134–137, 252.

135 "Duke at Carnegie Hail on Night of 'Blizzard,'" *People's Voice*, January 3, 1943, 22; 'Duke' Plays Liberian Composition," *New York Amsterdam News*, January 10, 1948, 4. Writing for *Down Beat*, Michael Levin criticized the orchestra for its lack of fire and technical execution. Levin was one of Ellington's strongest defenders of his *Black, Brown and Beige*, but his support of *Liberian Suite* was lukewarm at best, even though he concluded that it was the standout piece of the concert. See Michael Levin, "Ellington Pleases Concert Crowd," *Down Beat*, January 14, 1948, 3.

136 "Duke at Carnegie Hail on Night of 'Blizzard,'" *People's Voice*, January 3, 1947, 22; "'Duke' Plays Liberian Composition," 4.

137 "'Duke' Plays Liberian Composition," 4.

138 See Anders, "Pathology of Freedom," 305–308; and R. Williams, *Marxism and Literature*, 121.

139 See "Ellington Concert Will Face Boycott," *Afro-American*, January 27, 1951, 8; "Duke Cancels Richmond Concert after Boycott Threat," *Philadelphia Tribune*, January 30, 1951, 1; "Boycott Splits Duke, NAACP," *Chicago Defender*, February 3, 1951, 1.

140 "Duke Involved in New Row," *Philadelphia Tribune*, November 6, 1951, 1.

141 "'We're Not Ready Yet,' Duke Says of Jim-Crow Fight," *Philadelphia Tribune*, November 20, 1951, 9; "Duke Calls Fight for Rights 'Silly,'" *Afro-American*, November 24, 1951, 7; "What Our Readers Say . . . ," *Afro-American*, December 15, 1951, 4.

142 "The Case of Duke Ellington," *Courier*, February 10, 1951, 20.

143 Cf., for example, Monson's explanation of such clashes to the rising moral standards of the civil rights movement (*Freedom Sounds*, 61).

144 Jacobs, "Avant-Garde Production in America," 132–133.

145 See Stauffacher, *Art in Cinema*; and Sexton, "Alchemical Transformations."

146 Jacobs, "Avant-Garde Production in America," 139. See also Guldemond, Bloemheuvel, and Keefer, "Oskar Fischinger," 10–11.

147 Smith to Hilla von Rebay, June 17, 1950, Box 11, Folder 4, Harry Smith Papers.

148 On multiplicities and arborescent schema, see Deleuze and Guattari, *Thousand Plateaus*, 11–17.

149 See Singh, "Anthology Film Archives," 14–15; "Harry Smith (1923–1991)," Harry Smith Archives, accessed March 10, 2015, http://www.harrysmitharchives.com/1 _bio/index.html.

150 Singh, "Anthology Film Archives," 14.

151 "The Art in Cinema Society of the San Francisco Museum of Art presents Five Friday Nights at Eight O'Clock," program, Box 11, Folder 5, Harry Smith Papers; "Art in Cinema," *San Francisco Chronicle*, October 23, 1947, 13; "Art Films at Museum," *San Francisco Chronicle*, February 10, 1949, 13. See also Jacobs, "Avant-Garde Production in America," 151. For explanations of his hand-painting techniques, see Sitney, "Film Culture," 52–54; and Sitney, *Visionary Film*, 276.

152 "Nat, Diz, Keep S.F. Fly," *Down Beat*, June 30, 1948, 16.

153 Sitney, "Film Culture," 56.

154 Ralph J. Gleason, "Small Crowds Grow as Diz Bops Frisco," *Down Beat*, August 25, 1948, 16.

155 For contemporaneous examples of articles that addressed or disseminated such associations, see "Dizzy's Music Leads to Blows in the Night!," *Melody Maker*, March 6, 1948, 3; Harry Henderson and Sam Shaw, "And Now We Go Bebop," *Collier's*, March 20, 1948, 16–17, 88; "Claims Beboppers Are Drug Addicts," *New York Amsterdam News*, May 8, 1948; "Dizzy Gillespie Defends His Be-Bop against Outside Kick," *Chicago Defender*, June 12, 1948, 9; and Richard Boyer, "Profiles: Bop," *New Yorker*, July 3, 1948, 28–37. See also Gennari, *Blowin' Hot and Cool*, 24, 54, 109, 120, 160–161.

156 See Gennari's analysis of Cold War intellectual thought and jazz criticism of the late 1940s through the 1960s (*Blowin' Hot and Cool*, 165–170).

157 Sitney, "Film Culture," 53. According to Smith's "Curriculum Vitae," available on his online archive, he edited his *Film No. 3* down from its original thirty minutes to match "Guarachi guaro" (Harry Smith Archive, accessed March 12, 2015, http://www.harrysmitharchives.com/).

158 Smith to Hilla von Rebay, June 17, 1950.

159 For example, see "Record Reviews," *Down Beat*, April 22, 1949, 14.

160 Gillespie with Fraser, *To Be, or Not . . . to Bop*, 322–323 (my emphasis).

161 "Diz to Put Bop Touch to More Standard Tunes," *Down Beat*, March 11, 1949, 3.

162 André Hodier, "Dizzy Gillespie à Paris," *Jazz Hot*, March 1948, 6–7. See also Garcia, "We Both Speak African."

163 See Gillespie with Fraser, *To Be, or Not . . . to Bop*, 290.

164 See Dizzy Gillespie and His Orchestra, *Dizzy Gillespie: The Complete RCA Victor Recordings. Metronome* and *Down Beat* published the first record reviews of "Guarachi guaro" in April 1949.

165 Smith to Hilla von Rebay, June 17, 1950.

166 A recording of this interview, conducted by P. Adams Sitney in New York City in 1965, is available on YouTube, "Interview with Harry Smith and P. Adams Sitney: Part 1," accessed March 17, 2015, https://www.youtube.com/watch?v =DEVauFDiy-o. For an edited transcription of this interview, see Sitney, "Film Culture," 55.

167 Smith, interviewed by P. Adams Sitney, New York City, 1965.

168 The San Francisco Museum of Art, Art in Cinema, Sixth Series, program, Box 11, Folder 5, Harry Smith Papers.

169 San Francisco Museum of Art, Art in Cinema, Sixth Series, program, Friday, May 12, 1950, Box 11, Folder 5, Harry Smith Papers. See also "Museum Presenting Art Film Program," *San Francisco Chronicle*, May 12, 1950, 13.

170 "Bop Band Accompanies Non-Objective Films," *Down Beat*, June 30, 1950, 3.

171 Gillespie with Fraser, *To Be, or Not . . . to Bop*, 138, 265.

172 Smith to Hilla von Rebay, June 17, 1950.

173 Smith claimed to have recorded similar jam sessions, which took place following the showing, but no such materials apparently have survived (see Smith to Hilla von Rebay, June 17, 1950).

174 See Ginsberg, "Introduction," 2.

175 See Gray, "John Coltrane," 47–48.

176 See Jacobson, *Whiteness of a Different Color*, 109–113.

177 See Butler, *Bodies That Matter*, 171, 275n4.

178 Deleuze and Guattari, *Anti-Oedipus*, 34.

Chapter 5. Desiring Africa

1 Carlos Dorante, "Pérez 'Prado' en La Picota: Nueve Intelectuales Opinan Sobre los Mambos del Cara de Foca," *El Nacional* (February 24, 1951): 1.

2 In his *Folklore y cultura* Liscano cites Oswald Spengler's *The Decline of the West* as his main source for defining folklore as an actively generating force of culture and civilization as the provenance of the folk "cultured" and not the urban intellectual class, among which he lists folklorists (12, 16). For his discussion of "civilization" and the tensions between the city and province, see Spengler, *The Decline of the West*, 24–27. Cuban music critic and novelist Alejo Carpentier helped establish a specifically Latin American rendering of magical realism, beginning

with his first novel *El reino de este mundo* (The kingdom of this world), which he completed in 1948. He referred to this Latin American version of magical realism as *lo real maravilloso* (Carpentier, *El reino de este mundo*, 9–11). The significance of real maravilloso to this chapter pertains specifically to Carpentier's *El reino de este mundo* and its critical analysis by others.

3 Liscano, *Folklore y cultura*, 14–23.

4 For Sartre's explanations of anguish, see his *Being and Nothingness*, 66–78 and *Existentialism Is a Humanism*, 25–27.

5 "Propositos," *Afroamérica* 1, nos. 1–2 (January and July 1945), 3.

6 It is important to stress that the emergence of Afroamerican studies or *estudios afroamericanos* named as such did not occur only in the United States but indeed throughout the Caribbean, Mexico, and South America in the 1940s. Melville J. Herskovits, himself, regarded Juan Liscano's research on the festivals of San Juan among Afro-Venezuelans in Barlovento as of "first rate importance for our work in Afroamerican cultures" (Herskovits to Concha Romero James, January 16, 1948, Box 39, Folder 6, Melville J. Herskovits [1895–1963] Papers).

7 Diop, "Niam n'goura," 8. See also Mouralis, "*Présence Africaine*," 5.

8 Diop, "Niam n'goura," 7.

9 S. Ramos, *Historia de la filosofía*, 161.

10 Carpentier, *El reino de este mundo*, 5–11. See also Delbaere-Garant, "Psychic Realism," 252.

11 Sartre, *Black Orpheus*, 9. I have substituted "the gaze" as it appears in this translated version with Sartre's original *les regards* since the gaze is associated more with Jaques Lacan's later work (see Sartre, "Orphée noir," ix).

12 Gide, "Avant-propos," 5.

13 See Deleuze and Guattari, *Anti-Oedipus*, 262–271.

14 See Deleuze and Guattari, *Anti-Oedipus*, 33–35, 183.

15 It is worth noting that the publication of Freud's *Civilization and Its Discontents* in Germany in 1930 coincided with Melville Herskovits's initiation of his fieldwork and correspondences with Erich von Hornbostel and Fernando Ortiz on the African origins of New World Negro culture. Also, Zoila Gálvez and Modupe Paris had added the Negro spiritual to their repertories, and the League of Nations charged Liberian government officials with the forcible export of labor of the nation's native individuals. In each of these co-occurrences the human inclination to cruel aggressiveness was of concern, as demonstrated in the horrors of World War I (as noted by Freud and anticipated by Oswald Spengler), in the study of race relations and the performance of the history of slavery in the United States, or under Western Europe's and racial progress's capitalist regime in West Africa (see Spengler, *Decline of the West*, xiv, xxi).

16 Freud, *Civilization and Its Discontents*, 58 (my emphasis).

17 Freud, *Civilization and Its Discontents*, 100.

18 Jacques Attali theorizes silence as a form of capitalism's violence emanating not in the literal silencing of music but rather in its commodification, consumption, and

thus repetition. As he notes, the "triumph of capitalism" is that it made "people accept identity in mass production as a collective refuge from powerlessness and isolation" (Attali, *Noise*, 121–124).

19 For an explanation of "movement" and perception as utilized here, see Deleuze and Guattari, *Thousand Plateaus*, 280–282. Their key explanation is: "It is in jumping from one plane to the other, or from the relative thresholds [of perception] to the absolute threshold [of imperceptions] that coexists with them, that the imperceptible becomes necessarily perceived" (282).

20 Aguilar and Craddock interview. Pedro Aguilar, in spite of the implications of his professional name, "Cuban Pete," was born in Bayamón, Puerto Rico.

21 Aguilar, personal communication to author, December 8, 2002.

22 See Deleuze and Guattari, *Thousand Plateaus*, 474–500.

23 The charanga is an ensemble format whose instrumentation includes flute, violins, piano, bass, timbales, congas, guiro, and vocals. The repertories most associated with charanga ensembles are danzón and chachachá.

24 Cuéllar Vizcaíno, "La revolución del mambo," 20.

25 Urfé, "La verdad sobre el 'mambo,'" 2.

26 For analytical examples of the mambo rhythm, see Garcia, *Arsenio Rodríguez*, 41–55. See also López Cano, "Apuntes para una prehistoria del mambo."

27 Deleuze and Guattari, *Thousand Plateaus*, 294–295.

28 Cuéllar Vizcaíno, "La revolución del mambo," 98.

29 Cuéllar Vizcaíno, "La revolución del mambo," 99.

30 For an analysis of contratiempo in the music of Arsenio Rodríguez, see Garcia, *Arsenio Rodríguez*, 47–48.

31 Urfé, "La verdad sobre el 'mambo,'" 7; Cuéllar Vizcaíno, "La revolución del mambo," 21, 97, 99.

32 Deleuze and Guattari, *Thousand Plateaus*, 296; see also 300–302.

33 Urfé, "La verdad sobre el 'mambo,'" 7.

34 Juan S. Ramos, "La virtud del mambo," *Diario de la marina*, December 27, 1950, 4 (my emphasis).

35 Dorante, "Pérez 'Prado' en La Picota," 1.

36 Dorante, "Pérez 'Prado' en La Picota," 1.

37 See Carpentier, *El reino de este mundo*, 5–7.

38 Cané interview.

39 "The Glass of Fashion," *Sun*, February 5, 1950, A5.

40 "Pan American Group Tea Program to Have Mexico as Its Theme," *Chicago Daily Tribune*, February 17, 1950, A9; "Weekly Radio Program," *Jewish Advocate*, February 23, 1950, 11.

41 *New York Times*, October 10, 1948, X13.

42 *Chicago Daily Tribune*, May 25, 1949, B10; *Los Angeles Times* (June 19, 1949), A6.

43 Aguilar and Craddock interview.

44 *New York Times*, January 3, 1954, X9.

45 Mrs. Arthur Murray, "What the Heck Is the Mambo?" *Down Beat*, December 1, 1954, 2.

46 See Don Byrnes and Alice Swanson, "Mambo: A Vest Pocket Analysis," *Dance Magazine* 25, no. 10 (October 1951): 29; "Uncle Sambo, Mad for Mambo," *Life* 37, no. 25 (December 20, 1954): 16.

47 "This Is Dancing on Main Street," *Dance Magazine* 23, no. 4 (April 1949): 50.

48 Michael Levin, "Notes between Notes," *Down Beat*, February 14, 1948, 5.

49 "Granz Overseer of Mercury Bop," *Down Beat*, February 25, 1949, 1.

50 "Record Reviews," *Down Beat*, May 20, 1949, 14.

51 "Good-by, Bebop." *Newsweek*, September 4, 1950, 76; Nat Hentoff, "Mambo Rage Latest in Latin Dance Line," *Down Beat*, December 1, 1954, 2.

52 "Tele-Radiolandia," *Bohemia*, February 18, 1951, 42.

53 Ortiz, *Los bailes*, 99.

54 "Pow! Everything Happens in Circles," *Down Beat*, January 27, 1950, 5.

55 See Attali, *Noise*, 122.

56 "Television Highlights," *Washington Post and Times Herald*, January 12, 1956, 50.

57 *Los Angeles Times*, September 27, 1953, D12; Barbara B. Jamison, "Oddities in Person: 'Confidential File' Has Unusual Guest Stars," *New York Times*, May 29, 1955, 59.

58 "Look and Listen with Donald Kirkley," *Sun*, November 1, 1955, 10.

59 The Classic TV Archive, "Confidential File," accessed May 1, 2015, http://ctva.biz /US/Reporter/ConfidentialFile.htm.

60 Jess Stearn, "Touch of Jungle Madness," *New York Daily News*, May 6, 1951, 7; Foucault, *History of Madness*, 434–435.

61 Foucault, *History of Madness*, 3–8.

62 Foucault, *History of Madness*, 94–96.

63 For Deleuze and Guattari's critique of capitalism's creation and use of Oedipus as its internalized limit, see *Anti-Oedipus*, 50, 262–271. See Jacobson, *Whiteness of a Different Color*, 246–273.

64 "Sambo" is an Anglicization of the Latin American *zambo*, a term that originated in the colonial period to denote the Afro-Indian racially mixed caste (see Andrews, *Afro-Latin America*, 48, 203–205). All issues of *Life* are available digitally at http://books.google.com/books?id=N0EEAAAAMBAJ&source=gbs _navlinks_s#all_issues_anchor.

65 "Uncle Sambo, Mad for Mambo," *Life* 37, no. 25 (December 20, 1954): 14.

66 See E. P. Thompson, "Time, Work-Discipline," 91, 93–94.

67 Ernest Borneman, "Big Mambo Business," *Melody Maker*, September 11, 1954, 2.

68 J. S. Ramos, "La virtud del mambo," 4.

69 "Band Review," *Variety*, August 29, 1951, n.p.

70 "Mambo Island," *Sun*, August 12, 1951, F14.

71 "Cubanos son triunfos," *Bohemia*, February 13, 1949, 40.

72 "Rating the Records," *Atlanta Daily World*, May 23, 1950, 3; "Record Reviews," *Down Beat*, June 2, 1950, 14; "Platter Chatter," *Chicago Daily Tribune*, June 5, 1950, A3; "Feature Prado in New Album," *New York Amsterdam News*, August 26, 1950, 20.

73 "Pow! Everything Happens in Circles," *Down Beat*, January 27, 1950, 5; "Feature Prado in New Album," *New York Amsterdam News*, August 26, 1950, 20; "El Mambo," *Newsweek*, September 4, 1950, 76.

74 "Top Tunes," *Down Beat*, November 3, 1950, 5.

75 For an analysis of this film, see Garcia, "Going Primitive," 514–518.

76 García Márquez, "El mambo," 124–126.

77 McBride, "Existentialism," 51. During his time as a columnist, García Márquez wrote about and cited the work of Sartre and Camus (see García Márquez, *Textos costeños*, 594–595, 636–638).

78 See "Defensa de la guaracha" and "Mambo de Nueva York" reprinted in García Márquez, *Textos costeños*, 339–340 and 510–512.

79 "Dámaso Pérez Prado, creador del 'mambo,' " *La Prensa*, March 6, 1951.

80 Fausto, "La gran vía blanca," *La Prensa*, March 17, 1951; Fausto, "La gran vía blanca," *La Prensa*, March 24, 1951, n.p.

81 "Protestan en Perú por bailes de Amalia Aguilar," *La Prensa*, March 27, 1951, n.p.; "The Mambo," *Time* 57, no. 15 (April 9, 1951): 38, 41.

82 "Pérez Prado no llegó," *La Prensa*, March 25, 1951, n.p.

83 *Excelsior*, December 4, 1950, 25; *El Universal*, December 5, 1950, 23.

84 "Protestan en Perú por bailes de Amalia Aguilar," *La Prensa*, March 27, 1951.

85 See Holland, *Modern Catholic Social Teaching*, 114, 171, 233–235.

86 See Klaiber, *The Catholic Church in Peru, 1821–1985*, 208–209, 235–206.

87 Pius XII, *Evangelii praecones*, pars. 17–18.

88 Holland, *Modern Catholic Social Teaching*, 282.

89 Gerassi, *Jean-Paul Sartre*, 30.

90 "El mambo," *Newsweek*, September 4, 1950, 76.

91 García Márquez, *Textos costeños*, 542–543; *El nacional*, February 27, 1951, n.p.

92 García Márquez, *Textos costeños*, 542–543.

93 "Mambo King," *Ebony*, September 1951, 48.

94 Sartre, "Commentary on *The Stranger*," 78.

95 "The Mambo," 41.

96 "Mambo King," *Ebony*, September 1951, 45–48.

97 "Diggin' the Discs with Mix," *Down Beat*, December 15, 1950, 14.

98 This explanation of existential naturalism is based on Friedrich Nietzsche's philosophy. See Hatab, "Nietzsche," 139, 152.

99 Attali, *Noise*, 121.

100 "Mambo King," 45.

101 Sartre, "Commentary on *The Stranger*," 78.

102 Sartre, *Black Orpheus*, 50–51.

103 Fanon, *Black Skin, White Masks*, 133–135.

104 Mikics, "Derek Walcott and Alejo Carpentier," 385.

105 Federico Ortiz, Jr., "El mambo y su influencia malsana," *La Opinion*, July 9, 1951, 7.

106 See Zea, *El positivismo en México*, 28.

107 Zea, *El positivismo en México*, 29.

108 Vasconcelos, *La raza cósmica*, 33, 35.

109 Zea, *El positivismo en México*, 118–120.

110 For an analysis of *Víctimas del pecado*, see Garcia, "Afro-Cuban Soundscape."

111 See Foucault, *History of Madness*, 277–290.

112 Pérez Prado's orchestra with featured vocalist Beny Moré recorded this song in Mexico City in October 1949.

113 "Diggin' the Discs with Mix," *Down Beat*, December 15, 1950, 14.

114 *Excelsior*, December 1, 1950, 46; *Excelsior*, December 8, 1950, 39; *Excelsior*, December 11, 1950, 33.

115 "'El Rey del Mambo' en Nueva York," *El diario de Nueva York*, April 5, 1951; American Federation of Musicians, *Minutes of the Executive Board*, April 12, 1951.

116 *El diario de Nueva York*, April 11, 1951, *El diario de Nueva York*, April 14, 1951, *El diario de Nueva York*, April 20, 1951.

117 See Díaz-Ayala and Florida International University, *Encyclopedic Discography of Cuban Music*.

118 William Leonard, "Tower Ticker," *Chicago Daily Tribune*, May 24, 1951, B9.

119 "Prado, Mambo Creator, in U.S. Maestro Bow," *Variety*, August 15, 1951, 43; "Perez Prado Sets West Coast Dates," *Down Beat*, November 16, 1951, 2; "En entrevista relampago con el Rey del Mambo, Maestro Dámaso Pérez Prado," *La Opinion*, November 17, 1951, n.p. Some American dancers, too, believed Pérez Prado was Mexican, while some writers contested his claim that he was the creator of the mambo (see "Letters," *New York Times*, October 7, 1951, 181).

120 "L.A. Having Band Boom; Brown, Prado in Records," *Variety*, August 22, 1951, 51. See also "Prado One-Niter Sets L.A. on Ear," *Down Beat*, September 21, 1951, 1; Ralph J. Gleason, "Swingin' the Golden Gate: Prado's West Coast Tour Proving a Huge Success," *Down Beat*, October 5, 1951, 15.

121 See "Record Reviews," *Down Beat*, August 24, 1951, 14; "Band Review," *Variety*, August 29, 1951, n.p.

122 "Mambo King," *Ebony*, September 1951, 47.

123 See Monson, *Freedom Sounds*, 31–49. As Monson mentions, New York's Local 802 and Detroit's Local 5 were the only integrated locals in the AFM. Official efforts to integrate Los Angeles's Local 47 began in November 1951, the same month of Pérez Prado's tour of California. Local 47 would not officially become integrated until 1953.

124 See "Band in Bus Crash; One Dead, 12 Injured," *New York Times*, October 28, 1951, 74; "Pérez Prado está ya muy aliviado," *La Opinion*, October 30, 1951, "Pérez Prado viene al Paramount en fecha próxima," *La Opinion*, November 8, 1951; "Prado, Troupe Present Show Despite Injuries," *Los Angeles Times*, November 16, 1951, A7; "Prado, Bandsmen Injured in Bus Crash," *Down Beat*, November 30, 1951, 1; "Four Still Hospitalized after Prado Accident," *Down Beat*, December 14, 1951, 5.

125 "Bus Crashes Bring Cries for AFM to Investigate," *Down Beat*, December 28, 1951, 1.

126 Jacobson, *Whiteness of a Different Color*, 258.

127 Garcia, "Going Primitive," 517. See also Hernández Cuevas, *African Mexicans*.

128 Vasconcelos, *La raza cósmica*, 39–40.

129 These ads were published between November 10 and 21, 1951.

130 See Paz, *El laberinto de la soledad*, 12–16.

131 See Foucault, *History of Madness*, 286–289.

132 El Duende Filmo, "Nuestro Cinema," *El Universal*, November 22, 1951, 1.

133 See Paz, *El laberinto de la soledad*, 135–140.

134 Paz, *El laberinto de la soledad*, 137.

135 Meyer, *Testimonios*, 17.

136 Deleuze and Guattari, *Thousand Plateaus*, 175–178.

137 Deleuze and Guattari, *Thousand Plateaus*, 171 (emphasis in original).

138 Benítez-Rojo, *Repeating Island*, 248.

139 Fanon, *Black Skin, White Masks*, 51.

140 Deleuze and Guattari, *Thousand Plateaus*, 175 (my emphasis); see also 184–187, 190.

141 Benítez-Rojo, *Repeating Island*, 233.

Conclusion

1 "A Syllabus of Fifteen Lectures on the History of Jazz," Box 17, Folder 28, Marshal Winslow Stearns Collection.

2 See Deleuze and Guattari, *Thousand Plateaus*, 21.

Archival Collections

African Academy of Arts and Research. African Dance Festival. Performing Arts Research Collections, Dance. Performing Arts Library, New York Public Library.

African Academy of Arts and Research Collection. Manuscripts, Archives and Rare Books Division. Schomburg Center for Research in Black Culture, New York Public Library.

American Federation of Musicians. Local 802. *Minutes of the Executive Board, 1922–1985*. Reel nos. 5257–5335. Robert F. Wagner Labor Archives of the Tamiment Institute Library, New York University.

Asadata Dafora Papers. 1933–1963. Manuscripts, Archives and Rare Books Division. Schomburg Center for Research in Black Culture, New York Public Library.

Century of Progress. Series I. University Library, University of Illinois at Chicago.

David Benjamin Mudge Paris. Hampton University Archives, Hampton University.

Díaz-Ayala Cuban and Latin American Popular Music Collection. Green Library, Florida International University.

Duke Ellington Collection. 1927–1988. #301. Archives Center. National Museum of American History, Smithsonian Institute.

Franklyn Bliss Snyder (1884–1958) Papers. Northwestern University Archives.

Gary Kenton Collection. 1971–1989. Southern Folklife Collection, University of North Carolina at Chapel Hill.

George Herzog Correspondence. Archives of Traditional Music, Indiana University.

Harold Courlander. Cuba, 1940. Archives of Traditional Music, Indiana University.

Harry Smith Papers. 1888–2010. Bulk 1987–1990, 2013.M.4. Getty Research Institute, Special Collections, Los Angeles, CA.

Katherine Dunham Papers. Special Collections Research Center. Morris Library, Southern Illinois University Carbondale.

Katherine Dunham Photographs. Special Collections Research Center. Morris Library, Southern Illinois University Carbondale.

Marshal Winslow Stearns Collection. 1935–1966. Institute of Jazz Studies, Rutgers University Libraries.

Melville J. Herskovits (1895–1963) Papers. 1906–1963. Africana Manuscripts 6. Northwestern University Archives.

Melville J. and Frances S. Herskovits Photograph Collection. Photographs and Prints
Division. Schomburg Center for Research in Black Culture, New York Public
Library.
Melville J. Herskovits and Frances S. Herskovits Papers. 1902–1972. Sc MC 261. Schom-
burg Center for Research in Black Culture, New York Public Library.
Moses and Frances Asch Collection. 1926–1987. Center for Folklife and Cultural Heri-
tage. Ralph Rinzler Folklife Archives and Collections, Smithsonian Institution.
Richard Waterman. Cuba, 1948. Archives of Traditional Music, Indiana University.
William R. Bascom Papers, BANC MSS 82/163 c. Bancroft Library, University of
California, Berkeley.

Audio and Video Sources

Confidential File. "Mambo." 1 videocassette. Confidential Telepictures, 1955.
Courlander, Harold. *Cult Music of Cuba* (EFL P410). New York, NY: Folkways Rec-
ords and Service Corp., 1949.
———. *Music of the Cults of Cuba.* DICS Ethnic Album 131. New York, NY: DISC
Company of America, 1947.
Dizzy Gillespie and His Orchestra. *Dizzy Gillespie: The Complete RCA Victor Record-
ings.* 2 compact discs with program notes by Ira Gitler. New York: BMG Music, 1995.
Duke Ellington and His Orchestra. *Duke Ellington: Complete Prestige Carnegie Hall,
1943–1944 Concerts.* 3 compact discs. Andorra: Definitive Records, 2001.
———. *The Duke Ellington Carnegie Hall Concerts, December 1947.* 1 compact disc
with program notes by J. R. Taylor. Berkeley, CA: Prestige Records, 1977.
*From Spirituals to Swing: The Legendary 1938 and 1939 Carnegie Hall Concerts Produced
by John Hammond.* 3 compact discs; booklets with program notes by John Ham-
mond, Charles Edward Smith, Steve Buckingham, and Harry "Sweets" Edison, and a
facsimile of the original 1938 program. Santa Monica, CA: Vanguard Records, 1999.
Gilberto Valdés y Su Orquesta. *Cuban Big Bands, 1940–1942.* 1 compact disc with
program notes by Cristóbal Díaz Ayala. East Sussex, UK: Harlequin, 1995.
Herskovits, Melville J. *Afro-Bahian Religious Songs from Brazil.* Washington, DC,
Library of Congress Music Division, 1947.
Julio Cueva y su Orquesta. *Desintegrando.* 1 compact disc with program notes by Jordi
Pujol. Switzerland: Tumbao Cuban Classics, 1996.
———. *La Butuba Cubana.* 1 compact disc with program notes by Jordi Pujol. Switzer-
land: Tumbao Cuban Classics, 1994.
Katherine Dunham and Ensemble. *Afro-Caribbean Songs and Rhythms.* 1 ten-inch LP
disc. New York: Decca Records, 1950.
Orquesta Casino de la Playa. "Consuélate." 1 ten-inch 78-RPM disc. Camden, NJ: RCA
Victor, 1945.
———. *Fufuñando.* 1 compact disc with program notes by Jordi Pujol. Switzerland:
Tumbao Cuban Classics, 1995.
———. *Miguelito Valdés with the Orquesta Casino de la Playa.* 1 compact disc with
program notes by Gilbert Mamery. East Sussex, UK: Harlequin, 1994.

Orquesta Maravilla de Arcaño. "Rarezas." 1 ten-inch 78-RPM disc. Camden, NJ: RCA Victor, 1940.

Perez Prado and His Orchestra. *Go Go Mambo!* 1 compact disc with program notes. Switzerland: Tumbao Cuban Classics, 1992.

———. *"Kuba-Mambo."* 1 compact disc with program notes. Switzerland: Tumbao Cuban Classics, 1991.

Pozo, Chano. *El tambor de Cuba.* 3 compact discs with program notes by Jordi Pujol and David Garcia. Barcelona, Spain: Tumbao Cuban Classics, 2001.

Valdés, Miguelito. *Bim Bam Boom: An Album of Cuban Rhythms.* 1 ten-inch LP DISC. New York: Decca Records, 1949.

Interviews

Aguilar, Pedro, and Barbara Craddock. Interview by author. June 2, 2006. Tape recording. Miami, FL.

Cané, Humberto. Interview by author. August 28, 1996. Tape recording. Monterey Hills, CA.

Secondary Literature

Abraham, Otto, and E. M. von Hornbostel. "On the Significance of the Phonograph for Comparative Musicology" in *Opera Omnia*, edited by Klaus P. Wachsmann, Dieter Christensen, and Hans-Peter Reinecke, in collaboration with Richard G. Campbell, Nerthus Christensen, and Hans-Jürgen Jordan; English translation by Ray Giles, 185–202. The Hague, Neth.: Martinus Nijhoff, 1975.

Agawu, Kofi. *Representing African Music: Postcolonial Notes, Queries, Positions.* New York: Routledge, 2003.

Aiello, Thomas. Introduction to *Dan Burley's Jive*, edited by Thomas Aiello, ix–xxxi. DeKalb: Northern Illinois University Press, 2009.

Amira, John, and Steven Cornelius. *The Music of Santería: Traditional Rhythms of the Batá Drums.* Reno, NV: White Cliffs Media, 1999.

Anders, Günther. "The Pathology of Freedom: An Essay on Non-Identification." *Deleuze Studies* 3, no. 2 (2009): 278–310.

Andreu, Enrique. "Los 'Spirituals negro songs' y su acción étnico-social." *Estudios Afrocubanos* 1, no. 1 (1937): 76–91.

Andrews, George Reid. *Afro-Latin America, 1800–2000.* Oxford: Oxford University Press, 2004.

"Announcements for 1940–1941." *Lincoln University Bulletin* 45, no. 1 (January 1940): 1–96.

Arredondo, Alberto. "El arte negro a contrapelo." *Adelante* 2, no. 26 (July 1937): 5–6, 20.

———. *El negro en Cuba.* Havana, Cuba: Editorial "Alfa," 1939.

———. "Eso que llaman afrocubanismo musical." *Adelante* 4, no. 26 (April 1938): 5–6.

Aschenbrenner, Joyce. *Katherine Dunham: Dancing a Life.* Urbana: University of Illinois Press, 2002.

Ash, Mitchell G. *Gestalt Psychology in German Culture, 1890–1967*. Cambridge: Cambridge University Press, 1995.

Attali, Jacques. *Noise: The Political Economy of Music*. Translated by Brian Massumi. With a foreword by Frederic Jameson, and an afterword by Susan McClary. Minneapolis: University of Minnesota Press, 1985.

Averill, Gage. *A Day for the Hunter, a Day for the Prey: Popular Music and Power in Haiti*. Chicago: University of Chicago Press, 1997.

Awokoya, Janet T. "Reconciling Multiple Black Identities: The Case of 1.5 and 2.0 Nigerian Immigrants." In *Africans in Global Migration: Searching for Promised Lands*, edited by John A. Arthur, Joseph Takougang, and Thomas Owusu, 97–116. Lanham, MD: Lexington Books, 2012.

Azikiwe, Ben N. "In Defense of Liberia." *Journal of Negro History* 17, no. 1 (January 1932): 30–50.

———. Review of *Slaves Today, A Story of Liberia*, by George Schuyler. *Journal of Negro History* 17, no. 3 (July 1932): 382–383.

Bakhtin, M. M. *The Dialogic Imagination: Four Essays by M. M. Bakhtin*. Edited by Michael Holquist. Translated by Caryl Emerson and Michael Holquist. Austin: University of Texas Press, 1981.

Baugh, Bruce. "Body." In *The Deleuze Dictionary: Revised Edition*, edited by Adrian Parr, 35–37. Edinburgh, Scot.: Edinburgh University Press, 2010.

Becker, Judith. *Deep Listeners: Music, Emotion, and Trancing*. Bloomington: Indiana University Press, 2004.

Beckwith, John. "Kolinski: An Appreciation and List of Works." In *Cross-Cultural Perspectives on Music*, edited by Robert Falck and Timothy Rice, xvii–xxiv. Toronto, Ont.: University of Toronto Press, 1982.

Benítez-Rojo, Antonio. *The Repeating Island: The Caribbean and the Postmodern Perspective*. Translated by James Maraniss. Durham, NC: Duke University Press, 1996.

Bethune, Mary McLeod. "Hands across the Waters." In *Africa, Today and Tomorrow, April 1945*, edited by H. A. B. Jones-Quartey, 18–19. New York: African Academy of Arts and Research, 1976.

Bijsterveld, Karin, and Trevor Pinch. "New Keys to the World of Sound." In *The Oxford Handbook of Sound Studies*, edited by Trevor Pinch and Karin Bijsterveld, 1–59. Oxford: Oxford Handbooks Online, 2011.

Black, Allida M. Introduction to *Courage in a Dangerous World: The Political Writings of Eleanor Roosevelt*, edited by Allida M. Black, 1–16. New York: Columbia University Press, 1999.

Blesh, Rudi. *Shining Trumpets: A History of Jazz*. New York: Alfred A. Knopf, 1946.

Bourdieu, Pierre. *The Logic of Practice*. Translated by Richard Nice. Stanford, CA: Stanford University Press, 1990.

Bowler, Peter J. *The Invention of Progress: The Victorians and the Past*. Oxford: Basil Blackwell, 1989.

Brady, Erika. *A Spiral Way: How the Phonograph Changed Ethnography*. Jackson: University Press of Mississippi, 1999.

Brock, Lisa. "Introduction: Between Race and Empire." In *Between Race and Empire: African-Americans and Cubans before the Cuban Revolution*, edited by Lisa Brock and Digna Castañeda Fuertes, 1–32. Philadelphia, PA: Temple University Press, 1998.

Brock, Lisa, and Digna Castañeda Fuertes, eds. *Between Race and Empire: African-Americans and Cubans before the Cuban Revolution*. Philadelphia, PA: Temple University Press, 1998.

Brown, Carol. "Making Space, Speaking Spaces." In *The Routledge Dance Studies Reader*, edited by Alexandra Carter and Janet O'Shea, 58–72. 2nd ed. London: Routledge, 2010.

Burford, Mark. "Mahalia Jackson Meets the Wise Men: Defining Jazz at the Music Inn." *Musical Quarterly* 97, no. 3 (fall 2014): 429–486.

Burley, Dan. *Dan Burley's Jive*. Edited by Thomas Aiello. DeKalb: Northern Illinois University Press, 2009.

Butler, Judith. *Bodies That Matter: On the Discursive Limits of "Sex."* New York: Routledge, 1993.

Cabrera, Lydia. *El monte*. Miami: Ediciones Universal, 1992.

Camara, Babacar. "The Falsity of Hegel's Theses on Africa." *Journal of Black Studies* 36, no. 1 (September 2005): 82–96.

Carmichael, Stokely. "From Black Power Back to Pan-Africanism." In *Stokely Speaks: Black Power Back to Pan-Africanism*, edited by Ethel N. Minor, 221–227. New York: Random House, 1971.

———. "Power and Racism." *New York Review of Books*, September 1966. Reprinted in *Stokely Speaks: Black Power Back to Pan-Africanism*, edited by Ethel N. Minor, 17–30. New York: Random House, 1971.

Carpentier, Alejo. *El reino de este mundo*. Caracas, Venez.: Organización Continental de los Festivales del Libro, 1958.

Christensen, Dieter. "Erich M. von Hornbostel, Carl Stumpf, and the Institutionalization of Comparative Musicology." In *Comparative Musicology and Anthropology of Music: Essays on the History of Ethnomusicology*, edited by Bruno Nettl and Philip V. Bohlman, 201–209. Chicago: University of Chicago Press, 1991.

Clark, VèVè A. "Performing the Memory of Difference in Afro-Caribbean Dance: Katherine Dunham's Choreography, 1938–1987." In *Kaiso! Writings by and about Katherine Dunham*, edited by VèVè A. Clark and Sara E. Johnson, 320–340. Madison: University of Wisconsin Press, 2005.

Clark, VèVè A., and Sara E. Johnson, eds. *Kaiso! Writings by and about Katherine Dunham*. Madison: University of Wisconsin Press, 2005.

Clegg, Claude A., III. *The Price of Liberty: African Americans and the Making of Liberia*. Chapel Hill: University of North Carolina Press, 2004.

Cole, Sally. "Ruth Landes and the Early Ethnography of Race and Gender." In *Women Writing Culture*, edited by Ruth Behar and Deborah A. Gordon, 166–185. Berkeley: University of California Press, 1995.

Collins, Patricia Hill. *Black Feminist Thought: Knowledge, Consciousness, and the Politics of Empowerment*. Perspectives on Gender. Vol. 2. New York: Routledge, 1991.

Colman, Felicity J. "Rhizome." In *The Deleuze Dictionary: Revised Edition*, edited by Adrian Parr, 232–235. Edinburgh, Scot.: Edinburgh University Press, 2010.

Comte, Auguste. "A General View of Positivism, Chapters I and IV (abridged)." In *The European Philosophers: From Descartes to Nietzsche*, edited and with an introduction by Monroe C. Beardsley, 732–764. New York: Modern Library, 2002.

Corbitt, Duvon C. "Immigration in Cuba." *Hispanic American Historical Review* 22, no. 2 (May 1942): 280–308.

Courlander, Harold. "Abakwa Meeting in Guanabacoa." *Journal of Negro History* 29, no. 4 (October 1944): 461–470.

———. "From the Field: Recording in Cuba in 1941." *Resound: A Quarterly of the Archives of Traditional Music* 3, no. 4 (October 1984): 1–5.

———. *Haiti Singing*. Chapel Hill: University of North Carolina Press, 1939.

———. "Musical Instruments of Cuba." *Musical Quarterly* 28, no. 2 (April 1942): 227–240.

———. *Music of the Cults of Cuba*. Liner notes. New York: DICS Company of America, 1947.

Cox, Aimee Meredith. "In the Dunham Way: Sewing (Sowing) the Seams of Dance, Anthropology, and Youth Arts Activism." In *Katherine Dunham: Recovering an Anthropological Legacy, Choreographing Ethnographic Futures*, edited by Elizabeth Chin, 127–144. Santa Fe, NM: School for Advanced Research Press, 2013.

Cuéllar Vizcaíno, Manuel. "La revolución del mambo." *Bohemia* 40, no. 22 (May 30, 1948): 20–21, 97–99.

Cull, Laura. Introduction to *Deleuze and Performance*, edited by Laura Cull, 1–21. Edinburgh, Scot.: Edinburgh University Press, 2009.

Cyrille, Dominique. "Sa Ki Ta Nou (This Belongs to Us): Creole Dances of the French Caribbean." In *Caribbean Dance from Abakuá to Zouk: How Movement Shapes Identity*, edited by Susanna Sloat, 221–246. Gainesville: University Press of Florida, 2002.

Darnell, Regna. *Invisible Genealogies: A History of Americanist Anthropology*. Lincoln: University of Nebraska Press, 2001.

Davis, Darién. "Nationalism and Civil Rights in Cuba: A Comparative Perspective, 1930–1960." *Journal of Negro History* 83, no. 1 (winter 1998): 35–51.

de Certeau, Michel. *The Practice of Everyday Life*. Translated by Steven Rendall. Berkeley: University of California Press, 1984.

de la Fuente, Alejandro. "Two Dangers, One Solution: Immigration, Race, and Labor in Cuba, 1900–1930." *International Labor and Working-Class History* 51 (spring 1997): 30–49.

Delbaere-Garant, Jeanne. "Psychic Realism, Mythic Realism, Grotesque Realism: Variations on Magic Realism in Contemporary Literature in English." In *Magical Realism: Theory, History, Community*, edited and with an introduction by Lois Parkinson Zamora and Wendy B. Faris, 249–264. Durham, NC: Duke University Press, 1995.

Deleuze, Gilles. *Cinema 2: The Time-Image*. Translated by Hugh Tomlinson and Robert Galeta. London: Continuum, 2005.

———. *Difference and Repetition.* Translated by Paul Patton. New York: Columbia University Press, 1994.

Deleuze, Gilles, and Félix Guattari. *Anti-Oedipus: Capitalism and Schizophrenia.* Translated by Robert Hurley, Mark Seem, and Helen R. Lane. With a preface by Michel Foucault, and an introduction by Mark Seem. New York: Penguin Books, 2009.

———. *A Thousand Plateaus: Capitalism and Schizophrenia.* Translated and with a foreword by Brain Massumi. Minneapolis: University of Minnesota Press, 1987.

Demaison, M. André. "Nunca me conmovido tanto África como escuchando a Gilberto Valdés." *Estudios Afrocubanos* 1, no. 1 (1938): 151–156.

Denby, Edwin. "Asadata Dafora." *New York Herald Tribune*, December 19, 1943. Reprinted in *Dance Writings*, edited by Robert Cornfield and William MacKay, 183–186. New York: Alfred A. Knopf, 1986.

———. "Dance Criticism." *Kenyon Review* 10, no. 1 (winter 1948): 82–88.

———. *Dance Writings*, edited by Robert Cornfield and William MacKay, 183–186. New York: Alfred A. Knopf, 1986.

———. "Katherine Dunham." *New York Herald Tribune*, September 26, 1943. Reprinted in *Dance Writings*, edited by Robert Cornfield and William MacKay, 142–143. New York: Alfred A. Knopf, 1986.

Departamento de Turismo del Municipio de La Habana. "El concierto afrocubano de Gilberto S. Valdés." *Estudios Afrocubanos* 1, no. 1 (1937): 139–145.

Derrida, Jacques. *Of Grammatology.* Translated by Gayatri Chakravatory Spivak. Baltimore, MD: Johns Hopkins University Press, 1997.

Diawara, Manthia. *In Search of Africa.* Cambridge, MA: Harvard University Press, 1998.

Díaz-Ayala, Cristóbal, and Florida International University. *Encyclopedic Discography of Cuban Music.* Last modified January 9, 2013. http://latinpop.fiu.edu/discography.html.

Diop, Alioune. "Niam n'goura ou les raisons d'être de *Présence Africaine*." *Présence Africaine* 1, no. 1 (1947): 7–14.

Du Bois, W. E. B. "Africa and the Slave Trade," excerpts from *The Negro*, 1915. Reprinted, with an introduction by Eric J. Sundquist, in *The Oxford W. E. B. Du Bois Reader*, edited by Eric J. Sundquist, 628–637. New York: Oxford University Press, 1996.

———. "Little Portraits of Africa," 1924. Reprinted, with an introduction by Eric J. Sundquist, in *The Oxford W. E. B. Du Bois Reader*, edited by Eric J. Sundquist, 647–653. New York: Oxford University Press, 1996.

———. *The Souls of Black Folk*, 1903. Reprinted, with an introduction by Eric J. Sundquist, in *The Oxford W. E. B. Du Bois Reader*, edited by Eric J. Sundquist, 97–240. New York: Oxford University Press, 1996.

———. "The Star of Ethiopia," 1913. Reprinted, with an introduction by Eric J. Sundquist, in *The Oxford W. E. B. Du Bois Reader*, edited by Eric J. Sundquist, 305–310. New York: Oxford University Press, 1996.

———. "What Is Civilization?" 1925. Reprinted, with an introduction by Eric J. Sundquist, in *The Oxford W. E. B. Du Bois Reader*, edited by Eric J. Sundquist, 645–647. New York: Oxford University Press, 1996.

Dunham, Katherine. *Dance of Haiti*. Los Angeles, CA: Center for Afro-American Studies, 1983.

———. "The Dunham Schools." 1964 (unpublished). Reprinted in *Kaiso! Writings by and about Katherine Dunham*, edited by VèVè A. Clark and Sara E. Johnson, 479–480. Madison: University of Wisconsin Press, 2005.

———. "Ethnic Dancing." *Dance* (September 1946): 22–23, 34–35.

———. "Goombay." *Mademoiselle*, November 1945. Reprinted in *Kaiso! Writings by and about Katherine Dunham*, edited by VèVè A. Clark and Sara E. Johnson, 267–271. Madison: University of Wisconsin Press, 2005.

———. *Island Possessed*. 1969. Chicago: University of Chicago Press, 1994.

———. *Journey to Accompong*. New York: Henry Holt and Company, 1946.

———. "Katherine Dunham School of Arts and Research." 1946–1947. Brochure. Reprinted in *Kaiso! Writings by and about Katherine Dunham*, edited by VèVè A. Clark and Sara E. Johnson, 472–478. Madison: University of Wisconsin Press, 2005.

———. "A Lecture-Demonstration of the Anthropological Approach to the Dance and the Practical Application of This Approach to the Theater." Delivered at the University of California at Los Angeles, CA, October 1942. Reprinted as "The Anthropological Approach to the Dance" in *Kaiso! Writings by and about Katherine Dunham*, edited by VèVè A. Clark and Sara E. Johnson, 508–513. Madison: University of Wisconsin Press, 2005.

———. "Survival: Chicago after the Caribbean: Excerpt from 'Minefields.'" In *Kaiso! Writings by and about Katherine Dunham*, edited by VèVè A. Clark and Sara E. Johnson, 85–124. Madison: University of Wisconsin Press, 2005.

———. "Thesis Turned Broadway." *California Arts and Architecture*, August 1941. Reprinted in *Kaiso! Writings by and about Katherine Dunham*, edited by VèVè A. Clark and Sara E. Johnson, 214–216. Madison: University of Wisconsin Press, 2005.

Dunham, Katherine [writing as Kaye Dunn]. "L'ag'ya of Martinique." *Esquire* 12, no. 5 (November 1939): 84–85, 126. Reprinted in *Kaiso! Writings by and about Katherine Dunham*, edited by VèVè A. Clark and Sara E. Johnson, 201–207. Madison: University of Wisconsin Press, 2005.

Edwards, Brent Hayes. *The Practice of Diaspora: Literature, Translation, and the Rise of Black Internationalism*. Cambridge, MA: Harvard University Press, 2003.

———. "The Uses of Diaspora." In *Social Text* 19, no. 1 (Spring 2001): 45–73.

Eidsheim, Nina Sun. "Marian Anderson and 'Sonic Blackness' in American Opera." *American Quarterly* 63, no. 3 (September 2011): 641–671.

Ellington, Edward Kennedy. *Music Is My Mistress*. New York: Da Capo Press, 1973.

Embree, Edwin R. *Julius Rosenwald Fund: Review of Two Decades, 1917–1936*. Chicago: Julius Rosenwald Fund, 1936.

Erlmann, Veit. *Reason and Resonance: A History of Modern Aurality*. New York: Zone Books, 2014.

"Estatutos de la Sociedad de Estudios Afrocubanos." *Estudios Afrocubanos* 1, no. 1 (1937): 7.

Evans, Dylan. *An Introductory Dictionary of Lacanian Psychoanalysis*. London: Routledge, 1996.

Fabian, Johannes. *Time and the Other: How Anthropology Makes Its Object*. New York: Columbia University Press, 1983.

Fajardo Estrada, Ramón. *Rita Montaner: Testimonio de una época*. Havana, Cuba: Fondo Editorial Casa de las Américas, 1997.

Fanon, Frantz. *Black Skin, White Masks*. Translated by Charles Lam Markmann. New York: Grove Press, 1967.

———. *Peau noire, masques blancs*. Paris: Éditions du Seuil, 1952.

Feith, Michel. "The Syncopated African: Constructions of Origins in the Harlem Renaissance (Literature, Music, Visual Arts)." In *Temples for Tomorrow: Looking Back at the Harlem Renaissance*, edited by Geneviève Fabre and Michel Feith, 51–72. Bloomington: Indiana University Press, 2001.

Ferguson, Jeffrey B. *The Sage of Sugar Hill: George S. Schuyler and the Harlem Renaissance*. New Haven, CT: Yale University Press, 2005.

Fernández Robaina, Tomás. *El negro en Cuba, 1902–1958: Apuntes para la historia de la lucha contra la discriminación racial*. Havana, Cuba: Editorial de Ciencias Sociales, 1994.

———. "Marcus Garvey in Cuba: Urrutia, Cubans, and Black Nationalism." In *Between Race and Empire: African-Americans and Cubans before the Cuban Revolution*, edited by Lisa Brock and Digna Castañeda Fuertes, 120–128. Philadelphia, PA: Temple University Press, 1998.

Floyd, Jr., Samuel A. *The Power of Black Music: Interpreting Its History from Africa to the United States*. New York: Oxford University Press, 1995.

Fontaine, W. T. "An Interpretation of Contemporary Negro Thought from the Standpoint of the Sociology of Knowledge." *Journal of Negro History* 25, no. 1 (January 1940): 6–13.

Foucault, Michel. *The Archaeology of Knowledge and the Discourse on Language*. Translated from the French by A. M. Sheridan Smith. New York: Pantheon Books, 1972.

———. *Discipline and Punish: The Birth of the Prison*. Translated from the French by Alan Sheridan. New York: Vintage Books, 1995.

———. *History of Madness*. Edited by Jean Khalfa. Translated by Jonathan Murphy and Jean Khalfa. London: Routledge, 2009.

———. *The Order of Things: An Archaeology of the Human Sciences*. A translation of *Les Mots et les choses*. New York: Vintage Books, 1973.

Freud, Sigmund. *Civilization and Its Discontents*. Translated and edited by James Strachey. With an introduction by Christopher Hitchens, and a biographical afterward by Peter Gay. New York: W. W. Norton, 2010.

———. *General Psychological Theory: Papers on Metapsychology*. Edited and with an introduction by Philip Rieff. New York: Touchstone, 1991.

Frisbie, Charlotte J. "Women and the Society for Ethnomusicology: Roles and Contributions from Formation through Incorporation (1952/53–1961)." In *Comparative Musicology and Anthropology of Music: Essays on the History of Ethnomusicology*, edited by Bruno Nettl and Philip V. Bohlman, 244–265. Chicago: University of Chicago Press, 1991.

Fuller, B. A. G. *A History of Philosophy*. Revised by Sterling M. McMurrin. 3rd ed. New York: Holt, Rinehart and Winston, 1955.

Gaines, Kevin. "Duke Ellington, *Black, Brown and Beige,* and the Cultural Politics of Race." In *Music and the Racial Imagination,* edited by Ronald Radano and Philip V. Bohlman, 585–604. Chicago: University of Chicago Press, 2000.

Gálvez, Zoila. "Una melodía negra." *Estudios Afrocubanos* 4 (1940): 23–26.

Garcia, David. "The Afro-Cuban Soundscape of Mexico City: Authenticating Spaces of Violence and Immorality in *Salón México* and *Víctimas del Pecado.*" In *Screening Songs in Hispanic and Lusophone Cinema,* edited by Lisa Shaw and Rob Stone, 167–188. Manchester, UK: Manchester University Press, 2012.

———. *Arsenio Rodríguez and the Transnational Flows of Latin Popular Music.* Philadelphia, PA: Temple University Press, 2006.

———. "Contesting Anthropology's and Ethnomusicology's Will to Power in the Field: William R. Bascom's and Richard A. Waterman's Fieldwork in Cuba, 1948." *MUSICultures* 40 no. 2 (2014): 1–33.

———. "Embodying Music / Othering Dance: The Mambo Body in Havana and New York City." *Ballroom, Boogie, Shimmy Sham, Shake: A Social and Popular Dance Reader,* edited by Julie M. Malnig, 165–181. Urbana: University of Illinois Press, 2008.

———. "Going Primitive to the Movements and Sounds of Mambo." *Musical Quarterly* 89, no. 4 (winter 2006): 505–523.

———. " 'We Both Speak African': A Dialogic Study of Jazz." *Journal of the Society for American Music* 5, no. 2 (May 2011): 195–233.

García Agüero, Salvador. "Presencia africana en la música nacional." *Estudios Afrocubanos* 1, no. 1 (1937): 114–127.

García Márquez, Gabriel. "El mambo." *El Heraldo,* Barranquilla, Colombia, January 12, 1951. Reprinted in *La soledad de América Latina: Escritos sobre arte y literatura, 1948–1984,* edited and prologue by Víctor Rodríguez Núñez, 124–126. Havana, Cuba: Editorial Arte y Literatura, 1990.

———. *Textos costeños: Obra periodística 1 (1948–1952).* Compiled and with a prologue by Jacques Gilard. Barcelona, Spain: Mondadori, 1999.

Gennari, John. *Blowin' Hot and Cool: Jazz and Its Critics.* Chicago: University of Chicago Press, 2006.

Gerassi, John. *Jean-Paul Sartre: Hated Conscience of His Century.* Chicago: University of Chicago Press, 1989.

Gershenhorn, Jerry. *Melville J. Herskovits and the Racial Politics of Knowledge.* Lincoln: University of Nebraska Press, 2004.

Gershoni, Yekutiel. *Africans on African-Americans: The Creation and Uses of an African-American Myth.* New York: New York University Press, 1997.

———. *Black Colonialism: The Americo-Liberian Scramble for the Hinterland.* Boulder, CO: Westview Press, 1985.

Gide, André. "Avant-propos." *Présence africaine* 1, no. 1 (1947), 3–6.

Gillespie, Dizzy. With Al Fraser. *To Be, or Not . . . to Bop.* New York: Da Capo, 1979.

Gilroy, Paul. *Against Race: Imagining Political Culture beyond the Color Line.* Cambridge, MA: Harvard University Press, 2000.

———. *The Black Atlantic: Modernity and Double Consciousness.* Cambridge, MA: Harvard University Press, 1993.

Ginsberg, Allen. Introduction to *Think of the Self Speaking: Harry Smith—Selected Interviews*, edited by Rani Singh, 2–12. Interview with Hal Willner. Seattle, WA: Elbow/Cityful Press, 1999.

Glassberg, David. *American Historical Pageantry: The Uses of Tradition in the Early Twentieth Century*. Chapel Hill: University of North Carolina Press, 1990.

Goldsmith, Peter D. *Making People's Music: Moe Asch and Folkways Records*. Washington, DC: Smithsonian Institution Press, 1998.

Goodman, Ezra. "Nights Out." *Dance* (January 1947): 35.

Gramsci, Antonio. *Selections from the Prison Notebooks of Antonio Gramsci*. Edited and translated by Quintin Hoare and Geoffrey Nowell Smith. New York: International Publishers, 1971.

Gray, Herman. "John Coltrane and the Practice of Freedom." In *John Coltrane and Black America's Quest for Freedom: Spirituality and the Music*, edited by Leonard L. Brown, 33–54. Oxford: Oxford University Press, 2010.

Grossberg, Lawrence. *Dancing in Spite of Myself: Essays on Popular Culture*. Durham, NC: Duke University Press, 1997.

Guadarrama González, Pablo, and Miguel Rojas Gómez. *El pensamiento filosófico en Cuba en el siglo XX (1900–1960)*. Santa Clara, Mex.: Universidad Autonoma del Estado de México, 1995.

Guldemond, Japp, Marente Bloemheuvel, and Cindy Keefer. "Oskar Fischinger: An Introduction." In *Oskar Fischinger, 1900–1967: Experiments in Cinematic Abstraction*, edited by Cindy Keefer and Jaap Guldemond, 10–12. Amsterdam, Neth.: EYE Filmmuseum; Los Angeles, CA: Center for Visual Music, 2012.

Guridy, Frank Andre. *Forging Diaspora: Afro-Cubans and African Americas*. Chapel Hill: University of North Carolina Press, 2010.

Hall, Stuart. *Cultural Studies 1983: A Theoretical History*. Edited by Jennifer Daryl Slack and Lawrence Grosberg. Durham: Duke University Press, 2016.

Harrison, Faye V., and Ira E. Harrison. "Introduction: Anthropology, African Americans, and the Emancipation of a Subjected Knowledge." In *African-American Pioneers in Anthropology*, edited by Ira E. Harrison and Faye V. Harrison, 1–36. Urbana: University of Illinois Press, 1999.

Hatab, Lawrence J. "Nietzsche: Selfhood, Creativity, and Philosophy." In *The Cambridge Companion to Existentialism*, edited by Steven Crowell, 137–157. Cambridge: Cambridge University Press, 2012.

Heard, Marcia Ethel. "Asadata Dafora: African Concert Dance Traditions in American Concert Dance." PhD diss., New York University, 1999.

Hegel, Georg Wilhelm Friedrich. "Introduction to the Philosophy of History." In *The European Philosophers: From Descartes to Nietzsche*, edited and with an introduction by Monroe C. Beardsley, 537–644. New York: Modern Library, 2002.

———. *The Phenomenology of Mind*. Translated and with an introduction and notes by J. B. Baillie. Mineola, NY: Dover Publications, 2003.

———. *The Philosophy of History*. With prefaces by Charles Hegel and the translator, J. Sibree, and a new introduction by C. J. Friedrich. Mineola, NY: Dover Publications, 1956.

Heidegger, Martin. *The Basic Problems of Phenomenology*. Translated and with an introduction and lexicon by Albert Hofstadter. Bloomington: Indiana University Press, 1982.

———. *Being and Time*. Translated by John Macquarrie and Edward Robinson. London: SCM Press, 1962.

Hernández Cuevas, Marco Polo. *African Mexicans and the Discourse on Modern Nation*. Dallas, TX: University Press of America, 2004.

Herskovits, Melville J. "African Gods and Catholic Saints in New World Negro Belief." *American Anthropologist* 39, no. 4 (1937). Reprinted in *The New World Negro*, edited by Frances S. Herskovits, 321–328. Indiana: Minerva Press, 1969.

———. "The Contribution of Afroamerican Studies to Africanist Research." *American Anthropologist* 50, no. 1 (1948): 1–10.

———. "Freudian Mechanisms in Primitive Negro Psychology." In *Essays Presented to C. G. Seligman*, edited by E. E. Evans-Pritchard et al., 75–84. London: Kegan Paul, Trench, Trubner, 1934. Reprinted in *The New World Negro*, edited by Frances S. Herskovits, 135–144. Indiana: Minerva Press, 1969.

———. *Life in a Haitian Valley*. New York: Alfred A. Knopf, 1937.

———. *The Myth of the Negro Past*. 1941. With a new introduction by Sidney W. Mintz. Boston: Beacon Press, 1990.

———. "The Negro in the New World: The Statement of a Problem." *American Anthropologist* 32, no. 1 (1930). Reprinted in *The New World Negro*, edited by Frances S. Herskovits. Indiana: Minerva Press, 1969.

———. "On the Provenience of New World Negroes." *Social Forces* 12, no. 2 (December 1933): 247–262.

———. "The Significance of West Africa for Negro Research." *Journal of Negro History* 21, no. 1 (1936): 15–30. Reprinted in *The New World Negro*, edited by Frances S. Herskovits. Indiana: Minerva Press, 1969: 89–101.

———. "Social History of the Negro." In *A Handbook of Social Psychology*, vol. 1, edited by Carl Murchison, 207–267. New York: Russell and Russell, 1935.

Herskovits, Melville J., and Frances S. Herskovits. *Dahomey, an Ancient West African Kingdom*. New York City: J. J. Augustin, 1938.

———. *Suriname Folk-lore*. With transcriptions of Suriname songs and musicological analysis by Dr. M. Kolinski. New York: Columbia University Press, 1936.

———. *Trinidad Village*. New York: Alfred A. Knopf, 1947.

Herzog, George. Review of *Suriname Folklore*, by Melville J. Herskovits and Frances S. Herskovits. *Journal of Negro History* 22 no. 4 (October 1937): 503–506.

———. "Speech-Melody and Primitive Music." *Musical Quarterly* 20, no. 4 (October 1934): 452–466.

Herzog, George. With the assistance of Charles G. Blooah. *Jabo Proverbs from Liberia: Maxims in the Life of a Native Tribe*. London: Oxford University Press and H. Milford, 1936.

Hill, Constance Valis. "Collaborating with Balanchine on *Cabin in the Sky*: Interviews with Katherine Dunham." In *Kaiso! Writings by and about Katherine Dunham*, edited by VèVè A. Clark and Sara E. Johnson, 235–247. Madison: University of Wisconsin Press, 2005.

Hill, Donald R., and John H. Cowley. "Calypso at Midnight: The 1946 Town Hall Calypso Concert." In *Calypso after Midnight! The Live Midnight Special Concert, Town Hall, New York City, 1946*, produced by Anna Chairetakis and Jeffrey A. Greenberg, 6–25. Cambridge, MA: Rounder Records, 1999.

Hofstadter, Richard. *Social Darwinism in American Thought*. With a new introduction by Eric Foner. Boston: Beacon Press, 1992.

Holland, Joe. *Modern Catholic Social Teaching: The Popes Confront the Industrial Age, 1740–1958*. New York: Paulist Press, 2003.

hooks, bell. *Feminist Theory: From Margin to Center*. New York: Routledge, 2015.

Hornbostel, Erich M. von. "African Negro Music." *Africa: Journal of the International African Institute* 1, no. 1 (January 1928): 30–62.

———. "American Negro Songs." *International Review Missions* 15 (1926): 748–753.

Hubbard, James P. *The United States and the End of British Colonial Rule in Africa, 1941–1968*. Jefferson, NC: McFarland, 2011.

Hurok, Sol. *S. Hurok Presents: A Memoir of the Dance World*. New York: Hermitage House, 1953.

Introvigne, Massimo. "Cults and Sects." In *Encyclopedia of Religion*, edited by Lindsay Jones, 2084–2086. Detroit, MI: Macmillan Reference USA, 2005.

Iyanaga, Michael. "On Flogging the Dead Horse, Again: Historicity, Genealogy, and Objectivity in Richard Waterman's Approach to Music." *Ethnomusicology* 59, no. 2 (spring/summer 2015): 173–201.

Jackson, Walter. "Melville Herskovits and the Search for Afro-American Culture." In *Malinowski, Rivers, Benedict, and Others: Essays on Culture and Personality*, edited by George W. Stocking, Jr., 95–126. Madison: University of Wisconsin Press, 1986.

Jacobs, Lewis. "Avant-Garde Production in America." In *Experiment in the Film*, edited by Roger Maxwell, 113–152. London: Grey Walls Press, 1949.

Jacobson, Matthew Frye. *Whiteness of a Different Color: European Immigrants and the Alchemy of Race*. Cambridge, MA: Harvard University Press, 1998.

James, C. L. R. "Popular Art and the Cultural Tradition." In *The C. L. R. James Reader*, edited and introduced by Anna Grimshaw, 247–254. Oxford: Blackwell, 1992.

James, C. L. R., et al. *Fighting Racism in World War II*. New York: Pathfinder, 1980.

Jiménez Román, Miriam, and Juan Flores, eds. *The Afro-Latin@ Reader: History and Culture in the United States*. Durham, NC: Duke University Press, 2010.

Johnson, James Weldon. *The Book of American Negro Spirituals*. Edited and with an introduction by James Weldon Johnson. Musical arrangements by J. Rosamond Johnson. Additional numbers by Lawrence Brown. New York: Viking Press, 1925.

Johnson, Sara E. "Introduction: Diamonds on the Toes of Her Feet." In *Kaiso! Writings by and about Katherine Dunham*, edited by VèVè A. Clark and Sara E. Johnson, 3–18. Madison: University of Wisconsin Press, 2005.

Jones, LeRoi.. *Blues People: The Negro Experience in White America and the Music That Developed From It*. New York: Morrow Quill Paperbacks, 1963.

Joseph, Peniel, ed. *The Black Power Movement: Rethinking the Civil Rights–Black Power Era*. New York: Routledge, 2006.

"Katherine Dunham School of Arts and Research (Brochure, 1946–1947)." In *Kaiso! Writings by and about Katherine Dunham*, edited by VèVè A. Clark and Sara E. Johnson, 472–478. Madison: University of Wisconsin Press, 2005.

Kelley, Robin D. G. *Freedom Dreams: The Black Radical Imagination*. Boston: Beacon Press, 2002.

Khanna, Ranjana. *Dark Continents: Psychoanalysis and Colonialism*. Durham, NC: Duke University Press, 2003.

Klaiber, Jeffrey. *The Catholic Church in Peru, 1821–1985: A Social History*. Washington, DC: Catholic University of America Press, 1991.

Kleingeld, Pauline. "Kant's Second Thoughts on Race." *Philosophical Quarterly* 57, no. 229 (October 2007): 573–592.

Koffka, Kurt. "Perception: An Introduction to the *Gestalt-Theorie*." *Psychological Bulletin* 19, no. 10 (October 1922): 531–585.

———. *Principles of Gestalt Psychology*. New York: Harcourt, Brace and Company, 1935.

Köhler, Wolfgang. *Gestalt Psychology*. New York: Horace Liveright, 1929.

Krehbiel, Henry Edward. *Afro-American Folksongs: A Study in Racial and National Music*. New York: G. Schirmer, 1914.

Kuper, Adam. *The Reinvention of Primitive Society: Transformations of a Myth*. London: Routledge, 2005.

Las comparsas populares del carnaval habanero, cuestión resuelta. Havana, Cuba: Molina y CIA, 1937.

Lefebvre, Henri. *The Production of Space*. Translated by Donald Nicholson-Smith. Malden, MA: Blackwell Publishing, 1991.

Lévi-Strauss, Claude. *The Savage Mind [La Pensée sauvage]*. Oxford: Oxford University Press, 2004.

Lindgren, Allana C. "Civil Rights Strategies in the United States: Franziska Boas's Activist Use of Dance, 1933–1965." *Dance Research Journal* 45, no. 2 (August 2013): 25–62.

Liscano, Juan. *Folklore y cultura: Ensayos*. Caracas, Venezuela: Editorial Avila Grafica, 1950.

"List of Papers Read at Annual Meetings, 1943, 1944." *Bulletin of the American Musicological Society*, nos. 9/10 (June 1947): 34.

Locke, Alain. "Apropos of Africa." 1924. Reprinted in *The Works of Alain Locke*, edited and with an introduction by Charles Molesworth, and a foreword by Henry Louis Gates Jr., 262–268. Oxford: Oxford University Press, 2013.

———. "Slavery in the Modern Manner." 1931. Reprinted in *The Works of Alain Locke*, edited and with an introduction by Charles Molesworth, and a foreword by Henry Louis Gates Jr., 297–306. Oxford: Oxford University Press, 2013.

López Cano, Rubén. "Apuntes para una prehistoria del mambo." *Latin American Music Review* 30, no. 2 (fall/winter 2009): 213–242.

Lowenthal, Ira P. "Ritual Performance and Religious Experience: A Service for the Gods in Southern Haiti." *Journal of Anthropological Research* 34, no. 3 (autumn 1978): 392–414.

Lowinger, Rosa, and Ofelia Fox. *Tropicana Nights: The Life and Times of the Legendary Cuban Nightclub*. Orlando: Harcourt, 2005.

Lynch, Hollis R. "K. O. Mbadiwe, 1939–1947: The American Years of a Nigerian Political Leader." *Journal of African Studies* 7, no. 4 (winter 1980–1981): 184–203.

———. "Pan-African Responses in the United States to British Colonial Rule in Africa in the 1940s." In *The Transfer of Power in Africa: Decolonization, 1940–1960*, edited by Prosser Gifford and Wm. Roger Louis, 57–86. New Haven, CT: Yale University Press, 1982.

Macnamara, John. *Through the Rearview Mirror: Historical Reflections on Psychology.* [eBook Full Text] 1999. Accessed December 18, 2013. http://libproxy.lib.unc.edu/login?url=http://www.netlibrary.com/urlapi.asp?action=summary&v=1&bookid=12550

Malinowski, Bronislaw. Introduction to *Cuban Counterpoint: Tobacco and Sugar*, by Fernando Ortiz, lvii–lxiv. Durham, NC: Duke University Press, 1995.

Malnig, Julie. Introduction to *Ballroom, Boogie, Shimmy Sham, Shake: A Social and Popular Dance Reader*, edited by Julie M. Malnig, 1–18. Urbana: University of Illinois Press, 2008.

Manning, Susan. *Modern Dance, Negro Dance: Race in Motion.* Minneapolis: University of Minnesota Press, 2004.

Martin, Ronald E. *The Languages of Difference: American Writers and Anthropologists Reconfigure the Primitive, 1878–1940.* Newark: University of Delaware Press, 2005.

Matory, J. Lorand. "The 'New World' Surrounds an Ocean: Theorizing the Live Dialogue between African and African American Cultures." In *Afro-Atlantic Dialogues: Anthropology in the Diaspora*, edited by Kevin A. Yelvington, 151–192. Santa Fe, NM: School of American Research Press; Oxford: James Currey, 2005.

Mbadiwe, K. Ozuomba. "Africa in the War of Destiny." *Opportunity: A Journal of Negro Life* 20, no. 9 (September 1942): 260–264.

———. "The African Academy of Arts and Research." In *Africa: Today and Tomorrow*, edited by H. A. B. Jones-Quartey, 9, 17, 66. New York: African Academy of Arts and Research, 1945.

———. *Rebirth of a Nation.* Enugu, Nigeria: Fourth Dimension, 1991.

McBride, William. "Existentialism as a Cultural Movement." In *The Cambridge Companion to Existentialism*, edited by Steven Crowell, 50–69. Cambridge: Cambridge University Press, 2012.

McCluskey, Audrey Thomas. Introduction to *Mary McLeod Bethune: Building a Better World*, edited by Audrey Thomas McCluskey and Elaine M. Smith, 3–20. Bloomington: Indiana University Press, 1999.

Meier, August, and Elliott M. Rudwick. "Negro Protest at the Chicago World's Fair, 1933–1934." *Journal of the Illinois State Historical Society* 59, no. 2 (summer 1966): 161–171.

Melton, McKinley. "Speak It into Existence: James Weldon Johnson's *God's Trombones* and the Power of Self-Definition in the New Negro Harlem Renaissance." In *The Harlem Renaissance Revisited: Politics, Arts, and Letters*, edited by Jeffrey O. G. Ogbar, 109–126. Baltimore, MD: Johns Hopkins University Press, 2010.

Merriam, Alan P. "The Northwestern University Laboratory of Comparative Musicology." *Folklore and Folk Music Archivist* 1, no. 4 (December 1958): 1, 4.

———. "Richard Alan Waterman, 1914–1971." *Ethnomusicology* 17, no. 1 (January 1973): 72–94.

Meyer, Eugenia. *Testimonios para la historia del cine mexicano*. Mexico City, Mex.: Cineteca Nacional, 1976.

Mikell, Gwendolyn. "Feminism and Black Culture in the Ethnography of Zora Neale Hurston." In *African-American Pioneers in Anthropology*, edited by Ira E. Harrison and Faye V. Harrison, 51–69. Urbana: University of Illinois Press, 1999.

Mikics, David. "Derek Walcott and Alejo Carpentier: Nature, History, and the Caribbean Writer." In *Magical Realism: Theory, History, Community*, edited and with an introduction by Lois Parkinson Zamora and Wendy B. Faris, 371–406. Durham, NC: Duke University Press, 1995.

Miller, Karl Hagstrom. *Segregating Sound: Inventing Folk and Pop Music in the Age of Jim Crow*. Durham, NC: Duke University Press, 2010.

Miller, Ivor L. "A Secret Society Goes Public: The Relationship between Abakuá and Cuban Popular Culture." *African Studies Review* 43, no. 1 (April 2000): 161–188.

———. *Voice of the Leopard: African Secret Societies and Cuba*. Jackson: University Press of Mississippi, 2009.

Modupe, Prince. *I Was a Savage*. New York: Harcourt, Brace and Company, 1957.

Molesworth, Charles, ed. *The Works of Alain Locke*. With a foreword by Henry Louis Gates Jr. Oxford: Oxford University Press, 2013.

Monson, Ingrid. *Freedom Sounds: Civil Rights Call Out to Jazz and Africa*. Oxford: Oxford University Press, 2007.

Montejo Arrechea, Carmen. "*Minerva*: A Magazine for Women (and Men) of Color." In *Between Race and Empire: African-Americans and Cubans before the Cuban Revolution*, edited by Lisa Brock and Digna Castañeda Fuertes, 33–48. Philadelphia, PA: Temple University Press, 1998.

Moore, Robin. *Nationalizing Blackness: Afrocubanismo and Artistic Revolution in Havana, 1920–1940*. Pittsburgh: University of Pittsburgh Press, 1997.

———. "Representations of Afrocuban Expressive Culture in the Writings of Fernando Ortiz." *Latin American Music Review* 15, no. 1 (spring/summer 1994): 32–54.

Moreno, Jairo. "Bauzá—Gillespie—Latin/Jazz: Difference, Modernity, and the Black Caribbean." *South Atlantic Quarterly* 103, no. 1 (winter 2004): 81–99.

Morgan, Robert P. *Twentieth-Century Music: A History of Musical Style in Modern Europe and America*. New York: W. W. Norton, 1991.

Morris, Gay. "Modernism's Role in the Theory of John Martin and Edwin Denby." *Dance Research: Journal of the Society for Dance Research* 22, no. 2 (winter 2004): 168–184.

Mouralis, Bernard. "*Présence Africaine*: Geography of an 'Ideology.'" In *The Surreptitious Speech: Présence Africaine and the Politics of Otherness, 1947–1987*, edited by V. Y. Mudimbe, 3–13. Chicago: University of Chicago Press, 1992.

"Mr. Mudge Paris, African Baritone." *Virginia Intercollegian* 3 (March 1929): 7–8.

Mudimbe, V. Y. *The Invention of Africa: Gnosis, Philosophy, and the Order of Knowledge*. Bloomington: Indiana University Press, 1988.

Nattiez, Jean-Jacques. *Music and Discourse: Toward a Semiology of Music*. Translated by Carolyn Abbate. Princeton, NJ: Princeton University Press, 1990.

"Nécrologie." *Revue de Musicologie* 17, no. 59 (1936): 160.

"Notas y noticias." *Estudios Afrocubanos* 1, no. 1 (1937): 163–164.

Ogbar, Jeffrey O. G. *Black Power: Radical Politics and African American Identity*. Baltimore, MD: Johns Hopkins University Press, 2004.

———. Introduction to *The Harlem Renaissance Revisited: Politics, Arts, and Letters*, edited by Jeffrey O. G. Ogbar, 1–4. Baltimore, MD: Johns Hopkins University Press, 2010.

Ochoa Gautier, Ana María. *Aurality: Listening and Knowledge in Nineteenth-Century Colombia*. Durham, NC: Duke University Press, 2014.

Ohman, Marian M. "African and African-American Musicians Seeking Progress at *A Century of Progress*." *Journal of the Illinois State Historical Society* 102, no. 314 (fall–winter, 2009): 368–401.

Olmsted, Tony. *Folkways Records: Moses Asch and His Encyclopedia of Sound*. New York: Routledge, 2003.

Olupona, Jacob K., ed. *African Spirituality: Forms, Meanings, and Expressions*. New York: Crossroad Publishing Company, 2000.

Orovio, Helio. *Cuban Music from A to Z*. Durham, NC: Duke University Press, 2004.

Ortiz, Fernando. *El engaño de las razas*. 1946. Reprint, Havana, Cuba: Editorial de Ciencias Sociales, 1975.

———. *La africanía de la música folklórica de Cuba*. 1950. Reprint. Havana, Cuba: Editoria Universitaria, 1965.

———. "La música sagrada de los negros yorubá en Cuba." *Estudios Afrocubanos* 2, no. 1 (1938): 89–104.

———. *Los bailes y el teatro de los negros en el folklore de Cuba*. 1951. Reprint. Havana, Cuba: Editorial Letras Cubanas, 1993.

———. "The Relations between Blacks and Whites in Cuba." *Phylon (1940–1956)* 5, no. 1 (1944): 15–29.

Osumare, Halifu. "Katherine Dunham, a Pioneer of Postmodern Anthropology." In *Kaiso! Writings by and about Katherine Dunham*, edited by VèVè A. Clark and Sara E. Johnson, 612–623. Madison: University of Wisconsin Press, 2005.

Patterson, Karin. "Prince Modupe: An African in Early Hollywood." *Black Music Research Journal* 31, no. 1 (spring 2011): 29–44.

Paz, Octavio. *El laberinto de la soledad*. México, DF, Mexico: Fondo de Cultura Económica, 1973.

Pérez Derrick, Yoslainy. "Afro-Cuban Women in Opera: Stories, Coincidences and Realities." *Revista Islas* 23 (May 26, 2013): 56–60.

Perkins, Alfred. *Edwin Rogers Embree: The Julius Rosenwald Fund Foundation Philanthropy and American Race Relations*. Bloomington: Indiana University Press, 2011.

Philippoff, Olga. "Enforced Holiday: The De Basil Company in Cuba." *Dancing Times* 31, no. 10 (July 1941): 660–662.

Pierre, Dorathi Bock. "Katherine Dunham: Cool Scientist or Sultry Performer?" *Dance* 21, no. 5 (May 1947): 11–13.

Piñeiro Díaz, José. *Cronología artística de Zoila Gálvez (soprano y pedagoga)*. Havana, Cuba: Museo Nacional de la Música, 1989.

Pius XII (pope). *Evangelii praecones*. Rome: Libreria Editrice Vaticana, 1951. Accessed May 13, 2015. http://w2.vatican.va/content/pius-xii/en/encyclicals/documents/hf _p-xii_enc_02061951_evangelii-praecones.html.

Portell Vilá, Herminio. "El folklore en Jovellanos." *Archivos del folklore cubano* 4, no. 1 (1929): 53–59.

Porter, Eric. *What Is This Thing Called Jazz?: African American Musicians as Artists, Critics, and Activists*. Berkeley: University of California Press, 2002.

Price, Richard. "On the Miracle of Creolization." In *Afro-Atlantic Dialogues: Anthropology in the Diaspora*, edited by Kevin A. Yelvington, 115–148. Santa Fe, NM: School of American Research Press/Oxford: James Currey, 2005.

Price, Richard, and Sally Price. *The Root of Roots: Or, How Afro-American Anthropology Got Its Start*. Chicago: Prickly Paradigm Press, 2003.

Priestley, Brian and Alan Cohen. "'Black, Brown & Beige' (1974–1975)." In *The Duke Ellington Reader*, edited by Mark Tucker, 185–204. New York: Oxford University Press, 1993.

"Propósitos." *Afroamérica* 1, nos. 1–2 (January–July 1945): 3–4.

Radano, Ronald. *Lying Up a Nation: Race and Black Music*. Chicago: University of Chicago Press, 2003.

Radano, Ronald, and Philip V. Bohlman, eds. *Music and the Racial Imagination*. With a foreword by Houston A. Baker, Jr. Chicago: University of Chicago Press, 2000.

Ramos, Arthur. "Acculturation among the Brazilian Negroes." *Journal of Negro History* 26, no. 2 (April 1941): 244–250.

Ramos, Samuel. *Historia de la filosofía en México*. México, DF, Mexico: Imprenta Universitaria, 1943.

Ramsey, Kate. "Melville Herskovits, Katherine Dunham, and the Politics of African Diasporic Dance Anthropology." In *Dancing Bodies, Living Histories: New Writings about Dance and Culture*, edited by Lisa Doolittle and Anne Flynn, 296–217. Banff, AB: Banff Centre Press, 1999.

Redfield, Robert, Ralph Linton, and Melville J. Herskovits. "Memorandum for the Study of Acculturation." *Man* 35 (October 1935): 145–148.

Reed, Christopher Robert. "A Reinterpretation of Black Strategies for Change at the Chicago World's Fair, 1933–1934." *Illinois Historical Journal* 81, no. 1 (spring 1988): 2–12.

Rice, Timothy. "Comparative Musicology." *Grove Music Online*. Last accessed Nov. 25, 2016. http://www.oxfordmusiconline.com.libproxy.lib.unc.edu/subscriber/article /grove/music/46454.

Roberts, Helen H. "Melodic Composition and Scale Foundations in Primitive Music." *American Anthropologist* 34, no. 1 (January–March 1932): 79–107.

———. "Possible Survivals of African Song in Jamaica." *Musical Quarterly* 12, no. 3 (July 1926): 340–358.

———. "A Study of Folk Song Variants Based on Field Work in Jamaica." *Journal of American Folk-lore* 38, no. 148 (April–June 1925): 149–216.

Roffe, Jonathan. "Nomos." In *The Deleuze Dictionary: Revised Edition*, edited by Adrian Parr, 189–191. Edinburgh, Scot.: Edinburgh University Press, 2010.

Roosevelt, Eleanor. "Prejudice Springs from Ignorance." In *Africa, Today and Tomorrow*, edited by H. A. B. Jones-Quartey, 18–19. New York: African Academy of Arts and Research, 1945. Reprinted by Nendeln, Liechtenstein: Kraus Reprint, 1976.

Rose, Albirda. "Dunham Technique: Barre Work and Center Progressions." In *Kaiso! Writings by and about Katherine Dunham*, edited by VèVè A. Clark and Sara E. Johnson, 488–494. Madison: University of Wisconsin Press, 2005.

Rosenberg, June. "African Rhythm in the West." In *Africa, Today and Tomorrow*, edited by H. A. B. Jones-Quartey, 26–27. New York: African Academy of Arts and Research, 1945. Reprinted Nendeln, Liechtenstein: Kraus Reprint, 1976.

Ruppli, Michel, compiler. *The Decca Labels: A Discography*. Vol. 2, *The Eastern and Southern Sessions (1934–1942)*. Westport, CT: Greenwood Press, 1996.

———. *The Decca Labels: A Discography*. Vol. 3, *The Eastern Sessions (1943–1956)*. Westport, CT: Greenwood Press, 1996.

Sánchez Reulet, Aníbal, ed. *Contemporary Latin-American Philosophy: A Selection*. With an introduction and notes by Aníbal Sánchez Reulet. Translation from the Spanish and Portuguese by Willard R. Trask. Albuquerque: University of New Mexico Press, 1954.

Sargeant, Winthrop. "Cuba's Tin Pan Alley." *Life* 23, no. 14 (October 6, 1947): 145–146, 148, 151–152, 154, 157.

Sartre, Jean-Paul. *Being and Nothingness: A Phenomenological Essay on Ontology*. Translated and with an introduction by Hazel E. Barnes. New York: Washington Square Press, 1984.

———. *Black Orpheus*. Translated by S. W. Allen. Paris: Présence Africaine, 1976.

———. "A Commentary on *The Stranger*." *Cahiers du su*, February 1943. Reprinted in *Existentialism Is a Humanism* [*L'Existentialisme est un humanism*], including A commentary on *The Stranger* [*Explication de L'Étranger*]; translated by Carol Macomber; introduction by Annie Cohen-Solal; notes and preface by Arlette Elkaïm-Sartre; edited by John Kulka, 73–98. New Haven, CT: Yale University Press, 2007.

———. *Existentialism Is a Humanism* [*L'Existentialisme est un humanism*], including A Commentary on *The Stranger* [*Explication de L'Étranger*]; translated by Carol Macomber; introduction by Annie Cohen-Solal; notes and preface by Arlette Elkaïm-Sartre; edited by John Kulka. New Haven, CT: Yale University Press, 2007.

———. "Orphée noir." In *Anthologie de la nouvelle poésie nègre et malgache de langue française*, edited by Léopold Sédar Senghor, ix–xliv. Paris: Presses Universitaires de France, 1969.

Seashore, Robert H. "Convergent Trends in Experimental Psychology." In *Fields of Psychology: An Experimental Approach*, edited by Robert H. Seashore, 621–634. New York: Henry Holt, 1942.

———. "Convergent Trends in Psychological Theory." In *Fields of Psychology: An Experimental Approach*, edited by Robert H. Seashore, 601–620. New York: Henry Holt, 1942.

Seeger, Charles. "Notes and News." *Ethnomusicology* 1, no. 6 (January 1956): 1–10.

Selcer, Perrin. "Beyond the Cephalic Index: Negotiating Politics to Produce UNESCO's Scientific Statements on Race." *Current Anthropology* 53, no. S5 (April 2012): 173–184.

Seniors, Paula Marie. "Jack Johnson, Paul Robeson, and the Hypermasculine African American *Übermensch*." In *The Harlem Renaissance Revisited: Politics, Arts, and Letters*, edited by Jeffrey O. G. Ogbar, 155–176. Baltimore, MD: Johns Hopkins University Press, 2010.

Shannon, Magdeline W. *Jean Price-Mars, the Haitian Elite, and the American Occupation, 1915–1935*. New York: St. Martin's Press, 1996.

Shelemay, Kay Kaufman. "Recording Technology, the Record Industry, and Ethnomusicological Scholarship." *Comparative Musicology and Anthropology of Music: Essays on the History of Ethnomusicology*, edited by Bruno Nettl and Philip V. Bohlman, 277–292. Chicago: University of Chicago Press, 1991.

Shepherd, Gary. "Cults: Social Psychological Aspects." In *Blackwell Encyclopedia of Sociology*, edited by George Ritzer. Last modified September 2, 2014. www.blackwell reference.com.libproxy.lib.unc.edu.

Sherwood, Marika. " 'There Is No New Deal for the Blackman in San Francisco': African Attempts to Influence the Founding Conference of the United Nations, April–July, 1945." *International Journal of African Historical Studies* 29, no. 1 (1996): 71–94.

Singh, Rani. "Anthology Film Archives." In *American Magus: Harry Smith*, edited by Paola Igliori, 13–17. New York: Inanout Press, 1996.

Sitney, P. Adams. "Film Culture No. 37, 1965." In *Think of the Self Speaking: Harry Smith—Selected Interviews*, edited by Rani Singh, 44–65. Seattle, WA: Elbow / Cityful Press, 1999.

———. *Visionary Film: The American Avant-Garde*. New York: Oxford University Press, 1974.

Small, Christopher. *Musicking: The Meanings of Performing and Listening*. Middletown, CT: Wesleyan University Press.

Spengler, Oswald. *The Decline of the West*. An abridged edition by Helmut Werner; English abridged edition prepared by Arthur Helps from the translation by Charles Francis Atkinson. New York: Vintage Books, 2006.

Spivak, Gayatri Chakravorty. "Translator's Preface." In *Of Grammatology*, by Jacques Derrida, translated by Gayatri Chakravatory Spivak, ix–xc. Baltimore, MD: Johns Hopkins University Press, 1997.

Stauffacher, Frank, ed. *Art in Cinema*. San Francisco, CA: San Francisco Museum of Art, 1947.

Steady, Filomina Chioma. "African Feminism: A Worldwide Perspective." In *Women in America and the African Diaspora: A Reader*, edited by Rosalyn Terborg-Penn and Andrea Benton Rushing, 3–21. Washington, DC: Howard University Press, 1996.

Sterne, Jonathan. *The Audible Past: Cultural Origins of Sound Reproduction*. Durham, NC: Duke University Press, 2003.

Sundiata, Ibrahim. *Brothers and Strangers: Black Zion, Black Slavery, 1914–1940*. Durham, NC: Duke University Press, 2003.

Sundquist, Eric J. "Introduction: W. E. B. Du Bois and the Autobiography of Race." In *The Oxford W. E. B. Du Bois Reader*, edited by Eric J. Sundquist, 3–36. New York: Oxford University Press, 1996.

Swiboda, Marcel. "Becoming+Music." In *The Deleuze Dictionary*, edited by Adrian Parr, 27–29. Edinburgh, Scot.: Edinburgh University Press, 2010.

Thompson, E. P. "Time, Work-Discipline, and Industrial Capitalism." *Past and Present* no. 38 (December 1967): 56–97.

Thompson, Robert Farris. "Teaching the People to Triumph over Time: Notes from the World of Mambo." In *Caribbean Dance from Abakuá to Zouk*, edited by Susanna Sloat, 336–344. Gainesville: University Press of Florida, 2002.

Trippett, David. "Carl Stumpf: A Reluctant Revolutionary." *The Origins of Music*. Oxford: Oxford University Press, 2012.

Tucker, Mark, ed. *The Duke Ellington Reader*. New York: Oxford University Press, 1993.

———. "The Ellington Orchestra in Cleveland (1931)." In *The Duke Ellington Reader*, edited by Mark Tucker, 50–54. New York: Oxford University Press, 1993.

———. "Interpretations in Jazz: A Conference with Duke Ellington (1947)." In *The Duke Ellington Reader*, edited by Mark Tucker, 255–258. New York: Oxford University Press, 1993.

———. "Interview in Los Angeles: On *Jump for Joy*, Opera, and Dissonance as a 'Way of Life' (1941)." In *The Duke Ellington Reader*, edited by Mark Tucker, 148–151. New York: Oxford University Press, 1993.

———. "A Landmark in Ellington Criticism: R. D. Darrell's 'Black Beauty' (1932)." In *The Duke Ellington Reader*, edited by Mark Tucker, 57–65. New York: Oxford University Press, 1993.

———. "Previews of the First Carnegie Hall Concert (1943)." In *The Duke Ellington Reader*, edited by Mark Tucker, 155–160. New York: Oxford University Press, 1993.

———. "Program for the First Carnegie Hall Concert (23 January 1943)." In *The Duke Ellington Reader*, edited by Mark Tucker, 160–165. New York: Oxford University Press, 1993.

———. "Two Early Interviews (1930)." In *The Duke Ellington Reader*, edited by Mark Tucker, 41–45. New York: Oxford University Press, 1993.

———. "Wilder Hobson: 'Introducing Duke Ellington' (1933)." In *The Duke Ellington Reader*, edited by Mark Tucker, 93–98. New York: Oxford University Press, 1993.

Turino, Thomas. "Peircean Thought as Core Theory for a Phenomenological Ethnomusicology." *Ethnomusicology* 58, no. 2 (spring/summer 2014): 185–221.

United Nations Educational, Scientific, and Cultural Organization (UNESCO). *Basic Texts*. Paris: UNESCO, 2014.

———. *The Race Concept: Results of an Inquiry*. Paris: UNESCO, 1952.

Urfé, Odilio. "La verdad sobre el 'mambo.'" *Inventario: Mensuario polémico de arte y literatura* 1, no. 3 (June 1948): 2, 7.

Vasconcelos, José. *La raza cósmica: Misión de la raza iberoamericana*. Paris: Agencia Mundial de Librería, 1925.

Verharen, Charles. "'The New World and the Dreams to Which It May Give Rise': An African and American Response to Hegel's Challenge." *Journal of Black Studies* 27, no. 4 (March 1997): 456–493.

Wald, Elijah. *Josh White: Society Blues*. Amherst: University of Massachusetts Press, 2000.

Waterman, Christopher A. "The Uneven Development of Africanist Ethnomusicology: Three Issues and a Critique." In *Comparative Musicology and Anthropology of Music: Essays on the History of Ethnomusicology*, edited by Bruno Nettl and Philip V. Bohlman, 169–186. Chicago: University of Chicago Press, 1991.

Waterman, Richard A. "African Influence on the Music of the Americas." In *Acculturation in the Americas: Proceedings of the 29th International Congress of Americanists*, edited by Sol Tax, vol. 2, 207–218. Chicago: University of Chicago Press, 1952.

———. "African Patterns in Trinidad Negro Music." PhD diss., Northwestern University, 1943.

———. "'Hot' Rhythm in Negro Music." *Journal of the American Musicological Society* 1, no. 1 (spring 1948): 24–37.

———. "On Flogging a Dead Horse: Lessons Learned from the Africanisms Controversy." *Ethnomusicology* 7, no. 2 (May 1963): 83–87.

———. "Percussion Rhythms in the Music of the Negroes of Trinidad (abstract)." *Bulletin of the Chicago Anthropological Society* 1 (April–May 1945): 7–8.

———. Review of *Journey to Accompong*, by Katherine Dunham. *Notes* 4, no. 2 (March 1947): 179–180.

Wieschhoff, H. A. "The Social Significance of Names among the Ibo of Nigeria." *American Anthropologist* 43, no. 2 (April–June 1941): 212–222.

Williams, Drid. *Anthropology and the Dance: Ten Lectures*. With a foreword by Brenda Farnell. Urbana: University of Illinois Press, 2004.

Williams, Raymond. *Marxism and Literature*. Oxford: Oxford University Press, 1977.

Williams Jr., Vernon J. *Rethinking Race: Franz Boas and His Contemporaries*. Lexington: University Press of Kentucky, 1996.

Wolfe, Katharine. "From the Archive: Introduction to Günther Anders' 'The Pathology of Freedom.'" *Deleuze Studies* 3, no. 2 (2009): 274–277.

Yelvington, Kevin A. "The Invention of Africa in Latin America and the Caribbean: Political Discourse and Anthropological Praxis, 1920–1940." In *Afro-Atlantic Dialogues: Anthropology in the Diaspora*, edited by Kevin A. Yelvington. Santa Fe, NM: School of American Research Press/Oxford: James Currey, 2005.

Zea, Leopoldo. *El positivismo en México*. México, DF, Mexico: El Colegio de México, 1943.

Znaniecki, Florian, et al. "Abstracts from the Annual Meeting," *Midwest Sociologist* 5, no. 3 (March 1943): 3–8.

Aguilar, Amalia, 18, 246, 247–249, 256
L'ag'ya, 60–61
Al son del mambo (film), 246, 247, 252
American Council of Learned Societies (ACLS), 43, 98, 112, 118
American Labor Party, 149, 157
American Negro women's clubs, 126, 150
American Section of the International Society for Comparative Musicology, 38
American Society for Comparative Musicology, 38, 112
Americo-Liberian, 20, 177, 198–199, 201–203
Ammons, Albert, 181, 184–185
Amphitheater, 82, 84–85, 87, 90, 108, 144, 228, 229
Analyzing, 8–10, 12, 18, 19, 173, 188
Anderson, Marian, 195, 208
Andreu, Enrique, 127, 128, 132, 143, 144, 166; Cuban popular musicians, 142; spiritual, 141–142, 144; spiritual musicians, 142
Angelitos negros (film), 114
Anguish, 221, 226, 253, 316n4. *See also* existentialism; Sartre, Jean-Paul
Anthropological field, 9, 14, 24, 25, 55, 57, 60, 67, 73, 125, 126, 144, 176, 179. *See also* fieldwork
Anthropologist, 14, 24–25, 78, 108, 115, 176, 180
Anthropology, 18, 31, 53, 54, 56–57, 61, 77, 79, 111, 155, 180–181, 185–187, 194, 219; cultural, 29; dance study, 55; gender, 67, 69–71; physical, 29, 63, 70; racism, 67; sexism, 68, 70
Antonio Arcaño y sus Maravillas, *See* Orquesta Maravilla de Arcaño
Anxiety, 77, 94, 147, 158, 159, 219, 222
Arará, 113, 118–119
Arcaño, Antonio, 230, 232
Archive of Primitive Music (Columbia University), 112
Arredondo, Alberto, 79, 86–87, 89, 123, 142, 230
Art in Cinema Society, 209; film series, 211, 217–218
Artaud, Antonin, 178
Articulation, 8, 278n17
Aryanism, 25, 28, 65, 140
Asch, Moe, 117, 121
Assemblage, 3, 19
Assen, Abdul, 169
Atlantic Charter, 160–161, 168, 305n156
Atomic age, 8, 18, 20, 178, 212, 223, 225, 229, 254
Attali, Jacques, 93; silence, 252–253, 316n18
Auditory space-level, 74, 102, 106, 120, 127
Aurality, 8, 42, 76, 93, 107, 214, 229, 253, 269
Authenticity, 15–16
Avant-garde film, 178, 209–210, 217, 219, 308n20; dance, 209; music, 209–210; space, 209–210; time, 209–210
Azikiwe, Nnamdi, 130, 168, 195, 199

Bakhtin, Mikhail M., 12, 125, 149
Ballet Ruse, 154, 157
Baraka, Amiri, 1, 2, 5, 18
Barclay, Arthur, 198
Barreda, Gabina, 256
Bascom, William R., 96–97, 104, 105, 114
Batá, 85–86, 90, 92, 123, 290n49
Bebop, 5, 211–214, 218, 238, 257. *See also* jazz
Becker, Judith, 78
Becoming, 8, 9, 88, 121–122, 154, 157, 232, 275
Being-for-the-other, 12, 128
Belaire, 60, 62–63
Benedict, Ruth, 62, 185
Benítez-Rojo, Antonio, 267
Bernstein, Leonard, 195
Beruff Mendieta, Antonio, 80, 84
Bethune, Mary McLeod, 130, 161–162, 164–165, 195, 206; Federal Council on Negro Affairs, 165
Black dance, 192, 222, 227, 253, 275; modern, 5
Black internationalism, 4
Black music, 43–46, 51, 53, 79, 94–95, 101, 140, 149, 192, 196, 222, 224, 227, 253, 275; pathological, 86; syncopation, 44
Black nationalism, 3, 54, 65, 129, 195, 219
Black Other, 12, 16, 125, 127–128, 136, 144, 146, 207, 214

Black Power, 4, 6, 129, 158–159
Black rhythm, 86, 221
Black Skin, White Masks, See Fanon, Frantz
Blackness, 81, 204, 224, 289n28. *See also*
  whiteness
Blesh, Rudi, 105, 180–185, 187, 196, 209,
  211, 309n36, 309n38; *Shining Trumpets,
  A History of Jazz*, 182–184
Blooah, Charles G., 138–139
Boas, Franz, 26, 27, 29, 47, 48, 62–63, 68,
  127, 185; diffusionist paradigm, 35;
  Franziska, 310n68
Body, 10, 304n141; Africanized, 152, 154;
  Cartesian, 269; dancing, 56; disciplined,
  125; docile, 125; gendered, 144, 229,
  241, 257, 264; Jewish, 166; mambo, 241,
  257, 264; raced, 10, 14–17, 23, 93, 123,
  124–126, 129, 139, 144, 151–156, 164,
  166, 173, 175, 182, 188, 192, 229, 241,
  269; sexed, 126, 192; temporalized, 151.
  See also mind; Sydenham's Chorea;
  un-raced; whiteness
Body politic, 86, 108
Bongo, 63
Borneman, Ernest, 243
Bourdieu, Pierre, 8, 77
Brewster, Walter S., 150
British colonialism, 148, 152, 161
Brito, Alberto, 114
Brock, Lisa, 4
Brown, John, 137
Brujo, 115–116, 118, 120, 241
Burley, Dan, 185–186, 191–192, 194
Bush, 8–10, 14, 24, 31, 34, 39, 44, 53–54,
  60, 72, 73, 78, 79, 95, 99, 108, 125, 229,
  280n19
Bush Negro, 6, 25, 31–32, 34, 40, 43, 97;
  field recordings, 42; musical traits, 42
Butler, Judith, 126, 127, 219, 266–267,
  277n8

Cabrera, Lydia, 12, 115–116
Calypso, 19
Campbell, Donald T, 96
Campo, Pupi, 239
Camus, Albert, 246–247, 253
Capitalism, 6, 9, 19, 176, 178, 220,
  224–226, 233, 241–243, 249, 253;

alienation, 220; machines, 233, 235,
  239–240, 249; madness, 226–227, 229;
  mambo, 225–226, 229, 232, 243;
  schizophrenia, 220, 225, 226, 242–243,
  278n10; strictures, 270. *See also*
  Catholic Church; nationalism; Oedipal
  family
Capo, Bobby, 181, 187, 190
Caribbean, 9
Cariso, 63
Carmichael, Stokely, 129, 158
Carpentier, Alejo, 18, 221, 223, 226,
  233–234, 239, 246, 253, 254, 267; *lo real
  maravilloso americano*, 221, 223
Case study, 278n12
Catholic Church, 5, 224–226, 245, 247,
  251; Catholic Action groups, 247–249;
  Catholicism, 256; Mexico, 256, 258;
  Peru, 247–248; Venezuela, 249
Caucasian, 27, 28
Cesaire, Aimé, 222
Charanga, 229, 230, 232, 239, 317n23
Chase, Gilbert, 98
Chicago, 147, 157; African exhibit, 138;
  Chicago World's Fair, 136, 137, 139,
  145, 157, 299n66
Christianity, 16
Chronotope, 125, 126, 149, 152–154,
  156, 158, 164, 213, 229, 241, 251, 264,
  297n1
Civil rights movement, 3, 4, 195
Civilization, 5, 22–23, 25, 52; Western, 11,
  16, 19–20, 25, 32
Clark, VèVè A., 176, 308n15
Class, 14, 277n8
Clegg III, Claude A., 177, 201
Club Atenas, 27, 82, 88, 133, 141, 166
Coates, Paul 240
Coeval, 13
Coker, Norman, 162
Cold War, 3, 8, 171, 178, 195, 219–220
Cole: Fay-Cooper, 70; Sally, 68
Collins, Patricia Hill, 161
Colonialism, 6, 8, 12, 14, 16, 127, 130, 172
Commercial recordings, 72
Comparative method, 282n69
Comparative musicologist, 14, 24–25, 29,
  33, 42, 78, 79, 101, 115

Comparative musicology, 13, 24, 28, 33–34, 37, 40–41, 47–48, 51–52, 57, 72, 94–96, 99, 107, 111, 113, 155, 180, 219; Germany, 38–39; Gestalt psychology, 74–76; listening, 77–78; sexism, 33, 46, 68; United States, 38

Comparsa, 79–81, 86–87, 113, 116, 157, 188, 230. *See also* congas

Comte, Auguste, 77–78, 87, 255; Comteanism, 9, 11, 79, 89, 95, 108

Conceptual equipment, 16, 89, 93–94, 279n42, 290n68

Concert hall, 182, 229

Confidential File (television program), "Mambo" (episode), 239–241

Conga Pantera (ballet), 154–156

Congas, 81, 113, 116. *See also* comparsas

Congo, 79, 113, 114, 117–119

Contra-acculturation, 53–54, 65

Contratiempo, 231–234, 317n30

Controls, 31, 35

Cooper, Helen, 84, 143, 144

Council on African Affairs, 194–195, 207

Courlander, Harold, 4, 14, 16, 91, 99–100, 112, 117–123, 155, 214; *Adventures in Music* (radio program), 121; "Blen, blen, blen," 113; cults, 112–113, 118–123, 296n181; "Carabali Cult Song," 122; "Eluba Changó," 113, 121; folk, 118–121; Guanabacoa field recordings, 112–113, 119, 155; Haiti field recordings, 112; Havana field recordings, 112, 155; toque Ilé, 121, 122; Jovellanos field recordings, 112–113, 155; "Osain adádará mádá o," 122; popular, 121. *See also Cult Music of Cuba; Music of the Cults of Cuba*

Couzin, 'ti, 64–65

Covarrubias, Miguel, 222

Cowell, Henry, 37

Cruz, Celia, 235

Cuba, 28; African past/presence, 81–94, 119, 128, 142, 156, 230–231, 241; race, 81–82; race relations, 27–28, 83, 124, 127, 142; racial terror, 127; Spanish past, 87, 142; topography, 118

Cuban: identity, 120; music, 79, 85–86; historicism, 230, 233, 241;

nationalism, 81–84, 108, 116, 233; youth, 231, 233, 238, 242–243. *See also* danzón; mambo

Cuban Pete (Pedro Aguilar), 227–229, 235, 242

Cubop, 6, 213–214

Cuéllar Vizcaíno, Manuel, 229–232, 235, 238, 240, 245, 246

Cult Music of Cuba, 121, 156

Cultural relativism, 23, 53

Cunard, Nancy, 151

Dafora, Asadata, 2, 3, 4, 7, 16, 56, 126, 128, 131, 148–149, 151, 153, 154, 156, 159–160, 161–172, 179, 183, 191, 192, 194, 197, 222, 224, 260, 302n106, 302n108, 302n109; *African Dance and Music Festival* (dance drama), 168; *African Dances and Modern Rhythms* (dance drama), 168; *African Tribal Operetta* (dance drama), 168; *Batanga (African Freedom Rings)* (dance drama), 171; Caribbean, 168–169; *Festival at Battalakor* (dance drama), 169; jazz, 166; *Kykunkor* (dance drama), 7, 149, 162, 165–167, 169, 305n162; Latin America, 168–169; Western music education, 148; World War I, 166; *Zoonga* (dance drama), 148, 302n111; *Zunguru* (dance drama), 162, 305n162

Dahomey, 35

Dance, 6–7, 9, 12, 162–164, 175, 232; art, 55; black, 57; dancing, 14; primitive, 55–56; scientific study, 55. *See also* dance-music; music

Dance-music, 7, 14, 175, 228, 231–233; 251, 254, 270–271, 275. *See also* mambo

Dance studies, 3, 72

Dance studio industry, 233, 235–236, 239

Danzón, 229–233, 238, 239

Darwinism, 9, 11, 279n30; social, 131

Davidson, Will, 111, 187

Décalage, 157, 175

de Certeau, Michel, viii, 8

Del can can al mambo (film), 227, 261–265; el mal de San Vito, 264. *See* Sydenham's Chorea

Gillespie, John Birks "Dizzy," 7, 18, 178, 211–215, 217–219, 250, 251, 257; "Guarachi guaro," 178, 213, 214, 217, 315n164; "Manteca," 178, 205, 210, 212–214, 217; "Second Balcony Jump," 212

Gilroy, Paul, 4, 65, 67, 166; historicality, 277n3

Gleason, Ralph J., 211–213

Gold Coast, 35

Goldsmith, Samuel A., 50

Goodman, Ezra, 192–194

Gramsci, Antonio, 145

Granz, Norman, 238

Great Depression, The, 3, 28

Green Pastures, The (Broadway), 145

Green Pastures (film), 267

Gross, Nelson, 189

Gualberto Guevara, Cardinal Juan, 18, 247–249

Guaracha, 234

Guattari, Félix, 8, 19, 130, 220, 225, 226, 230, 232, 266–267, 268, 278n10

Guerra, Orlando "Cascarita," 234

Guridy, Frank Andre, 4, 127, 133, 142

Habitus, 8, 35, 51, 75, 77–78, 80, 88, 94. See also listening

Hague, Eleanor, 143–144

Haiti, 24, 199, 204

Hall, Stuart, 278n17

Hall of Races, 150, 157

Hammond, Jr., John, 105, 144–145, 149, 181, 182, 184, 212; From Spirituals to Swing (concert), 145, 149, 180, 181, 183, 187, 308n31

Haptic perception, 9, 25, 59, 76, 228

Harlem Renaissance, 1, 3, 56–58, 285n155

Havana, 5, 15, 29, 75, 78–79, 93, 113, 147, 154, 157; Carnival (1937), 80, 82, 113, 116, 142; Department of Tourism, 82, 84–85, 90, 92, 116, 127

Heard, Marcia, 148

Heat Wave, From Haiti to Harlem, 18

Hegel, G. W. F., 12, 78, 87, 127–128

Hegelianism, 9, 11, 79, 89, 108

Heidegger, Martin, 12, 94

Hentoff, Nat, 238

Herndon, Coy, 133

Herskovits, Francis S., 31

Herskovits, Melville J., vii, 2, 7, 14, 15, 22–25, 26–37, 38–54, 55–60, 62, 64–73, 79, 80, 86, 95–100, 102, 105, 118, 122, 127, 137, 139, 140, 144, 178, 182, 184, 185, 219, 222; acculturation, vii, 27, 30, 37, 39, 42, 44, 45, 53, 55, 57, 59, 65–66, 73, 103, 112, 137, 159; Africanisms, 35; *Afro-Bahian Religious Songs from Brazil*, 122; anthropometric research, 30; Brazil, 96; Brazil field recordings, 79, 104–105; calypso, 99; cultural determinism, 22, 29, 58; cultural focus, 44–45, 283n106; Freudian psychology, 97, 99, 106; Gestalt psychology, 75; Haiti field recordings, 48; historical-ethnographic method, 35, 48, 51; *The Myth of the Negro Past*, 23, 26, 72; Nigeria fieldwork, 105; sexism, 33, 46, 72; Suriname field recordings, 34, 39–40, 43–44, 51, 53, 122, 144, 316n15; *Suriname Folk-lore*, 31, 39–41, 45–48; syncretism, 43; Toco, 99, 101, 104, 106; Trinidad field notes, 104; Trinidad field recordings, 53, 79, 96, 97, 99, 101, 293n115; West Africa field recordings, 39, 40, 43–46, 48, 50–51, 144

Herzog, George, 33, 36, 37–38, 43, 45–49, 99, 103, 112, 295n158; research in Liberia, 138

Historians, 78

Historicism, 2, 4, 10, 19, 126, 129, 145, 165, 172, 232, 253, 277n3, 278n9; Spenglarian, 221

History, 7, 176, 182, 271, 274, 276; punctual system, 230–232

Hitler, Adolf, 27, 37, 64

Hodier, André, 213

Hoffman, Malvina, 150–151

Hollywood, 157

Home, 15, 108, 114, 121, 156–157, 182

hooks, bell, 15, 17, 143, 277n8

Hornbostel, Erich von, 13–15, 24, 29–30, 33–37, 38–40, 43–45, 47, 52, 72, 75, 95, 99, 139, 144; Scotch snap, 44; spiritual, 44

Horton, James Africanus B., 148

Metropolis, 9, 78, 124–127, 139, 147, 163, 224, 226, 229, 239, 251, 253–254; Caracas, 253; Havana, 239, 253; Latin American, 225; Lima, 253; Mexico City, 253, 262; New York City, 253; noise, 253, 265. *See also* modernity

Mexican film industry, 114, 226, 227; racial erasure, 261

Mexico, 11, 18, 227; Catholicism, 256, 258, 261; nationalism, 258; pachuco, 262; Pan-American Highway, 263; political economy of gender, 264; political economy of race, 255, 260, 263–265; positivism, 255–256, 261, 262, 266

Mikics, David, 254

Miller: Ivor, 119–120; Karl Hagstrom, 7

Mind, 15; Cartesian, 269; unconscious, 80, 96, 97, 99. *See also* body

Modern, 8–9, 11, 15, 23; African, 139; city, 9, 78; Cuban, 87, 89; family, 225; moderns, 14, 35, 66, 76–77, 126, 146–147, 221; ontology, 223–224; present, 76, 222, 225, 231; society, 51; world, 8–9, 12, 15, 20, 32. *See also* primitive

Modernism, 172, 213, 250, 291n69

Modernity, 2–13, 14, 16–20, 25, 34, 53, 83, 108, 109, 120, 123, 127, 158, 166, 168, 172, 174, 178, 188, 207, 210, 211, 219, 222, 227, 242–243, 252, 254, 267, 268–269, 277n8, 278n11; absurdity, 247; authority, 269; machines, 225; madness, 226–227; mappings, 3, 7, 9–10, 19, 83; neurosis, 226; primitive past, 125, 225, 227; psychosis, 226; topography, 159. *See also* metropolis; pathology of freedom; regimes of truth; subjective anchoring/assurance

Monson, Ingrid, 260, 314n143

Montaner, Rita, 18, 85, 257, 289n46

Montero-Sánchez, Berta, 114, 292n103

Moore, Robin, 81

Morales, Aguedo, 85, 88, 91

Moss, Carlton, 149

Motor behavior, 29–30, 33, 46

Movement, 9, 14, 78, 91, 93, 123, 128, 143, 146, 149, 152, 156, 158, 162–164, 175, 178, 188, 191–192, 219, 221, 224,

226–228, 230–231, 250–252, 270, 317n19

Mowrer, Ernest R., 97

Mudimbe, V. Y., 17; gnosis, 286n183

Murray, Arthur, 18, 235; basic step, 235–236; Kathryn, 236

Music, 6–7, 12–13, 29; notation, 86, 215; style, 30; time, 175; transcription, 95, 99. *See also* dance; dance-music

Music of the Cults of Cuba, 91, 109–110, 117, 120. *See also* DISC; Courlander, Harold

Musicking, 7–8, 10, 13, 14, 17, 18

Myal, 59

NAACP, *See* National Association for the Advancement of Colored People

NACW, *See* National Association of Colored Women

Ñañiguismo, 115–116, 118, 120, 241

National Association for the Advancement of Colored People (NAACP), 27, 207–209

National Association of Colored Women (NACW), 128, 150, 157, 165

National Council of Negro Women, 150, 161, 165

Nation of Islam, 54, 65

Nationalism, 6, 224–226, 241

Native African Union of America, 148

Naturalism, 252–254, 319n98. *See also* existentialism

Nazism, 3, 8, 14, 21, 24, 27–29, 37, 38, 47, 52–53, 63, 73, 140, 280n16

Neale, Vivian J., 140, 151

Negritude, 73, 223, 253

Negro, 16, 29, 174–175, 277n9; African, 24, 30, 42, 127, 129, 139, 158, 161; American, 8, 12, 15–16, 24–27, 29–30, 32, 35, 40, 44–45, 51, 63–66, 70, 94, 106, 124–125, 127–129, 131, 139–144, 145–147, 149, 151–152, 158, 161, 177, 195, 197, 229; Cuban, 117, 127, 129, 144, 158; men, 200; modern, 11, 106; nationalism, 170; slave, 125, 156; soul, 166; West Indian, 151; woman, 150, 171, 176, 193. *See also* black music; Bush Negro; New World Negro

Ramos: Arthur, 21, 222, 283n99; Juan S., 233, 243; Samuel, 223
Ramos Calles, Raúl, 224, 240–241
Ramsey, Kate, 65
Rebay, Hilla von, 210, 211, 213, 214
Recording industry, 233, 235, 239
Recordings, 77, 108, 112, 114–115, 120; field, 16, 34–35, 42, 51, 72, 77, 95, 99, 102, 108, 112, 117, 144, 181–182; film, 114; studio, 75, 77, 108, 109, 112, 114, 144
Reddick, L. D., 168
Redfield, Robert, 44, 53–54, 55, 69–70, 178
Regimes of truth, 5, 6, 269. *See also* modernity
Retention, 15, 44, 89; cultural, 23. *See also* African
Reynolds, George M., 71
Rhizome, 19, 274–275
Ritmos del Caribe (film), 227, 235, 247–248, 256–258, 266; Magali, 257–258, 266; "Negra," 257 "Rarezas del siglo," 257
Roberts, Helen H., 33, 37, 45–46, 67–68, 72, 287n201; anhemitonic, 46; pentatonicism, 46
Robeson, Paul, 16, 17, 125, 129, 137, 144, 145, 152, 154, 156, 172, 176, 178, 195, 197, 303n126; *Sanders of the River*, 151–153
Robinson, Bill "Bojangles," 146, 170, 187
Roche, Pablo, 85, 88, 89, 91
Rockefeller Foundation, 69
Rodríguez, Arsenio, vii, 228
Romero: Cesar, 240; Delia, 260; Fernando, 97
Roosevelt: Eleanor, 130, 161–162, 164–165, 195; Franklin D., 18, 161, 165, 168; "Four Freedoms," 18, 161, 164, 168, 177, 202, 203

Sachs, Curt, 38
San Francisco Museum of Modern Art, 180, 182, 209
Sanders of the River (film), 144, 151–153, 156
Santamaria, Ramón "Mongo," 260
Santería, 78, 85, 90, 92, 115, 116; Regla de Ocha, 288n20

Santos, Daniel, 257
Sapir, Edward, 55
Sargeant, Winthrop, 108, 116, 118, 241; "Cuba's Tin Pan Alley," 116–117, 120, 242
Sartre, Jean-Paul, 11, 18, 224, 226, 250, 253–254; absurd, 253; books banned by Pope Pius XII, 249. *See also* existentialism
Schneider, Marius, 38
Schomburg Collection of Negro Literature, 168
Schünermann, Georg, 38
Schuyler, George, 23, 185, 195, 197–198
Science, 6, 11, 14, 15, 18, 23, 25–26, 27; social practice, 51
Scotch snap, 44
Scott: Kermit, 218; Walter Dill, 52
Scottsboro case, 19, 132, 141–142, 151, 157
Seashore, Carl E., 72, 96; Robert H., 96–97, 102
Seeger, Charles, 37–38, 98
Self, 12
Selassie, Haile, 57, 285n159
78-RPM disc, 232
Sevilla, Ninón, 258
Sexism, 5, 14, 33, 143, 172, 279n34. *See also* comparative musicology; New World Negro studies
Sexuality, 125, 220, 277n8
Shelemay, Kay Kaufman, 112
Shologa Aloba Dance Group, 162
Singh, Rani, 210
Sissle, Noble, 145–146
Small, Christopher, 7, 175
Smets, Georges, 49
Smith, Harry, 3, 12, 16–18, 175–176, 177–178, 209–219; alchemy, 211; anthropologist, 210, 215, 218–219; bebop, 210, 211–212, 218; comparative musicologist, 210; cubop, 212, 214; drug use, 210–212; *Film No. 1*, 211, 217; *Film No. 2*, 178, 211, 213–215, 217; *Film No. 3*, 211, 217, 314n157; *Film No. 4*, 178, 211, 215–217; *Five Instruments with Optical Solo* (film), 217–218; "Guarachi guaro," 215; *Manteca* (painting), 178,

Western, 77, 159, 270; world, 23. *See also*
chronotope; space
Tongolele, 238
Town Negro, 34, 40, 43
Transculturation, 12
Trinidad, 63; Shango, 64, 102
Tropicana Nightclub, 154–155
Truman, Harry, 168
Tubman, W. V. S., 198, 201–202
Turner, Lorenzo Dow, 73

Ulanov, Barry, 183, 212
UNCIO, *See* United Nations Conference on
International Organization
UNESCO, *See* United Nations Educational
Scientific and Cultural Organization
UN Conference on International
Organization (UNCIO), 168, 169, 194,
209
UN Educational Scientific and Cultural
Organization (UNESCO), 21–23, 25–26,
172, 223, 307n9
United States, 4–5, 11, 15, 26, 35, 43, 51;
communism, 171; identity, 120; political
economy of race, 28, 63–65, 124, 160,
203, 212, 219, 260; racial logic, 120, 141,
242; racial terror, 127, 142, 162,
165–166, 306n176; racism, 68, 86, 127,
140–141. *See also* Jim Crow
Universal Africa Nationalist Movement, 195
University of Chicago, 54–55
Un-raced, 5, 16, 18–19, 75–76, 79, 120,
219, 264, 277n8. *See also* body; race
Urfé, Odilio, 229–233, 235, 238–240, 253
Urueta, Chano, 18, 246, 261, 266

Valdés: Alfredo, 85; Bebo, 234, 251
Valdés, Gilberto, 15, 78, 82–92, 103, 122,
123, 141, 144, 153, 183, 190, 213, 251,
290n50, 290n51; "Ilé-nko Ilé-nbe," 88,
191; "Sangre Africana," 88, 89, 92, 213;
"Tambó," 85–86, 88, 92, 213
Valdés, Miguelito, 113; *Bim Bam Boom, An
Album of Cuban Rhythms*, 109, 111, 115;
"Enlloro," 115
Vargas, Pedro, 263
Vasconcelos, José, 226, 227, 255, 265–266;
La raza cósmica, 255, 261

Víctimas del pecado (film), 256, 258,
319n75
Vodun, 58, 66; hounci kanzo, 64; lave-tête,
64
Voodooism, 166

Waterman, Richard, 3, 13–15, 68, 72,
79–80, 90–91, 94, 101, 107–108, 112,
114, 139, 155, 159, 182, 186, 214, 219,
222, 283n100; "African Influence on the
Music of the Americas," 105; "Angelitos
negros," 114; "Blen, blen, blen," 114;
Cárdenas field recordings, 114;
dissertation, 97, 101–105; faculty
instructor, 98–99; Freudian psychology,
96, 99, 102, 104; Gestalt theory,
102–103, 106, 182–183; graduate
studies at Northwestern University,
95–98; Havana field recordings, 104;
Herskovits's Trinidad field recordings/
notes, 101–104; "hot," 103–106; "'Hot'
Rhythm in Negro Music," 103, 105,
293n123; Jovellanos field recordings,
114; "La barca de oro," 114; Laboratory
of Comparative Musicology, 97–99, 107;
Manantiales Villiers field recordings,
114; psychology, 79, 96, 105–106,
291n93; Puerto Rico fieldwork,
292n103; State Department, 98;
worksheet, 99–101, 123. *See also*
metronome sense; off-beat phrasing
Weeyums, Ba,' 59, 66
Welfish, Gene, 185
Wertheimer, Max, 74, 75
West Africa, 24; colonial, 124
Western civilization, 25, 32, 221–226, 267;
barbarism, 224, 225; binary logics, 227,
241; machines, 224, 226, 229, 238; past,
226; strictures, 270. *See also* metropolis
White, Josh, 181, 183–185, 309n40
White supremacy, 166, 185, 207
Whiteness, 5, 24; Cuba, 81, 84, 120, 277n8,
289n28; Latin America, 266; Mexico,
256, 258, 261, 263–264; United States,
18, 27, 120, 178, 219–220, 242, 260. *See
also* blackness; faciality
Williams: Eric, 222; Raymond, 129
Williams Jr., Vernon J., 47